Skinny Bitch

Home, Beauty & Style

RUNNING PRESS
PHILADELPHIA · LONDON

To Stephane and Jack—my two great loves.

And to Keesha, my soul sister.

I wouldn't want to be here without you guys.

TABLE OF CONTENTS

Introduction

When I was a little girl, I tagged along with my mom to the drugstore whenever I could. Getting her to *let* me go usually involved a little begging. She wasn't stupid—the woman knew that I was going to ask for at least a dozen things that weren't designed for a ten year old. Why I wanted anti-aging cream and a Danielle Steel novel is still beyond me.

Unlike the supermarket (bo-oring), the drugstore was an amazing emporium of cool stuff. Over here you had mascara, deodorant, nail polish, perfumes, and body wash. In the next aisle you were drowning in greeting cards. Walk another ten feet and you could take your pick from teen mags and paperback books. And there was always the fascinating aisle that had no rhyme or reason at all. You know, the one with cotton balls, laundry detergent, lawn chairs, dog toys, and holiday décor all stuffed into one. What can I say? For a budding beauty product junkie, it was better than Disneyland.

Boy, was I young and stupid. Had I known then, thirty years ago, what I know now, I probably would have stayed home and learned to sew—playing with needles would have been a much safer infatuation for a young kid.

What I know now is that most of those products—from my acne skin wash to the perfumes that promised to make me smell like a celebrity—were filled with scary chemicals all tarted up in savvy marketing. In addition to fighting acne or BO, they were weakening my immune system and setting me up for bad allergies, anxiety, and chronic colds. I was a sucker, a prime target for big brands that built a following with cool packaging and peer pressure.

The fact is I could learn to deal with all of these health problems. What I would have a much harder time doing is watching my little boy go through it.

I first started learning about all the junk in our beauty and household products when I was working on my third book, *Skinny Bitch: Bun in the Oven.* I was pregnant with my one and only, Jack. I started doing some research, because like any protective mom, I wanted to make sure I brought him into this world right. Come to find out, that's not all that easy to do. The shit I came across made my stomach turn. Flame retardants in cribs and pajamas that may play a role in causing leukemia, dangerous preservatives in baby sunscreens and shampoos, endocrine disruptors in plastic baby bottles, and toxic lead in paint chips . . . the list went on. The health implications are obvious. We aren't winning the war

on cancer, and more and more children are suffering from allergies, ADHD, and other disorders. Women are struggling with fertility issues, turning to in vitro to get knocked up. I was also finding that not only did our food and fashion reek of animal cruelty, but so did our carpets, mattresses, sheets, and silky robes.

I was livid. Outraged. Pissed off. And you don't want to piss off a bitch with a big mouth and a baby in her belly. She just might write a book about it.

So I started making changes, but as it turned out, not nearly enough. By the time my son, Jack, was two years old, he was getting sick all the time. It wasn't just a cold or stuffy nose. We're talking full-blown upper respiratory and sinus infections. Every virus that went around, he caught, usually with back-to-back illnesses. I started seeing an allergist who did a shitload of blood tests, to find out that Jack had a weakened immune system. The poor kid just wasn't strong enough to handle the things he was exposed to. I couldn't help but think that I had done something wrong.

So don't just take my word for it, read the source materials at the end of this book and decide for yourself.

After I beat myself up for a month, I sucked it up and quit feeling sorry for myself. Poor Kim. How is any of that crying going to help my kid? That's right—it didn't and it wasn't. I realized that I did nothing wrong, but here's the deal: When it comes to this crap, what you don't know can hurt you. It can make you very sick.

I had to pick myself up, and continue educating myself to make Jack's life better. Every day, I learn something new. My husband and I have ripped apart Jack's entire room. From his mattress and bedding, to an air purifier, to the paint in his room, to healthier flooring, we're making sure we get this kid healthy. I've tested the house for mold. I use all nontoxic cleaners. I dust like a goddamn bat out of hell. And things are getting better—for me, my husband, and my child. It's a journey and there will always be something else to worry about. So I take it one baby step at a time.

With that said, it should come as no surprise that the inspiration behind this book is my son, and all the women out there who are doing their best to juggle a million things on a daily basis and still keep their families' health in check. There was only so much I could fit in *Bun in the Oven*. And frankly, there was only so much research out there. But for the last few years, I've been keeping tabs on the government and their actions on consumer safety; I've been paying attention to cowardly manufacturers and their sneaky marketing tactics; and I've had my eye on a few businesses that are doing the right thing for our safety. And I've saved it all for this book. It's a natural step in the *Skinny Bitch* saga.

I'm gonna say it up front: Much of what I say throughout this book is my opinion based on all the research I've compiled. So don't just take my word for it, read the source materials at the end of this book and decide for yourself. You are going to come across a lot of shocking information, but it's not meant to scare the shit out of you. That wasn't my intention. My intention was to tell you what I wish someone had told me: Every little thing you put on or near your body—or your child's—is going *in* your body. Your skin is like a sponge, soaking up anything and everything it comes into contact with. Treat it with care. Introduce it to healthier products, and you will feel healthier. As it so happens, most of these safer products and brands are actually better for the environment, to boot. By supporting them, you're making it very clear that you won't stand for toxic products that are bad for your health and the planet. Not on your dollar.

And who says you can't look and feel smokin' hot while you save the planet and protect your family? Not me. I'm not one of those earthy-crunchy tree-huggers. I don't have hairy armpits and dreadlocks. Oh. No. I l-o-v-e beauty products. I am completely and dangerously obsessed with having great hair, and I'm always on the lookout for a fierce pair of winter boots. I just happen to want it all without being cruel to animals, poisoning my body with parabens, or taking advantage of the earth and its resources. Is that too much to ask? Hell, no.

Throughout the book, I've compiled helpful tips and some of my favorite rules of thumb to make this all easier on you. It's not supposed to hurt. You should be able to just take the advice and use it. Whatever you do, don't jump in and try to change *everything* at once. Now, that would be painful … and expensive. Pick the things that matter most to you and make changes in phases. Get familiar with what to look for, and for the love of God, look for it. Give yourself a pat on the back every now and then. You will appreciate the things in your life and the purchases you make when you know they stand for something.

Don't doubt for a second that they don't stand for something. For every conscious decision you make, some other broad is doing the same thing. Then add another one to the equation. Before you know it, that's a lot of broads who aren't giving their business to the system. And that, ladies, speaks louder than anything we can ever say.

Keep that in mind next time an extra dollar or two is what stands between a safe product and a toxic one. Don't be a cheap ass. You're not doing it for my health, honey. You're doing it for yours.

Love + Peace,
Kim Barnouin

PART I
Your Home

Ah, the filth we breathe. For decades, we've been warned about all that smog, carbon dioxide, and dirty exhaust that's pumped into our atmosphere.[1] We get it—it's real bad for us. Check the air quality before you step foot outside and slather on the sunscreen. It's a goddamn swamp out there.

In 2010, the EPA released a little report saying our air was getting cleaner. But nobody gave a shit. In fact, the air out there *is* much better. We're talking fourteen percent better for ozone and seventy-eight percent for lead over the past four decades. In Southern California—where it once burned our lungs to breathe—outdoor pollution has dropped by sixty percent since the early 1970s.[2] But the air didn't just clear up magically. No, no. The government actually toughened up with new laws, and then companies and people had to start making changes.

The real slap in the ass is that the whole time we've been freaking out about the war outside our doors, there's been another one heating up *inside*

our homes. Yeah, get this: You may feel safe when you're sitting on your couch watching some dumb reality show, but you're not. You're in deep shit. The toxic spray cleaners under your sink. The cancer-causing air fresheners. The pots and pans that leach crap into your food. Even our mattress is preparing for DEFCON 5. Every year, more than two thousand chemicals get thrown into our products, and only about seven percent have undergone any type of testing for safety.[3] Sit on that for a minute . . . *seven* percent. And you thought that coffee stain on your white couch was eating away at you.

The air inside the average American home is anywhere from two to five times worse than the air outside.[4] All those glass cleaners, tub and tile scrubs, dishwashing soaps, and laundry detergents are contaminating your home. Look around you for a minute. You have walls. Those things block much of anything from going out. When you tally up all the hours you spend indoors sleeping, working, relaxing, knocking the boots, cooking—whatever it is that you do—you breathe around nine out of every ten breaths inside.[5] Now I wonder why childhood asthma has doubled in the last twenty years.[6] Beats me.

All our woes don't just come from the hazardous cleaning products. Home furnishings, fabrics, paint, carpets, candles, and almost anything plastic are also doing a number on our homes. I'll bet you're wondering how these innocent little material things could do any wrong. Wake up and smell the napalm. There are diesel trucks leaking oil all over the highway that are more innocent.

Every chemical has its own set of damages, but here are the three broad categories that the worst fall under.

▪ Volatile Organic Compounds (VOCs)

Not everything that's organic is good, honey. In scientific talk, organic just means it contains carbon. That's the definition chemists play by. In that case, you are organic. The grass is organic.[7] Most VOCs just happen to fall under the category "not so great" organic things. They are chemicals that evaporate from products at different concentrations and get released as harmful gases that sit in the air.[8] You can't stop them. They were born to fly. When they leave the product they rode in on, it's called *offgassing* (or *outgassing*).[9] Offgassing occurs at normal room temperatures, but spits out even more VOCs when exposed to heat or sunlight.[10]

You don't have to be a genius to see that VOCs have a screw loose. Formaldehyde is a VOC. Alcohol, toluene, xylene,[11] methylene chloride, perchloroethylene, and benzene[12] are all VOCs. There are about two hundred that are commonly found in everyday home products.[13] Once they're in your indoor air, you inhale them. And that folks, is when you've got a little problem.

▪ Plasticizers

There is a whole mob of other chemicals that don't qualify as VOCs because they don't offgas into the air. But they're not less dangerous. Plasticizers such as bisphenol A (BPA) and phthalates have been getting more attention lately than celebrities and their DUIs. The former is used to harden plastic and the latter makes it more flexible. Both have something in common that's a real bummer: they are hormone disruptors (aka endocrine disruptors). It sounds fancy, but it's really a medical term for chemicals that enter your body and start to imitate your natural hormones.[14] Hormone disruptors are like the chick from *Single White Female*. They are a group of toxins that imitate your natural hormones and start copying everything they do. This fools your body so your hormones start getting blocked from their normal sites.[15] Then they try and make up for it, and

everything gets real jacked up. What you're left with are cells that promote a handful of cancers and some screwy reproductive problems.[16] The frightening part is that BPA and phthalates do the most damage in infants and kids—yet we still haven't gotten enough balls to ban them from children's products in the United States.

▪ Perfluorinated Compounds (PFCs)

It's great that you can clean dog piss right out of your couch, but I wouldn't say it's exactly natural. PFCs are a class of chemicals that have been used since the 1950s to make materials stain- and stick- resistant. They're in your upholstery, fabrics, and clothing under names such as Scotchguard, Stainmaster, and Gore-Tex. And they're also coating your nonstick cookware to make sure your hash browns don't stick to the pan. Yes, I'm talking about Teflon. But like VOCs, they don't like to stay in one place. They creep out and end up a) getting absorbed by your skin and inhaled through dust; and b) leaching into your food. There have been some serious concerns that they can cause cancer, and weaken or impair our organs. Many companies have phased them out, or are in the process of doing so, but we're going to feel their pain for years to come.[17]

In this section, we're going to chit-chat about what some of the most popular things in our home have to hide, and your best alternatives. As much as all this bites the big one, it doesn't mean you need to live in a bubble. Just quit inviting these crazies into your home. After all, they didn't just walk themselves in there. You threw down some hard cash for all that toxicity.

Aa BITCHIONARY: SYNTHETIC Something made by the hands of man through a chain of chemical reactions. There is nothing natural about it.

THE SHIT LIST
The Worst Toxins in Your Home

Here are a few of the worst chemicals that hang out in your home, where they're hiding, and how to kick them to the curb.

I'm not saying that products that contain these nasty chemicals are surely going to kill you. Quite frankly, I don't think anybody really knows exactly what they can do to you in the long run. But I, for one, am not going to wait around to find out.

AMMONIA

A chemical found naturally in the environment, ammonia is also added to household cleaners in higher concentrations because it's a cheap and effective way to clean your home. The problem is it's landed itself on the EPA's *Community Right-to-Know* list for potential health effects when inhaled, and is known to irritate the lungs, nose, mouth, and eyes.[18] (Seriously, have you ever taken a whiff?) It's especially uncomfortable for those with allergies or asthma.

BENZENE (Nickname: Naphtha)

One of those vicious VOCs derived from petroleum, benzene is a known carcinogen common in oven cleaners, detergents, furniture polishes, and spot removers. With longer exposure—it's even in your paint and furniture—benzene has some serious effects on the blood, leading to anemia, lymphoma, and leukemia. So it makes perfect sense that it's one of the top twenty chemicals the industry produces by volume![19] Right . . .

BISPHENOL A (BPA)

Used to harden plastics and coat the inside of food cans, BPA can be found in plastic bottles, baby bottles, food storage containers, microwaveable dinners, kids toys, and oh, ninety percent of Americans.[20] Over time, it starts to break down in plastics and leaches into food and water. Give it a little heat with a blast from the microwave, and it leaches fifty-five times faster than normal.[21] Now ask yourself how many times you've reheated baby formula, leftovers in a plastic container, or maybe drank from a plastic water bottle left in a hot car. Yeah, sleep on that one. Once in our bodies, it imitates our hormones—in this case, estrogen—and has been linked to early puberty, and increased risk of developmental problems, and cancer.

2-BUTOXYETHANOL (Nicknames: Butyl Cellusolve, Ethylene Glycol Monobutyl Ether)

A very popular chemical in all-purpose and floor cleaners, liquid soaps, and stain removers, heavy doses of this one can damage your nerve tissues. It has the potential to rupture blood cells, leading to internal bleeding, and liver and kidney damage.[22] In animal studies, 2-butoxyethanol really goes to town on the reproductive organs.[23]

CHLORINE BLEACH (Nicknames: Hypochlorite, Sodium Hypochlorite, Hydrochloric Acid)

Also known as plain ole bleach, it's in mildew removers, toilet cleaners, fabric brighteners, and disinfectants. I'm not one to point fingers—psyche!—but chlorine is to blame for the most household poisonings in the United States.[24] When it's mixed with ammonia, it releases poisonous chlorine gas. Since you release ammonia everytime you take a whiz—it's in your pee-pee—you're creating a little chemical reaction every time you clean your bathrooms with this stuff.[25] The damage starts with corrosion of your lungs, skin, and eyes, and works up to wearing down the enamel on your teeth.[26]

ETHANOLAMINES (Nicknames: Diethanolamine (DEA), Monoethanolamine (MEA), Triethanolamine (TEA))

A family of chemicals found in detergents, furniture polishes, and all-purpose cleaners that reduce the surface tension of water so it can penetrate materials easier to remove dirt and grease. The ethanolamines are another set of hormone disruptors that build up in your organs. The big fuss is in some cases they can react with nitrates in the air, or possibly in your body, to cause nitrosamines.[27] Nitrosamines can cause cancer.[28] The end.

FORMALDEHYDE

It's used to preserve frogs for science projects and as an embalming solution for cadavers. Maybe you recall the nauseating odor from Biology 101 when you were dissecting Kermit. You thought you would drop dead from the smell. Turns out, you just might. This one pops up in adhesives, paneling, carpets, plywood, pressed fabrics, wood products, and even air fresheners. It can set off allergic reactions that affect the entire respiratory system, and the International Agency for Research of Cancer (IARC) classifies it as a *known* carcinogen—not to be confused with a "potential" carcinogen.[29] Even at the lowest of levels, it triggers headaches, fatigue, eye and throat irritation, and shortness of breath.[30] Because your body naturally produces it in very small amounts, some argue it's nothing to be concerned about. Bullshit.

ETHYLENE GLYCOL (Nicknames: Ethylene Dihydrate, Ethylene Alcohol)[31]

A clear liquid antifreeze found in many all-purpose cleaners and mildew stain removers, it can slow down the central nervous system, and lead to kidney damage or heart failure if ingested.[32]

POLYBROMINATED DIPHENYL ETHERS (PBDE)

More than twelve million pounds of these flame retardants are produced every year for use in foam products such as mattresses, couches, pillows, and blankets. So it won't come as a shock that it's found in the bodies of almost every American. You absorb more of them than your body can get rid of, so they just hang around, banging up the nervous and reproductive systems. In one study, kids had 3.2 times more flame retardants polluting their blood than their mothers did. (Maybe that's because cribs and toddler beds are covered in them.)[33] Studies have indicated that even tiny doses of PBDEs at a child's critical stage of development may slow down their motor skills, learning, memory, and hearing.[34]

PETROLEUM DISTILLATES (Nickname: Naphtha)

A very broad category that covers pretty much all chemicals derived from petroleum, these bad boys can be found in furniture polishes, paints, adhesives, air fresheners, and all-purpose cleaners.[35] The EPA says they pose the biggest risk when they are inhaled, even in small amounts. Here's the problem: They are all over your house. And unless you're holding your breath, you're inhaling them.[36] Once they're in your system, they can irritate and damage your lungs, and may also contain small amounts of benzene, toluene, and xylene.[37]

PHENOLS

These toxins are commonly found in detergents, all-purpose cleaners, and disinfectants to cover offensive odors. But they are rapidly absorbed by your body when inhaled, and can trigger toxic effects throughout the entire body. Symptoms of overexposure include shock, delirium, dark urine, and damage to the respiratory and circulatory systems.[38]

PHOSPHATES

Phosphates are added to detergents to "soften" hard water minerals and keep the dirt from settling back onto materials. It's not what these guys do to our health that has everyone up in arms (they're actually pretty nontoxic to humans). But in the environment, they do some nutty stuff. When you let nature do its thing, phosphates are essential to animal and plant growth. But all that changes when man adds more phosphates to the equation with pollution from our everyday household products. Let me break it down for you. For the algae that exists in our natural habitats, phosphates might as well be cupcakes. Algae finds them delicious and just eats them right up. But when algae feed on phosphates, they go buck wild and bloom like crazy, invading rivers, lakes, and oceans.[39] Algae isn't all that bad. But too much algae isn't the best thing for these waters—it depletes oxygen and suffocates marine life.[40]

PHTHALATES

A family of industrial chemicals used to give polyvinyl chloride (PVC) plastics like shower curtains, paint, and teething rings that nice, flexible feel. Like BPA, phthalates are hormone disruptors that mimic estrogen, which makes our natural estrogen go haywire. This is especially a problem for the kiddies, whose hormones are still telling their growing bodies how to develop properly. When phthalates start screwing with a child's hormones, they are known to "feminize" little boys by slowing down the growth of their little johnson. It may not mean much when they're five, but it will be a pretty damn big deal when they reach college. Trust me. Other possible developmental problems that would scare the pants off any mother include autism, testicular cancer, and lowered sperm counts.[41]

PERFLUOROOCTANOIC ACID (PFOA) (Nickname: C8)

A sneaky chemical that gets released as a toxic vapor from nonstick cookware, furniture, stain resistant carpets, and microwave popcorn bags. It's been linked to infertility, high cholesterol, and thyroid disease in humans. But in animals, it causes everything from liver and immune system failure, to birth defects and all types of cancers.[42]

SODIUM HYDROXIDE (Nicknames: Lye, Caustic Soda)

A far-too-familiar chemical in detergents, stain removers, and disinfectants that can burn the crap out of your bodily tissues. Even the lowest of levels gets your nose, throat, and airways in a funk, but don't get it on your skin or in your eyes. It can cause severe burns and may leave you blind.[43]

SODIUM LAURYL SULFATE AND SODIUM LAURETH SULFATE (SLS or SLES)[44]

A questionable pair of sulfates added to detergents, liquid soaps, and all-purpose cleaners to work up a good lather and prevent dirt from settling back onto clean materials.[45] SLS can produce a deadly chemical called 1,4-dioxane, which is known to cause cancer according to the State of California and is considered a probable human carcinogen by the Environmental Protection Agency (EPA).[46] Aside from that minor concern, they are known to irritate your skin, eyes, and mucous membranes. I almost forgot—they are also used to degrease car engines. You hear that? Car. Engines.[47] Sounds real safe for something you're wiping all over your counters and lathering onto your scalp.

TOLUENE

A toxic VOC found in everything from paint to furniture to mattresses to car seats.[48] It's considered a drug in "higher" concentrations, doing its worst damage on the brain. The solvent has also been linked to a higher risk of spontaneous abortion and miscarriage in women.[49] Experts say to treat it like a teratogen—an agent that interferes with fetal development.[50] How do we know all this? Because some chicks are dumb enough to "sniff" paint and glue purely for shits and giggles when they're pregnant, leading researchers to some pretty disturbing potential side effects.[51] Though it may not be as toxic if you're not sniffing it for recreation, it leaks out of paint and furniture for years into the air you breathe.?

TRICHLOROETHYLENE

A chemical potent enough to degrease metals, but also common in paints, stain removers, and furniture. It can cause headaches and dizziness, as well as kidney, nerve, and liver damage. But more importantly, the IARC says the odds are good that it also causes cancer. The National Toxicology Program (NTP) seconds that.[52]

The Vegan Taboos:
CRUELTY FABRICS AND MATERIALS IN YOUR HOME

DOWN

Down feathers are ripped from the breasts of ducks and geese. The birds are often thrown into large warehouses—another way to say factory farm—and some allege that in certain countries their feathers are plucked "live" while they are restrained. They can be plucked when they're dead, too. However some say their dead, rotting bodies don't produce the best quality feathers.

It's also been alleged that in certain places, waterfowl may go through this torture three to five times during their life. (Imagine if someone pulled out each one of your fingernails out.) After their feathers are spent, they are slaughtered for their meat. Others are force-fed until their livers swell ten times their normal size, and then they're killed for food. We call this diseased, fatty liver *foie gras*. Vomit.

WOOL

Wool gets around in "natural" carpets, fabrics, and as an alternative to polyurethane foam in furniture padding. It has its health benefits because it's hypoallergenic and naturally fireproof, but not without a societal cost. Don't let them pull the wool over your eyes: Animals aren't just getting a harmless haircut. The farm is no day spa, honey. And Mary's little lamb isn't the only one being sacrificed for your home and apparel. Wool is also shaved off the backs of angora rabbits, and cashmere and mohair goats.

Sheep. Sheep have it baaaad. Every year, more than six million are raised in the United States for meat and wool production. Within weeks of popping out of their mother's womb, a baby lamb's ears are punched with holes, their tails are cut off, and males are robbed of their manhood without anesthesia. Nowadays, they are also genetically modified to produce wool in droves. Since they have wool coming out their ears, they don't shed naturally anymore. So someone with a forceful hand "trims" the sheep, often cutting and injuring the poor thing during shearing. Their wool is cut so close to the skin that they have no protective layer to shield them from frigid weather or the blaring sun. So they get painful sunburns.

If you want to talk some real pain, let's chat about mulesing. In Australia—where more than fifty percent of the world's Merino wool is manufactured—lambs are painfully mutilated to remove excessive skin folds near their ass. Since these wrinkles are filled with shit, flies start to infest their backside. So farmers cut large strips of flesh out of their bums, sometimes as early as four weeks into the little lamb's pathetic life. Thanks to pressure from PETA, ranchers have agreed to start phasing this fun little hobby out, but wouldn't you know it, not everybody is living up to the agreement. For the ones that are, the method they're replacing it with isn't much better. They put clamps onto the lamb's rump to cut off any blood circulation. The flesh eventually dies and falls off.[53]

To save the sheep from the pain of mulesing, ranchers may consider tail docking—a much less painful procedure. [Cough] Bullshit. They take a knife and slice off the skin on both sides of the tail stump. No anesthesia for any of these barnyard surgeries. Just lots of pain.[54]

When sheep age and stop producing as much wool, they are shipped off to slaughterhouses. Otherwise, they get labeled "downers." That's just a fancy way of saying they leave them to suffer and die from pure neglect. What a way to go.

Angora. Bunnies are cute, but not on coats. Angora rabbits are stuffed in wire cages for their entire lives. Except for the males, who are traditionally killed at birth because they don't produce as much fur. They are alone the entire time with no sort of interaction in these unbearable cages. That can't feel too good. Since they can't fit in their cages as they get bigger, their bones deform. That *really* can't feel too good. When it's time for a shaving, they are roughly trimmed, which often freaks them out and traumatizes them for their short, miserable lives.

Cashmere and Mohair Goats. Animal shearers cut off a goat's balls and horns without any anesthesia. What farmers are really after is that wool. When goats get shorn for the first time, their bodies usually haven't even had the time to produce enough hair to shed. Nobody gives a shit. They're left to suffer through the chill temperatures and put up with parasites without their protective fleece. Meanwhile, the filthy and overcrowded environment they live in makes them prone to getting sick. [55] When they do, they're left to die without food, water, or care of any kind. Sounds like a great bedtime story.

For more on the toxic chemicals in your home and animal-friendly materials, visit healthybitchdaily.com.

CHAPTER 1

The Skinny: Air Quality

★ (Dis)comfort Zone:
FURNITURE WITH A HIDDEN AGENDA

Your bed. The coffee table. Even that hideous couch your husband bought unsupervised. All of this stuff has some serious shit to get off its chest. And whether you like it or not, you and every living thing under that roof are suffering its wrath.

You think you didn't ask for any of this? Oh, but you did. You asked for trouble as soon as you slapped down your credit card and told them Friday morning after your bikini wax was a perfect time for delivery.

Why wouldn't you assume that every new piece of furniture and accessory you bring into your home is totally safe? I mean, it's *new*. It's not like it's chipped or about to burst into flames. Yeah, about that . . .

FLAME RETARDANTS IN YOUR LOVE SEAT

Your couch is actually soaked in chemicals that are there to keep it from catching fire.[56] Why would anyone be so concerned about your love seat starting a wildfire? Well, because most padded furniture is made with polyurethane foam—a soft plastic that is superflammable. Actually, it's so flammable that firefighters compare it to gasoline.[57] Put it too close to a heater or maybe a candle in the heat of the moment, and up in flames it goes. To calm your couch down, manufacturers spray it with fire-retardants. But don't get blinded by the light. They may stop your couch from getting all hot and bothered, but they've got their own baggage.

The most widely-used industry flame retardants are polybrominated diphenyl ethers (PBDEs). Try saying that in one breath.[58] While I'm sure they are super at fighting a flame, these chemicals aren't bound to the foam. Nope, the stuff in your foam likes to roam. Most of our exposure to PBDEs and other flame retardants comes from dust, believe it or not. They sneak out of the upholstery and get caught up in dust bunnies on floors and carpets, which we eventually inhale.[59] If you have kids crawling around the house amidst all this dust, chances are they're probably putting PBDEs in their mouths like a pacifier.

Let me tell you why you don't want PBDEs fiddling with your body. These guys accumulate in your blood, breast milk, and fatty tissues. It's just sitting in there, bringing down the entire house. PBDEs can botch your thyroid, mess with the way your brain functions, and even push cells to turn cancerous.[60] As loose as the Environmental Protection Agency (EPA) may be, even they classify PBDEs as a "potential" carcinogen.[61]

On the bright side, PBDEs are slowly being phased out. States such as California, Maine, Hawaii, Illinois, and New York are pushing them out completely. Some major retailers—like, believe it or not, global furniture giant IKEA—have even decided they're not waiting for a law to exhaust them. The problem is that the government isn't just phasing out flame retardants altogether. They're replacing them with other chemicals that haven't been properly tested. Two of the alternatives, TDCPP and TCPP—more commonly known by their street name, "*Tris*"—are known to affect a male's sperm. Not in a good way. In the 1970s, Tris were removed from kids pajamas after they figured out the skin can absorb them. This was sort of a problem since they can mutate your genes.[62]

Another flame retardant the industry will start using more often is hexabromocyclododecane (HBCD). Don't even try to pronounce it. All you need to know is that it's another one that collects in your blood, breast milk, and fatty tissues. Studies suggest you should be concerned. It's highly toxic to fish and may mess with your reproductive system and brain.[63]

STAIN-FREE FABRICS

Since *some* of us are slobs, manufacturers have found ways to keep fabrics stain-free. God forbid your couch or chaise take the blow of some spilled pasta sauce. Couldn't let that happen.

These chemicals that keep everything free of stains—known as perfluorinated compounds (PFCs)—are bad, bad, boys. Like PDBEs, they are known to build up in your body and stay there. One of the PFCs, PFOA, rapidly accumulates in your fatty tissues and your body doesn't get rid of it *ever*. Studies have shown that PFOA has a half-life in the body of 4.4 years. That's just a fun way of saying that even if you absorbed not a single drop more, your system would still take almost 10 years to dump it out.[64]

Everybody has some PFCs in their blood. But it's what they do when they are in your blood that freaks me out. They've been shown to mess with our thyroid, fetal development, and a male's baby maker. In animal studies, they've also been linked to a handful of different cancers.[65] You will hear more than you like in this book about the notorious stain repellants (see page 45).

DANDER AND DUST MITES

It's a bird. It's a plane. You wish. It's hairy microscopic bugs that lounge in your furniture and feed on your dead skin! Barf.

You may not be able to see them, but they are there. Dust mites are house bugs that under a microscope look like mini cockroaches. They hang out in mattresses, pillows, carpet, and frequently-used furniture, getting high off of skin cells and pet dander all day. Oh, by the way: You shed enough skin every day to feed one million of these dudes.[66] Keep exfoliating.

The pro is that dust mites don't carry diseases and are pretty harmless to most people. But for the rest of us, they can cause sneezing, wheezing, watery eyes, runny nose, itching, and a bunch of other allergic reactions.[67] Don't look to Nyquil to cure these symptoms. Mites can also cause nasal polyps to grow in the back of your nose and sinuses. These can eventually affect your sense of smell and make it tougher to breathe.[68] Even if you don't start out with a dust mite allergy, you can develop one. Your body just needs to be exposed to them long enough. Double barf.

> **Aa** **BITCHIONARY: HALF-LIFE**
> The period of time it takes for a substance that is decaying to decrease by half of its initial value.

CANCER YOU CAN BREATHE

Got wood? Whether your home smells of rich mahogany or cheap plywood, you got more than that. You have a lung full of cancerous chemicals. Lucky you.

You can blame your furniture for a majority of bad indoor air. But if you're going to point fingers, point right toward all that pressed wood. It sounds like an industrial term, but pressed wood is really just a pile of wood materials that are slapped together with a fancy-schmancy adhesive.[69] Now bear with me while I make you want to scratch your eyeballs out for a minute. This is some important stuff.

The materials that go into making pressed wood are your bottom of the barrel scraps—wood chips, shavings, and sawdust, to name a few. Most people call them by seductive names such as plywood, medium density fiberboard (MDF), hardboard, or particleboard.[70] Oooh, tell me more. It requires some heavy-duty crap to fuse all these scraps together. Elmer's Glue just won't cut it. Furniture makers use toxic glues and adhesives that trash our air with VOCs like formaldehyde. That's just Step One. For the finishing touch, they top it off with paints, lacquers, and varnishes. Again, we're talking more formaldehyde.[71] This is the chemical known to cause cancer in both humans and animals.[72] Not just one cancer, but a handful.[73]

All these layers of toxic gunk don't know how to sit still and behave. Just days after getting comfortable in your house, the VOCs start to evaporate into the air at room temperature. This goes on for years. This offgassing releases formaldehyde, along with other deadly toxins, which all screw with the air you breathe.[74]

Inhaling even a small dose of formaldehyde can mess up your immune system. Think watery eyes, burning throat, difficulty breathing, and nausea. All those side effects are considered pretty darn normal for formaldehyde levels set at about 0.1 parts per million (ppm) in your home. Interesting. Because the EPA says that a home with significant amounts of pressed-wood products would put your indoor levels at 0.3 ppm, or more.[75]

Let's be honest—we really don't know what the hell we're getting when it comes down to it. The European Union (EU), China, and Japan run a tight ship when it comes to formaldehyde. But here in America, we're more chill about what some countries are quick to call "dangerous." There have been *no* government standards for formaldehyde in this country. Zilch. So when countries like China export wood to America, they don't care about the formaldehyde levels. Why would they? We sure don't. If you want some proof, here it is. China has been shipping pressed woods with lower formaldehyde levels to Japan and Europe for years to meet their strict standards. When someone tested similar birch wood planks imported from China at a Home Depot in Portland, Oregon, Americans looked like suckers. The wood released one hundred times more formaldehyde than what's legal in Japan, and thirty times more than what's allowed in Europe and China.[76]

The sickest part is that some manufacturers, even the luxury brands, are using this crap in nursery furniture. While your bundle of joy is sound asleep, he could be surrounded by formaldehyde in cribs, toddler beds, changing tables, rocking chairs, dressers, and armoires.[77] It's considered to be one of the most dangerous chemicals in the world, people. Studies link it to leukemia—a deadly disease that usually picks on children.[78] Well, who do you think is napping in those cribs and getting their poopy diapers changed on that table? It sure ain't your husband.

If there is anything good we can take from this disaster, it's this: President Barack Obama has cracked the whip against formaldehyde. As of January 2013, any product sold in the Red, White, and Blue will have to meet some hardcore emission standards. Actually, the new law will be the toughest in the world against formaldehyde.[79] It's about damn time.

Aside from formaldehyde, there are plenty of other toxic VOCs fleeing from wood; which ones always involve a good guess since every coffee table is different. Some of the other air pollutants are toluene, ethoxyethanol, and lead. Acetone doesn't have to be listed on the label because it's not a VOC, but pressed wood is loaded with it. It's a major skin irritant that can be mistaken for the flu. And they spray that stuff on thick.[80]

HASTA LA VISTA, RAINFORESTS

There are other reasons to question wood products. Let's just say, it doesn't grow on as many trees as it used to. Partly because here in America, we are paving the road to mass deforestation. Our country makes up almost one-third of the world's total wood-buying market. If we were more careful, we could get all the wood we need from just twenty percent of the earth's forests. But what's the fun in being careful? It doesn't feel nearly as exhilarating. So we've thrown out the blueprints and gone all Paul Bunyan on our forests, chopping down trees like they're weeds. Now our reckless asses are seeing the problem very clearly: Almost half of the world's original forests are gone. Toodles. And every year, we kiss goodbye another forty million acres. Some experts project that we may lose our rainforests *entirely* in less than forty years.

When these natural habitats go extinct, the animals do, too. Shockingly, they get their food and shelter from the trees. As the trees go, so go fifty thousand animal, insect, and plant species every year.[81]

It's also a good idea to remember that those trees we're chopping down suck up carbon dioxide—the main greenhouse gas that's behind global warming. Not only do we lose these natural defenders, but cutting them down *releases* tons of carbon dioxide. It's a lose-lose situation.[82]

CLEARING THE AIR: MAKING SMARTER CHOICES

All this can make you feel pretty helpless. But you're not. Even when it comes to the toxic stuff you already own. Just because your furniture is on a rampage doesn't mean you should sell it on eBay and splurge on an entire new living room set. I don't care if you're rich and have an island named after you. That would be plain silly.

Tossing it would be even dumber. That just adds to our massive landfill problem and releases even more toxins into our groundwater and air. Let's save the melodrama, and keep everything right where it is. By being proactive, you can limit furniture from offgassing and even tame the flame retardants and mites.

IF YOU'RE STUCK WITH WHAT YOU'VE GOT

LOOK FOR NONTOXIC SEALANTS. Sealants put a cork in offgassing, by stopping VOCs such as formaldehyde, benzene, and heavy metals from spewing out all over your living room. They are easy to find at your local hardware store, and come in different variations to match any style of wood. You don't have to be a carpenter to use a sealer. Using a clean bristle brush, just paint it over the wood—chill out, it goes on clear—let it dry, and apply a second coat. Or you could always just read the directions. What a concept.

Kim's Pick: Safe Coat Safe Seal

KEEP YOUR HOME COOL. The hotter it is in your house, the more VOCs will break loose. That's how they work. While they do escape at room temperature, heat and humidity will push emissions to new levels. Keep your home cool. Move pressed wood furniture away from sunlight, and turn on the air conditioner if necessary. You may also want to think about investing in a dehumidifier if you live where it's warm and muggy (I'm looking at you, Florida). These help suck moisture out of the air, and keep mold and mildew from cramping your style.

OPEN UP THOSE WINDOWS. Ventilate, baby! The best thing you can do is open up windows to cool down your home, and send the bad air packing.

WATCH FOR FOAM GONE BAD. Whether it's your couch, pillows, or mattress, keep an eagle eye on upholstery that lies between you and foam. If it starts to tear or rip, sew it up or seal the area tightly. If you think flame retardants leach out of foam when it's covered, just think about what they can do with no boundaries. If you notice the foam is starting to deteriorate, it's time for a replacement. Don't try and get all crafty and fix it. Your health is more important.

VACUUM LIKE IT'S YOUR JOB. Since we get most of our exposure to flame retardants from dust in the house, don't let it get out of hand.[83] Vacuum like it's nobody's business. Some say every day, but we do have lives outside of pushing that monster around the house. Shoot for every other day.

Not only does vacuuming get rid of chemicals caught up in dust balls, but it also sucks up dust mites and their tiny little craps. Vacuums with true HEPA filters are your healthiest option because they don't release dust and dander right back into your air.

IF YOU'RE BUYING SOMETHING NEW

The only way we are going to start phasing out bad, destructive furniture is to stop buying it. Quit throwing your money at companies that could care less about your health (nevermind the planet's). Once you start buying wisely, and the next gal starts using her brain, guess what? The companies who don't care about our health won't have a pot to piss in unless they make some changes.

Here is a laundry list of things to consider next time you're in the market to upgrade your interiors.

DITCH THE CHEAP WOODS. In their natural state, the leftover wood chips and scraps aren't so bad. Actually, they're pretty green. It's the glues that bring them down, and they almost always go hand-in-hand. If you are in doubt, do some research on the company or product before you buy. After all, furniture is a splashy purchase—some time and energy should go into the process.

LOOK FOR WATER-BASED GLUES AND ADHESIVES. Just because companies use formaldehyde and other foul toxins to press all that wood together doesn't mean you have to settle for it. Even when the formaldehyde levels are "lowered" in all wood products, they will still be there. Water-based adhesives won't offgas solvents and they perform just as well at the task. Soy-based glues for wood are starting to get some attention, too.[84]

One caveat: Some companies boil animal parts or use milk to make water-based glue with casein, so check the ingredients or ask your retailer if you're gung-ho. Looks like even your wood can suffer cruelty.[85]

BE DOWN WITH THE FSC. The Forest Stewardship Council (FSC) is like the FBI of the forest. We're talking one tough cop. The nonprofit organization was created in 1993 to put an end to illegal logging and set some standards that would finally force companies to take responsibility for their recklessness with nature. Hallelujah. The FSC basically works to educate both retailers and the consumer—that's you, toots—on how to be smarter with our resources. They then reward companies that harvest trees in a way that does right by the environment and the economy with a nifty certification. That certification, by the way, is considered the toughest in the world to get. Bow down, tree people.

The organization now oversees fifty countries around the globe. They run a tight ship on everything from the use of filthy pesticides and genetically modified trees (GMOs), to protecting the forests and habitats that are still standing. When a company or retailer earns the FSC stamp of certification, the buyer can trace where the wood came from.[86]

If you're going to buy anything made with wood, use your brain and take home furniture that has the stamp of approval. It's actually more common than you think and getting more affordable by the day. Now you see how consumer demand changes everything. *Check out fscus.org/productsearch/retailers to get your hands on a list of retailers that carry the FSC logo.*

BUY FURNITURE FINISHED IN LOW- TO ZERO-VOC PAINTS OR STAINS. Toxic finishes and stains aren't exclusive to particleboard and cheap woods. Even when you're dealing with veneers or solid wood, steer clear of finishes or topcoats that emit VOCs. I dig more into low- and zero-VOC paints for your walls in the next chapter, but it's important to keep in mind that manufacturers plaster your furniture in the nasty stuff (see "Color Me Badd" on page 30). If you can't get a straight answer from retailers about what's in their finishes or varnishes, then don't reward them with a commission.

Buying unfinished furniture is cool, too. You can rest assured that nothing fishy is sneaking out. Just take it home and paint it with whatever nontoxic paint or finish you damn well please.

> **KIM'S TIP:**
> Don't waste another minute stalking furniture stores for nontoxic glues. Cut to the chase. Columbia Forest Products—the biggest hardwood maker in the country—didn't think it should be so tough or expensive to locate safe, quality furniture. So they introduced the PureBond Fabricator Network, an online list of U.S. and Canadian companies that make formaldehyde-free wood products. Obviously there is something in it for them—all of the retailers on the sought-after list use their Columbia PureBond soy-based adhesive. But who cares? You just need the goods without getting ripped off. *Check out columbiaforestproducts.com/PFN.*

IF THE ENVIRONMENT IS A TOP CONCERN

As you'll quickly realize, the environment and your health may often times clash. Lesson #1: Let's say buying new isn't really an option for you because you don't want to support the mass consumption that has contributed to a Landfill America. Well, buying used may earn you some points from Mama Earth, but it may also leave you with a dining room table that hasn't finished its violent offgassing. Oh, snaps! On the other hand, purchasing a new desk with water-based glues means you're handing your cash over in support of forest destruction. A girl just can't win.

Here's one thing to consider: When you buy lower-VOC products and safe finishes, you are doing a better thing for the earth. As much as they ravage your health, chemicals also put our ecosystem through hell. But whether you decide to buy new, used, or just want to get something off your hands, here are a few things to keep in mind that may offer a healthy ecobalance.

THINK RECLAIMED, REPURPOSED, AND RECYCLED.
You know what they say: One man's trash is another woman's treasure. No need to dig through the dumpsters (though that's an option) but think about this next time you go to buy "new" wood: Ninety-percent of everything made in the United States ends up in landfills less than a year after it's produced.[87] Look for furniture that's been reincarnated from landfills, or a piece made from wood that's been salvaged from forest beds or even underwater. Reclaimed lumber can also come from old barns, factories, warehouses, trains, and wine barrels.

Buying salvaged wood furniture saves virgin trees from getting the axe, and doesn't call for any new materials. You can also look for the SmartWood Rediscovered label, another arm of the FSC that certifies companies taking the even more responsible route.

A list of retailers can be found at rainforest-alliance.org.

If none of that works for you, think about buying lower-grade woods over higher-grade. Lower-grade woods are simply those with natural defects on the wood surface such as knots, twists, and crooks. To get high-grade products, they just smooth out the kinks.[88] Personally, I think the kinks give it some character.

HELP GET WOODS OFF THE ENDANGERED SPECIES LIST.
Stop yourself from buying furniture made from endangered woods such as teak,[89] Brazil wood, Spanish cedar, mahogany, and rosewood.[90] Choose "secondary species" which are in less demand. Some of these include sweet gum, madrone, and California oak.[91]

BUYING LOCALLY ISN'T JUST FOR FOOD.
Get to know your local furniture artisans. Visit craft fairs and skim through online community resources to find ones that fit your style. You'll run across some true hippies at local markets that only use salvaged wood and recycled fabrics. Buying furniture locally also calls for *a lot* less petroleum and packaging to get to your doorstep. To ensure you don't put your health in jeopardy, just do your due diligence and engage in some conversation with the artisan before buying to find out what glues and finishes were used. Open your big mouth and let them know what's important to you.

IF YOU'RE BUYING USED, TAKE A VACUUM TO IT.
When you get home, use the attachment hose to eat up any dust mites. (I know, again, *gross.*) If you're not too lazy, remove any upholstery and wash in hot water before getting comfortable.

BUY VINTAGE FURNITURE. Like George Clooney, some things just get better with age. Old is the new, well, *new*. A big advantage to vintage is that it's probably offgassed as many VOCs as it can. Since vintage furniture may contain lead, it's smart to get it sealed before bringing it into your home. Lead is a motha of a problem when it starts chipping away. Look for a furniture refurbisher in your area, and leave it to a professional.

IF YOU'RE OVER IT, GIVE IT A SECOND LIFE. Stop polluting our landfills when your indecisive ass is tired of something you own. Craigslist and eBay weren't created out of boredom; they were developed out of necessity. Take advantage of these tools by selling, trading, or even giving it away for free to someone else who might actually think it's cool. List it on freecycle.org or even kick it to the curb—literally (just attach a "free" sign). Also, take a stab at upcycling: Make it into something else that will fit your needs or lifestyle. Just remember how creative you were when you made the solar system out of styrofoam balls in second grade. See you do have a creative bone in that hot body.

THE SKINNY: FURNITURE UPCYCLING

Women are fickle. Don't expect us to like something forever. We may not even like it next month. But that doesn't mean we should just cut it loose. (That's cold.) So we went to Dianne Kraus, a LEED AP-certified designer and owner of ecoboutique and design consultancy, GreenTangerine, for crafty ways to remake items that have lost their luster, but not outlived their usefulness. (For those scratching their heads, LEED is a third-party certification system that basically recognizes a building or community for design that embodies sustainable elements.)

The upcycling guru calls her mantra the five "Rs"—reclaim, repurpose, redesign, recycle, and rethink. "No sturdy artifact should have to live out eternity in the landfill," she says. "If it's your mission to get deeper into the green furniture space, put on your designer's smock, and start tinkering."

If that dresser doesn't look so hot with your new bedspread, she suggests freshening it up with low- or VOC-free paint or finish. Drawers from an old armoire or nightstand can be repurposed as planters for the garden. If you own way too many cookbooks and are drowning in recipes, stack books about three- to four-feet-high for a table stand. Top with candles, knick-knacks from your travels, or a lamp. Old rugs can even make a stand-in window shade when you want to block out sunlight (nasty hangover, eh?).

One of Dianne's favorite resources is Etsy.com for one-of-a-kind items from artists around the globe. She also looks to Drap-Art's creative recycling festivals and workshops out of Spain, which is ripe with ideas (drapart.org). She says upcycling is on the upswing. "I am finding my clients wanting to upcycle more often than not these days, and it is a great design challenge."

Check out GreenTangerine at greentangerinela.com

TRY AND DITCH THE POLYURETHANE FOAM. Find retailers that offer organic cotton or polyester fill over polyurethane foam. Polyurethane is not only a pyromaniac, but it's also a petroleum project. If the flammable foam is the only option, make sure it's covered or wrapped in thick-ass upholstery or fabric. Build the barrier between you, your dust, and flame retardants.

If retailers brag about a "natural" filling, you might want to ask just how natural. Wool and down are common fills when replacing the plastic variety.

Soy isn't just for your burgers, either. One of your best options is BiOH polyols, a soy-based foam that is becoming more popular in furniture, bedding, and carpet backing.[92] It's as flexible and soft as foam made from petroleum. It lasts as long as foam made from petroleum. But I'll be darned, it's not made from petroleum. BiOH has made it ridiculously easy for you to score furniture that uses this less-toxic foam.

Just visit bioh.com/biohlocator for retailers and locations in your neighborhood.

Here's an idea: practice some caution, too, and don't be so clumsy. Move candles away from upholstery or anything that could spell trouble. Put some distance between your couch and lamps. And for crying out loud, make sure it's not blocking a heater.

WRAP IT IN ORGANIC COTTON. If you're customizing a used or new couch, doll that baby up in organic cotton. Requiring an obscene amount of pesticides and insecticides to grow, conventionally farmed cotton is outright cruel to our health and the planet's[93] (see page 38). Eco-friendly retailers like Mod Green Pod have it down pat. Their organic cotton upholstery comes in the cutest prints and are silk-screened with low-impact, water-based inks.

Visit modgreenpod.com to view the goods.

BAMBOO:
THE BANGIN' ALTERNATIVE TO WOOD

Bamboo has got it going on. Though it's actually a grass and not even related to wood, it's taking a load off of our virgin forests.

It's not hard to see why. First off, bamboo shoots up like a weed and doesn't need much water to grow. There is no need to hose it down with pesticides since it's naturally pest-resistant. And this wonder grass absorbs up to thirty-five percent more carbon dioxide than trees of a similar size. In furniture, it's actually more durable than oak.[94]

What makes bamboo a real freak of nature is that it can grow to its full height in as little as three to four months. And when you cut bamboo down, there's no replanting required. Bamboo just starts replenishing itself right away. An oak tree, on the other hand, can take up to 120 years to reach maturity, and it won't exactly pop back up anytime soon.

So what's the catch? How come I'm not living in a decked-out bamboo hut in the middle of Santa Monica, California? Well, nearly all of the commercial bamboo sold in the U.S comes from China. That's a whole lot of oil burned on the way to your doorstep. On balance, it's still a better choice as long it's not caked in toxic finishes and glues.[95] In that way, bamboo can suffer from the same woes as pressed wood.

Check to make sure it meets Greenguard standards, an independent nonprofit that makes sure products meet some indoor air quality and off-gassing standards. For more information, visit Greenguard.org.

BITCH WE LOVE:
EMILY KROLL
Q&A WITH THE FOUNDER
OF EKLA HOME

Emily Kroll isn't exactly the type that comes to mind when you think of home furnishings. The sharp blonde is a far cry from your showroom hustler hard-selling you to clear a couch from her showroom floor.

And to that, we should all be saying, *Rock on.*

The CEO and founder of the Los Angeles-based EKLA Home—an eco-chic furniture design and lifestyle company—Emily's nothing like the norm. She's the granddaughter of a furniture designer on one end of the family tree, and a scrap metal recycler on the other. Hell, her family's roots have been in the recycling business since the early 1900s.

In the early 1990s, Emily got savvy to something that just wasn't all right with her: The furniture industry was credited for raping two-thirds of the world's rainforests. So she got down and dirty researching ways to build furniture with the lowest impact possible. After seeing Al Gore's seminal speech at The Milken Institute in 2005—the basis for *An Inconvenient Truth*—she made the critical decision to make her company one-hundred percent green or go home.

Today Emily is still making and designing furniture for interior designers, celebrities, and large businesses, but with even more thought. EKLA's designs focus on organic cotton and sustainable materials with no VOCs, chemical flame retardants, or toxic dyes.

If anyone knows what's wrong with our furniture industry, it's this woman. And she's not afraid to speak up.

KIM : *Many of us don't realize where a bed has been before it reaches the showroom floor. How far is most of our furniture traveling?*

EMILY KROLL: These days most furniture travels from Asia. While some companies will try to play down their import practice by claiming they are offsetting a high carbon footprint by using water transport [ships], they don't tell you that their products are compiled of raw materials that are sourced in many different countries and then shipped where labor is cheapest. The finished goods are then transported again to U.S. and European consumers, thus nullifying the low impact of a one-way ship.

K: *How is the production process in making furniture wasteful?*

EK: Most furniture today is made in China and Vietnam. The Chinese are most concerned with moving a large volume of product at the lowest possible price point. To achieve these goals, they are using techniques that are not environmentally friendly. The dying process for textiles overuse natural resources and pollute groundwater, not to mention they are dangerous to the people working with them. The chemicals used in furniture production are not monitored and regulated in the same way as they are in the United States. Because of all this, the environment in China and other developing countries is suffering. It's not good.

K: *What are a few of the most dangerous chemicals being used in furniture?*

EK: PBDEs, pesticides, formaldehyde, and petroleum.

K: *Why are manufacturers still using these chemicals if there are safer options?*

EK: The chemical companies have tremendous lobbying power and money, which they use to silence the opposition. State and federal law regarding fire requires the use of chemical flame retardants in furniture, which doesn't help our cause.

K: *We've talked about FSC-certification, nontoxic glues and stains, but what about natural rubber?*

EK: Natural rubber is otherwise known as natural latex. In the United States, a product need only contain six percent natural latex rubber to be labeled as "natural latex." The other ninety-four percent of the product may contain chemicals and petroleum that is potentially toxic. Consumers should ask when buying natural latex (or rubber) products whether it is certified organic natural latex—new to the market—, meaning it is bound with nontoxic ingredients.

K: *As far as upholstery and fabrics, what is important to know before you make that next home furnishing purchase?*

EK: Make sure to purchase products that have ingredients that are organic and third-party certified. This means that an independent organization—not a trade organization—has certified the ingredients to be nontoxic.

Secondly, try to support local production of furniture products to ensure that the products are not traveling halfway around the world before reaching your home.

K: *What tips would you give to the gal who just realized her home is full of crap but she just doesn't know where to start?*

EK: I would say start with your bed. We spend an average of one-third of our lives in our beds, and conventional bedding products in this country are loaded with chemical flame retardants. This includes mattresses, mattress pads, pillows, and comforters. Switch to organic bedding first, and then tackle the next item where your family spends the most time—your sofa.

For more information on Emily Kroll and EKLA, visit eklahome.com.

★ Color Me Bad:
PAINT

So you're saying you're ready to paint. You got the paint roller, the old sweats you wear when you're on the rag, and nothing but white walls ahead of you—did you even bother to check what you're planning to splash all over them? Let me guess . . . it was a pretty color.

Lesson #1: If walls could talk, they'd never shut the hell up.

Ever wonder why that new paint smell gets you higher than a doobie in high school? It's the fumes. That paint you bought at your local home big-box store could be loaded with up to ten thousand chemicals.[96] These chemicals spoil the air in your home for longer than they take to dry. We're talking years, toots.

Let's break down what you're getting when you buy a can of paint.

THE "BAD" ORGANICS: VOLATILE ORGANIC COMPOUNDS (VOCS)

Remember that woman-to-woman chat we had about VOCs in the beginning of the book? Well, they take the cake as the most dangerous stuff in paint. They are messed up in the head. These freakish chemicals evaporate at room temperature and don't just walk out the door. Your house is full of these noxious gases thanks to that "pretty color."

What you might be breathing in depends on the type of paint. But VOCs can come from ethylene, propylene glycol, formaldehyde, toluene, benzene,[97] and white spirit to name a few. No, not the kind in your vodka, you lush. White spirit is a solvent made from paraffin—the sludge at the bottom of the oil barrel. You can also find it in candles. It's known best for slowing down your central nervous system, impairing your coordination and reaction time.[98] By reaction time, I mean in situations like when you have to break at a stoplight or see a car coming straight for you on your morning jog. Kind of important stuff.

The VOCs in paint are especially demented. According to the EPA, you can expect nose and throat discomfort, headaches, vomiting, nosebleeds, fatigue, dizziness, and some funky skin reactions. The American Lung Association decided to add muscle pain and liver and kidney damage to that list.[99] Anything else, people?

VOCs can also react with oxygen in the presence of sunlight to form ozone. The bad kind of ozone—the kind causing global warming and that gigantic hole over Antarctica that makes it dangerous for you to get your tan on. Consider this: Americans buy about two gallons of paint per person every year.[100] If you get a lot of sunlight in your home, there's a chemical reaction going on in your living room, producing ozone. Of all that paint, more than sixty-four million gallons gets wasted and tossed every year. It should go to a hazardous waste dump, but most is going to our landfills where it reacts with even more sunlight.[101] Ouch.

I've said it before, but this offgassing inside your

home happens at room temperature. You don't need to turn on the heat, or bang pots and pans against the wall for VOCs to come out and play. They just do.

THE OTHER GUYS

There are several working parts in a can of paint. Binders hold everything together, solvents affect the texture and how fast it dries, and pigments give it the color. Great. Why should you care? Because they all contain a mob of man-made additives that aren't too hot for your health.

Toxic binders can be made from petroleum, polyurethane (a plastic), polyester (a fabric), or epoxy. The latter can contain BPA, the chemical that gives plastic a soft, flexible feel and gets absorbed by your body before targeting your hormones. Say hello to some major reproductive issues and cancer.[102]

Let's not forget about the color. How do you think that paint gets all canary yellow? It's not from wildflowers, honey. Try heavy metals. Since lead got phased out, chromium and cadmium still find their way into paints.[103] Chromium is the dangerous shit Erin Brockovich fought to get out of a town's water supply. It's highly toxic to your lungs, throat, and mucous membranes. If you inhale it for long enough—say for the two years it gets offgassed into your freakin' home—it can lead to ulcers and cancer. You saw the movie. Cadmium isn't any friendlier. It's a known carcinogen that can cause renal failure. Even at low levels, you can be overexposed to both.[104]

While lead was phased out of new paints in 1978, older homes may still have it. Deteriorating lead paint is still the number-one source of lead exposure in kids. Let's be real: Adults inhale it, too. But kids have a funny habit of putting their dirty hands all over walls and then sucking their thumbs. Lead particles also fall off the walls and get mixed up in dust bunnies in your carpet or floor. There are no safe levels established on lead. None.[105] When adults come in contact with lead, they absorb about eleven percent of this heavy stuff. Your tots absorb anywhere from thirty to seventy-five percent.

What a difference a few birthdays makes. Doctors say that lead in a child's blood can lower his IQ by about one to three points.[106] Were you trying to raise a kid who can't pass the SATs? Somehow I doubt it.

If you live in a house that may have lead on the walls, nontoxic paint strippers can remove it. Even though you can get these at home improvement stores, take my word for it: Hire a professional. Typically, your friendly local painter can handle the gig, but you can also cruise local listings on Craigslist or another local community Web site. Don't get all independent on me and try and do it yourself.

COLOR YOU GOOD: BUYING PAINT THAT DOESN'T SUCK

Don't turn your back on your walls. There are healthier paints out there. Get armed with some knowledge and you won't let that pretty color sway you into making any more stupid decisions.

GO FOR LOW- TO VOC-FREE PAINTS. To find the VOC levels, just read the back of the label. VOCs are measured in grams per liter (gm/l). You really want to shoot for zero-VOC paint, but since the color options are still growing, if you are dead set on something with more pop, go for low-VOC. That's as soft as I'm going to get on you.

Current federal EPA limits for "low-VOC" are set at a max of 250 gm/l for flat paints. What that means: A paint labeled "low-VOC" can contain anywhere from 5 gm/l to 250 gm/l. Here's where things get tricky. These guidelines were based on lowering VOC emissions from levels that react with ozone and turn your home into a war zone. They don't look at the impact of VOC emissions on your health and indoor air, which could be toxic at lower concentrations. That is why I say go with zero-VOC.[107] Though "zero" or "no" would normally mean what it says—none at all—zero-VOC paints can still contain up to 5 g/l. But that's it.[108]

★ What Lies Beneath:
CARPETS AND FLOORING

CONSIDER PAINTS DERIVED FROM NATURAL SOURCES. Natural paints are just that . . . natural. They're made with plant- or mineral-based ingredients. Natural paints are a stellar alternative because they contain few VOCs and fewer risks to your health. Common active ingredients are clay, soy by-products, and milk. Watch out for milk. Do you really want your walls going *mooo*? Milk paint has been around for hundreds of years, but it's made with casein (milk protein) from animals, lime, and natural pigments.[109] Gross. Go with a natural paint that's free of dairy.

Going with green paints doesn't mean you have to literally paint the walls green anymore. All of these alternatives are pretty easy to find. Check out your local home improvement store or just order online. And ask them to send you color swatches if you're worried it's not going to match the drapes.

THE SKINNY:
You may dig the color, but tone it down there, Rainbow Bright. As a rule of thumb, lighter paints contain fewer VOCs than those superbold colors.[110] They also absorb less heat so they last longer.

KIM'S PICKS: PAINTS
Benjamin Moore Natura Line (benjaminmoore.com)
Mythic Paints (mythicpaint.com)
YOLO Colorhouse (yolocolorhouse.com)

Kiss the ground you walk on. Go ahead. Give it a big wet one. Dirty feet and lint won't be the worst thing sitting on your tongue. You'd be better off licking the tile in the guy's locker room.

The cheap floors in your home reek of toxins that put Chernobyl to shame. These chemicals—usually products of petroleum—are some of the same offenders you'll find in your furniture. They are a bitch to get away from. Mostly because these chemicals were used to make the floors or carpet, and then were reapplied to super glue them to the concrete floor. Wood and vinyl floors usually get the triple whammy—petrochemicals are also used to give them that shiny look.

The problem isn't just the stench (Think: new car). Over time, these chemicals deteriorate. Some things speed up the break down process: heat, sunlight, water, and walking all over it in your ghastly four-inch heels. When the chemicals deteriorate, they evaporate and pollute your air.[111] And this, after all, is what you breathe. Depending on what you're dealing with, this offgassing of toxins and VOCs can last for two months and up to five years.[112] You're in for the long haul.

CHEAP MATERIALS UNDER YOUR FEET

All commercial builders care about is laying that floor down, and what it's going to cost them. They don't care what's in it. It's all about using the cheapest materials and installing by the cheapest means possible, so they can get on to their lunch break. There aren't any regulations that push them to use safer products.

We can blame all these cheapo materials for turning our homes into a living hell. Some of them contain some pretty harsh VOCs, and others are downright evil.

There's a big scare about phthalates in vinyl floorings. When you consider that babies and toddlers spend a majority of their days crawling around on floors, it has moms shitting bricks.

Phthalates aside, vinyl flooring is made of petroleum. The stuff you fill your gas tank with. It can offgass heavy metals into the air, including lead and cadmium. Lead builds up in your body, and is toxic to almost every organ you've got.[113] During the production process, vinyl creates a toxic cocktail of dioxins and vinyl chloride that sabotages the environment and our health. Once you decide you're sick and tired of it, it sits in a landfill f-o-r-e-v-e-r, without degrading. It can be burned at high temperatures, but that just releases more dioxins.[114] We really don't need any more.

Wood floors, carpet, or anything with a shiny laminate can emit formaldehyde.[115] This one is actually nicknamed a VVOC, which stands for *very* volatile organic compound. The International Agency on Research for Cancer (IARC) says formaldehyde causes cancer,[116] and even the EPA says it's a probable human carcinogen. It causes lung cancer in rats, could alter your DNA, and actually may react with other chemicals to produce more carcinogens and mutagens.[117]

Carpet really gives me the heebie-jeebies. It's the cheapest of all types of flooring, and emits a mess of VOCs on top of formaldehyde. Take your pick: benzene, styrene, toluene, and xylene. When you inhale any of these freakish four, your body rapidly absorbs them. Once inside, they slow down the central nervous system.[118] This is the cockpit for the entire body. It tells everything else what to do.

That's not even why carpets make me cringe. They are a good hiding spot for just about anything and everything you don't want chillin' in your house. Dust mites, pesticides, pet hair, mold spores, bacteria, and viruses all love to sink into the fibers.[119] Ewww. The dust mites are what really piss me off. Dust mites may be smaller than a grain of rice, but they feast on dead skin cells, and they're tough to spot. In just one square yard of carpet, you can have up to one-hundred thousand of these crazy Mo Fos that leave behind about twenty droppings each a day. These little turds contain a protein that many people are allergic to.[120]

Oh, and if you'd prefer not to have an exploited farm animal in your carpet, stay away from goat hair or wool (see The Vegan Taboos on page 16). This crap is everywhere in carpet because it's a biodegradable option. Don't let a carpet rep try to convince you that they just give sheep a haircut. Ask her if she'd like the skin around her anus removed without anesthesia. See how she likes that . . .

It's natural to be floored by all this. Luckily, a new age of green and clean flooring has dawned and it's giving us plenty of stylish alternatives.

FLOORS WITH SUSTAINABLE STYLE

Some of you just like the way carpet feels under your feet—it's soft, helps muffle sounds, and retains heat when it's cold outside. But now you know conventional carpeting is a bunch of fluff. Homebuilders use synthetic glues to assemble and nail them down. So now you have glues *and* the carpet unleashing VOCs into your home. What a team.

If you're a sucker for softness, you don't have to abandon your carpet *completely*. Just know what you want before you walk into a bad decision.

Rather than paving your floors with petroleum, look for natural fiber carpets in earthy materials. Sea grass, sisal, and coir (coconut husk fiber) are some of the more popular options. These are easier to keep clean and the dust mites just don't go all gaga over them.

If natural fibers seem like your cup of tea, keep these tips in mind:

CHOOSE A DENSE, CLOSELYKNIT WEAVE. The closer the weave, the less dust build-up you'll get. It beats vacuuming every day.

MAKE SURE CARPETS WERE NOT TREATED WITH CHEMICALS IN THE MANUFAC-TURING PROCESS. Hello?! The chemicals are the jerks that leave your floors and pollute your air.

THINK ABOUT A CARPET THAT HASN'T BEEN DYED OR USES VEGGIE-DYED FIBERS. Dyes contain chemicals that stink for your health and the environment. If you're going to go natural, why not go all the way?

OPT FOR A BACKING THAT IS ALSO MADE FROM NATURAL FIBERS. Think felt, natural rubber, recycled rags, or burlap. See above. Why screw up the natural plan?

FASTEN THE CARPET TO THE FLOOR WITH WATER-BASED GLUES OR GRIPPER STRIPS. Adhesives that contain no solvents, or low- to no VOCs will keep your air the cleanest.

WHEN INSTALLING NEW CARPETS, LEAVE THEM HOME ALONE FOR A FEW DAYS. Open up the windows to increase ventilation and send any toxins outdoors. You can always ask the retailer to let new carpets sit in their warehouse for three or four days before installing in your space.

IF YOU CAN'T DECIDE WHETHER YOU WANT CARPET OR WOOD FLOORING, ROLL WITH BOTH. The manufacturer Interface offers a rad alternative to conventional carpeting with low-VOC FLOR tiles made with natural fibers and recycled rubber backing. The pieces fit together in any fashion like a puzzle. When you're sick of them, return them to Interface to be recycled. You can also use the carpet tiles to make a living room rug.

Visit interfaceflor.com.

KEEPING AN EXISTING CARPET IN GOOD SHAPE

For those of us stuck with the carpet we've been dealt, often just treating it with kid gloves is enough to limit its toxic outbursts. Here is where it pays dividends to be a clean freak.

VACUUM LIKE A MAD WOMAN. Everyone will tell you something different, but your best bet is to vacuum every other day or at least once a week. It feels like a daunting chore, but so does blowing your nose fifty times an hour after a severe allergy attack. Touché. For tips on buying the right vacuum, see page 71.

STICK WITH "DRY" CLEANING. Avoid cleaning your carpets with wet steam or dousing a stain in hot water. Leave a carpet wet and you might as well post a huge "vacancy" sign for the likes of mold, mildew, and dust mites. If you're going to use a wet steam cleaner, open the windows and turn on the fans to encourage quick drying.

Instead, use a dry steam cleaner or hire a professional service that uses natural carpet-cleaning solutions. Once dry, give those carpets a quick vacuum to properly dispose of dead dust mites and allergens camping out on top.

CHECK THE SHOES AT THE DOOR. Make guests go barefoot in your house. It's your house, not theirs. If they've got a problem with it, maybe *they* should host a dinner party once in a blue moon. Shoes can drag in pesticides and dog poop from outdoors that stick to carpet fibers. As for pets, keep wet wipes at the back door and pat down their paws before they come back in.

PUT AN END TO CONTINUOUS CARPET OFF-GASSING. You can actually seal your carpet with a non-toxic floor sealant or vapor barrier that puts an end to any more offgassing. Companies like SafeChoice Carpet Seal (afmsafecoat.com) offer a sealant that blocks chemicals such as toluene, formaldehyde, xylene, styrene, and benzene from offgassing for up to five cleanings. The only kink is you *cannot* apply the product to dry carpets—it should be applied to carpets right after shampooing by misting the sealant over the surface with a pump sprayer. Again, just make sure you speed up the drying process so wet carpets don't sit around soaking up moisture.

GO NATURAL

Vinyl is easy to clean up after a spaghetti disaster. But it's also just another name for polyvinyl chloride (PVC) or plastic. And let's get another thing straight: Vinyl and linoleum aren't the same thing. They have little in common but a nice, shiny surface.

The good news? Natural linoleum is made from green materials including linseed oil, ground limestone, cork flour, and tree rosin. The right ingredients are mixed together like a smoothie and pressed onto a

---

B BITCHWORTHY: MARMOLEUM
Next time you make a trip to the gyno, check out the floor. The linoleum alternative, Marmoleum, is a favorite for hospitals because it's antibacterial and a cinch to clean. Just because your doctor picked a boring color doesn't mean you have to. Choose from 150 colors that also come in tiles and sheets. *Visit marmoleumclickstore.com.*

chemical-free backing. Linoleum flooring is naturally nontoxic and hypoallergenic—it repels dirt and dust. Linoleum floors can last up to forty years if cared for and are better than vinyl at standing up to nicks and scratches.[121] The bad news? Linoleum does cost a bit more and usually requires a professional to install it, unless you were going for that botched flooring look.

WOOD ALTERNATIVES

We all dig a home that smells of rich mahogany, but hardwood floors raise some eyebrows for toxic varnishes as well as formaldehyde glues and adhesives. Also on the downer side: Its existence is the reason our forests are now open plains.

Look for reclaimed or salvaged wood that doesn't require virgin trees to be cut down. Whether it came from an old barn, winery, railroad ties, or an estate sale, it will tell a story. Make one up if you want to. Like furniture, you can often find an artisan dealer in your hood to prevent all the transport. If you must buy new hardwood floors, always look for the FSC logo or SmartWood certification. No excuses.

Another option is to refinish weathered wood floors with a nontoxic varnish. By working with what you've got, you save transportation costs (to the environment) and some trees.

> B **BITCHWORTHY: SCATTER RUGS**
> An easy way to add contrast to your flooring is to lay down a few area or scatter rugs made from natural fibers or unbleached organic cotton.

Bamboo

You can also score the hardwood look with bamboo. Though it's actually a grass, bamboo can also earn FSC certification stating that it's been harvested sustainably. This look is super sharp in any home, and is naturally resistant to bacteria and moisture. Bamboo floors are also simple to install, low-maintenance, and comparable in price to hardwoods.

So how does it hold up in your home? Bamboo is more durable, but much softer than hardwood. If you love playing dress-up in Carrie Bradshaw stilettos, you may hate it. The heels will eventually start to leave their mark. If you go with bamboo, double check with the manufacturer to make sure it hasn't been treated with toxic chemicals and adhesives.

Cork

A retro throwback to the '70s, cork flooring might just be the most renewable flooring option on the market today. Cork flooring is made from the bark that sheds from trees every nine to fifteen years. It's hypoallergenic, naturally resistant to nasty mold and mildew, and ultradurable. For those living in colder climates, it maintains a pretty neutral temperature with great insulation so you stay warm and toasty.

Do think about how much sunlight you get. Cork eats up sunlight and starts to discolor with age. Another negative is the dent it can put in your wallet and carbon footprint. It's not sourced locally—it's native to Europe and Africa—so it can also rack up carbon emissions. Regardless, it still has clout in the health department.

TILE AND TILE ALTERNATIVES

Tile floors seem to be a good match for chicks who live near a beach or just love the outdoors. They're low-maintenance, as long as you're willing to make like Cinderella and get on those hands and knees to scrub. If you're living in an older home, tiles can contain asbestos—a group of twisted mineral fibers that can cause lung and abdominal cancers. When these tiles start to wear down and deteriorate, like say in that 1920s home you might be living in, asbestos leaches into the air and then your lungs.

If you do have asbestos in your humble abode, you have a few options. Once you start to see damage, always hire a professional to remove the tiles or seal the asbestos back together with a nontoxic sealant. Whatever you do, don't try to patch this up yourself.

Recycled Glass or Ceramic Tiles

Recycled glass floors, mosaic glass, or ceramic tiles add character to a place (and prevent used glass from going to the landfills). Terrazzo is a hybrid of crushed glass and concrete that is immune to chemicals and bacteria. No asbestos. No cancerous chemicals. And no sealants required. It will also last you a lifetime. You do want a long one of those.

B BITCHWORTHY: BEDROCK INDUSTRIES
Allow me to get sappy here. This collection of colorful tiles is made from purely recycled glass with no artificial pigments or colorants. One word: beautiful. The company packages with all recycled materials and rallies the local community with elementary school bottle drives. *Visit bedrockindustries.com.*

Recycled Rubber Floors

For those with kids running around the house, rubber floors aren't just for the Gold's Gym down the street. Check out recycled rubber floors made from old tires or other sources. They come in different colors and designs, but they got my attention for one big reason: Girl, they can take a beating! Let your kids or pets go to town on these things.

Subflooring

What lies beneath your flooring can be a hell of a headache, too. Subflooring—the layer underneath your carpet, cork, or bamboo floors—can contain the conventional plywood and particleboard that spits out formaldehyde. If you're building from scratch, you're in luck. Choose a solid wood subfloor that is FSC-certified or post-consumer recycled.

THE SKINNY: FLOOR CLEANERS
Dirty floors aren't going to clean themselves. Get to work. But work with a natural floor cleaner.

When you buy one of those cheap, petrochemical solvents or steam cleaners, you're just fueling the problem. Go figure, name-brand floor cleaners don't have to list their chemicals so chances are they won't. That is probably because they contain wicked chemicals such as dipropylene glycol, 2-butoxyethanol, and ammonium hydroxide. Some may even contain traces of benzene.

HOMEMADE NATURAL FLOOR CLEANER
What You Need:
¼ cup club soda
1 tablespoon liquid castile soap
¼ cup distilled white vinegar
2 gallons (8 liters) hot water

Mix well to dissolve liquid soap and mop floors with a microfiber mop.

★ Good in Bed:
EVERYTHING YOU NEED TO GET HEALTHY ZZZZS

We don't get nearly enough beauty sleep. Just ask the seventy million Americans with insomnia who can't take a phone call until they're hopped up on three lattes.[122]

Maybe we should retire the poor sheep clearing hurdles in our heads, and take a look at the damn bed. It's about as restful as a Big Gulp of caffeine.

"Wrinkle-free" and "no iron" bedding can be treated with formaldehyde. And for all you walking zombies, one of the side effects of formaldehyde is insomnia. Your bed could be the very thing keeping you awake at night.[123] Go ahead and ask the question: Why in the world would someone be nuts enough to douse our sheets in formaldehyde? Well, how else do you think they avoid the iron? Nature is good, but not that good.

CONVENTIONAL COTTON

The toxicity doesn't end at formaldehyde. Cotton is nicknamed the world's "dirtiest" crop.[124] Conventional cotton fabrics are bleached and doused in chemicals to unsettle the waxes and get rid of the harmful gunk. Usually this is done with chlorine monoxide,[125] which gains some credit for depleting the ozone layer.[126] Whatever the bleaching agent, this process sets dioxins and extremely toxic chemicals loose in the wild. Once those fabrics have put the environment through the ringer, they're typically dyed and treated with heavy metals.[127]

Aside from all the water cotton production sucks up, almost one-quarter of the world's insecticides are dumped on cotton crops to keep the bugs at bay.[128] That doesn't even cover pesticides—somewhere around fifteen pesticides go into harvesting cotton. Nine of the ten most commonly sprayed pesticides are said to be "moderately to highly hazardous" to our health, with seven classified as "probable or known" human carcinogens by the EPA. To show you just how foul these pesticides are, aldicarb—cotton's second bestselling insecticide—can kill a person with just one potent drop absorbed by the skin. As whack as that sounds, aldicarb is still used in twenty-five states with sixteen of them showing traces of it in their groundwater.[129]

PETROLEUM IN YOUR BED

Don't look at the person sleeping next to you—your bed is the one passing gas all night long. If you don't sleep in the throes of cotton, you probably snore to the tune of nylon or polyester. [Do you love the smell of phthalates in the morning?] Nylon and polyester are synthetic fabrics made from petroleum that emit plastic vapors.[130] When you take a breath, you inhale these vapors. It's that easy.

Plastic aside, the main ingredient used to make polyester is ethylene glycol. When inhaled or absorbed by your skin, it may interfere with your central nervous system and kidneys.[131] Does that sound like a good night's sleep to you? Um, no! Nylon also has a reputation in the sack for irritating skin and causing dermatitis.[132]

A BED WITH BENEFITS:
FEEL- GOOD SHEETS

Quit sleeping around with pesticides and ruthless chemicals. Fabrics and linens that are safe and still good in bed are easy to find and affordable nowadays. If your bed needs a makeover, here are a few things to look over before the sale rack pulls you in.

BUY ORGANIC COTTON THAT IS UNBLEACHED AND UNDYED. Organic cotton is grown without any pesticides or chemicals, leaves no residues behind, and is free of genetically modified organisms (GMOs). It is the golden ticket to a healthier you and a happier planet. You can't argue with that.[133]

When buying organic cotton fabrics, look for a material that hasn't been bleached or has been colored with low-impact dyes. Though organic cotton isn't produced with harsh chemicals, some manufacturers dye the material with artificial colors that make you itchy and hivey. The term "artificial" should set off an alarm in your head by now. An even better alternative is organically colored cotton, which is basically strains of cotton that naturally grow on the stem in earthy shades—not the modern-day white cotton used to make fabrics. It's actually twenty to forty percent cheaper than regular dyed cotton, so quit your cryin'.

LOOK FOR NATURAL FIBERS. Natural fiber is a fancy way of saying materials that come straight from the earth. But don't get swindled by the buzzword "natural"—look for specific references to the type of fiber. Besides organic cotton, look for hemp, flax, bamboo, and legna.

Bamboo

Bamboo grows like a grass on steroids without the need for chemicals or pesticides. It's ideal for bedding and linen because it's really soft with a cashmere-like feel. You'll want to swim in bamboo sheets. Another big-time benefit is that bamboo is wrinkle-resistant by nature, and washer-dryer friendly. Throw them in the wash as often as you like, and they won't start unraveling. The grass also has deodorizing properties that resist smelly odor and bacteria. If you have pets, kids, or a partner that too often smells like he just ran a marathon, I suggest making the investment. For tips on how to make sure you're getting sustainable bamboo, see page 193.

Some activists argue that, on the downside, bamboo can be treated with harmful solvents that defeat the purpose. But there is a safer solution. Look for bamboo fiber or linen products made with the *lyocell* process. This method uses low-toxicity chemicals in a closed-loop system. In layman's terms, the chemicals are captured every time they are used, and then recycled for the next set of sheets.[134]

Hemp

One of the most versatile fibers to work with, hemp isn't just popular among your stoner friends. Used in everything from textiles and clothing to rope and building materials, hemp calls on no nasty fertilizers and needs little water to grow. It does lack the soft texture of bamboo and legna, but it's still lightweight and comfortable.

Legna

The brainchild of the Italians, legna (LANE-ya) is a biodegradable silk-like fabric made from sustainable wood. Legna is also produced in a primarily closed-loop system similar to the lyocell process. The soft material is also colored using low-impact dyes. You can buy legna in a variety of styles, and not just bedding. Pick up some matching sheets, towels, and bathrobes. *Visit www.sdhonline.com.*

PILLOWS

Don't expect your pillows to help you get a good night's sleep. They are getting their revenge for all that sweat, drool, and zit cream they have to soak up. Just like your soft sheets, pillows offgas a bunch of petrochemicals that you breathe and absorb. But what really makes me want to rest my head on concrete is that they are a hideout for dust mites. I repeat: There are dust mites—both dead and alive—making themselves at home in the soft cushion you billow your face in all night. It's one hell of a pillow fight.

There's more that can go wrong with that bag 'o fun. Pillows can be packed with down feathers from ducks and geese to make you think you're sleeping on marshmallows. The feathers are often ripped out of the bird while they're alive, because manufacturers feel the quality is better. This trauma starts when birds are ten weeks, and can go on until they are four years old. Aside from the cruelty, down pillows attract mold as they age.

Silk is another downer. Sleeping in the lap of luxury costs more than what is on the price tag. You may know that silk is the fiber silkworms weave to make their cocoons. But what you probably don't know is that the worms are steamed or gassed alive in their cocoons to satisfy your superficial needs.[135]

Here are a few animal-friendly alternatives that are filled with natural goodies.

NATURAL LATEX PILLOW Like your mattress, natural latex pillows conform to your head and neck for some firm support. If you live in a colder area with frigid winters, natural latex regulates heat. But let me just stop right there and tell you what you really want to hear—natural latex is inherently resistant to bacteria, mold, and dust mites.[136]

If you want something fluffier, try shredded natural latex. The shredded rubber gives the pillow a more elevated feel, but you still get the neck support.

KAPOK PILLOWS Kapok is a lightweight alternative to cotton with super-soft natural fibers that come from the flower seeds of wild fruit trees in the rainforest. It feels like silk or down, but without the allergies and animal cruelty. The material is hypoallergenic and also repels moisture so you don't have to deal with dust mites, mold, and mildew.

BUCKWHEAT HULL PILLOWS Filled with buckwheat hulls, these pillows are a good choice for those with chronic pains. You name it—bad shoulders, back pain, a stiff neck, and migraines. It contours well to your body and offers some nice elevation for your head. But if you're a light sleeper, forget it. They are noisy and kind of feel like you're sleeping on a beanbag.

ORGANIC COTTON PILLOWS Organic cotton pillows are good if you are allergic to latex or buckwheat. They start out offering firm neck support and then compress by nearly one-third over time to become just plain firm. If you want to avoid dust mites and mold—can I see a show of hands?—look for spelt organic cotton. It's a little coarser, but made of untreated and unbleached cotton husks.

Kapok pillows are definitely going to be a challenge to find in stores, so look to online retailers like Amazon and Pristine Planet. Natural latex, buckwheat hull, and organic cotton pillows are pretty easy to find at major retailers including Target and WalMart.

SLEEPING WITH THE ENEMY: A HEALTHIER MATTRESS WITH A SHELF LIFE

It's the Goldilocks approach. You want a mattress that feels "just right." As long as there's enough cushion for the pushin', and it's sturdy enough to hold your weight when you let yourself go in ten years . . . consider it sold.

But chances are your mattress is anything but *right*. In fact, it's probably all wrong. And considering you spend an upwards of twenty-five years in bed over the course of a lifetime, it's something you should seriously consider splurging on.

Here's why I'm bagging on your mattress: most of them are made with a ticking or filling made from polyurethane foam, another product of Big Oil. Before it makes its way to the place where all the magic happens, the foam is soaked in flame retardants, then wrapped in those infamous chemical-laden fabrics such as polyester or conventional cotton, and then topped with formaldehyde to resist stains. Sometimes, when they're feeling extra kind, they dunk that entire mattress in flame retardants to keep your bed from causing a forest fire.[137] Unless you're getting freaky under the sheets, your bed is the last thing you want to catch fire. But it will. We've had this discussion: conventional foam mattresses are extremely flammable. To meet federal regulations, manufacturers have to bathe those mattresses in fire retardants. As a trade-off, your health pays the price.

Mattress makers can turn to a handful of flame retardants, but they seem to be infatuated with PBDEs (see page 14.) Our homes have gotten very familiar with PBDEs, but our bodies know them even better because they nest in our fatty tissues until we're dead.[138]

Rather than sleep your life away inhaling toxins from a cheap bed every night, you have a few healthier options depending on your lifestyle and the life expectancy you're looking for in a mattress.

ORGANIC AND NATURAL-LATEX MATTRESSES

For the eco-obsessed and health-crazed (like *moi*), as long as you go with a 100 percent organic mattress, you're sleeping on something completely free of chemicals, fire retardants, pesticides, and toxic glues and dyes. Organic mattresses are made with more natural materials such as (organic) cotton, hemp, coconut husks, natural latex, or wool. (Wool is a no-no. Go ahead and count sheep if it helps you get some shut-eye, but don't sleep on them.)

The latest and hottest on the market today, and rightfully so, is pure natural latex. It comes from the sap of a rubber tree that starts to heal itself within an hour of being tapped. Natural rubber is naturally fire-resistant so it doesn't need to be treated with any flame retardants. As far as comfort, it contours to your body at any temperature—compared to memory foam, which call for the room to be at least 65 degrees Fahrenheit—and pops right back into place when you crawl out of bed.

Like all organic mattresses, natural latex is also resistant to bacteria, perfect for those with chemical sensitivities, won't irritate your allergies, and very absorbent.[139] Remember, moisture is what attracts mold, mildew, and dust mites, so that's reason enough.[140] You don't want your sweaty ass bringing all the bugs to the yard.

Organic mattresses are also designed to biodegrade entirely without leaving behind any toxic residues. Since almost forty million mattresses get tossed into landfills every year, don't turn your bed into a nightmare for the environment.

If you're set on getting your beauty sleep on something that is 100 percent natural, make sure you are buying "natural" latex, and not just a latex mattress. There's a big difference—natural latex comes from the rubber tree and synthetic latex comes from petroleum. Yeah, you get it. Same goes with buying an organic mattress. If it's simply labeled "organic" and not "100 percent organic," you could still be conking out on a mattress treated with formaldehyde, coated with plastic, and then wrapped in polyester with small percentage of organic materials. If that's the case, why even bother?

MOSTLY NATURAL-PART SYNTHETIC

For those who appreciate durability above sustainability or health factors, a natural latex mattress with synthetic fillers might just be your best bed buddy. You're still sleeping on something that offgasses fewer chemicals, but it will stand the tests of time. According to eco expert, Danny Seo, the key is to limit the amount of petroleum-based foam. "A 100 percent natural latex bed may sound like the greenest solution, but it breaks down in a shorter period of time," said Danny. "Think of it like a gold bracelet: a 24K bracelet is the purest gold, but it's too fragile and unrealistic to wear everyday. That is why synthetic fillers give it strength and durability."

Though Danny is always the first to side with the environment, he admits that in beds, 65 percent natural latex mixed with 35 percent traditional foam has been found to be the highest amount of natural content you can incorporate to ensure you still have a bed that will last twenty to twenty-five years. In other words, it's the 18K gold of eco mattresses. His general rule of thumb is to limit the amount of petroleum-based foam as much as possible, without ruining the quality of the bed.

PROPER CARE AND CLEANING FOR SUSTAINABLE PILLOWS

Every two to three months, it's good to give the actual pillow a good cleaning. You do lay your face on it every night. But pillows are more fragile than other bedding, so you don't want to just throw them in with the rest of the load.

If you're worried about putting your pillow in a washer and dryer, take a pointer from eco-expert Danny Seo on detoxing your pillow overnight.

DANNY'S TIP:
One easy way to detox your pillows is to pop them in the freezer overnight—any dust mites that might be in there will freeze to death. Also, I like to wrap my pillows with three layers of pillowcases. Every two days I just peel off the top layer until I'm down to my last case on laundry day. You should also replace your bed pillows every two years, which can come as a shock to people.

STEP 1: Wash in pairs. This helps maintain some balance in the washer. If you own a supersized pillow, wash it alone.

STEP 2: Dilute a small amount of natural detergent with cold water. This isn't rocket science. Just pour the detergent in the washer and let the cycle run for a few minutes before you throw the pillow in the mix.

STEP 3: Once the detergent is diluted, toss the pillow in the washing machine on the gentle cycle. Squeeze the pillow tightly to let out the air before you submerge it in water.

STEP 4: Add a teaspoon of white distilled vinegar during the final rinse cycle to kill any leftover residue. As long as you keep it to a teaspoon, the pillow won't stink of vinegar.

STEP 5: Get that pillow dry as quickly as possible. Throw it in the dryer on a low setting, fluffing frequently. If it's a hot, sunny afternoon, you can also set it near a window to dry naturally.

DANNY SEO'S HANDY MATTRESS CHECKLIST

Since Danny seems to be in bed with green, I turned to the bestselling author, television personality, and eco-product developer to help me assemble more tips for a mattress-buying checklist. If you're unconvinced, Danny is the author of seven books including his latest *Upcycling*, the founder of his own organic skincare line, Wholearth, and markets his own self-titled collection of eco-friendly home products at stores including TJ Maxx, Marshalls, and HomeGoods. And ladies, he now has his own Simmons Natural Care by Danny Seo mattress line. He was born on Earth Day. I mean, *really*.

TIP #1: NEVER, EVER BUY A USED MATTRESS. While reusing something is generally the greenest thing you can do, buying a used bed is one of the riskiest things you can do. All those advertisements you see on Craigslist proclaiming someone bought a $2,000 bed, slept on it "once and only once," and they're happy to sell to you for a bargain basement price are almost always too good to be true. In fact, some people drive around in pick-up trucks looking for old beds near trash bins, re-cover them with new fabric and plastic, then sell them to unknowing folks as "factory sealed" on the side of the road or online. Crazy but true.

TIP #2: LOOK FOR A LONG WARRANTY. Mattresses are nearly impossible to recycle, and 99 percent of the time they get tossed into a landfill. Choosing a mattress with a long warranty—twenty or twenty-five years—is the best way to get long wear for long-term use.

TIP #3: PROTECT IT. Once you get your new bed, be sure to protect it with a 100 percent organic cotton mattress protector or encasement cover. This creates a breathable barrier between you and the bed, while preventing anything from getting inside.

TIP #4: NOT JUST ORGANIC ON THE OUTSIDE. If buying an organic bed is important to you, be sure it's not just organic on the outside. Many companies are using organic cotton ticking to cover conventional foam mattresses, which in my eyes, is greenwashing. Be sure to ask what's inside the bed. In fact, it's the inside that really counts—not the fabric on the outside.

TIP #5: AIR OUT YOUR MATTRESS. Air that mattress out. Ultraviolet light is a great natural disinfectant. Unwrap the whole bed and place it by the sunniest window to let it "bake" in the sun. The ultraviolet light will help disinfect odor and detox the bed. There are products you can buy with UV light bulbs inside that you wave across the bed to kill germs and bacteria. But why waste money when sunlight is free?

ASK DANNY:

If you have a conventional mattress and can't afford to buy a new one, is there anything you can do to help limit the amount of toxins it produces?

Answer: Wrap the bed in an encasement cover.

Trap the VOCs and chemicals with an encasement cover that is 100 percent (organic) cotton. Though a mattress pad will provide extra comfort and protect the durability of the mattress, encasement covers are used specifically to trap any chemical offgasses, and to keep bed bugs, pet dander, and other allergens out. Look for them at major retailers and online.

For thousands of insightful tips and do-it-yourself home projects, visit dannyseo.com. Check out Simmons Natural Care mattress collection by Danny Seo, which features natural latex tapped from the rubber tree. Visit naturalcarebed.com.

★ Nonstick Nonsense:
COOKWARE AND STAIN-RESISTANT FABRICS

Since the early 1950s, people have flocked to non-stick cookware. It was revolutionary. Cleaning was a breeze when you no longer had to scrub until your hands bled. The same went for stain-resistant fabric coatings. Entertaining was suddenly stress-free, too. No more worrying about the clumsy bimbo next door spilling red wine all over your white couch. A little splash of water and a pat down, and that couch looked right off the show-room floor again.

We praised these nifty new designs for better living, but nobody questioned how they worked. It was enough that they did. Meanwhile, the companies making the stuff were keeping some scary DEETs under wraps. True, the food and stains weren't "sticking," but neither were the risky chemicals used to make them. You may remember these punks. They're called PFCs (perfluorinated chemicals)—or more precisely, PFOA (perfluorooctanoic acid) and PFOS (perfluorooctanyl sulfonate). And they were leaching right out of products for anyone to inhale. The garbage was building up in our fatty tissues and spreading like crazy in the environment. Wildlife was showing traces of it.[141] But nobody knew how sticky the situation really was.

Back in the day, both DuPont and 3M corporation began manufacturing PFOA, though it became best known under DuPont as the chemical used to manufacture Teflon. Soon PFOS showed up in the form of Stainmaster, Gore-Tex[142] and Scotchguard to nip stains in the bud. Carpets, fabrics, upholstery, and clothes were soon stain-free, as well.[143] Apparently, housewives were lazy and tired of doing laundry and dishes.

PFOS

The first real hint that PFCs might be shady came in 2000. That year, the manufacturer of Scotchguard, 3M, announced that they were going to phase out PFOS, the chemical behind this signature product.[144] (They also made a point to say they were done making PFOA.) *Really?* You're suddenly calling it quits on a chemical you've produced for more then forty years? This raised a big red flag to consumers. Something glaring had to be wrong with PFOS. 3M tried to put a positive spin on the phase-out, sensationalizing the move as that of a stand-up corporate citizen, by saying "small" levels were showing up in the environment. But watchdogs including the EPA called bullshit. For very good reason. They were coming across some freakish findings, that many presumed 3M had known about for years. According to studies, PFOS showed signs of toxicity, persistance in the environment, and bioaccumulation in organisms—meaning we absorb it at a rate greater than we get rid of it—to "an extraordinary degree." Lab tests found that PFOS killed baby rats born to mothers who were themselves exposed in the womb. It may be dawning on scientists that exposures to the chemical may be more harmful during fetal development than they are to adults.[145] Oh crap.

PFOAS

After 3M said buh-bye to PFOS, the spotlight turned to PFOA. The EPA had had its eye on this one for a while. A few mothers who worked at a Teflon plant in the '80s had claimed that PFOA might have something to do with their babies' birth defects.[146] Other studies showed that the dirty chemical pummeled the immune system in lab animals.[147] Something was fishy.

Then DuPont really started to feel the heat. An independent study commissioned by the EPA found that PFOA was a *likely* human carcinogen.[148] Who would have ever thunk?! Fourteen trusty Teflon users then stepped up with a $5 billion class-action lawsuit against DuPont. They were—hmm, how to put this?—*pissed,* that the company failed to warn people of the dangers. DuPont fired back saying that "cookware coated with DuPont Teflon nonstick coatings does not *contain* PFOA."[149] Smart play on words there. PFOA is used to manufacture Teflon and doesn't actually contain it—it just releases it as a deadly gas when heated to high temperatures.[150] Like, say, the temperatures we cook at. DuPont said that such leaching, or as they like to call it, "significant decomposition," should only occur when temperatures exceed 660 degrees Farenheit.[151] But, c'mon, that just doesn't happen, they argued. *Oh really*, said the Environmental Working Group (EWG). *That's news to us.* The environmental watchdog and advocate of public health found that nonstick coatings could reach 700 degrees Farenheit in as quick as three to five minutes when overheated. While leaving an empty pan on a hot burner would easily reach these temperatures, it just happened that such extremes could also be reached by cooking everyday meals on high heats, like stir-fry. When that nonstick shit reaches high heats, it spews out fifteen toxic gases and chemicals; two of them just happen to cause cancer.[152]

But this lawsuit didn't stick either. It was dismissed and the company still says Teflon is safe for its intended uses.

Finally, The EPA brought DuPont down for what many called the most groundbreaking win in the agency's history. They claimed that DuPont straight up hid information for more than twenty years about PFOA. Everything pointed to the fact that they knew it was a big risk to humans and the environment. The maker of Teflon had to pay $10.25 million for violating the law and another $6 million toward environmental projects.[153]

With all this information, the government could finally do something. The EPA asked eight big manufacturers—including DuPont—to be responsible and stop it with the PFOA already. There was no reason to hide. Cut the shit. All eight gave in and have agreed to phase it out by 2015.[154]

At the time this book went to press, DuPont said that PFOA had mostly been removed from new products since 2007, and 3M completed the phase-out as of 2009.[155]

THE STICKY SITUATION

It's a good thing that PFOA is on its way out because it's one mean dude. Nine out of ten Americans have it in their blood, including most newborns.[156] Studies are linking PFCs to higher "bad" cholesterol in kids and teens.[157] It's known to wear down the thyroid and alter male reproductive hormones (boys kind of need those.)[158] Now PFOA is linked to breast, testicular, liver, and pancreatic cancers and tumors.[159] If you ask me, I'd say the jackasses at DuPont have been getting away with murder.

And let's not be stupid and let the stain-repellants off the hook. 3M may have phased it out, but companies outside the United States still use PFOS.[160] This stuff gets around. We're finding it in polar bears in the Arctic, and in dolphins, seals, and otters on opposite coasts.[161] All this suggests that it's still in the food chain. So it's safe to say it might still be in your blood.

With PFOA "Judgment Day" still years away, we need to watch the products we're bringing into our homes. That doesn't even cover the whacked-out cookware we already own. But there are a few things you can do to make sure PFCs steer clear of your food and fabrics.

HOW TO KICK PFCS

DON'T BUY TEFLON-COATED COOKWARE. Um, duh. Why take chances with something that might give you cancer. For nonstick action without teflon, many people are also turning to good 'ole cast iron and learning to season it like our grandmothers did. (Yes, a well-seasoned cast iron skillet is effectively nonstick.) Thermolon is a new material being used by some manufacturers that is reputed to be both PTFE- and PFOA-free. If you already own Teflon, cut your losses. You have two choices. Ring your local Household Hazardous Waste Center and ask for the date and location of their next collection day. Just drop it off and they handle the rest. You can also ship it back to its maker with a cute little stick figure of you flipping the middle finger, and a note that says, *Thank you for considering my health, asshole.*

Visit earth911.com to find a center in your neighborhood.

JUST SAY NO TO SOLUTIONS, FINISHES, OR FABRICS LABELED AS STAIN, DIRT, OR GREASE RESISTANT. That includes upholstered furniture, upholstery, or fabrics labeled as stain- or water-resistant. Stay away from the stain-resistant sprays and cleaners, too. Talk about buyer's remorse. If you have little ones or are really worried about stains, mix a dash of white vinegar and baking soda in a spray bottle. It works every time. See page 63 for more home recipes.

WATCH OUT FOR INGREDIENTS THAT INCLUDE THE TERMS FLUORO OR PERFLUORO. Companies are sneaky. PFCs can be found in everything from dental floss to cosmetics. Read your labels carefully.[162] SKIP THE MICROWAVE POPCORN. While it's fun to pop the microwaveable crap every now and then during a good horror flick, microwaveable popcorn is usually coated with nonstick chemicals.[163] Stick with stovetop-popped corn, or put some kernels in a brown paper bag and fold the top a few times to make your own DIY version of microwave popcorn. Toss with Earth Balance Natural Buttery Spread and salt.

KIM'S TIP: RECYCLE TEFLON
Rather than toss Teflon, take it to a metal scrap recycler or see if your curbside recycling program accepts metal. If you have no clue where one is in your area, visit recycleinme.com.

Stank Scents: ★
CANDLES AND AIR FRESHENERS

Candles are like a damn tattoo. You get one and suddenly you want ten in every room—all lit at the same time. But with candles, more is definitely not the merrier. They can mask stank odors and set a mood, but the conventional brands are not what you'd call "aromatherapy." Unless your idea of aromatherapy is an incense of toxic fumes choking up the air in your home. Then by all means . . . light 'em up.

Sadly, most scented candles are made from paraffin. It may have a pretty ring to it, but paraffin is a petroleum by-product born from the sludge that sits at the bottom of the oil barrel. The wax is bleached and firmed with a nasty chemical known as acrolein.[164] Then they throw in some synthetic fragrance oils. When you light that baby in your bedroom to sex things up, a candle releases black soot into your air (that's the film that covers the top of the candle jar). That dark soot may be laced with at least eleven known toxins, including benzene, lead, acetone, toluene, and carbon monoxide.[165] Frisky? More like *risky.*

Risky doesn't even cover it. One notable study even found that scented candles carry an uncanny resemblance to diesel exhaust.[166] Why not just start up the car in the garage and close all the windows in the house?

WAXES

When we breathe in all the artificial dyes, perfumes, and petrochemicals in candle wax, they just sit in our organs and fatty tissues.[167] Benzene can beat up your bone marrow and weaken your immune system. Light those wicks for a long enough period, and you're just asking for a higher risk of anemia or leukemia.[168] Lead is another doozy. Think you can handle a whiff? No safe levels of lead have *ever* been defined. No safe level means even the smallest amount can start to get in the way of how your body functions.[169]

Did the label on the back of that candle tell you about the muscle pain, diarrhea, loss of appetite, and depression? No? Must have been an oversight.[170] Low exposure to carbon monoxide will explain similar side effects.[171]

This might all seem like a big misunderstanding. Why would manufacturers continue to make candles with paraffin if it's so bad for our health? Well, aside from the simple answer that they could give a rat's ass, in short, paraffin is cheap to produce. It also melts at the right temperature and burns quickly. As a by-product of petroleum, it's just the leftover crap from all those fossil fuels we never get tired of burning.[172]

The best thing for you to do is to quit buying cheap scented candles that make empty promises of turning your living room into an apple orchard or bed of clean linens.

KIM'S TIP:
The candle industry has its own cheerleader. The National Candle Association crosses its heart that paraffin wax is perfectly safe. They even point to FDA approval (you guys should be comedians!). The NCA says consumers should recognize that one candle produces only a small amount of soot. Yeah, one candle. Some of us burn enough over a lifetime for a worldwide vigil.

The NCA does make one point worth jotting down. Choose reputable candle retailers. Don't buy homemade candles from craft fairs or online unless you trust the brand. They often go bonkers on artificial fragrance, using too much of the wrong stuff.[173]

BITCHWORTHY: A SCENT OF SCANDAL CANDLES
Show everyone you don't have a stick up your ass with vegan candles from A Scent of Scandal. The scents play second fiddle to their scandalous names, which include "Sleep Around," "Gold Digger," and "Walk of Shame." As crass as they sound, brother-and-sister duo Ari Solomon and Heather Brancaccio make sure each one smells heavenly. The 8-ounce candles are hand-poured with 100 percent soy wax, and metal-free cotton wicks. They even have a candle called "Skinny Bitch" (I think that qualifies me for a discount). *Visit ascentofscandal.com.*

TIPS FOR HEALTHY BURNING:
PARAFFIN ALTERNATIVES

TELL PARAFFIN TO SUCK IT. No matter which wax gets you going, vegetable- and plant-based waxes emit less soot and spew no toxic fumes into your home. Plant-based waxes are also biodegradable, so they will feed the soil once they decompose.[174] Greener alternatives also have a lower melting point and burn cooler and more evenly than paraffin wax. Longer shelf life. Safer home. Any complaints?

CHOOSE SOY CANDLES LABELED 100 PERCENT ORGANIC SOY. If you like soy candles, read the label carefully to make sure you're only inhaling soy. Don't let companies fool you by parading the term "soy" all over the packaging. There may be soy in the candle . . . along with paraffin. Boy, are they sly. Choosing organic soy is also a sure sign you are not supporting genetically modified soybeans (GMOs).[175]

CHOOSE UNSCENTED CANDLES OR SCENTS FROM (ORGANIC) PURE ESSENTIAL OILS. The terms "fragrance," "parfum," and "fragrance oils" are code names for more than three thousand hidden additives. I don't know what they are. You don't know what they are. So don't roll the dice.[176]

The FDA has almost no control over the term *fragrance*. Here's why: Companies use the lame excuse that disclosing the ingredients will make their scent fair game for cheap brands to copy it. For years, they've been self-regulated, testing the safety of their own ingredients then turning the results over to the FDA. Of course, the FDA takes their word for it—*and bam!*—it's safe enough to scent our beauty and household products. But these so-called "secret ingredients" are typically toxins such as acetone, ethanol, toluene, camphor, benzaldehyde, and formaldehyde.[177] There are more, but I'll save you the melodrama.

The solution is simple: Either go for unscented candles, or don't buy into bold and brazen marketing terms. Look for candles with 100 percent true essential oils, preferably organic or wild harvested, so you can be sure you're not burning agrochemicals. Pesticides, herbicides and fungicides can react with or weaken essential oils during the distillation process, leaving behind toxins.[178] (See page 130 for tips on buying essential oils)

CHOOSE PURE COTTON, PAPER, OR HEMP WICKS. Don't subject yourself to wire wicks, which love to emit heavy metals like lead and zinc. Pure cotton or hemp wicks release clean fumes. Mmmm . . .[179]

CHOOSE RECYCLABLE PACKAGING. Pay it forward by supporting companies that believe in recyclable packaging. More often than not, you will find that those companies that care about our health also care about the health of the planet.

THE SHIT LIST: BEESWAX

Vegans should pay attention to what they're burning. Most eco-conscious candle makers are trading paraffin for beeswax (some use both). Burning beeswax might be better for us than petroleum, but it's killing off the bee population. Bees have become a cash cow for honey producers, and they're no strangers to their own style of a factory farm.

Like slaves, worker bees are holed up for their honey. Queen bees get their wings clipped so they can't fly, and they are usually killed every season to make room for a new one. The tight living quarters they live in also make them susceptible to insect attacks and viruses. Beekeepers don't like to deal with viruses. So they just set the hive aflame with the bees inside. Does that sound like a fair way to die?[180]

THE NOT-SO-SWEET SMELL OF AIR FRESHENERS

Sit in front of the television for a few minutes and it's not tough to figure out that big brands think we are idiots. Catchy commercials paint a picture of the everyday woman lifting couches, clicking her heels, and gliding through the house like Mary Poppins, spraying a can of air freshener like it's a fix-all. Get a big whiff. A pump here, a spray there, and everything is fresher than a bed of roses.

Let's get real. You'd probably throw your back out lifting a goddamn sofa. And you sure as hell don't clean in pumps. Shouldn't you wonder then if maybe your pine forest air freshener is an imposter, too? *Absofreakin-lutely.*

Get this: There is nothing fresh about air fresheners. Nothing. It's just a bunch of petrochemicals sucked into a spray bottle that can't wait to infect your home like the H1N1 virus. But we are obsessed. Every year, we spend almost $2 billion to get our homes smelling sweet. Open up those sinuses. That's enough dough to buy 82,100 brand- spankin'-new Toyota Priuses.[181]

Air fresheners are a sneaky gimmick. Many actually release chemicals that deaden your nerves and coat your nasal passages with a film. The smell is literally stuck on you.[182]

WHY AIR FRESHENERS REALLY STINK

There's not one, not two, but stacks of studies that leak what scents you're really smelling. None of them tell you what you want to hear.

One University of Washington study found nearly one hundred VOCs emitted from just six air fresheners. Man, that's some muscle. Not one of the chemicals emitted were listed on the product label. Out of the six "unnamed" brands, five released at least one or more cancer-causing chemicals that the EPA calls unsafe at any level of exposure, according to the study. Take a deep breath, bitches. It doesn't get much fresher than that.[183]

Now what about those tatas? Your girls are telling you to quit it with the aerosol. Women who rely heavily on solid air fresheners have been shown to be at double the risk of getting breast cancer than those who don't.[184]

The newest fad is to market girly plug-in fresheners to tweens and teens. Some of them come in flirty flavors that match their lip gloss or twinkle with pretty lights. They've stooped to a new low. Like it's so tough selling to girls with money from the tooth fairy burning a hole in their pockets. *Puuhlease?!* All this marketing to kids is freaky. A recent study that followed the development of 14,000 kids from before birth looked at the effects of air fresheners in their homes. They found that babies in homes where air fresheners were used daily had suffered chronic diarrhea and earaches more often than homes where it was used once a week or less. As for their moms, headaches were only the half of it. Daily users were 26 percent more likely to be depressed.[185] That would make for a great Prozac commercial.

Believe it or not, ozone—a cute name for the outdoor air pollution from cars and factories—is a regular in your home. (Experts say indoor ozone levels are about 50 percent of outdoor levels.) And it has a funny way of reacting with the chemicals in air fresheners. When the two meet, sparks fly. Sparks like formaldehyde, acetaldehyde, 2-butoxyethanol, and a shitload of other byproducts that I don't even want to write down.[186]

FRAGRANCE

The chemicals at work here hide under the same ubiquitous term found in scented candles: *fragrance*. Have you ever relished the scent of summer breeze in your living room and wondered just how it lasts so long? Of course not. You were too busy clicking your heels and lifting couches.

The long-lasting aroma is a product of phthalates—the chemicals responsible for making plastics more flexible. They're in fragrances because they help the scent last and "stick" in the air.[187] Phthalates delude our hormones and make them do funny shit (see page 74). They can lead to infertility as well as breast, prostate, and testicular cancer.[188] They also impair our brains and collect in our fatty tissues.[189]

The most alarming news is that nearly 75 percent of U.S. households use some sort of plug-in, spray, or aerosol freshener.[190] But guess what? We don't need no stinkin' air fresheners to get our air in clean mode. We don't even have to go completely natural (though that's the way I prefer it). Here are some things to consider instead of turning your home into a Glade testing facility.

NATURAL WAYS TO FRESHEN YOUR HOME

KEEP IT CLEAN. Quit reacting and start being proactive. Tidy up after yourself. Open the windows for ventilation. Don't be a slob—take out the trash instead of letting it sit there for days. If you want to disguise odors, wipe down counters and surfaces with white vinegar and baking soda (see page 63). A ramekin of vinegar sitting on your counter will also keep funky smells at bay.

MIX SOME PURE ESSENTIAL OILS AND WATER. Fill a spray bottle with water and squeeze in a few drops of your favorite essential oil. My general rule is eight to ten drops of essential oils diluted in one-half cup of filtered water. Shake it up and spritz evenly throughout the desired room.

Just an FYI: Lemon essential oil acts as a deodorizer; cedar and tea tree kill pet odors; and lavender, rose, and orange give off a fresh, floral scent.

> B BITCHWORTHY:
> Place little tins or open jars of baking soda throughout the house to absorb nasty odors. Boiling herbs and spices in water can also jazz up the aroma.

★ Girl Seeking Plant:
INDOOR HOUSEPLANTS FOR A CLEANER HOME

A houseplant doesn't ask for much. Until it dies. Then we say it was high-maintenance. Fess up, slacker. You just forgot to water it for five days. All a plant really needs is sunlight, water, maybe an occasional pat on the stems telling it to *keep on truckin'*, and some VOCs.

You heard me, toots: V-O-C-s. As in, the toxic gases you're inhaling because you love the smell of new furniture. I'll bet you love the scent of gasoline, too.

Plants have been suave air filters for a long time. Maybe you knew that. Give yourself a gold star. But only in the last few years have NASA scientists figured out that plants can absorb CO_2 *and* some pretty harsh chemicals, then pump out fresh, clean oxygen. They're so efficient at eating up contaminants that NASA is sending them to space to support biological life at space stations.[191]

As dirty as your indoor air is, you better start showering your plants with a bit more water from the tap.

GO LOCAL, GO ORGANIC

These plants may be gifted, but man will always find a way to screw it up. Commercial farmers spray down plants with the same ole fertilizer and insecticide bunk that's on our food. Pesticides, as you can figure, are capable of reversing the plant's ability to grab indoor air pollutants. One study found that four of the praised chemical-sucking houseplants were belching out more VOCs than they were sucking up. The peace lily heaved up a whopping twenty-three; sixteen for the areca palm; thirteen for the weeping fig; and twelve in the snake plant. Does that sound clean to you?[193]

It's a no-brainer: Buy indoor plants at your local farmer's market, natural health store, or ring your local sustainable farming association. Ask if the plant is organic. If you call ahead and do your research, you won't run all over town for nothing.

> **KIM'S TIP:**
> If you want your air cleaner than the top of the Alps, how many plants should you stock up on? One plant for every ten square yards of floor space is the general rule. This adds up to two to three plants for the average 25-square-foot living room with eight- to ten-inch ceilings.

THE TOP PLANT PURIFIERS

Don't just head to the Home Depot and drag out the biggest palm tree you can find. Not all houseplants are good at sucking up the really bad pollutants (like formaldehyde, benzene, and trichloroethylene, to name a few).[192] But these guys have a special talent.

Reed palm (*Chamaedorea siefritzii*)
Areca palm (*Dypsis lutescens*)
English ivy (*Hedera helix*)
Spider plant (*Chlorophytum comosum*)
Pothos ivy (*Epipremnum aureum*)
Peace lily (*Spathiphyllum Mauna Loa*)
Chinese evergreen (*Aglaonema modestum*)
Snake plant or mother-in-law's tongue
     (*Sansevieria trifasciata 'Laurentii'*)
Heart leaf philodendron (*Philodendron scandens*)
Lacy tree philodendron (*Philodendron selloum*)
Elephant ear philodendron (*Philodendron domesticum*)
Red edge dracaena (*Dracaena marginata*)
Corn plant (*Dracaena fragrans 'Massangeana'*)
Janet Craig dracaena (*Dracaena deremensis
     'Janet Craig'*)
Striped dracaena (*Dracaena deremensis 'Warneckii'*)
Weeping fig (*Ficus benjamina*)
Gerbera daisy or Barberton daisy (*Gebera jamesonii*)
Pot mum or florist's chrysanthemum
     (*Chrysanthemum morifolium*)
Rubber plant (*Ficus elastica*)

THE XX FACTOR:

HOW WOMEN ARE CARVING A PATH FOR A BETTER, GREENER TOMORROW

BY SARAH BACKHOUSE

As we enter a new era of sustainability, there is a unique opportunity for women to lead. As strong communicators, collaborators and nurturers, women are perfectly positioned to become the decision makers of tomorrow. Women have the power to change mindsets and behaviors in their homes, workplaces, and communities. All we need to do is recognize that we can carve a path to a greener tomorrow.

Women will reach the epiphany that *they* are the solution to many of our planetary woes at different moments in their lives. For many, pregnancy is a time when the environmental bell not only rings, but deafens. While it might have been OK to OD on sushi or slather on wrinkle-erasing face creams when it was "just us," growing another person inside of us can completely change our perspective.

From lead-based household paint to mercury-laden fish, beauty products that mask phthalates to fresh produce doused in pesticides, expectant mothers are often horrified to learn of the many environmental toxins that threaten to harm their unborn child. Suddenly everything they eat, drink, drive, clean with, and sleep on has to meet new standards of health and sustainability.

Switching to a greener lifestyle is easy. Women are already the CEOs of their own households, making 85 percent of all purchasing decisions. We're the ones buying organic blueberries or bamboo sheets or paraben-free shampoos. With the global market for organic food and drink rising steadily—increasing threefold from $18 billion in 2000 to $60 billion in 2010—it appears many women have already hopped on the sustainable bandwagon.

Purchasing power aside, women are more likely to take action on environmental matters, too. Consulting firm Tiller LLC's survey of 1,000 adults yielded not-so-surprising results: According to the survey, 52 percent of women said they are "very likely" to recycle more, compared with 33 percent of men; 51 percent plan to carry their own bag to the supermarket, compared with 30 percent of men; 48 percent intend to reduce their household's energy usage, compared with 32 percent of men.

Not only are women making changes to their own lifestyles, they're encouraging their friends and families to follow suit, quietly inspiring the community at large.

But it's not just in the home where a woman's impact is being felt. We're effecting change in the workplace, too. For the first time ever, women have overtaken men to make up the majority of the workforce, which means we have the potential to make a huge contribution to the green economy.

How can women transition to a greener career path? The answer is often simpler than you might think. You don't need to erase the past and start from scratch. Going green doesn't mean ditching your job at the law firm to dig wells in the developing world.

Whatever your profession, there's a way to "green" it from the inside. Waitresses can ensure their place of work is polystyrene-free. Office workers can demand double-sided photocopying. Money managers can choose to invest in socially responsible mutual funds. In my case, mainstream television hosts can dedicate themselves to environmental media.

So to all the women of the world, know that the positive changes you are making in your homes and in your jobs are influencing the world in profound ways. Push yourself to do more. Become the leaders you know you can be.

The time is right now. Today. Because tomorrow will be too late.

A TV host, writer, and producer, Sarah Backhouse has lived in Sydney, London, and Los Angeles, where she's worked for such media powerhouses as CNBC, BBC, PBS, Fine Living, Sci Fi Channel, and Discovery. Since 2006, Sarah has dedicated herself to environmental media. Sarah currently anchors The Planet 100, a daily online news show for Discovery's Planet Green. Learn more about her at Sarahbackhouse.com.

CHAPTER 2

The Skinny: Household Crap

★ The Genies in the Bottle

THE TOXIC SUBSTANCES CONTROL ACT OF 1976: LIKE, *SO* OUTDATED

Once upon a time, we scoured a tub with a little Arm & Hammer and vinegar to get it spankin' clean. And—*gasp*—it worked! These days, unless a cleaning product has got warning labels and maybe a phone number for the poison control hotline, people leave it on the shelf. Just give 'em the chemicals and nobody gets hurt.

This whole "more is better" mentality really hasn't done us much good. Instead of a home, we live in a goddamn power plant. Someone please tell me—where in the hell did we get the idea that chemicals we can't pronounce would make our lives better? Oh wait, that would be the companies selling them to us. *Right.*

Obviously, we need to dust off the ole dictionary. It doesn't matter which Webster's you pick up, the definitions all pretty much agree on what *clean* means: free of dirt and impurities, free from foreign matter or pollution; characterized by a fresh, wholesome quality.

Free from pollution? Wholesome? Either someone's lying to us or the definition of clean is way overdue for a tune-up. (Hint: Somebody's lying to you.)

All the cheap crap in household cleaners is anything but clean. And, believe me, the people making them know it. Manufacturers, industry lobbyists, and even the regulatory agencies that were built to protect us have long been fighting to hide the facts from us. But let me tell you, it really hasn't been that tough for them to do. Actually, it's been a piece of cake. Because of a little loophole in a law created in 1976, companies don't have to label what's in the stuff we are buying.[194] That law is the Toxic Substances Control Act (TSCA) of 1976. The clause under TSCA that's caused a big stink is called Confidential Business Information (CBI.)[195] In a nutshell, the clause was set up to encourage healthy competition. It gave companies the right to slap "trade secret" on ingredients they used in products so that other companies couldn't produce cheap knock-offs.[196] Just like the "secret sauce" at your local fast food joint. In the beginning, it made some sense. I mean, what dumb broad would spend $10 on a window cleaner when another company sold the same exact thing for $3? That's right—nobody. By revealing the ingredients, a company would be setting itself up for failure. But it backfired on us. Companies are hiding the ingredients from their competition all right. But they are hiding them from us, too. And by law, that is a-okay. We have given greedy manufacturers the right to conceal whatever they damn well please from the people. And girlfriend, you best believe they have some shit to hide.

Under TSCA, whenever a company brings a new chemical to market, they have to let the EPA know about it ninety days before they start selling it. They don't have to attach any kind of health or safety information to it. That's a big relief, because chances are the companies don't even have it. As mentally insane as it sounds, manufacturers are *not* required to do any type of testing. It's encouraged, but nobody is pushing them. So it's perfectly fair to say that a chemical may be sitting in your everyday dishwashing soap that didn't go through any type of testing. Actually, only about 7 percent have ever been tested for your safety.[197]

Somewhere around 95-freakin'-percent of these so-called "pre-manufacture notices" that come through the EPA have some sort of trade secret, or CBI, claim on them. Usually the EPA doesn't have time to ask questions. They've got other shit to worry about. They stamp the big "approved" sticker on there and add it to the TSCA inventory of chemicals.[198] Thousands of confidentiality claims are sent in, and the EPA has only challenged an average of fourteen every year.[199] Even more unsettling is that about 1.3 billion pounds of chemicals on the market are secret.[200]

As you can see, the EPA places a load of trust in these companies that the chemicals are safe; if a company has even the slightest inkling that a chemical they're using may pose a "substantial risk" to human health or the environment, they're supposed to tell the EPA. Real funny. Unless consumers complain of health issues associated with a product, what are the chances that a company will have evidence that a chemical isn't safe for human use when they aren't required to test it?[201] Like zero to one. But let's say consumers do complain, giving manufacturers or Big Chem companies just enough reason to believe a chemical may be unsafe. The chances that the company making the product is going to rat on themselves to the EPA are again highly doubtful.

In 2010, the EPA started to crack down . . . well, if that's what you want to call it. They can reject the confidentiality claim if they have reason to believe a chemical may pose a substantial risk to human health or the environment. But in order to have reason, they need to have proof before they can act. And it's kind of hard to get proof when nobody is required to submit any health data.

The EPA would have to conduct their own studies—which I would pay to see—or they'd have to gather a pile of consumer complaints.[202]

Then there's the punishment. If the EPA succeeds in rejecting the confidentiality claim, all of the rats get listed on the EPA Web site as posing "substantial risk."[203] That's their spank on the ass. The companies don't have to stop using the chemicals, nor do they have to slap them on the label since there are no full disclosure laws on ingredients.[204] No, instead, they get posted on a Web site that I doubt the head of the EPA even checks once a week, let alone the general public. Weak.

The one thing we can all agree on is that TSCA of 1976 is one of the most outdated and screwed-up laws we have. But a few bills are trying to change that. With the help of thirty pissed-off nongovernmental organizations, we continue to push for the Kid-Safe Chemicals Act (KSCA)—a bill created to push Congress to fix the major holes in TSCA of 1976. Plus, we've stepped up our game and introduced the Safe Chemicals Act of 2010, which would change the industry, as we know it. Both bills have set out to basically reverse the embarrassingly outdated TSCA. If the bills were passed, they would make manufacturers provide proof of safety of each ingredient before it can go on the shelves.[205] What a wild idea?! They will also require chemical manufacturers to show proof that chemicals are indeed safe if they want to keep selling them to companies for their products. And I'll be darned, the bills will finally grant the EPA some authority, for once. If the new legislation passes, the EPA will be able to ask for additional information and safety tests on chemicals whenever they feel like it. They won't need any proof it's risky, and the company has to hand that information over.[206]

All this lobbying and political bullshit begs the question: What exactly are these companies hiding? Well, just about anything they can get away with.

SQUEEZING THE LIFE OUT OF US

You have to hand it to the big brands. They know we're clean freaks and that bacteria scares and fears of viruses have turned us into paranoid whack jobs. So they spend billions of dollars every year to convince us that we can't have a clean and healthy home without them. We want whiter whites, squeaky-clean floors, and, just to be safe, a kitchen that smells like a Clorox factory. We've even been grateful to these brands for saving us from elbow grease. There was no good reason to second-guess their motives.

To cut them some slack, when chemicals started to invade our lives right after World War II, nobody could have guessed the hazards they pose to our health (and to nature). But today, with all the evidence in hand, there is really no excuse.

Money-hungry companies continue to pour toxic chemicals in our cleaners because they're cheap, easy to get their hands on, and potent. These chemicals also have been linked to side effects that sound like a freakin' lab experiment—dizziness, nausea,[207] problems breathing, chronic infections, reduced sperm count, infertility, birth defects,[208] and irreversible damage to the liver, kidneys, and bone marrow.[209] That just covers a handful of products. A study in the United Kingdom found that women who regularly use conventional household cleaners are twice as likely to get breast cancer than those with enough common sense to use natural products.[210]

That's some scandalous stuff. Yet unless you're buying from credible brands you can trust, you don't know know what's in the bottle; only one percent of ingredients are listed on the label. We can't expect any transparency from dishonest brands driven by profit.

Then again, why would companies list ingredients or test for safety if nobody makes them? Beats me. If your dad allowed boys to be in your room with the door closed when you were thirteen, would you leave the door open? Hell no! Manufacturers just continue to laugh at what they're getting away with. Meanwhile, they're bathing in billions of dollar bills while we soak in a bubble bath of sulfates and solvents wondering why we can't afford our medical bills.

But let's quit focusing on the negative, and shift to how we're going to get that act of yours cleaned up. It's easier than you think. By now you should know about most of the dirty chemicals in your household products. If you don't, I suggest you revisit The Shit List on page 13. That will get you off to a nice start.

> **! FAT FACT:**
> Today, the average home is packing sixty-two toxic chemicals—more than a chemistry laboratory contained a hundred years ago.[211]

★ Chicks With Choices:
THE ABCs OF HEALTHY CLEANING

READING LABELS: WHAT TO BELIEVE AND WHEN TO CALL BULLSHIT

I'm thinking it's time to tell Mr. Clean, Drano, and Pine-Sol to look for another home.

Greener and healthier products are not tough to find nowadays. Really, they're not. The more questions we asked—like, say, why the hell we need a surgical mask to polish the floors—the more demand grew for businesses with a conscience. Funny how that works. You will even find safer products and aisles dedicated to natural household solutions at major grocers now. However, since greenwashing has become fair practice, you need to arm yourself with the tools and resources to ensure that a product is indeed "natural" or "green."

> **! FAT FACT:**
> A study found that 70 percent of stream water contained traces of detergent and 66 percent contained disinfectant cleaners.[212]

> **Aa BITCHIONARY: GREENWASHING**
> A catchy term that refers to the phony use of green buzzwords to make people think a company's policies or products are better for our health and the environment—when in reality, it's a big fat lie.[213]

Don't ignore the label, ladies. Even if all the ingredients aren't required to be listed, there are telltale signs that some companies are trying to dupe you. And most of them are. Show them they are messing with the wrong girl.

LOOK FOR PLANT-BASED INGREDIENTS. Think: from the soil, not foreign oil. Plant-based implies they came from fruits, vegetables, grains, trees, herbs, and other minerals that are renewable. Take your pick: Would you prefer to breathe in citrus or sludge? Up to you.

SKIP THE ANIMAL INGREDIENTS. A product can be all-natural and still contain a pulverized animal part or two. I know, disgusting. While beauty products tend to use more animal by-products (check out The Shit List in the beauty section on page 114), household items aren't in the clear.

The company may also fall into the group of losers that test on animals. At the time this book went to print, household brands such as Clorox, Procter & Gamble, S.C. Johnson, Reckitt Benckiser, and Colgate-Palmolive all tested on animals.[214] That works out nicely for you because these are also the companies that offer a shitload of toxic cleaners. Don't support them.

Look for the "cruelty-free" logo, or check PETA's Web site (peta.org) for a huge database of animal-friendly household products. Just lay your eyes on one photo of a bunny with severe burns all over his body from product testing, and you'll be convinced. Trust me.

LOOK FOR FULL DISCLOSURE OF INGREDIENTS.
Again, companies aren't required to list their ingredients. So if they choose not to, it's a damn good reason not to buy it. I assure you, if they had something to brag about, they would. Choose products that practice full-disclosure by listing all of their ingredients (it will say "full ingredients" or something similar). Companies such as Seventh Generation, Ecos, and Method practice this transparency, but more and more are popping up. You also want to make sure those ingredients are primarily plant-based and free of harmful chemicals. (Case in point: Clorox now practices full disclosure of ingredients on their Web site, which is one way to be transparent. But what they tell you is that you probably don't want their products in your home.)

AVOID SYNTHETIC FRAGRANCES AND DYES.
You have no clue what's in that "fragrance." Honestly, the makers of the product may not even know what's in it. Since it can be more than three thousand exotic chemicals—some of which cause cancer or birth defects—don't take the risk. In one EPA study, 100 percent of perfumes tested contained toluene. [215] You familiar with that one? It causes brain damage and poisons your nervous system.[216]

Then there are the dyes. Chemical dyes are rough on the environment, but they can also contain glycol ethers and other unknowns.[217] Hey, I love a good mystery, too, but let's leave that to Sherlock Holmes. Not here, not now. Just suck it up and buy household cleaners that are fragrance-free, or have scents that are derived from essential oils.

CHECK FOR THIRD-PARTY CERTIFICATIONS.
If a company has the blessing of a third-party agency, that's usually a good sign. This tells you that an independent source says the product is safe. All of them stand for something different or represent a sole industry. A few of the best are the Green Seal, EcoLogo, The Carpet and Rug Institute's (CRI) Green Label Plus, Cradle to Cradle, and the EPA's Design for the Environment (DfE) Formulator Program. Jump on the Internet to get some background on what each of these mean. Keep in mind that certification can be pricey, so it's tougher for smaller brands to obtain. Don't use it as a crutch—use it simply as validation.

SCAN THE LABEL FOR WARNINGS LIKE "DANGER," "POISON," OR "CAUTION." If I have to explain this one, then we should go back to the dictionary. Activists and environmental groups are doing a lot of ball-busting to get companies to fully disclose ingredients. Until then, check the label for "Danger," "Poison," "Caution," and "Warning." The Consumer Products Safety Commission (CPSC) requires this labeling when a product is corrosive, flammable, combustible, irritating, or has the ability to cause serious personal injury as a result of normal use. Hot diggity damn! That should tell you something.[218] Nearly all of the chemicals on The Shit List will come with one of these taglines. Where there's smoke, there's a fire.

GREENWASHING: UNREGULATED TERMS TO SERIOUSLY QUESTION

There's a reason the bajillionaires behind our major household products are so big. They listen. They hold fun little market research powwows with suburban housewives to find out what we want. If they find out we want greener and cleaner products, they don't remove the toxic ingredients or environmental poisons. Oh, no. That would cost a lot of money. They just change up the label and greenwash us with fancy words and bold catchphrases to reel us in. Don't fall for it. You're smarter than that.

If you see any of the following key words on a product, make sure they back up the claim. Study the ingredients closely for signs that these brands aren't being so true to their word. If you have any doubt—here's a bright idea—don't buy it. Screw them.

MISLEADING TERM: NATURAL Really? Prove it. Make them back it up with specific ingredients, or look for terms that aren't so wildly vague ("solvent-free" or "no phosphates" for example). The term "natural" isn't regulated by the FDA or any governmental agency. So brands slap it on every product they can get their dirty hands on.[219] To give you an idea of just how bad it is out there, a study done by environmental marketing agency, TerraChoice, found that 98 percent of so-called "natural" products on the shelves are getting away with potentially false claims.[220]

MISLEADING TERM: ECO-FRIENDLY A company learns how to recycle paper and suddenly they think they're green. Before you know it, they're calling their entire line of dishwashing detergents "eco-friendly" because they got rid of one ingredient that isn't so natural. But there are a dozen others in there that will kill off our wildlife and poison our oceans! *Puuhlease*. If a brand shouts "eco-friendly" on the front of the label with nothing to support it, chances are they are compulsive liars. Would you care for an example? Many aerosol spray cleaners flaunt "no CFCs" (or chlorofluorocarbons) on the front of the package to let you know they're not depleting the ozone layer and thereby selling an "eco-friendly" product. Hmm, that's weird. CFCs were banned from aerosols in 1978. That means companies cannot legally use them. That doesn't make you environmentally conscious, dipshits. That's called abiding by the law.[221]

MISLEADING TERM: NONTOXIC Let me tell you something very interesting about the term "nontoxic": It has no official definition. While I throw it around like it's going out of style, I actually back it up with facts. If you spot this claim, check for a third-party certification or dig a little deeper, Nancy Drew.

MISLEADING TERM: ORGANIC Just when you thought you knew how to navigate the "organic" label with ease, chew on this: Only foods and herbs can be certified organic. Unfortunately, the term doesn't carry much weight on a household cleaner.[222] So if they start mouthing off on the front of the label that the product is "organic," question it. In chemistry, "organic" refers to chemicals that are carbon based. Yes, that would include VOCs, those harmful fumes offgassing in your home. In that case, they are most certainly organic—just not the kind you were hoping for.

On a happier note, the ingredients inside a household product can be organic if they are plant-based. These are good. The more of these in a product, the safer your home is going to be. Look for plant-based ingredients or oils that are labeled "certified organic" by the USDA.

MISLEADING TERM: BIODEGRADABLE When used responsibly, this term refers to something that will naturally decompose into matter that the soil can absorb. But companies exploit this term. Think about it—in due time, everything will biodegrade. Plastic bottles biodegrade. They just require about seven hundred years to even begin the process.[223] By then, you'll be living your sixth afterlife as an Egyptian goddess or something. The problem is they get thrown in landfills where there's little air, moisture, or sunlight to help them biodegrade. So they go down v-e-r-y slowly. Even DDT, which is considered one of the most toxic carcinogens that has ever existed, most certainly biodegrades, but as it does, it actually breaks down into two compounds that are even more dangerous—DDD and DDE.[224]

The key is looking for plant-derived ingredients that belong in the soil, so will break down there quicker. Harsh chemicals don't. Look for products that put a timer on this ecological claim, like "biodegradable in 3 to 5 days."

CLEAN HOUSE WITH YOUR PANTRY

Don't feel like you have to choose between cleanliness and a functioning liver or kidneys. You don't. You can have both. There are plenty of safe, nontoxic household cleaners out there that are fantastic.

While greener products are lovely, I personally prefer the truly all-natural stuff already in my pantry—the ingredients I could eat afterwards if I wanted to. I don't need to spend any money. I know for sure I'm not killing any animals by using them. And, big surprise, I still get a clean house. Below, I lay out a dozen or so that work wonders and won't cost you more than a few bucks. Try and argue with that.

BAKING SODA If it's just hanging out in the back of your fridge, it's time to wise up to some serious kitchen wisdom: Baking soda is a foolproof all-purpose cleaner, and even helps keep laundry fresh and clean. It's also a better scouring agent than half the crap on grocery shelves.

All-Purpose Household Cleaner: Sprinkle baking soda on a damp cloth and wipe down countertops or tile surfaces. Rinse with water. For heavier duty cleaning, create a paste with baking soda and a plant-based liquid castile dish soap. Add a few drops of your favorite essential oil for a natural fragrance. Use it regularly to disinfect sinks, countertops, toilets, and tubs.

Carpet Deodorizer: Sprinkle baking soda all over carpet and let it sit for about 15 minutes. Then just vacuum up. Take a whiff. Isn't that heavenly?

Grime Remover: No matter how hard you scrub a pot, sometimes burnt-on food just doesn't want to come loose. Sprinkle that grimy pot with baking soda and add hot water. Let it soak overnight. Any dried food or grime will come right off.

Drain Cleaner: Pour 1 cup of baking soda down a clogged drain, and follow it up with 3 cups of boiling water. This opens everything up.

DISTILLED WHITE VINEGAR I'll bet you didn't know that vinegar can even get grass stains out of carpet. It's nuts. It works for just about any household chore, too. Dab on a paper towel to clean glass, spot clean carpets and linoleum floors, or scrub away soap scum. White vinegar is also bang-up at cleaning toilets. (Wish I could say the same!)

All-Purpose Household Cleaner: Fill a spray bottle with equal parts vinegar and water for a nontoxic disinfectant. For dirtier tasks, use 100 percent vinegar concentration (no water). Use it to clean glass or windows, sterilize any kitchen surface, get rid of odors, and fend against mold and mildew in the shower.

Oven Cleaner: Make a paste using 1 cup vinegar and ¼ cup nontoxic powdered laundry detergent (try Seventh Generation or Ecos). Preheat the oven to 350°F; once it reaches that temperature, let it heat for 5 minutes, then turn if off. You want it warm when you apply the paste, but wait until it's cool enough for your hands to be in there. Duh. Apply the paste to greasy areas and leave it on for 1 hour. Use a spatula to scrape the mess away.

Odor Repellant: The next time you forget to take the garbage out or leftover Indian food gets the best of your house, boil 2 cups white vinegar on the stove. Vinegar absorbs odors in minutes.

Ant Repellant: Spray some on the windowsill to scare off ants.

Static Fighter: If static cling is driving you crazy, pour ½ cup of vinegar into the rinse cycle.

MUST-HAVE: LIQUID CASTILE SOAP OR NONTOXIC LIQUID DISH SOAP

I really don't care which natural cleaners you use. Just use them. If there is any foolproof advice I can give you, it's to get yourself a natural liquid castile soap, and keep extra on hand. It's the most versatile thing you will ever own. You can use it to do the dishes and then take it in the shower to wash your dirty ass. Whatever works. It's awesome on its own, and it also adds extra strength to your homemade cleansers.

Castile soap is simply an odorless soap made with vegetable fat from oils such as coconut, hemp, avocado, almond, and walnut. It's gentle on skin and surfaces, and won't aggravate your allergies as long as it's made with natural additives. That last part is key. Look for one that is chemical-free with plant-based ingredients. Some brands still slip artificial fragrance and preservatives in there so you have to be careful.

Whatever you do, don't be a buffoon and squirt conventional dish soap like Dawn into your DIY all-purpose cleaner, honey. Make that mistake and you're only injecting something natural with sodium lauryl sulfate, alkyl dimethyl amine oxide, sodium chloride, and fragrance. These are the nasties we're trying to wean you off of. Clean that wax out of your ears and listen.[225]

COARSE SALT Sea salt isn't just yummy in recipes. Use it to get rid of rust stains on copper pans and cast-iron cookware. A pinch of salt on fresh spills in the oven also makes them easier to pick up, and hides gross odors.

Cast Iron and Copper Cleaner: Mix about 2 tablespoons of grapeseed or vegetable oil with 4 tablespoons coarse salt to form a thick paste and heat it up over medium-low heat for a few minutes to warm. Wipe down your cast-iron or copper pots with a fresh towel, then scrub them with the paste. Rinse with cool water and let dry. Rust won't be able to compete with the abrasive surface of the salt.

Rust Remover: If you're not one to get your hands dirty, Ms. Priss, you can sprinkle salt on rust. Top it with a lime or lemon squeeze. It does the job on its own.

Tile or Floor Cleaner: Sprinkle on tile or linoleum and scrub with an old bristle brush and water. Mop with a microfiber mop when done. Once dry, sweep up any remaining salt. You can also add essential oils for a fresh aroma. Keep salt away from wood floors. It will scratch them up and I'm not taking the blame for that.

GRAPEFRUIT SEED EXTRACT (GSE) If you've never heard of grapefruit seed extract, you are in for a real treat, babe. It eats up mold and mildew like it never existed. And unlike other mold killers, this one's odorless and nontoxic. GSE is extremely potent at killing hundreds of parasites and bacteria such as salmonella and staphylococcus. Just how strong is grapefruit seed extract? In lab tests, it's been proven to be ten to one hundred times more effective as a disinfectant than chlorine.[226] Woot!

With GSE, try and buy the extract from companies or brands you trust. GSE can be contaminated with parabens and propylene glycol, which act as preservatives in themselves (kind of defeats the purpose to use synthetic preservatives to *preserve* natural preservatives—but it is done).

> **KIM'S TIP:** Grapefruit seed extract can be found at any natural health retailer such as Whole Foods. You can also get it online at HerbalRemedies.com or Amazon.com

All-Purpose Cleaner: Pinch about 15 to 20 drops of grapefruit seed extract into a spray bottle filled with 2 cups of water. Shake it up and spray away, sister. When disinfecting problem areas, spray and let it sit for a while without rinsing. The same goes with disinfecting cutting boards—rub in 15 drops and let it sit for 30 minutes. Then rinse the board with water, and voilà!

Fruit and Veggie Wash: Fill a spray bottle with water and add 20 drops of grapefruit seed extract. Shake up and spray down produce. Tasty, huh?

ESSENTIAL OILS Oils have natural antibacterials so they are great for sanitizing. The real upside is that you know you're not getting phthalates or any jacked-up chemicals so you can feel comfortable inhaling it. Well, as long as you buy the right oils (check out page 130 for a guide). Lavender, citrus, and tea tree are some of my go-to oils. But some of the best for cleaning are cinnamon, clove, eucalyptus, thyme, spruce, lemon, lemongrass, pine, and grapefruit seed.

All-Purpose Cleaner: Fill a spray bottle with 2 cups of water and a quarter-size squirt of liquid castile dish soap. Add 5 drops of essential oils and shake well. The dish soap isn't necessary but some like a deeper clean.

Dust Mite Killer: To make sure those dust mites don't stand a chance, add 25 drops of eucalyptus to each load of laundry. Studies have shown that eucalyptus in particular kills pesky mites that were living in your bedding. Yuck. It also deters new ones from taking up residence. Finally some sanity.

TEA TREE OIL It's one of the pricier oils, but tea tree oil is also the most useful at everyday household tasks. It is awesome for those with health conditions or allergies. Why? It's a natural antiseptic with germicidal, antifungal, and immune-boosting qualities. Tea tree oil also kills mold and mildew, right along with stank odors.

All-Purpose Cleaner: Combine 2 teaspoons of tea tree oil and 2 cups of water in a spray bottle. Shake it up and use to clean kitchen countertops, tile floors, and tubs.

LEMON JUICE When life gives you lemons, put that citric acid to work. Lemon's god-given acidity makes it a gentler household alternative to bleach. Use it as an all-purpose disinfectant, or as a polishing agent on wood furniture. And who doesn't love a fresh lemon scent? Nobody on my speed dial.

Glass Cleaner: In a spray bottle, mix equal parts lemon juice and water. Wipe down.

Grease Cutter: Add 1 cup of lemon juice to the rinse cycle of your dishwasher to add some shine and cut grease.

Armpit Stain Fighter: Pit stains aren't cute. Say adios to yellow discoloration by squeezing lemon juice on the affected area and letting it sunbathe until dry.

OLIVE OIL Keep olive oil on hand specifically for polishing and shining wood furniture. Your wood coffee table is toxic enough. Don't double up on the poisons with conventional polishes.

Furniture polish: Mix up 1 cup olive oil with 1/2 cup lemon juice for a safe and long-lasting polish for hardwood furniture. If you squeezed your last lemon, replace with one part distilled white vinegar to three parts olive oil.

TOOTHPASTE There are dozens of ways to get crafty with toothpaste. A little squeeze scrubs away stains, shines up chrome sinks, and removes water rings from coffee tables or other wood furniture. I use it to make sinks and silverware look spiffy again.

Rust Remover: Rub tarnishes out of silverware with a dab of toothpaste and a soft cloth. Just rinse under warm water and pat dry.

Stain Remover: For carpet or clothing stains, add a nickel-size dab of toothpaste to a toothbrush and scrub gently. Rinse and let dry.

Crayon Marks Remover: To erase those stick figures marking up your living room walls, squeeze a dollop of toothpaste on a damp cloth, gently scrub, and just wash off. Don't keep it up there just to make your kid feel good. He's no Picasso.

KIM'S PICKS: NATURAL DISH SOAPS

Dr. Bronner's Pure Liquid Castile Soap (drbronner.com)

Citra-Solv (citra-solv.com)

THE SHIT LIST: DAWN

Now, for a quick lesson on irony. While I commend Procter & Gamble for donating $1 of every bottle of Dawn sold to help rescue wildlife affected by the 2010 BP oil disaster, I'm calling bullshit. The very suds Dawn promoted to remove all the toxic sludge and coal tar from birds' feathers and beaks just happened to be made from the same shit that caused this whole mess. That's right—oil. Coincidence? I think not. You only have to do a little digging to find that Dawn, like most traditional liquid dish soaps, contains surfactants, detergents, and emollients derived from petroleum. *Petro,* meaning: oil. The only thing Dawn should win credit for is an ingenious marketing campaign that has consumers thinking they are making a meaningful difference by purchasing a chemical-laden dish soap. Things aren't always what they seem. Buy dish soaps with nontoxic, plant-based ingredients made by companies that are trying to make the environment safer for these animals every day. Not just during a national disaster.

HYDROGEN PEROXIDE If you still think you can't part with your economy-size tub of chlorine bleach, I have the perfect match for you, woman. Meet hydrogen peroxide. Yes, the same stuff you've used for years to clean wounds and bleach your hair so blonde it required a reflector. This safe, chemical-free solution costs you two bucks at your local drugstore and does everything that chlorine bleach can't. Like, say, keep the environment and your health intact. Hydrogen peroxide can brighten up soiled whites, purify a pool or spa, erase stains, get rid of shower scum and mold, and get blood out of clothing and upholstery. It also acts as a brilliant household cleaner for everything from tile floors to tubs to kitchen counters.

All you need is hydrogen peroxide (3 percent solution) to manage all your cleaning needs.

All-Purpose Cleaner: In a spray bottle, mix 2 cups water, one cup hydrogen peroxide, and ¼ cup lemon juice. This solution works on anything from countertops and tables to toilets and stoves.

Blood and Wine Stain Remover: Spray or apply undiluted hydrogen peroxide directly on the stain. Let it sit for 5 minutes and rinse with cold water. Repeat again if necessary.

Scum and Mold Fighter: In a spray bottle, combine equal parts hydrogen peroxide and distilled white vinegar to scrub away scum and kill mold.

Germ Killer: Soak toilet brushes, and yes, even toothbrushes, in hydrogen peroxide to kill germs and bacteria. Just don't soak them together in the same solution. I had to say it. Gross.

★ The Sick Rumor About Bacteria:
ANTIBACTERIALS

We have this crazy idea that all bacteria are bad. Like, '80s perm bad. Just why do we think it's the devil? Um, because everybody said so.

Go ahead and thank shrewd industry marketing for that. When we're faced with a few food recalls, a bad flu season, and super viruses, we freak out like we just lost our puppies. Consumer packaged goods and pharmaceutical giants can smell fear. And, boy, does it get them excited! Introduce a public relations campaign. Dangle the word "antibacterial" in front of us like a freakin' carrot and we're running to the drugstore like a bunch of nut jobs cleaning out entire stocks of hand sanitizer and soaps. Still wondering where we got that wacky idea? Glad we had this talk.

This whole "anti" bacteria craze may just be the biggest marketing scam since bottled water (I'm getting to that one, too). We've been suckered into thinking they will protect us from the snot and sniffles during cold season. But colds (and flus) are the work of viruses . . . not bacteria, sweetheart. Get it straight. Bacterial infections from the likes of salmonella, Listeria, and E.coli are usually food borne in raw or undercooked foods. You can wash your hands thirty times a day, and it won't fix that.

If there is any doubt that we're being sold, look at the numbers. In 2004, 322 new antibacterial products hit the shelves. In 2005, another 253 made bacteria into the Antichrist.[227] Today, there are more than 1,000 on store shelves.[228] These companies have cleaned up with antibacterials, taking in $45 billion in 2012.[229] I smell a profit motive.

Thanks to the campaign against bacteria, there's a whole new bacterial threat. They're called "superbugs." And they might just be the reason half of America waited in line for the H1N1 shot.[230] Go ahead and thank some of your favorite hand sanitizers for that.

TRICLOSAN AND SUPERBUGS

The two chemicals to blame might just be triclosan and triclocarban. The duo is added to most antibacterial products to stop or slow the growth of *all* bacteria and fungi.[231] Every time you wash up, these chemicals leave a little residue behind to continue killing bacteria. But, as the label promises, they only kill "99.9%" of bacteria. That 0.1 percent lives. It might sound like nothing to you, but that teensy 0.1 percent breeds. We're talking a lot of babies. And leave it to evolution for these babies to be bred with genetics that resist the antibacterials—then those bacteria breed. Suddenly, we have a bunch of "superbugs" running around like He-Men that our antibiotics can't kill.[232] So we develop new drugs to fight those.

One of the newer superbugs that has caused a ruckus is methicillin-resistant *Staphylococcus aureus,* or MRSA. Come down with this infection and expect anything from boils to even more severe infections of the blood and lungs. Doctors say it can kill and *disfigure* you. The only way to treat it is with a very pricey antibiotic that needs to be pumped into your veins. Are you at all curious where a deranged superbug like this might have come from? A built-up resistance to antibacterial wipes at hospitals.[233] Your hand soap isn't looking so hot right now, is it?

Triclosan is just one big problem after another. It's a hormone disruptor that upsets the thyroid hormones. When this happens, it can stunt growth, slow down the brain, and lead to infertility. Triclosan gets absorbed by your skin, and what do you think you're putting these antibacterials on?[234] Yes, that would be your skin. Even the FDA and EPA have got their panties in a bunch. Call me crazy, but maybe it's because triclosan has been found in the urine of 75 percent of the population.[235] And a Swedish study found triclosan in the breast milk of three out of five women.[236] Infants and toddlers are more vulnerable to its side effects since their bodies are still developing. This isn't child's play, people.

ANTIBACTERIALS KILL OFF "GOOD" BACTERIA

As you might have guessed at this point, not all bacteria are bad. Actually, most of them keep you out of harm's way. Our digestive tracts are lined with bacteria that help break down food into vitamins and nutrients, and then make sure the intestines absorb the nutrients to pass through the bloodstream. Without the "good" bacteria, we wouldn't be able to digest food properly.[237] But antibacterials don't know the difference between good and evil. They just open up fire on all bacteria, including the ones we need to stay healthy.

Our skin works the same way. Your body is covered in good bacterial species that help fight off virus and infection. When you use an antibacterial hand soap or sanitizer, you kill the good guys.

THE POWER OF GOOD OLE SOAP AND WATER

Want to keep your hands real clean? Dump the stupid antibacterial gimmick. Go back to washing up with soap and water. Studies show there is no evidence that antibacterial soap is any better at getting rid of germs and bad bacteria than regular soap.[238] Actually, evidence suggests that soap and water are *more* effective at removing viruses and bacteria than antibacterial soaps. A study billed as the most comprehensive of its kind, discovered that soap and water got rid of the common cold virus, hepatitis A, and a handful of other sick germs within ten seconds of scrubbing like

nobody's business. No kidding. Soaps bind to dirt, oil, and bacteria to remove it from your body, and remember, antibacterials don't kill viruses. But the study points to the conclusion that some viruses have indeed become fairly resistant to disinfection. It just gets better and better! In the study, the waterless, alcohol-based hand sanitizers seemed to fare the worst. They had unreliable and weak effects, which just got weaker every time they were used.[239]

Washing your hands with soap and water will do more than just keep you clean—it helps build your immune system to kick viruses, diseases, and microbes. In a child's case, even bad bacteria can be good. Being exposed to harmful bacteria when you're a tot helps you build a healthy immune system that can fight allergies.[240] Just let kids be kids already.

Instead of promoting new breeds of superbugs, use a plant-based soap with essential oils. Some essential oils—such as peppermint, tea tree, oregano, lemon, thyme, and eucalyptus—have natural antibacterial properties. But check the label before you buy just any natural soap. Some may contain tallow, which is animal fat from cows, sheep, and pigs. Um, gross. These ingredients don't only suck because they support a cruel business, but some beauty experts argue that tallow can clog your pores.

A WOMAN'S WEAPONS: HEALTHY AND SAFE CLEANING TOOLS

Your hands are only so good at cleaning. You need things that are going to scrub, suck, and soak up the scum that's making your house a disaster area. But some of the tools that go to work on your house come with their own set of problems. *As if!*

Since that spill ain't gonna clean itself, most of us rely on sponges to soak up our troubles and restore order to our kitchens. But where do you think all that raunchy residue goes? It ain't heaven, honey. No, it sits there in your sink, bathing in a filthy, bacteria-charged bubble bath until the next time you spread it around your countertops like you got shit under control. Newsflash: you don't.

Here's the dope on sponges: they may cut grime, but they are so dirty they make your garbage disposal look clean. Moist sponges are the number one source of germs in your entire home.[241] Yep, *numero uno.* They are the perfect real estate for bacteria such as *salmonella, E. coli,* and *staphylococcus.*[242] When you clean the fridge or sink with said sponge, you're just spreading all this dirty bacteria around like a sick kid on the playground. According to microbiologist Charles Gerba of the University of Arizona, kitchens actually host more *E. coli* bacteria from fecal matter than your toilet. And that's where you go poop.[243] Please tell me that freaks you the 'eff out.

But there's another big problemo with sponges—they are cheap, disposable, and full of chemicals. You think you're being thrifty by buying them in packs of three, but really you're just creating a bigger nightmare for the environment and your health.

Standard sponges are made with synthetic and petroleum-based materials. Polyurethane, a popular plastic in sponges, can emit formaldehyde that pollutes your air and soils your dishes with toxic residues.[244] Companies may also treat your trusty sponge with triclosan to fight odors and germs—the very same hormone disruptor that's added to antibacterials.[245]

Cellulose sponges are a little better; at least they're made from wood pulp, which gets some approval rating for reducing waste and the use of chemicals. It also comes from nature so it's designed to biodegrade quickly without harming the soil. But again, we're cutting down trees to get that wood pulp. It's not falling from the sky. But don't even think about natural sea sponges. Get it together—they are a living creature. One that actually shares 70 percent of our DNA. Leave them to play at the bottom of the ocean.[246]

If you must own a sponge, there are some better alternatives that won't be as harsh on your well-being, the environment, or your countertops. Avoid sponges that flaunt terms like "antimicrobial" or "antibacterial." That's a dead giveaway they've been treated with some

chemical that is arguably worse than a sponge full of bacteria. Look for sponges made from plant-based ingredients that naturally fight bacteria and fungi, but require little to no pesticides or fertilizers to grow.

Hemp sponges are super absorbent, and suck up about 150 percent of their weight in water. They're also mildew-resistant and don't require pesticides or fertilizers. Bamboo also fights bacteria and fungi when cleaning up spills and messes. Again, some argue that bamboo requires lots of energy to weave, but it's much better than polyurethane. One of my favorite sponges for both the kitchen and bath is natural loofah. Loofah in its natural state is sustainable and compostable. It comes from a type of vegetable often referred to as Chinese okra.

Even when you go for more eco-friendly sponges, you can't ignore basic upkeep.

Disinfect sponges every couple days. It's easy. Wet the sponge and stick it in the microwave for one minute. If the radiation from microwaves scares you, boil it in water for three minutes or run through the dishwasher. This will kill more than 99 percent of all bacteria. Practice safe sponging on a regular basis, and you won't need to throw the thing out with the trash every week. That just costs you more money and more problems for this planet you're living on.

DO THE TWIST

As much as I don't want to get on my boring soapbox about brands, Twist products are the only sponges you need to have in your kitchen. Twist's heavy-duty agave and hemp scrubbers, bamboo reusable cloths, and loofahs are all biodegradable. They are made from 100 percent plant-based ingredients, and they actually make cleaning look stylish. The Euro Sponge Cloth lasts for about one thousand uses to replace paper towels, too. You can find them nationwide at natural health retailers like Whole Foods, Sprouts Farmers Market, Henry's Farmers Market, Wegmans, and Natural Grocers. *Visit twistclean.com.*

CLEANING SUCKS: GREEN AND CLEAN VACUUMS

If there's one thing that should suck real hard, it's your vacuum. The harder the better, baby. With all the dust, dirt, and bacteria that build up on floors, you really want to push that beast around once a week. If you have carpet, vacuum every day or skip a day in between.

In the vacuum department, you don't want to go with a cheapo. Most vacuums just suck up dust, dirt, and household waste, then release it right back into your air. For the sake of your health, buy a HEPA vacuum. They can pick up the smallest of irritants including dust mite droppings, pet dander, and pollen to reduce asthma and allergy symptoms. The best ones even use UV light to kill bacteria, airborne viruses, and infections.[247]

Here is what you need to know to buy a real cleaner, and not a faker.

KNOW HEPA FROM HYPE. Avoid "HEPA-type" filters, which can be 55 percent lower in efficiency than a true-HEPA filter. Real HEPA vacuums sieve out more than 99 percent of airborne bacteria and microscopic pores. They also trap flame retardants, phthalates, and pesticides that bind to household dust. HEPA filters are easy to care for since they can be washed at home. Just remove the filter from the vacuum unit and disinfect.

LOOK FOR A COMMITMENT. Roughly one in five households buys a new vacuum cleaner each year. It's a vacuum, not a bikini, woman. Buy a good one and you won't be so fast to dismiss it. Look for a machine that comes with a long warranty and has a plan for part replacements. You may spend a little more up front, but just think of the long-term savings.

BAG IT OR DUMP CANISTERS OUTDOORS. Bagless vacuum cleaners help lighten the landfill load, but emptying compartments can disperse dust and allergens back into the air. If you've got some bad allergies, try cleaners with eco-friendly bags or make sure you're emptying the bagless varieties outdoors. Bagless vacuums can get clogged up easily, especially when picking up pet hair or dander. This muck sticks to the filter and restricts airflow to the motor, which wears it down. If you do decide to go with a bagless vacuum—like one of my favorites, the Dyson DC25 Ball—get a good warranty, clean it frequently, and dump the canister outside.

DON'T GET SUCKED INTO THE AMP GAME. More power doesn't mean it's going to clean better or faster. Try a vacuum with an 8-amp motor or at least one that offers a power-saving mode.

KIM'S PICKS: VACUUMS

Bissell 16N5 Healthy Home Upright Vacuum (bissell.com)

Dyson DC25 Ball All-Floors Upright Vacuum (dyson.com)

Electrolux Ultra Silencer Series EL6984A (ajmadison.com)

! FAT FACT:
Just one gram of dust holds more than one million bacteria, thousands of fungus spores, hundreds of pollen grains, and live dust mites. Now you know where all those nose boogies are coming from.

★ The Plastic Revolution

Anybody up for a challenge? Step right up, hot shot. I should probably tell you up front that you're going to fail miserably. *Nah.*

Here is your mission should you choose to accept it: *Cut plastic out of your life.*

Get it out of your home. Don't ever store another leftover in the stuff. Start thinking only glass and paper. Just cut your ties.

Think you got this one in the bag? (Not a plastic one, of course.) It won't take long to figure out that I just asked you to give up your freedom. But chances are you threw in the towel as soon as you figured out your cell phone was plastic. Fat chance you'll give up all that texting.

The reality is plastics are in just about everything we can get our eager little hands on. From the cars we drive, to the phones we abuse, to the sippy cups in our kid's mouths, to the clothes on our backs. There are few things that plastic hasn't left its mark on.

It all boils down to one word: convenience. After World War II ended, we turned into greedy materialists. Manufacturers needed something that was cheap to make and versatile enough to pump out all kinds of products to meet demand. Plastic was born. And with the right balance of chemicals, it could take on many forms, from soft to rigid. The public went apeshit. We begged for more, and Big Chem companies gave it to us in nylon, polyester, Styrofoam, and PVC.[248] Whatever our little hearts desired. Before we knew it, we were a culture of disposables. Once we're done with that 24-ounce cup, we just throw it out and get on to more important things like hair appointments and Pilates.

Come a new millennium and what was once our answer to everything has become one of the worst environmental threats in history. We screwed ourselves big-time.

On this great big planet of ours that we call home, we produce 100 million tons of plastic every year.[249] Holy cow. As convenient as that bottled water or to-go container might feel, it calls for more than 330 billion barrels of oil to produce the amount of plastics we consume every year in the United States alone.[250] Man do we have our priorities mixed up. Here we are asking the oil industry to wean the country off of fossil fuels with a bottle of Evian in hand. We couldn't look more ridiculous.

THE "NO-RECYCLING" PROGRAM

Plastic bottles are the scourge of our street gutters, trash cans, and oceans. Go ahead and roll out a recycling program. See if we care. We're just going to continue to toss stuff in the regular dump. And that right there is the big ole elephant in the room. Why we can't walk our lazy asses a little farther to a recycling can is a goddamn mystery to me. But it appears to be too much trouble. Even though 80 percent of U.S. households have access to a plastics recycling program, less than 1 percent actually recycle.[251] Recycled plastics can go to making carpets, clothing, upholstery, piping, and more plastic bottles. Instead, we treat the environment like one giant trash heap.

If the unrecycled stuff makes it to a landfill, it can take anywhere from one hundred to four hundred years to break down in the right conditions.[252] Plastic bottles made from BPA can take about seven hundred years to *begin* biodegrading.[253] But most of the time, it doesn't even get the opportunity to decompose. That's because plastic loves to get around. Most of the stuff we're tossing is tramping itself out in our oceans right next to the endangered sea creatures. There's no decomposing going on out there in the wide-open seas, honey. None.

WOULD YOU LIKE SOME OCEAN WITH YOUR PLASTIC?

Say hello to our beautiful oceans. Then say hello to their friend, plastic. There are more than forty-six thousand flippin' pieces of plastic junk floating in every square mile of ocean. Every square mile![254] Ten percent of all the plastic we produce across the globe every year makes its way out to our oceans. Most of that sinks, where it will never biodegrade.[255]

And don't think the ocean is going to let us live it down. It's sure to remind us just how stupid and negligent we are every day. Not symbolically. *Literally.* Somewhere in the middle of the North Pacific Ocean halfway between San Francisco and Hawaii sits a 3.5-million-ton vortex of trash.[256] The one I'm talking about, the Eastern Pacific Garbage Patch (aka the Pacific Trash Vortex) is twice the size of Texas. Created by giant rotating ocean currents, it's just a floating haze of plastic soup. This vortex has continued to grow tenfold every decade since the 1950s, just collecting debris in its path like an underwater tornado. Eighty percent of it is plastic.[257]

So there you have it—the environment is suffering. And so is our health, thanks to our cheap love affair with plastic. To get these plastics soft and rigid requires the handiwork of two chemicals we visited earlier in the book—BPA and phthalates. In this age of plastics, these guys have become so ubiquitous it's common to find them in our bodies.

THE HORMONE HEIST:
BISPHENOL A (BPA) AND PHTHALATES

BPA is a chemical used to "harden" plastic. Enough already. But what you probably don't know is that BPA showed warning signs before it even came to market. Scientists had run into evidence that BPA disrupted the hormones in our body. Once inside your body, it takes over for estrogen and starts doing its job without permission. Your body gets all discombobulated and tries to work out the problem, which just screws things up worse.[258] After sitting on this evidence, the reasonable move would have been to say, *It's been real,* and pull the plug. But why discontinue it when they can start adding it to plastics? So, that's what they did. And it's been leaching into our food and water ever since.

When the Toxic Substances Control Act was enacted in 1976, the boobs behind it just assumed that every chemical already on the market was "safe as used."[259] BPA was one of these sixty-two thousand chemicals "grandfathered" in by the act.[260] Safe as used? Funny, considering studies were showing clear evidence that even at the lowest exposure, BPA was poisonous to humans.[261]

Under consumer pressure, it's been tough for the federal government to continue to do squat. After years of denying it, the FDA caved in 2010, conceding that it held "some concern about the potential effects of BPA on the brain, behavior, and prostate gland in fetuses, infants, and young children."[262] But they still wouldn't admit that it was dangerous or unsafe.[263] Apparently. Are you freakin' kidding me? What more do you need—a dozen autopsies? The FDA continues to claim it can't ban BPA's use due to its hundreds of formulations. In other words: *This shit is in everything. Banning it would require a lot of manpower and time that we don't have. There's like five of us here managing the entire food industry, so suck it.*[264]

The EPA's idea of "safe levels" of BPA in products are twenty-five times higher than what some say are not safe.[265] When the agency set the standard back in 1988,

the levels may have seemed reasonable. But in the last twenty years, a crapload of studies has shown that BPA is toxic at levels far lower than what they recommend. They just haven't got around to updating them.[266] In the meantime, they have finally agreed to start measuring the impact of BPA on the water supply and parts of the environment, which is a start.

Because our government is too chicken shit to take action, plenty are busting their balls to get BPA out of our lives. Canada banned it.[267] Minnesota became the first U.S. state in 2009 to pass a ban on BPA in products for infants and toddlers.[268] Connecticut followed suit, adding food and drink containers. Wisconsin,[269] Massachusetts, Washington, Maryland, and the city of Chicago have all put a similar ban in place.[270] There are about a dozen other cities and states that are working on doing away with BPA.[271] Retailers aren't waiting for higher-ups to get their act together either. Retail giants such as Wal-Mart have already voluntarily removed it from their products.[272]

The companies with something to lose from all this continue to argue that they have industry research that BPA is safe. Yes, "industry research." Research sponsored by the companies that make billions of dollars each year producing 2.5 billion pounds of this scum.[273] That's like asking the fast food industry to sponsor a study on how factory-farmed meat prevents cancer. For fuck's sake. When you look at the more than one hundred independently funded experiments on BPA's effects on rats, 90 percent show adverse effects at levels pretty darn similar to what we're exposed to in our everyday lives.[274] There is a right and a wrong here.

Unfortunately, that's not the only toxic chemical floating in our blood streams courtesy of plastics.

BPA's degenerate cousins, phthalates, help soften plastics. They also pimp themselves out. The chemicals are used in everything from shower curtains to plastic wrap. In skincare products and cosmetics, BPAs are added to increase the penetration of other chemicals deeper into the skin.[275] In air fresheners and household cleaners, phthalates are responsible for making scents "stick around" in your indoor air. Because that's exactly where you want them hanging out, right?

Phthalates made their debut around 1950, but unlike BPA, concerns didn't start popping up until almost fifty years later.[276] By then it appeared we weren't just peeing the chemicals out when our bodies absorbed them. The Environmental Working Group (EWG) found that a common phthalate, bis (2-ethyl-hexyl) phthalate, was parked in the bodies of *every* single person they tested for industrial pollutants.[277]

Fast forward a few years and the U.S. Centers for Disease Control put together the first broad study on phthalate exposure. Of the results, the uneasiest finding was that some women of child-bearing age were testing positive for two phthalates[278] at levels that exceeded the government's safe levels to protect against birth defects.[279] Since phthalates act as hormone disruptors, you'd think this was something to stress about. Babies in the womb and infants need these hormones to tell their bodies how to grow and develop.[280]

Then researchers finally nailed a link between phthalate exposure in pregnant women and slowed genital development in their sons. The little boys' wieners just weren't growing.[281] Bingo! Once that cat was out of the bag, suddenly a bunch of studies were linking phthalates to endometriosis and infertility in women[282] and attention deficit hyperactivity disorder (ADHD) in kids.[283]

Another similarity that phthalates share with BPA is the whole lag on "safe levels." The last time the EPA updated safety standards for them, we were bidding Harry S. Truman a presidential farewell. It's been sixty years, people.[284]

The European Union nations, Canada, South Korea, Japan, Taiwan, and China have all gotten the clue and banned phthalates. But the U.S. isn't so cautious. We demand more proof—a level of proof that many scientists consider nearly impossible for them to obtain without testing on humans. Congress passed a bill banning six phthalates from cosmetics and children's toys,[285] while California banned the chemicals entirely.[286] But the verdict is still out on whether this is progress. Since companies still aren't forced to disclose their chemicals, we have no clue what they're using in place of phthalates. A provision on the ban would have made companies share this information. But, wouldn't you know it, Exxon Mobil—the largest producer of plasticizers in the world—put their lobbyists on the task and got the provision cut.[287] So continues the saga of lawmakers choosing incentives over public safety.

Today, more than one billion pounds of phthalates are produced each year across the globe for use in our home and beauty products.[288] More than 75 percent of Americans have substantial amounts in their bodies.[289] They really do cover some ground.

Enough of the depressing facts. Let's chat about how you can avoid the hormone wannabes.

> The European Union nations, Canada, South Korea, Japan, Taiwan, and China have all gotten the clue and banned phthalates. But the U.S. isn't so cautious.

BANNING BPA AND PHTHALATES FROM YOUR HOME

AVOID PLASTIC CONTAINERS LABELED #3 OR #7. The numbers stamped on plastic containers aren't just there to look pretty. These tell you what type of plastic you're dealing with, and whether it can be recycled. Number 3 is made with PVC, which is a good indication that you're at risk of one of these nasties leaching in your food. Number 7 can mean a few different plastics, but you can assume it's polycarbonate—a plastic hardened and lined with BPA. Neither are recyclable or good news. *Healthy Alternatives:* Products labeled numbers 1, 2, 4, and 5 are much safer if you're going to buy plastic. These plastics do not leach any known chemicals into your food and are generally recyclable.

STORE FOOD IN GLASS OR STAINLESS-STEEL CONTAINERS. Even when you're buying safer plastic alternatives, remember they're all capable of leaking chemicals. It might not be BPA or phthalates, but it's still junk you don't want to invite into your body. Try to use glass or stainless-steel containers. They are safe for hot foods and reheating foods, and will last for years if you take care of them. *Healthy Alternatives*: If you want to go the extra step, look for glass containers with BPA-free lids, as well. Snapware Glasslock containers use tight-fitting lids free of the hormone impersonators (snapware.com). Pyrex glass cooking dishes are made with BPA-free plastic lids, and double as food storage even for larger casserole dishes (pyrexware.com).

NEVER HEAT PLASTICS. Even if they claim to be heat-resistant, just resist the temptation to pop that plastic in the microwave. That is, unless you want leftovers seasoned with toxic spices. Yummy. When heated, the chemicals in plastic are very unstable, which causes them to break down and unleash hell into your food, beverage, or yes, even baby formula. Speaking of heat, wash *all* plastics by hand. The mixture of hot water and detergents can also wear down plastics, promoting even more leaching and deterioration.[290] Your microwave isn't the only instigator.

QUESTION PLASTIC WRAP. Conventional plastic wrap is also made with PVC. Shocking, I know. Some women are slightly infatuated with plastic wrap, so if this is the case, look for one that is PVC-free. Other healthier alternatives are unbleached wax paper, recyclable aluminum foil, and glass containers with lids. *Healthy Alternatives:* There is a load of options. If you want to get more of the stretchy, plastic feel, Natural Value offers a PVC- and plasticizer-free food wrap that keeps oxygen out to keep foods fresh longer (PVC wrap lets oxygen through to spoil food faster). Diamant Food Wrap is another food film that is recyclable and certified by the Environmental Choice Program. In the United Kingdom, BioWrap sells a polyethylene film that is biodegradable and recyclable.

B **BITCHWORTHY: PRESERVE FOOD STORAGE**
If you like your leftovers and don't trust yourself with glass, you may want to check out Preserve. It's the only brand you need to know for BPA-free products. Made from 100 percent recycled plastic (that can be recycled again). Preserve containers come in different sizes with screw-top lids for you clumsy ones. And I'm not the only one singing their praises. The Boston-based company has also been named "Greenest Product" by *National Geographic's* The Green Guide. *Visit preserveproducts.com.*

COOK WITH FRESH INGREDIENTS AND AVOID CANNED FOODS. Food manufacturers coat the inside of cans with BPA to keep them from rusting. Some brands including Trader Joes, Eden Organics, and Native Forest carry some product lines in BPA-free cans, but it's not a sweeping company policy. You can check the can, but the safest move is to go for fresh fruits, vegetables, legumes, and lentils whenever possible. Fresh is always better for the body and soul.

AVOID WORN-DOWN PLASTICS. Visible signs of scratching or damage indicate the plastic is leaching. Send it to the recycling can. If it's not recyclable, use it around the house for storage. Plastic containers make a perfect home for jewelry, hair bands and bobby clips, nail polishes, and office items.

BE SKEPTICAL OF THE TERM FRAGRANCE. Now you know why that fresh pine scent lingers in your kitchen for days. If it says "fragrance," the product may contain phthalates. There is a chance it doesn't, but the odds are not in your favor. Try to use products boasting essential oils, rather than artificial fragrance.

CHOOSE BPA-FREE PLASTIC BABY PRODUCTS. Most companies are voluntarily removing BPA from baby bottles (babies are more vulnerable to the toxin). Check into brands who have adopted this practice—this is your kid for heaven's sake.

MILK IT: BPA-FREE BABY BOTTLES AND SIPPY CUPS
I hunted down a dozen of the baby brands that are proud to be BPA-free. Some just offer glass options, which are usually naturally phthalate-, BPA-, PVC-, and lead-free, but there are plastic bottles ditching the chemicals, too.

BPA-FREE PLASTIC BOTTLES
Born Free Baby Bottles
Medela Baby Bottles
ThinkBaby Bottles
Green to Grow Baby Bottles
Adiri Natural Nurser Baby Bottle
MAM by Sassy
Nuby Non-Drip Bottles

SIPPY CUPS
SIGG Kids Bottles
Stainless Steel Sippy Cup by Thermos
Klean Kanteen Sippy Cup
The Safe Sippy
Fluid No-Spill Toddler Cup by Boon

GLASS BABY BOTTLES
WeeGo Glass Bottles by BabyLife
Dr. Brown's Natural Flow Standard Glass Bottles
Born Free Wide Neck Glass Bottle
Lifefactory Glass Baby Bottle with Silicone Sleeve
EvenFlo Classic Glass Bottle
Momo Baby Glass Feeding Bottle
Coddlelife Glass Bottle
Munchkin Mighty Grip Glass Bottles
NurturePure Glass Baby Bottles

BPA-FREE PLASTIC BOTTLE LINERS
Playtex Drop-Ins Bottles

Look for these BPA-free bottles at WalMart, Babies R Us, Whole Foods, and online at amazon.com.

BOTTLED WATER:
THE CONSPIRACY THEORY

Apparently, we're a thirsty bunch here in America. Or absurdly naive. However you want to look at it. The average person drinks more than 167 bottles of water every year. You could be standing right in front of a running faucet, but there's just something about the way that plastic hits your lips that persuades you to pay a markup of 1,900 times the cost of good ole tap water. But that's just pocket change for pure spring water from snow-capped mountain peaks, right? *Au contraire.* One bottler's "spring water" came from a well that sat in an industrial parking lot next to a hazardous waste dump. Chemicals had been leaking into the well at levels that put FDA standards to shame. You think I'm joking? I wish. True story right there.[291]

The bottled water industry, on the other hand, now that's a joke. Laugh it up.

When you count it all up, we buy almost thirty billion plastic water bottles a year.[292] That makes bottled water the second most popular beverage in the country.[293] It's water. In a bottle. Ninety percent of the cost of bottled water is actually the cost of the damn bottle itself.[294] Who's laughing now?

There's a little conspiracy around bottled water—it isn't any safer than tap water. During a four-year review, the Natural Resources Defense Council (NRDC) found that just because water comes out of a bottle doesn't make it any cleaner or safer than water from the tap.[295] Hold on, this just in—tap water might just be safer.

In the United States, tap water goes through some brutal testing for contaminants and bacteria as often as 480 times a month. If you do the math, that's as many as 16 times a day.[296] There are hundreds of federal staff members and state personnel that are in charge of overseeing that city water meets some pretty serious standards. But water bottlers play by a whole different set of rules. Silly me, there I go being nice again. Actually, they don't really have any rules at all. Somewhere between 60 and 70 percent of bottled water sold in this country doesn't cross state lines. That makes it exempt from FDA regulation. No need to clean the wax out of your ears . . . you heard me right. FDA rules go out the window when water is packaged and sold within the state. Just a small oversight. When it does cross state boundaries, the FDA admits that bottled water is low on their list of priorities. It's no big secret that they're incredibly understaffed over there. The agency has the equivalent of *less* than one staff person making sure water bottlers follow the rules. Leave it to the FDA to assign less than one person to something.[297]

THE BITCH FIGHT: BOTTLED WATER VS. TAP WATER

If you're curious just how unregulated that bottle of water is, I've got the dirt right here. Take a look at how the water you wash dishes with measures up against your guilty pleasure. It's guiltier than you think.

Tap water from a city source has to be filtered and dis-infected, or the local water system has to adhere to detailed protective measures.

Bottled water is subject to absolutely no filtration or disinfecting enforcements by federal law.

Tap water is tested at least one hundred times a month for coliform bacteria by certified labs.

Bottled water plants must undergo testing only once a week with no testing required.

Tap water cannot contain any *E. coli* or fecal coliform bacteria before it's made available to the public. It also has to be tested for two common water pathogens, cryp-tosporidium and giardia, which are known to cause diarrhea and other intestinal problems.

Bottled water is subject to no such rules under FDA guidance. Actually, a certain amount of *any* type of col-iform is actually "OK" by the FDA.

Tap water systems have to report lab and test results or notices of violations to state or federal officials.

Bottled water companies don't have to report squat.

Tap water systems have to issue annual reports to con-sumers telling them what's in their water.

Bottled water companies don't have to tell us jack shit (they crushed a provision that would require them to be open with consumers).

If you're one of the more than half of Americans who rely on bottled water for their only source of hydration, then this is really going to piss you off. Twenty-five per-cent of bottled water is just tap water in a fancy bottle.[298] The EWG even found that some bottled water samples had residues of arsenic, chlorine, and fertilizer.[299] That, ladies, is what you are paying for—waste in a bottle. California is the only state that requires water bottlers to tell you where the water came from or what standards it meets.[300] Otherwise, they just fill those plastic bottles with any water source, slap a pretty sticker of crystal clear geysers on there, and make a killing. Don't look at them—you're the one making them rich.

There's still more dirt. The plastic used for most single-serving bottled waters is one of the most unsafe types of plastic on the market. As the temperature of the bottle starts to get warmer from leaving it in a car or maybe in the pantry, it may leach phthalates into your water.[301]

CLEAN TAP WATER

There are contaminants that even tap water can't shed. And because of our pill-popping problem, remnants of prescription drugs like Prozac and Valium are starting to wander into our water supply.[302] Other pollutants that may find their way into our water are pesticides, rust, heavy metals, bacteria, and trace amounts of chlorine and fluoride.[303]

Don't flip out. At the end of the day, experts agree that your city tap water is still safer than the plastic bottled shit. Here are some things you can consider to fix your tap water right up.

INSTALL A WATER FILTRATION SYSTEM. Water filtration systems can get rid of up to 99 percent of chlorine and contaminants in drinking water.[304] But there are a few things you want to check into before you blow your wad on a water filtration system. The quality of your tap water really depends on where you live. Find out what contaminants are common in your region by reading the annual Consumer Confidence Report (if you have trouble finding it, ask your water supplier or visit the EPA's Web site). If the information looks like it's written in a foreign language, check out other online resources that help decipher the info (type in: *Making Sense of Drinking Water "Right to Know" Reports*). After you know what's in your water, here are a few basics for choosing the right water filter.

LOOK FOR NSF INTERNATIONAL CERTIFICATION. These dudes act as a watchdog over water filtration companies to make sure they meet the tough requirements. Their stamp of approval can be found on the packaging or you can visit the Web site to find a list of approved companies. *Visit nsf.org.*

CHOOSE A FILTER THAT TARGETS THE WATER CONTAMINANTS IN YOUR REGION. Carbon filters are the most inexpensive solution for most water pollutants. But if you want to make sure it's filtering exactly what you need it to, read the label.

Reverse osmosis and whole house filtration systems are also available if you have more serious water contamination issues. But remember not to drive yourself insane over it—no matter which filter you use, some pollutants are always going to find their way in.

CHANGE YOUR FILTERS. You can't keep the same filter in there for two years. Sorry, honey. Every filter is different, but most need to be changed every three to six months. If you don't change them, they don't filter. Funny how that works . . .

WATER FILTRATION SYSTEMS

AQUASANA Aquasana has countertop attachments and under-the-counter water filters that are easy to install and filter up to thirty gallons an hour. Aquasana filters retain the natural trace minerals and sift out 99 percent of chlorine, lead, VOCs, cysts, heavy metals, pharmaceuticals, and bacteria. *Visit aquasana.com.*

ZERO WATER BOTTLE SYSTEM If you have a stand-up water cooler, this nifty system just plugs right in. It prepares three gallons of filtered water in a large BPA-free plastic water bottle. Two carbon filters screen out the bad stuff. *Visit zerowater.com.*

FILTRETE WATER SYSTEM This one is really pushing the lines of innovation. Just turn on the faucet and let the water stream into a water docking station, which has valves that are attached to four grab-and-go bottles. The fast-flow technology filters and fills up the bottles as it goes. The bottles are removed from the docking station, and can be stored in the fridge until you're thirsty. Each one is BPA-free and safe to throw in the dishwasher. *Visit 3m.com.*

B BITCHWORTHY: WATER FILTERS VS. WATER PURIFIERS

A good choice for backpackers who may not have the best access to clean water, water purifiers do some extra work. While water *filters* can remove dirt, bacteria, and contaminants from water, only purifiers kill viruses from untreated water.[306]

REFRIGERATOR FILTRATION PITCHERS

Don't think you're getting the whole shebang when you buy a water filtration pitcher. Most do reduce the amount of chlorine, trace metals, and unwanted tastes and odors, but not everything. Brita even admits on their Web site that its pitcher filters don't meet the new industry standard for lead reduction.[305]

There aren't a ton of BPA-free options that still filter out the toxins and pollutants, but there are a few. Here are a few systems that are reliable.

RESTORE CLEAN WATER SYSTEM BY HOMEDICS It has an uncanny resemblance to all those other fridge filtration pitchers, but this one is free of BPA, and still reduces the nasty heavy metals, chlorine, and city pollutants. The pitcher also comes with a cool UV lightbulb in the bottom that purifies more than 99 percent of all bacteria, viruses, and microbes. You plug it into a wall socket for less than a minute to purify, and then just stick the pitcher back in the fridge. The UV purifier hikes the price of the system up to about $50, but at least you know your water is clean. *Visit homedics.com.*

REVOLVE WATER FILTRATION BOTTLE For my ladies who just need clean water for one, this stainless steel, BPA-free bottle is easy to lug from work to yoga and fits snuggly in your fridge. It may not be a pitcher, but it filters up to 99.99 percent of all tap water contaminants as you sip. Revolve, formerly known as Sovereign Earth, is the brainchild of its twenty-something CEO, Steve Hess, who started questioning bottled water standards in college. The 27-ounce filtration bottle meets EPA requirements and is certified by the standards of NSF International and ANSI (American National Standards Institute). One percent of all proceeds are donated to various environmental causes. Once you get one, you'll take it everywhere. Who am I kidding? Buy two. *Visit revolvewater.com.*

THE SHOPPER'S DILEMMA:
PAPER, PLASTIC, AND THE REUSABLE BAG

An unhealthy addiction to bottled water isn't our only plastic folly on this great big planet. Case in point: the abominable plastic bag. Plastic bags suck up around twelve million barrels of petroleum oil every year in the United States alone.[307] We just can't seem to kick the habit. Although San Francisco banned plastic bags from supermarkets and chain drugstores, other cities including Boston, Portland, and Phoenix pushed for similar bans with little progress. California got the closest to a statewide ban in 2010, before the state senate crushed it under pressure from industry lobbying (though Los Angeles county was able to push a ban through).[308] Despite all the efforts to ban them, one thing is always clear: Our government is extra good at falling flat on its ass. Either we have to start phasing out plastic bags ourselves, or shit just isn't going to get done.

It's not enough to go buy a cute reusable bag, throw it in the cabinet, and brag to everyone you "went green." Caught you, babe. The no-plastic-bag policy really needs to become a regular occurence.

There are one-hundred thousand marine animals that die every year mistaking these plastic bags for food.[309] And we're to blame. Plastic manufacturers are pumping out between five hundred billion and one trillion bags a year worldwide. That is more than one million bags a minute.[310] It's enough solid waste to fill the entire Empire State Building two and a half times. That's not something to be proud of.

Though plastic bags can be recycled, only about five percent of them actually are. It's no different from plastic bottles.[311] Billions are tossed as litter with no care in the world for where they are going. But they know exactly where they are going. Many start out by littering the streets and clogging up the city's sewage system. It may seem trivial, but try explaining that to Bangladesh. Plastic bags were found to be the cause of the 1988 and 1998 floods that submerged two-thirds of the entire country under water. The discarded bags choked the drainage system.[312] They even wreak havoc on sidewalks and in gutters, where, besides being an eyesore, they break down into little microscopic pieces that offgas toxic chemicals. These chemicals infect our soil and groundwater. Same ole story.[313]

If they end up making the journey to the landfills, the bags can take anywhere from four hundred to one thousand years to degrade by sunlight.[314] That's something even your great, great grandchildren won't live to see. Sometimes they're incinerated to get it over with. That's when the inks and chemicals in plastic leach dioxins and heavy metals into the air.[315]

More commonly though, the plastic bag's light and fluid nature carries it to our oceans and beaches. This is where things really start to suck. In some parts of the sea, there are six pounds of plastic for every pound of plankton. Marine animals such as whales, dolphins, and sea turtles think it's food so they eat it. Their bodies can't digest it and they die. Birds like the albatross get entangled in floating plastic bags, and they choke and die.[316] The Pacific Leatherback Turtle has officially landed itself on the endangered species list after years of mistaking floating plastic bags for its favorite food: the jellyfish. Their population has declined 95 percent in the past two decades, right as the plastic bag population has seen record numbers.[317] Are you seeing a trend here? Plastic is wiping out our wildlife.

On the other side of the shopper's conundrum is the paper bag. It's easier to recycle, biodegrades pretty quickly in a landfill, and leaves no petroleum in its wake.

But it's got its own set of issues. It takes about fourteen million trees to support the amount of paper bags we tote around every year. Paper bag production also spews out 70 percent more air pollution than plastic.[318] Before it ends up at the checkout, it's been washed, bleached, and colored. On the upside, paper bags can be recycled to avoid cutting down more virgin trees, but the recycling process relies on a lot of chemicals and energy. Not as green as you thought, huh?

So how's this for a shopper's stance: Say no to paper *and* plastic. Keep a handful of reusable bags in your car so you have them on hand at all times. Better yet, roll one up tightly in a zip-up compartment of your purse so you have no excuse. When you make it a habit of using reusable bags, you end up looking like a compassionate human being, while the plastic-user behind you looks like a heartless bitch. It's a win-win. Just one reusable bag has the opportunity to save more than twenty thousand plastic bags over the course of your lifetime.[319] In one year, a reusable bag can save three hundred to seven hundred plastic bags, depending on how often you *really* use it. Just think if you have three [wink, wink].

THE SKINNY: BIODEGRADABLE BAGS
Newsflash: Plastic bags don't have to be immortal. Though reusable bags are my first choice, biodegradable bags are better than their never-say-die alternatives. That is, if you buy the right ones. Look for the vendor certification symbols—ASTM D6400 and/ or DIN EN 13432. Any bags labeled *oxo-degradable, oxo-biodegradable, oxy-degradable, oxy-biodegradable*, or *degradable* are a dupe. It's just plastic with a chemical ingredient that helps them break down faster but leaves behind a hazardous residue.[320] Biodegradable bags can also replace those heinous kitchen trash bags and be used for throwing out pet poo.

One of my favorites is BioBag, made from GMO-free starch and other renewable resources, with absolutely no polyethylene. *Visit biobagusa.com.*

KIM'S SLIM PICKINS: REUSABLE BAGS
ChicoBag (chicobag.com)
Envirosax (envirosax.com)
Baggu (baggubag.com)

The Skinny:
A Healthier Soul

★ Clutter-Free:
ORGANIZATION FOR A HEALTHIER MIND

Letting go is not easy, and I'm not talking about an ex-boyfriend or your virginity. (Good luck getting those back.)

I'm talking about all the crap in your home. You know, the ancient textbooks from college, that tragic drawer full of unmatched socks and seven pairs of Spanx, empty shampoo bottles clogging up your bathtub, your old Barbie collection. You get the picture. So what if Barbie never got her Malibu beach house or the hot pink corvette? Get over it and move on, woman.

We're a nation of hoarders. There is so much junk on our counters, we wouldn't know a phone bill from a lingerie catalog. When are we going to realize that all of this clutter equals time? Time that is very valuable. The average person spends an average of thirty minutes, and as much as two hours every day just looking for things.[321] Thirty minutes. All that time wasted trying to find our sunglasses or an unpaid parking ticket is turning us into stress cases. Sure, we may brush stress off as normal, but it's not good. It screws us up mentally, and causes all sorts of physical problems—headaches, bad digestion, insomnia, mood swings, and lousy diet habits. Plus, it makes us more likely to hit the bottle, use drugs, and smoke disgusting cigarettes. How normal does that sound? Seriously.

The tricky part is that we're pretty set in our ways. It is much easier to fix the things around us, than it is to fix ourselves. But instead of throwing a bunch of plastic containers, bins, and boxes at the problem, we need to create lifestyle tools that help us simplify our lives and give our short-term memories a break.

Organizational experts agree—it isn't a space problem; it's a "person" problem. We need to change our behavior to get on the right track. Remember, this isn't an overnight life change.

Enter organizational lifestyle expert Jill Pollack. Jill isn't just another clean freak. She's the personal trainer you need riding your ass like a drill sergeant to shed unwanted clutter and gain back the peace in your life. The idea is to keep consumption down to ease the mind, body, and soul. And ease the pressure off our planet in the process.

Here are a few of Jill's tips to cutting down on junk and save precious time.

GET RID OF JUNK MAIL. The average adult receives forty-one pounds of junk mail a year.[322] That is a shit-load of catalogues and credit card applications you don't even want (remember, retail therapy=bad). If we all just put our foot down on mail we didn't ask for, we'd keep more than 100 million trees in the ground. Visit 41pounds.org and pay $41 to get your name off of 80 to 95 percent of junk mail lists for 5 years. That is less than $10 a year. Don't be a cheap ass. The non-profit service also donates one-third of your fee to an environmental organization of your choice. Trust me, shedding that useless paper weight will make you feel lighter on your feet. *Check out 41pounds.org.*

STOP WITH THE MAGAZINE SUBSCRIPTIONS ALREADY. There is no denying that magazines are alluring. But they also stare you in the face like a kid selling candy bars. *Have you read me yet? Are you planning on reading me? Or will I just be another thing in your life you don't get around to?* Get rid of the guilt and the paper weight. In the United States, magazine production uses up more than 2.2 million tons of paper every year! Hello?! That wipes out more than thirty-five million virgin trees.[323] Even worse, you're not reading them. Nearly three billion magazines every year never even get read. Nowadays, a majority of what you find in a magazine can be found online. Get with the times and stay on top of the trends digitally.

GO PAPERLESS, HONEY. Junk mail isn't the only paper waste that jams up our mailboxes. Shift all of your bank accounts, receipts, and monthly bills online. If you are someone who likes to have tangible records, save a second copy in a folder on an external hard drive and print when necessary. Mint.com is a complimentary online service that helps consolidate all of your bills, budget your finances, and keep your payments on time. A lifesaver for the scatter-brained.

PUT A PAD OF PAPER ON THE REFRIGERATOR. I know what you're thinking: How does writing something down on paper—the very thing destroying our rainforests—help me get organized and lighten my carbon footprint?" It's simple. When you write down the things you need, you cut down on time spent roaming the aisles. It also lowers the risk of impulse buying. Stick to the list and get out. Jotting down daily tasks, important dates, and birthdays also helps keep your mind in order and helps you visualize what you have accomplished. Greener Printer offers a selection of memo pads made from 100 percent recycled paper and vegetable-based inks. *Check out greenprinteronline.com.*

SHARE SOMETHING BEFORE YOU BUY SOMETHING NEW. Take a lesson from the sandbox and learn to share. Before you buy a book, cell phone, or new couch, you should sell, gift, or trade the one you already have. This cuts down on clutter and gives that special something a second or third life. Donate to a women's shelter, share with a neighbor, or make some money off of Craigslist.

LOSE THE JUNK IN THE TRUNK. The only thing that should be in your trunk is a spare tire and maybe a yoga mat. Why the hell does it look like Sport Chalet back there? Put it in your garage, store neatly in a closet, or donate it to Goodwill. Lighten the load and save gas. For every one hundred pounds you add to a car, you eat up 1 to 2 percent more gas.[324] *Visit goodwill.org.*

BITCH WE LOVE:
JILL POLLACK

Jill Pollack is a professional organizer whose clients include Marcia Cross, Felicity Huffman, and Jennifer Tilly. She's also been featured in *Self*, *O Magazine*, *Quick and Simple*, *InStyle Home*, and on *The Style Network*. Here's some of her advice for getting creative with what you've got:

"Skip the trip to The Container Store. Instead, work with what's already taking up space in your place. Used glass jars and tins make charming receptacles for loose items such as keys, change, and sunglasses. This is the beauty of 'upcycling,' and it works for nearly everything—not just the little stuff.

There are so many more reusable items in most households that can benefit from a second life. Here are a few ideas:

- Pretty candle votives, Granny's old teacups, and soap dishes can double as containers for essential oils, tweezers, and jewelry.
- Glass mason or food jars are awesome for cosmetic brushes and toothbrushes.
- An old step-up ladder makes a fun shoe rack in your entryway.
- Hotel shower caps make fabulous shoe and high-heel covers when traveling.
- Got an old wine rack? Roll up clean towels or magazines in the wine cubbies for creative bathroom storage.
- Remake an old dining room table into a clever coffee table by cutting or shortening the legs.
- Reuse newspapers or junk catalogs to wrap gifts or clean windows.
- Turn empty paper-towel rolls into a capsule for kid's artwork, rolled-up reusable bags, or diapers.
- Turn an old-school clawfoot bathtub into an indoor planter or outdoor ice cooler for backyard entertaining."

★ My Secret Garden:
SMALL-SPACE GARDENING

It's funny how our priorities shift with age. Yesterday all I wanted was bigger boobs, and today I'm perfectly happy sitting on the Itty Bitty Titty Committee as long as I got a spot to grow some damn tomatoes. Older and wiser.

Three years ago, I got my big girl's garden. So what if it was a patch of grass between a one-car garage and a litter box? A garden is a garden. Whether you have a small outdoor deck, a fire escape, or a backyard the size of an amusement park, homegrown fruits, veggies, and herbs help ensure we eat healthier. We control how they are grown, nurtured, picked, and served up on a platter. You can't get any closer to your food source than that.

I really don't care what style of gardening you're up for. It needs to make you happy. After all the long days at the office, wiping your kid's ass, and taking care of everyone else but yourself, it's a release to have something that's just for you. This chapter is going to give you some dummy-proof tips for getting your garden growin' and not wasting any more time.

THE DUMMY'S GUIDE TO STARTING AN ORGANIC GARDEN

You have the land. Though it's well, *quaint*, you are ready to start your own organic garden. Irises, rosemary, and whatever else can survive the ride of your ignorance. Right now, there's really only one thing standing between you and juicy heirloom tomatoes this summer—the slightest clue of what the hell you're doing.

Gardening is an art. Any true green thumb will tell you that a garden is like a child that requires constant nurturing. Only, with proper care, this one won't grow up so pissed off at you.

My goal is to make this as simple and as far from boring as possible. At times, I might slip and drag you down a black hole of ideal soil types and water conservation, but I promise, with Martha Stewart as my witness, I will bring you back to fun.

Now someone hand me a flippin' shovel.

STEP ONE: Set a Goal.

It's simple. Do you want to grow vegetables? If so, ask yourself what types of vegetables you want to plant. Creating your own personal vegetable and herb garden is a great way to feel useful, eat healthy, and save money. Once you buy the seeds, the only thing that plant is going to cost you is your time. When the economy dipped in 2009, vegetable seed sales shot up by 40 percent. The waiting lists at urban community gardens grew fourfold.[325] This is a trend worth following.

Whatever you chose to grow—vegetables, herbs, or flowers—find out what plants are native to your state or region. They will complement local wildlife and do not need as much water or extra TLC (for a list of native plants, visit Wildlife.org). If you are thinking about planting seeds and starting from scratch, study up to make sure that they will be in season when your garden is prepped. Lastly, be realistic for your own sanity. Just remember: You are a novice. You are not a professional. Start the journey with something that is easier to care for, and you can always work up to the exotics.

Here are a few varieties that are happy in just about any garden, and won't require an expert's care:

Flowers: Marigolds, sunflowers, snapdragons, zinnias, pansies, California poppies

Vegetables: Tomatoes (cherry), onions, lettuce, peppers, green beans, zucchini, and scallions

Herbs: Basil, parsley, mint, garlic, thyme, rosemary, cilantro, oregano

B BITCHWORTHY: EASY BLOOM PLANT SENSOR

Say you don't have the first inkling as what to put in your garden. You know you want to get your hands dirty, and you think flowers are pretty. *That's about it.* Why not ask your soil what it likes? Yes, your soil can talk—just in a different tongue. The urban girl's foolproof tool to simple gardening, the Easy Bloom Plant Sensor tells you what will work best with your soil. Just stick it in the ground for twenty-four hours and let it assess sunlight, humidity, temperature, and other factors. After a day's work, plug it into your computer USB port, and it will literally tell you what will do best in that spot. *Check out easybloom.com.*

STEP TWO: Pick the Location.

Do some research on those flowers or plants you are planning your garden around. Different varieties will call for different amounts of water and sunlight. Consider the soil and how well yours holds water. Vegetables and herbs prefer soil that drains well, especially in the spring and summer when they like to shine. Gauging how much sunlight a location will get is simple. Just observe. See if it gets more sun in the morning or late afternoon, and how long the sun sets on your garden to be. If it sits in the shade most of the day, don't be an idiot—find another spot. Unless you want a garden with no action.

HOW TO TEST YOUR SOIL: For the most part, soils are classified as clay, sandy, or loamy. To see which type you're working with, grab a handful of moist soil—be careful that it's not wet—and give it a nice, firm squeeze like you're grabbing someone's ass. Then open your hand. What happens?

Loamy soil If it holds its shape, but crumbles when you give it a light tap, it's loamy soil. Congratulations. Loamy is great at retaining moisture and nutrients but doesn't get all swamp like. Hint: This is exactly what you want. A few cartwheels would show some appreciation.

Clay soil If it holds its shape, but stays put when you give it a light tap, it's clay soil. Not bad. Clay is rich in nutrients but can retain too much water. Hint: Don't water as much.

Sandy soil If it falls apart as soon as you open your hand, you got sand, girl. All good. Sand drains water well but isn't so good at retaining nutrients. Hint: You're going to need some good compost, mulch, and nutrients for upkeep.

You're not done yet. Now you want to check the drainage. Herbs and veggies may die if their roots stay too wet. Just dig a hole about six inches wide and one foot deep, and fill the hole with water. Let it drain and repeat, checking to see how long it takes to drain. If it takes hours, you have poor drainage. That doesn't sound so hot.

STEP THREE: Make your bed.

By now, you should have your garden site. If you're like me, you just want to start planting seeds everywhere like somebody is timing you. This isn't *Supermarket Sweep* . . . take a step back. You want a nice manicured garden that makes neighbors incredibly jealous, not embarrassed to live next door. Revert to your kindergarten days and *plant* inside the lines. Take a few stakes or picks and stick one in each corner of your garden bed, drawing lines with a shovel to connect each corner.

Chances are your garden area isn't ripe for planting yet; you have grass, weeds, or gravel that stop you from getting started. Start digging, baby. Completely clear the area and I assure you, the rest is a piece of cake.

STEP FOUR: Dress Up the Soil.

If you really want a gorgeous garden, you want to feed it all the right nutrients. The best move is to lay down some compost. Some people will lay down fertilizer, but not in a *Skinny Bitch* garden. Traditional fertilizers are packed with chemical pesticides, fungicides, algaecides, and insecticides.[326] Save that shit for the factory farms. You want a healthy, organic garden.

Layer Compost. You have a few options here. You can use your own compost if you've already discovered how cool it is, or you can get it from somewhere else. If you want to start composting and use your own recycled matter to keep it all in the family, that's lovely. But it can take anywhere from several months to a year to produce useable soil, so you're going to need to get it from somewhere else for now (see page 105 for a composting how-to). Call your local gardening center(s) and ask for herbal organic compost—herbal compost is key. Some organic compost will contain animal by-products such as chicken shit, bone meal, fish products, and blood meal. Herbal compost will just be vegetable matter and minerals. Last thing and I'm done ranting about compost: Find out whether it's an all-purpose formula or specialized for flower or vegetable gardens. You don't want flower compost for a veggie garden, and vice versa. Make sure to buy enough to spread around your garden; a thin layer about an inch thick is perfect. Bravo. Now are you ready to get planting, or what?

STEP FIVE: Get Your Seeds or Plants.

Now for the fun part: It's time to go get your plants or flowers. I prefer to buy organic seeds since you get to watch them from the very beginning. When buying plants, choose locally and organically. You do not want chemical- and pesticide-ridden plants haunting your garden. Most major home improvement centers now carry a good selection of organic seeds and plants.

Before you proceed to checkout, survey your potential new plant. *Does it look weak or unhealthy?* Look for tiny holes in the leaves as an indicator that insects have been eating away at it. If it looks straggly or depressed, keep it out of your backyard.

> **B BITCHWORTHY:**
> You don't even have to leave the seat of your couch to get organic seeds. A few great online resources are Burpee.com, Johnnyseeds.com, Parkseed.com, and Thompson-morgan.com. The best time to shop is right after the New Year. New year, new plants.

STEP SIX: Get Planting.

Once you've brought your plants in, given them the house tour, and introduced them to significant others, kids, neighbors, and pets, they are ready to get acquainted. First, give them a big drink of water—even if you plan on planting them immediately. This helps alleviate soil shock.

When you are ready for the big moment, slice the root ball so the roots will be able to crawl their way through the soil. Dig a hole with your handheld shovel that is just as deep as the root ball of the plant, and twice as wide. Stick the plant in, replace the soil, and pat down. Done!

If you chose to go with seeds, follow the instructions on the seed packet. Some seeds are best started indoors in a controlled environment and then moved outdoors. But depending on the time of year you are planting, others must be sown directly into the soil. Each variety will be different.

After the seeds or plants are grounded, water them down, and—holy shit ladies and gentlemen—we have a garden.

Layer Mulch. Your garden still needs a little prep work to bloom. After the plants are in the ground and seeds are sown, the soil is primed for mulch. You want to lay down about a three-inch layer over the entire garden area. Give it a sprinkle.

Mulch is made from ground wood chips, leaves, and straw. It protects soil from weeds and disease, helps retain the moisture, and gives the soil some organic matter to do its best work. When you buy mulch, be cautious about contaminants and harmful chemicals like arsenic from pressed wood. Grass clippings, fallen leaves, and crushed peanut or pecan shells also make great natural mulch, so start collecting. If you are really gung-ho about closing the loop, put a call into a tree trimming service and ask them for leftover mulch from recent jobs. They won't think it's a crank call—this is a common request. To find certified chemical-free mulch, visit Mulchandsoilcouncil.org.

STEP SEVEN (Optional): Label the Goods.

If you are a beginner—sorry to keep reminding you—it's smart to label the goods in your garden. If you prefer not to decorate your garden with color-coded picks and names, you can create a garden map that you keep in a safe place. This is important so you know when each plant is expected to bloom, and what they are in the first place.

C'mon, was that so bad? Well, I'm not finished just yet.

URBAN COMMUNITY GARDENS

If real estate is what you are after, urban community gardens are a great way to grow organic produce and herbs, build a sense of community, and connect to your local environment. You know what else they are good for? Protecting our food supplies and taking money back from factory farms.

Perfect for the chick who can barely fit a welcome mat outside her front door let alone a plant, urban community gardens give you a cool and engaging alternative outside of container gardening.

When we live in big cities or metropolitan areas, it's easy to forget where our food comes from. Urban gardens bring us right back to our food sources, even when we can hear the fire engine sirens and angry horns across the street.

The grand idea is you are renting space to practice your new hobby. You can find a group and start one yourself, or apply to join an existing garden. Some people have become addicted because you can swap produce and herbs for ones you don't grow with friends and fellow gardeners. You can also give back by donating your harvest to local soup kitchens or homeless centers.

For a good resource, check out the American Community Gardening Association's Web site, communitygarden.org. There you can apply to an urban garden, start your own, ask questions, or take classes on Gardening 101. .

KIM'S TIP: WATCH OUT FOR INVASIVE PLANTS Some plants really find satisfaction in spreading their roots all over the place, and suffocating the roots of other plants. I know, it blows, but not everything in life is all sunshine and lollipops. Some of these include horseradishes, buckthorn, butterfly bush, honeysuckle, Japanese anemone, and creeping Jenny. As if that last one didn't offer quite the clue. For more invasive growers, cruise the Internet.

WATERING YOUR GARDEN

Every time we whip out a garden hose we seem to blank on the fact that we're in a major global water shortage. By 2025, two out of every three people in the world are expected to live in a place where water is scarce. I don't know about you, but I'm not looking forward to that.[327]

In most areas around the world, daily water consumption is limited to just 2.5 gallons per person, per day. But here in America, your average family uses almost 400 gallons per day.[328]

Constant flushing, bath time, and doing the dishes or brushing our teeth with the faucet running add up fast. But watering your plants, lawn, or garden is just as problematic. Spraying down your lawn and garden can account for up to 120 gallons a day. Water doesn't grow on trees, woman.[329]

Our goal here is not to contribute to our environmental issues, but help solve them. There are plenty of ways to conserve and recycle water for your mini garden and houseplants.

QUICK TIPS FOR RECYCLING H$_2$0 FOR GARDENING
Follow these creative reuse tips to recycle water for plants or flowers in your garden.
- Stick a bucket or bowl under the shower or tub faucet while you're waiting for the water to heat up.
- If you're washing dishes by hand and want to have the water running, put a large bowl or bucket underneath to catch the water.
- If you have ice left in a reusable water bottle or takeout cup, offer it to a plant.
- Rather than dumping your pet's water out in the sink, pour it into your garden

---

DON'T WATER WHEN IT'S HOT OUTSIDE. Heat and wind help evaporate water quicker. Try watering early in the morning or late at night to ensure plants suck up and retain moisture. And don't go crazy on the watering. Water less often but give it a good soaking to stimulate the roots.

CAPTURE RAINWATER. If you live in a rainier climate, collect rain water to water your plants, your garden, or the grass. It's pretty simple. You can buy ready-made barrels or urns that have openings at the top to collect rainwater and a hose plug-in at bottom so you can use the water when you're ready. For every inch of rain in a 1,000-square-foot area, you can collect an upwards of 600 gallons of rainwater. Rain barrels can run anywhere from $70 to $200. Call me old-fashioned, but I'm a fan of putting a bucket out in the rain, and putting a top on it when the water starts to overflow. Why spend the money if you don't need to?

LOOK FOR NATIVE PLANTS. We hit on this earlier, but plants native to your region do not require as much water. They naturally grow like weeds. Because summer and winter are more water-hungry seasons, try to plant new crops or seeds in fall or spring.

USE ORGANIC MULCH. Natural mulch such as shredded wood and leaves slow down the evaporation of water from the plant's roots. It also helps shade and cool the soil, so if you were thinking about skipping it, don't.

BUG OFF: A GUIDE TO ORGANIC PEST CONTROL

Not all bugs are bad, but most of them are if you ask me. But maybe that's because I can't even look at a praying mantis without losing my shit. It bites off its baby's daddy's head when it gives birth, for crying out loud.

The key is to let the right ones in. Gardeners will tell you there are more than a handful of bugs that you want in your garden—brachonoids, ladybugs, lacewings, wasps, hover flies, and, god help me, the praying mantis are all beneficial bugs.

Today, too many gardeners completely defeat the purpose of growing their own veggies and fruit. Spraying chemicals and synthetic fertilizers on your future food source isn't my idea of connecting with the environment or a healthier lifestyle. Even if you are just growing roses, these chemicals enter your bloodstream when you touch them and can be dragged into the home by kids, pets, and dirty shoes.

Sadly, Americans dump more than 136 million pounds of pesticides on their gardens every year. Um, yuck. In North America, residential gardens use three times more than commercial farmers. Hello?! You're growing plants not redwood trees, loons. [330]

Then there are the bugs. Everyone thinks the only way to get rid of insects is with a potent, deadly spray. The more chemicals to wipe those suckers out, the better. But we completely forget that these hazardous poisons in a bottle are bad for our health, too.

Just study the label of Ortho Bug-B-Gon MAX Garden Insect Killer Dust to understand my beef with bug sprays. It flat out says it's dangerous for humans and pets, and will kill fish. Then there's a bunch of caution signs and warnings to "Keep out of reach of children." But when you look at the ingredients, the bug masters disclose one measly additive, permethrin, at .25 percent, and 99.75 percent "other ingredients." The EPA classifies permethrin as a potential human carcinogen, while the "other" ingredients could be any of 313 "reportable" ingredients—many of which haven't been tested for human safety. But the Material Safety Data Sheets assure us "it's *practically* nontoxic if inhaled." [331] Call me impractical but I'm not taking that risk.

With some planning and regular maintenance, you should never need insect killers on steroids. The simple act of making sure the soil is healthy, and that your garden gets enough sunlight and drains water properly, helps keep pests at bay. But there are a few other ways to stop those annoying pests from eating up all your hard work:

REMOVE THE DEAD CRAP. Don't let the weak bring down the rest of your garden. Get out there and use your hands! Grab a hoe and remove weeds or plants that aren't looking so hot. Cut and remove old buds or diseased parts of plants to allow all the nutrients to go to the healthy parts of the plant. Proper trimming will keep all that's good in order.

ADD SOME MULCH AND COMPOST. Mulch and compost help protect your plants all through their life cycle. Keep extra on hand to sprinkle over plants every few weeks. Just pour an inch-thick layer over the soil. Seaweed or kelp also act as earthy fertilizers that speed up the growth and make the soil strong. If you live near the beach, you can throw fresh kelp directly onto the soil or in the compost pile. Nurseries and organic gardening brands also sell packaged seaweed fertilizer.

Side note: If you compost in your garden and find that pests are crowding it, just move the compost. Use your brain. Putting it in an area not so close to your crops will quickly help with your pest problem.

ADD COFFEE GRINDS OR MILKY SPORES. For you coffee drinkers who prefer to make it at home rather than support major chains, spent coffee grinds are actually useful. Since they have a very high carbon-to-nitrogen level—this is a good thing—grinds add a nice texture and acidity to compost. Mixing the grounds with a little soil helps keep off the slugs and snails, plus the worms love to eat them right up. You can even toss the biodegradable coffee filter into a compost pile.

Milky spore is another way to kill the grub (eggs) of Japanese beetles, a common pest that feeds on fruit, flowers, garden plants, and the roots of grass and other vegetation. It's a soil-dwelling bacterium that isn't actually made from milk, but gets its name from the milk-like substance that fills up the eggs. Milk spore bacterium discriminately attacks the white grub of Japanese beetles, so it won't hurt beneficial bugs, the birds, or the bees. It also adds healthy nutrients to your garden, and spreads through the soil to ward against future pests after the eggs are dead.

WATER EARLY IN THE MORNING. Fungus and insects are attracted to moist plants when the sun goes down; watering early gives the soil all day to dry out. You can't do anything about rain, but you can control your hose.

ROTATE PLANTS. Treat your garden to a game of musical chairs. Rotating just means moving your plants and crops to different areas of the garden every year. This fools soil-borne disease or pests that have settled in one area to feed on certain plants, giving them little time to regroup and attract all their nasty friends. Problem solved.

USE NATURAL INSECT SPRAYS. Instead of buying the toxic sprays, make your own all-natural bug spray using ingredients from the pantry.

NATURAL BUG REPELLANT

Safe and all-natural bug repellants are tough to find on store shelves. So when all else fails, whip up your own deterrent. Though the ingredients are harmless items in your kitchen, they can kill or repel *any* bugs or insects, even the good guys. Only use if necessary.

WHAT YOU NEED:
1 tablespoon distilled white vinegar
1 tablespoon olive oil
3 to 4 drops peppermint oil
3 to 4 squirts liquid castile soap
2 hot peppers, chopped

WHAT TO DO:
Combine all ingredients in a 12-ounce spray bottle and fill with water. Spray on your garden early in the morning or in the evening.

HOMEMADE WEED KILLER

This harmless solution isn't so harmless on weeds that spring up in sidewalk cracks and gardens. It just shrivels them up and wishes them well. Don't get all happy with the spray gun. Target the actual weeds, since it can bring down flowers and produce, too.

WHAT YOU NEED:
1 tablespoon gin
1 tablespoon cider vinegar
1 teaspoon liquid castile soap

WHAT TO DO:
Pour the gin and cider vinegar into a 32-ounce spray bottle. Fill with **hot** water until three-quarters full. Shake well to combine ingredients. Then add the castile soap and gently shake.

KIM'S TIP:
Add some chopped garlic to a homemade bug repellent to drive off neighborhood critters, too. Great for those who live in areas where rabbits, deer, and ticks run wild. Calm down, it won't kill them.

★ Life in a Pot:
CONTAINER GARDENING

Maybe the idea of a garden intimidates you; a bit grandiose at this point in your life. You can barely keep track of your periods, let alone gauge healthy soil. Hear ya loud and clear.

Container gardening isn't just for those with a small yard, or none at all. It's perfect for those with bad soil or sunlight, and pest issues like gophers and unicorns (just making sure you're still paying attention).

Even if you have a garden, decorative containers and bright pots add some color pop or texture to any yard. They also look fab in doorways, home entrances, kitchens, and on windowsills. For all you ladies who want to speed up the growing process, pots will heat more quickly than the ground. Once you get container gardening down, maybe you'll be ready to graduate to a real one. Stranger things have happened . . .

It's all about finding the right plant for the right pot and environment. The formula doesn't require a calculus degree. Here are a few do's and don'ts, before we move to the best plants for container growing.

DO CHECK THE WIDTH OF THE PLANT'S ROOTS. The larger the plant's roots, the larger the pot. For vegetable growers, at least five gallons of soil will help produce grow faster.

DON'T BUY A POT THAT IS TOO SMALL OR TOO LARGE FOR THE PLANT. If you buy a mini pot, the plant may fall over or dry out. If you buy a supersized pot, it retains too much water and you'll end up with some rotten roots.

DO BUY COLORED PLANT POTS IF YOU ARE LOOKING TO ATTRACT SUNLIGHT.

DON'T BUY DARKER-COLORED POTS IF YOU LIVE IN AN UNGODLY HOT CLIMATE like Arizona or Nevada. The heat will suck out the moisture and increase the soil temperature, damaging roots and foliage.

DO MAKE SURE THE POT HAS DRAINAGE UNDERNEATH. The biggest mistake new gardeners make is overwatering a pot with inadequate drainage.

DON'T PUT A POT WITH BOTTOM DRAINAGE ON YOUR LIVING ROOM FLOOR. *Duh.*

DO BUY GLAZED TERRA-COTTA POTS; THEY RETAIN MOISTURE BETTER.

DON'T BUY SMALL, UNGLAZED TERRA-COTTA POTS; they are cheaper but they allow water to move right through them and tend to dry out faster.

DO LOOK AT THE PURPOSE OF A CONTAINER. Clay pots, salvaged or reclaimed wooden tubs, and recycled or biodegradable containers are all good for organic gardening. In terms of wood, redwood and cedar insulate plants and won't rot. Consider upcycling some items around the house that are on their way out—wine bottles, old ceramic washtubs, coffee tins, milk cartons, old boots, and baskets can all make cool containers. Just drill or poke some holes in the bottom.

DON'T INVEST IN PLASTIC CONTAINERS. Now there's a bright idea! Plastic comes from petroleum. If you're growing food in that pot, BPA, phthalates, and other chemicals can leach into soil.[332] Cheap plastic pots also decay under sunlight.

If you must go with plastic, go for recycled. Your best bets are those labeled numbers 1, 2, 4, and 5. Avoid plastics labeled numbers 3, 6, and 7.

Now that we got planters out of the way, let's talk about the what and how—*what's* good to plant and *how* you're going to plant it.

You can grow whatever the hell you please in a pot, but I'm going to focus on food. The first trick is to pick something you really like. Standard-size fruits and veggies—meaning not watermelons—all herbs do really well in contained soil, but I do have a few favorites. Just a few . . .

MY FAVORITE CROPS FOR CONTAINER GARDENING

There are some crops that blossom in containers. Call them introverts—they just want their own space. No matter what you decide to plant, do some research on the best time of year to get it started. The rule of thumb is to plant warm weather crops in early spring, and cool weather types in late summer. But it does matter whether you're working with seeds or small transplants (or "starts"), so be prepared to ask questions.

TAKING CARE OF YOUR CONTAINER GARDEN

By now, you should have the pot, the plant (or seeds), and the organic potting mix. The rest is a breeze. Once you have followed the planting instructions and are ready to rock and roll, give it a good watering until you see water dripping from the drainage holes. This is a good way to get the soil moist so everything starts playing nicely together.

Again, not all plants are made equal. Most vegetables require six to seven hours of sunlight a day and regular trimming to make sure weeds and scraggly branches don't steal all the good nutrients. If your home is gets spotty sunlight, move the pots around the yard to catch more sunlight a few times a week. (If they are heavy, ask for help. Don't try and pick them up like you're a heavyweight champion.)

Vegetable crops also require more water than flowers or herbs, so don't skip town for four days and assume everything is a-okay. You made the decision to take on a new responsibility, so deal with it. Count on watering at least once a day. At times, when the forces of nature bring more heat, humidity, and wind than desired, soak that baby twice a day. Harsh weather causes water to evaporate quicker, and you don't want your carrots drying up.

Keep in mind that containers are not resistant to pests. They do provide more of a challenge to everyday small pests and insects, but when there is a will, there's a way. The simple act of spraying bugs down with a shot of water makes a statement that they shouldn't meddle near your plants.

Pick your veggies when they are good and ripe. Even if a plant produces more than you can possibly eat, don't just let it sit there on the plant and wither up. Instead, bottle up vegetables in the refrigerator or freezer in a glass jar tightly closed.

This is where I give you a little pat on the ass and wish you the best of luck. I hope your new garden or container brings you some happiness, and maybe drives you up the goddamn wall every once in a while. If it were that easy, what would be the fun in it? Bitches love a challenge.

★ Recycling and Composting:
THE DUMBED-DOWN VERSION

We all rack up trash. More than anybody could possibly know what the hell to do with. The average American household tosses out about 4.5 pounds of garbage a day. Add it up—that's 230 million tons a year.[333]

How about I paint a little picture to make it easier for you to understand? Line up a bunch of dump trucks, bumper to bumper, from here to the moon—that's the amount of trash we consume just in the United States. For you sports fanatics, it's the equivalent of burying more than 990,000 football fields under six-foot-high heaping piles of trash. Go team.

If I can be real candid for a moment, trash is not going away. We're human, and unless some wacky scientist finds a way to upgrade our digestive systems, we're not going to eat the plastic wrap on that tofu wrap anytime soon.

The only thing that separates the conscious from the wasteful is recycling. With some things like diapers and cat litter, the trash can is the only logical place to toss it. But for the other 70 percent of the junk overcrowding our landfills, there are much better alternatives.

Recycling is this idea of processing used materials to create new ones. And you play a big part by doing your citizen's duty to put the right items in the right cans. Nobody else has the time to do it for you, lazy ass. They are too busy figuring out where we're going to put all the stuff we can't recycle in about twenty years. According to the EPA, many of the country's landfills have been shut down indefinitely for two unavoidable reasons: a) they were full, or b) chemicals that were produced while all that crap was degrading were finding their way into our groundwater.[334] Chemicals like dioxins, one of the most toxic pollutants in our environment.[335]

When done right, recycling is actually one of the easiest ways to reduce your impact and slow global warming. Yes, there is a wrong and a right way. Just follow these basic guidelines and you'll feel much savvier on trash day.

THE DO'S AND DON'TS OF RECYCLING

THINGS THAT SHOULD ALWAYS BE RECYCLED: steel cans, aluminum cans, compact fluorescent lightbulbs, newspapers, magazines, catalogs, junk mail, plastic beverage bottles, milk jugs, glass bottles and jars, cereal boxes, and other clean and dry cardboard boxes.

THINGS YOU SHOULD THROW IN THE TRASH CAN: Styrofoam, incandescent lightbulbs, food-soiled paper, waxed paper, and ceramics.

THINGS THAT ARE HAZARDOUS AND YOU'D HAVE TO BE AN IDIOT TO TOSS IN THE TRASH: paint cans, poisons, solvents, cleaners, motor oil, car batteries, heat pumps, air conditioners, old refrigerators, pesticides, and pool chemicals. Check community resources for where to drop off household hazardous waste in your area.

THINGS THAT SHOULD BE TAKEN TO THE GROCERY STORE: Leftover plastic bags should be returned to grocery stores to be collected and reused to make plastic lumber. Many grocers will have recycling barrels for plastic bags, but just check with you neighborhood store.

TIPS FOR PROPER RECYCLING ETIQUETTE

PAPER PRODUCTS SHOULD BE CLEAN AND DRY. Newspapers, magazines, and white paper can all be recycled as long as the paper is clean and dry. Paper waste accounts for about 35 percent of total landfill waste, so recycling it makes a big ole difference. Plastic wrap, stickers, or rubber bands should be removed, but staples and plastic window envelopes are all right.

DON'T RECYCLE WET CARDBOARD. It can clog the sorting machines.

CHECK THE BOTTOM OF PLASTIC ITEMS TO IDENTIFY IF THEY ARE RECYCLABLE. Containers labeled 1, 2, 4, 5, or 6 are usually good for the recycling can. But plastics labeled 3 or 7 are usually a no-go.

DON'T TORTURE YOURSELF IF YOUR DOG CAN'T LICK ALL THE PEANUT BUTTER OUT OF THE JAR. Try to empty and rinse glass jars and containers when you can. But the recycler has ways of eliminating contaminants.

RINSE CANS, BUT DON'T WORRY ABOUT CRUSHING THEM. As far as recycling goes, aluminum is the closest thing to perfect as we're going to get. It's the only material that can be recycled again and again and . . . well, you get it. Plus, the shear cost of producing and buying new aluminum makes recycled aluminum the most valuable material to manufacturers, and the most recycled item in the United States. Each recycled can is regenerated and back on the shelf in as little as sixty days. Goooooo Waste Management!

TAKE DEAD RECHARGEABLE BATTERIES TO A RECYCLING CENTER. This includes worn-out rechargeable batteries like those in cell phones, computers, or power tools. Go to Rbrc.org to find a drop-off location in your area.

Visit Earth911.com to find recycling centers nearest you, and more specific information on recycling topics.

WHY RECYCLING IS COOL

Reusing and recycling are good for just about everything on the planet—from the water and the trees to even the economy. Here are just a few ways this simple act gives back to us:

FUELS THE ECONOMY. Recycling and reuse companies employ more than 1.1 million people every year. In the United States, it is a $236 billion industry. Plus, in this new age of sustainability, American companies count on raw materials from recycling programs to create new products.

SAVES ENERGY. Plain and simple, manufacturing virgin materials from steel, copper, glass, or paper, produces four to five times more carbon emissions than using recycled materials. For raw aluminum, emissions are 40 times higher.[336]

PRESERVES LANDFILLS AND REDUCES WASTE. We are running out of room for landfills. Recycling reduces the waste load and the toxic pollution that escapes into our air and groundwater from these trash dumps.

PROTECTS OUR WATER. Cutting down trees for paper is the most water-hungry industrial process in the country. Production of recycled paper uses up to 80 percent less water than new paper.[337]

PROTECTS OUR WILDLIFE. When you recycle, you're helping prevent wild animals from losing their habitats in forests and wetlands. Unlike us, they have nowhere else to go.

SAVES TREES. We turn to our forests when we need new goods. More than half of the planet's forests are already gone, and more than 95 percent of the original forests in the United States have been mutilated for commercial use.

SLOWS DOWN GLOBAL WARMING. Recycling just one ton of glass helps lower our carbon emissions by 300 percent. Making plastic from raw materials requires 70 percent more energy than making it from recycled plastic.[338]

COMPOSTING:
HOMEGROWN RECYCLING
FOR YOUR FOOD SCRAPS

I'm about to shake up your world, girlfriend. Remember all those years your mama gave you such a hard time for not cleaning up after yourself? I mean, why would you, right? That's what she was there for. Well, I'm about to tell you to throw all that garbage out the window . . . right into your backyard.

It may help to know that some of the stuff you've been dumping in the trash isn't really trash, after all. Apple rinds, orange and banana peels, coffee grinds, tea leaves, paper towels, potato peelings, peanut shells, newspaper. All of these things have one thing in common: They can be recycled back into the earth. If it came from the soil, chances are the soil will gladly take it back.

This wicked cool concept is called composting. To sum it up, composting is throwing food and kitchen scraps back into the soil to biodegrade and produce new life—life in the form of a dark, crumbly soil packed with beneficial nutrients that we can use to nurture our crops and reduce our waste. Since yard trimmings and food scraps make up 23 percent of the waste in the United States, there isn't any good reason to divert it for better uses. Compost also helps eat up some of the industrial pollution that we breathe, absorbing 99.6 percent of industrial VOCs in contaminated air.

The process of getting a compost system up and running is pretty basic. While this is far from comprehensive, here is a running list of everyday items that *can* and *cannot* be composted.

Things you can compost

Apple cores
Beer
Branches
Cereal
Coffee filters
Coffee grounds
Crumbs
Dryer lint
Egg cartons
Eggshells
Grass clippings
Hair (pet and human)
Hay and straw
Herbs and spices
Jelly, jam, or preserves
Junk mail, shredded
Leaves
Matches
Melted ice cream
Newspaper
Nutshells
Oatmeal
Paper towels, shredded
Pretzels
Raw fruit and vegetable peels (orange, grapefruit, lemon, banana, etc.)
Recycled cardboard, shredded
Saltine crackers
Seaweed and kelp
Tea bags (without staples)
Toothpicks
Twigs
Used paper napkins, shredded
Weeds, leaves only
Wine
Wine corks
Wood, shredded (tree bark, branches, etc.)

Things you should never compost

Meat products
Milk products
Cooking oil or grease
Feces or urine
Diapers
Personal products, used (condoms, tampon applicators)

CREATE YOUR OWN BACKYARD BIN

It must be said that some people compost every-thing—yes, even latex condoms, cardboard tampon applicators, and pee. But I'm going to go out on a limb and say I wouldn't want any of these guys in my com-posted soil. Some people also compost cooked rice, pasta, and breads. But unfortunately, they tend to attract pests and insects. Try it. If you have success with it, then maybe it's not such a bad idea for you.

Some of the items mentioned that come straight from nature will make the base of your compost pile, though you can continue to pile them on after your com-post starts to grow. These include branches, twigs, leaves, and wood chips. Again, we're getting to that.

So maybe you're wondering just where will you com-post all of these food and kitchen scraps? The answer: wherever best fits your lifestyle. Since we are talking about composting made easy, I'm going to focus on cre-ating a simple compost bin for your backyard as well as one that can sit in your home. There is a bunch of dif-ferent ways to compost. If you are interested in more, just hop online. There is enough information to make your freakin' head spin. I prefer not to do that.

Step One: Pick a home for your compost.
Look for sheltered or shaded areas that are level with good drainage. It's best to keep away from large trees, walls, or wooden fences, which tend to suck up moisture. The ideal amount of space is around four to six square feet. You can also set up a compost bin inside the con-fines of your garden.

Step Two: Build your compost.
You'll need four wooden slabs or stakes (approximately three feet in length), or some chicken wire to build your compost pile. The general rule is to keep your compost bin about three feet square for good aeration, but the size will really depend on your space constraints and how much compost you produce. If you don't have these materials around the house, try your local grocer or lum-beryard to see if they have any lying around in need of a second home. You can also buy bins from a nursery or hardware store, but sometimes the beauty of it is assem-bling it yourself. All you do is bind the four slabs or stakes together into a square using a hammer and nails or water-based adhesives. If you go with chicken wire, just use additional wire to bind the four sections together to form a square.

Last up, if you live in an environment of extreme con-ditions—really hot, frigid, or unbearably humid—consider making (or buying) a top to cover it. Your compost bin doesn't have to suffer through your misery.

Step Three: Prepare your compost.

Once the bin is constructed, create a moist underbelly for it to sit on. If you're dealing with pavement, don't throw your hands up in the air. Just lay down two to four inches of wet dirt or soil under the bin. Moisture is key to turning over good compost so setting it on top of a water heater is probably not the best idea, smart-ass.

Step Four: Lay down the base.

Cover the wet dirt or soil with roughly six inches of twigs, newspaper, branches, and leaves. This layer will provide good air circulation for the compostable items and scraps that you will add on top. After the base is laid, add an additional three to six inches of soil. Then alternate thin layers of soil and compostable matter, switching with each row until the pile is around three feet high. As you start to accumulate compost materials over time, let all of the items hang out with one another—this interaction between biodegradable materials promotes bacteria growth and produces the heat you need for everything to decompose.

Step Five: Nurture your compost.

Keep adding material over the following weeks and months. Once a week, it is smart to take a small shovel or hoe and mix up the material to let the pile get some air and allow biodegradable material to heat and break down. Just like your plants, you also want to water weekly to keep compost from drying up. One way to gauge the moisture levels of compost is by just taking a big whiff. It should give off an earthy scent. If not, add more water.

CREATING AN INDOOR BIN

If you live in tighter quarters, composting is not out of the question. In fact, indoor bins don't make your home any less clean. However, putting the "wrong" material in an indoor bin will quickly prove to be a bad idea. Keep the meat, dairy, and dog shit out. You'll have a stench on your hands that could send you running to the nearest motel.

Making your own indoor bin is quick and easy with materials you can often find around the house. Just look for a plastic trash bin, large pail, or bucket with fitted lids (about twenty-four inches high). Drill eight to ten small holes in the bottom of the container and in the lid to let it breathe. Now repeat Steps Four and Five as directed above.

You can put an indoor bin wherever is most convenient for you—most often, this is the kitchen, laundry room or garage. Just make sure there is proper aeration to help the materials along in the decomposition process. Anytime you add new compost to the heap, remember to put the lid back on to avoid attracting pests or rodents.

FINISHED COMPOST: IS IT READY YET?

Now for the big question eating away at us all: When will your compost be ready? Patience, patience. This bin doesn't produce the fancy stuff with a click of the heels. It's not a sugar daddy, for heaven's sake. Compost is more like a long-term relationship—the real magic happens after you've spent some time together. The length of time varies, but if you're feeding it the right organic matter, it can take anywhere from six weeks to two years. You will know when it's ready because none of the original organic matter you tossed into the compost bin will be identifiable anymore; only dark, crumbly soil. This composted soil is exactly what you will use to add to container planters and garden beds.

Part II: Your Body

My addiction to cosmetics started with a tube of bubblegum lip gloss. That day that I lost my innocence; I was only twelve.

After weeks of watching the cool girls at school apply and re-apply, I marched down to the drugstore and coughed up a week's allowance to cake my lips with the irresistible goop. Almost instantly, I felt different. One might say . . . *smokin' hot.* Before my first high school dance, I had graduated to a drawer full of sparkly eyeshadows, multicolored blush pallettes, eyelash-lengthening mascara, and so many scented perfume sprays you'd think I had a rare and incurable body odor condition. But I smelled like any other pubescent girl . . . just fine.

Just like all my friends, I was a walking beauty counter. Those big beauty companies had us right where they wanted us. Hook, line, and sink*her.*

They still do. Let's face it—the pressures to be beautiful have seriously impaired our brains. We'll give up lunch for a week to buy that beauty cream, and request an extension on rent to get a golden, fake tan. We will even pilfer our savings to buy an anti-aging serum that promises to take twenty years off our face in six weeks. That's a problem when you're only 25 years old, sweetheart.

What may have started as an innocent flirtation with Lip Smackers has turned into a fatal attraction. We created a freakin' monster—a $35 billion beauty industry that will gain our loyalty at any cost. Even if that means jeopardizing our health.

Today, there are roughly 279,000 beauty companies in the United States alone vying for our dollars.[1] To break through the cluster, they speak to us in a language they know we'll hear, using terms like "natural," "hypoallergenic," "organic," "eco-friendly," "herbal," "pure," and "clean."

Yada, yada, yada—talk is cheap. It's easy to throw these words around because none of them are regulated by a third-party organization and standard definitions haven't been established. That's right. In fact, the cosmetics industry is the most unregulated industry under federal law.[2] The FDA said it best when they admitted that manufacturers may use marketing claims "to mean anything or nothing at all."[3] They just use their wild imaginations like a toddler. It's this careless use of terms we commonly associate with "good" that has made it tough for consumers to sift through the bullshit to find the truth.

FDA VS. BEAUTY INDUSTRY

Rest assured, the beauty industry is weighed down by bullshit. There are approximately 10,500 industrial ingredients used today in cosmetic and personal care products, according to the FDA.[4] Of these, only 11 percent have been looked at for human safety. Yet we apply an average of 126 ingredients on our skin every goddamn day.[5] If your skin were as thick as a bulletproof vest, that would be splendid. But it's paper-thin. Our skin absorbs up to 60 percent of these foreign substances,[6] and then it's absorbed into our bloodstream and carried to our organs.[7]

For the past seventy years, the FDA has had no authority over cosmetics companies to require premarket safety assessment, except for color additives. The governing body doesn't even have the power to review or regulate what goes into cosmetics.[8] Instead, the FDA follows the lead of our criminal justice system: *innocent until proven guilty*. They don't even do any so-called regulating until products are already on the market, and their safety is considered only if and when health complaints are filed. And how many of those do you think are actually being filed? An epic 3 percent. Surprise, surprise. As if beauty companies are going to be quick to turn themselves in and tell people what their products are doing to everyone.[9] Once complaints pile up to prompt an investigation, the FDA has to prove that a product is harmful, falsely labeled or marketed, or is in violation of law to get legislators to ban a cosmetic product from the market.[10] Who are we kidding? This can take decades.

The sheer amount of chemicals and pollutants that women are exposed to every day was the motivation behind the Breast Cancer Fund—a nonprofit organization dedicated to finding an explanation for the one-half of new breast cancer cases that can't be attributed to known risk factors such as genetics or smoking.[11] Read: Chemicals aren't just being flushed out by our livers; they are making themselves at home in our bodies and trashing it like a frat party.

We're fooling ourselves if we think that activists are pushing the panic button over nothing. We may be neurotic, but we're also not complete idiots. The Environmental Working Group (EWG) has found that one in every five adults is likely exposed every single day to *all* of the top seven carcinogenic toxins that are prevalent in personal care products—hydroquinone, ethylene oxide, 1,4-dioxane, formaldehyde, nitrosamines, polycyclic aromatic hydrocarbons (PAHs), and acrylamide.[12]

> **Aa   BITCHIONARY: POLYCYCLIC AROMATIC HYDROCARBONS (PAHS)**
>
> PAHs are common contaminants in petrolatum, also known as petroleum jelly (the gooey stuff your mama used to basically bathe you in). PAHs are also found in 1 of every 14 products on the market, including 15 percent of lipstick and 40 percent of baby lotions and oils. The FDA places restrictions on its usage in food and drugs, but companies can use however much they damn well please in personal care products. A Columbia University study linked PAHs to breast cancer, and the National Toxicology Program identifies some PAHs as "reasonable" human carcinogens.[13]

The American beauty industry only continues to grow more ass-backwards by the day, while other countries play by a very different set of rules. The European Union (EU)—more than twenty-five countries strong—has banned more than 1,100 chemicals from cosmetics since making amendments in 2003 to its regulatory law, the Cosmetics Directive.[14] That's impressive. Under the new laws, any ingredients suspected to be carcinogenic, mutagenic, or cause reproductive harm—known collectively as CMRs—must be removed from cosmetics *asap*.[15] They even hold animals in higher regard than we do people in America. In 2000, the United Kingdom put a halt to testing ingredients on animals.[16] Even more impressive.

In this country, on the other hand, the FDA has banned or suspended only eleven chemicals in the more than seventy years it's been around. They are just sitting on their asses when it comes to cosmetics.[17]

Here's the big difference between the two continents: While the European Union depends on independent, third-party committees to review the safety of ingredients, the U.S. "equivalent" is a board of scientists entirely funded by the Personal Care Product Council (PCPC)—the very trade group that lobbies for more than six-hundred cosmetics companies in the country. Does that seem right to you? Uh-uh. Legalizing cocaine is more right than this.

To break it down for you, this power struggle came to a head in 1976 (a period in time when we were all smoking too much pot). At the time, cosmetics companies were coming up on thirty-eight years of freedom from being required to test their products, all thanks to the industry lobbyists that flexed their big muscles in 1938 and talked Congress into leaving them out of a new rule that would give the FDA regulatory control of drugs and food additives.[18] Although Congress was feeling the pressure to finally do something about how little power the FDA had over cosmetics, once again, beauty industry lobbyists persuaded the government to allow the industry to police *itself* by proposing the creation of its own internal watchdog.[19] The cosmetics industry was throwing a big temper tantrum to keep the safety of its ingredients under wraps. Yet nobody called them on their crap.

> Chemicals aren't just being flushed out by our livers; they are making themselves at home in our bodies and trashing it like a frat party.

So how exactly was the PCPC—formerly known as the Cosmetic, Toiletry, and Fragrance Association (CTFA)—going to police the beauty industry? Well, of course it would create and fund its own board of scientists to "review" the safety of the ingredients and chemicals going into our cosmetics. *Hello?* Did we really believe they were going to hire unbiased scientists? They're not that stupid. And so the Cosmetics Ingredient Review (CIR) was born.[20] Now the safety of millions of Americans was in the hands of a panel that gets their paychecks from the beauty companies trying to safeguard those chemicals in question. We were screwed. Case in point: Dibutyl phthalates (DBP)—found in fragrances, lotions, and nail polish—have been shown to mess with our hormones and can cause birth defects. Though DPB has been shown to build up in fatty tissues, the CIR claims their toxicity is irrelevant because "they go in and out of the body." Really? So do hardcore street drugs, people.

Next up: parabens. Another hormone disruptor, parabens have been found in the tissue of breast tumors in independent studies, leading to the theory that they may cause breast cancer. The CIR claims this is horseshit; they say all tests point to no safety risk.[21]

But hold on for a second. In its thirty-year history, the CIR would have to stumble across *some* chemicals whose risks were so indisputable that even they couldn't hide it. There are nine to be exact.

And there was an even bigger boo-boo in the system—the beauty companies never pinky swore they would listen to these recommendations, nor was anyone else saying they had to.[22] In the cases of coal tar and sodium borate (aka. boric acid), the CIR has reported that the ingredients are a big concern, yet you can still find them in U.S. cosmetics.[23] Coal tar, an ingredient in hair dye, has been linked to bladder cancer,[24] while sodium borate has been reported to mess with little boys' testes. As perverted as it sounds, you can find sodium borate in Desitin Creamy diaper-rash lotion. Moms are rubbing it all over their little boys' butts without even knowing what harm they are doing. The PCPC may be policing the industry, but the streets are corrupt with crooked cops disguised as beauty companies. Nothing has changed.

As you can see, chemical safety is determined singlehandedly by the companies making these products. They have something to gain in all this. The FDA requires that cosmetics brands "adequately substantiate safety"or show off a cute little warning label stating that the product's safety is undetermined. What the hell does "substantiate safety" mean? Apparently, the FDA doesn't know either; nor do the cosmetics companies. There is no definition or process for what it means, and of course, nobody is showing off the warning label (except now in California).[25] In 2004, the EWG called the FDA out and urged them to recall any products that were in violation of CIR's recommendations, investigate the most toxic ones, and educate everyone on what it means to "adequately substantiate safety." Not a chance, said the FDA. They denied the petition on all accounts, stating they didn't have the authority to do such a thing. [26] Funny, the PTA at my kid's school has more power than the FDA.

Still, the cosmetics companies continue to argue that their products are totally safe, despite the fact that EWG says 89 percent of the 10,500 ingredients in personal care products have never been tested for human safety—not by the FDA, not by the CIR, not by *anybody*.[27] They are just taking a wild guess. Big beauty companies and industry lobbyists keep telling the general public that the European Union is just exaggerating when it comes to outlawing ingredients. OK, let's assume for one second this isn't completely bogus. The European Union bases their decision to ban or restrict a chemical simply on whether it's toxic or not. That's it. They couldn't care less at what levels it may be safe for humans or whether it's added in small dosages that couldn't even hurt a fly. Instead of taking a chance, they just play it safe and tell manufacturers to find a safer and healthier alternative. Period. But the United States looks at the risks and decides whether those risks still exist when you consider how someone might be exposed. Oh—*wait for it*—yet another boo-boo. Part of the problem with that approach is that a majority of these chemicals haven't been tested for long-term effects, nor has it crossed their puny little minds that many Americans use at least ten different products a day.[28] Those "small" amounts add up over a day, a month, a year, a lifetime. Today, more than 750 beauty or personal care products sold in the United States would be in violation of safety standards in other countries.[29]

THE SAFE COSMETICS ACT

While cosmetic addicts continue to put themselves in harm's way, both individual states and government officials are trying to pick up the slack. California became the first state in the nation to pass its own act—the California Safe Cosmetics Act in 2005. Though it has its loopholes—like not requiring manufacturers to *remove* harmful or toxic ingredients—the California Safe Cosmetics Act does force companies to warn people of any ingredients that are known to cause cancer or birth defects. In 2008, Washington also put its foot down and banned phthalates from personal care products designed for children and infants.[30] But it was the Safe Cosmetics Act of 2010 that was shaping up to be the real game-changer. Introduced in the U.S. House of Representatives, it proposed nationwide legislation that would do away with the industry's self-regulation and require cosmetics companies to disclose all ingredients whether they like it or not.[31] In addition to full disclosure on ingredient labels, it also proposed the enforcement of safety information of all ingredients, regulations on distributing any products that contained ingredients on the FDA's "restricted" list, dismissal of the "trade secret" clause, and alternatives to animal testing. In other words, *Tell us what's in the goods or pay the price, assholes.* The bill was never passed and therefore needs to be reintroduced into Congress for further consideration, but it's a sign that our government is responding to consumer pressure.

The diehards behind this entire movement, the Campaign for Safe Cosmetics, also didn't sit around for law to go into effect. The nonprofit coalition launched the Compact for Safe Cosmetics to bully companies to voluntarily meet or exceed European Union standards in the spirit of transparency.[32] More than 1,500 companies signed on to remove known toxins from their products and replace them with safer alternatives. According to Stacy Malkan, author of *Not Just A Pretty Face* and communications director for the Campaign for Safe Cosmetics, nearly 450 of the companies that signed the compact have already fulfilled all parts of the Compact, including full disclosure of product ingredients (that even means listing fragrance components[insert

gasp!]). Plenty of jerks never signed it (though Revlon and L'Oréal agreed to start adopting EU guidelines).[33]

There is no doubt that the PCPC is crapping their pants over all this talk of harsher legislation. They do agree that the FDA needs to have a greater involvement, but instead is asking for tighter regulations rather than sweeping law. They say they are willing to submit more routine ingredient reports to the FDA, with lists of all the ingredients they are using. But that still wouldn't force them to tell the consumer what those ingredients are. The most laughable part of their proposal is suggesting that cosmetics manufacturers report any serious consumer health complaints or adverse reactions to the FDA.[34] Hmm . . . so what's considered *serious* to you, PCPC? Please, enlighten me. Are allergies and asthma serious, or is cancer? Judging by the modest 3 percent of health complaints that manufacturers have reported in the past, I'm taking a guess that we can't trust them to report these claims. Even if they did, it would still take the FDA light-years to ban these ingredients. It doesn't take a genius to see that the PCPC hasn't been accountable before, and I doubt they are completely focused on watching out for the safety of consumers. After all, consumers aren't the ones paying their generous salaries. The cosmetics companies are.

You get it. The only person that really cares about you and your family, is well, you and your family (OK, throw in the Environmental Working Group and a few hundred other health and environmental activists).

Whatever the case, it's time you knew what exactly is in your products and where to find them. We're going to chitchat about healthy vegan alternatives, what to be über cautious about, and how to be a narcissist when it comes to reading labels (like your neurotic friend, Kim).

I also thought we'd take this opportunity to hear from industry experts who got rid of the toxic shit a long time ago, powerful women who decided to zig when everyone else zagged, and admirable chicks who started brands to ensure we didn't sacrifice healthy for hotness.

Because we are worth it.

THE SHIT LIST

The Worst Ingredients in Your Medicine Cabinet

Reading beauty labels can really feel like a test of your intelligence. *Sodium lauryl sulfate, imidazolidinyl urea, para-aminobenzoic acid, phenoxyethanol* . . . come again? Since when do you need a Ph.D to buy shampoo? It's tempting to just buy the first product you find that has an ingredient you can pronounce. But that would be a big mistake. In this ugly business, ingredients such as mineral oil, parabens, talc, and fragrance may slip right off the tongue, but they shouldn't come near your body. Frankly, they suck hard . . . *real hard.*

You need to know what they are and where they may be lurking. Here is a cheat sheet of some of the worst ingredients in your personal care products.

CETEARETH (-12, -20, -25, -30)

A family of synthetic emulsifiers that helps other chemicals penetrate deeper into the skin. Potential carcinogens linked to breast cancer,[35] they are in moisturizers, hair conditioners and dyes, and tanning products. Even the useless CIR claims that "care should be taken" when they are added to beauty products.[36]

COAL TAR

A petroleum by-product used to make synthetic colors in hair dyes. Oddly enough, it also is commonly used to treat psoriasis, dermatitis, and dandruff.[37] It has been known to cause nosebleeds, coughing, rashes, and hives, and is a reported human carcinogen. Coal tar is banned or restricted from cosmetics in several countries,[38] and carries a caution in Canada because it can lead to blindness when used to dye eyebrows.[39] Yet we still mix it into hair dyes in this country.

FRAGRANCE

Thanks to "trade secret" laws designed to protect manufacturers, beauty brands can assign this term to cover up questionable ingredients (up to three thousand of them) in almost every product on the shelves. What those ingredients are is one big secret.

HYDROQUINONE

An antioxidant and skin-bleaching agent found in hair dyes and skincare products, it is used to lighten brown spots, age spots, freckles, and melasma. The CIR claims it's OK, but only for "discontinuous, brief use followed by rinsing from the skin and hair." Canada doesn't allow it in products that touch the skin, and the European Union has banned it from skin lighteners while requiring a warning label on any other products that contain it.[40]

IMIDAZOLIDINYL UREA

The most common preservative in cosmetics after parabens, this antimicrobial is often excreted from animal piss and other bodily fluids. It releases formaldehyde in products such as baby shampoo, eye and face makeup, hair products, and moisturizer, and may trigger major skin irritations. It's also believed to wreak havoc on the gastrointestinal system and liver in high dose testing on animals.[41] The CIR stated in the 1980s that it was safe, and it's not rethinking its decision.[42] Smart move, people.

LEAD AND MERCURY (Thimerosal)

Heavy metals used as coloring in mascaras, hair dyes, lipstick, and eye makeup that are easily absorbed by the skin where they build up in fatty tissues. Lead is the most hazardous and poisonous metal on the planet no matter how you slice it. It induces muscle cramps, numbness, depression, brain damage, coma, and almost done here—*death*. Side effects of mercury range from chronic inflammation and personality changes to nervousness and rashes. For some crazy reason, it has been banned from cosmetics but is still approved for use in eye makeup.[43]

NANOPARTICLES

These itty-bitty microscopic particles found in mineral makeup and sunscreens are becoming the cosmetic industry's darling. Nanos may be tiny but studies on laboratory rodents are causing a big uproar. They suggest that nanos may be able to penetrate the body easily, harm the lungs, and collect in nasal airways to cause inflammation of the mucous membranes.[44]

P-PHENYLENEDIAMINE

Welcome to the dark side of beauty salons. This chemical is a coal tar that's used as a dyeing agent and permanent hair dye.[45] Found in higher concentrations in darker colored dyes,[46] it's been rumored to trigger skin rashes, eczema, and asthma. But the real downer came when one study suggested that women who dyed their hair for ten years or more were at an increased risk of developing breast cancer. Though it's been highly debated, other salon studies suggest it may be linked to bladder cancer, lymphoma, and leukemia.[47]

In spite of the more than 440 studies surrounding its safety, the CIR says it's just fine (as long as the person using it has no sensitivities, of course). Unfortunately, this is one dye job that the FDA has tried to put an end to, but it's been no match for industry lobbying.[48]

PABA (Para-aminobenzoic acid, 4-aminobenzoic acid, p-aminobenzoic acid)

Best known for its starring role in sunblock, PABA blocks ultraviolet rays. Unfortunately, it also seems to damage DNA and assist in the release of free radicals, which leads to skin discoloration and increases your risk of skin cancer. Most sunscreen makers have voluntarily pushed it out the door after ruffling enough consumer feathers.[49] Not surprisingly, Canada has banned it from cosmetics but the CIR has never reviewed it for safety.[50]

PARABENS

The most popular synthetic preservatives in shampoos, makeup, lotions, and deodorants,[51] though research indicates they mimic estrogen and could make our natural hormones go absolutely berserk.

MINERAL OIL

A cheap and common additive in everything from baby products to hair conditioners to shaving creams, it suffocates your skin and clogs your pores, ultimately screwing with the body's ability to get rid of toxins. This slows down the cells so you look older than you actually are.

PROPYLENE GLYCOL (PG), POLYETHYLENE GLYCOL (PEG), BUTYLENE GLYCOL, ETHYLENE GLYCOL, DIETHYLENE GLYCOL

The most commonly used ingredient in many moisturizers besides water,[52] propylene glycol may cause serious problems, and been known to cause allergic reactions, hives, rashes, and eczema.[53] While butylene glycol and PEG are marketed as a tad safer, a report in the *International Journal of Toxicology* performed by the cosmetic industry's very own CIR, found that PEG can be contaminated with 1,4-dioxane, lead, nickel, and arsenic to name a few. [54]

TALC (Talcum powder)

A finely powdered mineral living in baby and bath powders, makeup, and facial masks and creams, talc has been linked to ovarian cancer with a freakish ability to work its way up the reproductive tract. Its properties strike a similar resemblance to asbestos—a banned lung irritant and carcinogen. [55]

TITANIUM DIOXIDE

Credited with giving cosmetics that spiffy white pigment, titanium dioxide gets lots of face time in sunblocks and toothpastes, but is really causing a stink in nano form in mineral makeup[56] (See "Nanoparticles"). Use this as a guide to get you started, but not as a comprehensive list. Remember that new chemicals and "miracle" ingredients get introduced every year.

The Vegan Taboos:
INGREDIENTS THAT AREN'T ANIMAL-FRIENDLY

Unfortunately, vegans have to worry about more than just what they stuff in their mouths. We also have to watch our backs when it comes to what we put on our bodies. Animal by-products hide behind inconspicuous ingredients, and are even getting more play in natural beauty products. While beeswax and lanolin—fat or grease from wool—are easy to spot, don't overlook your antiaging and hair products. Ingredients such as collagen, elastin, gelatin, and keratin are being used to boost, plump, fill, and smooth your troubles away. I wonder how vivacious you'll feel when you hear they are extracted from boiled animal skin, ground chicken feet, and the hooves, horns, nails, and claws of various other animals. Now if that's not sexy, than I don't know what is. Carmine is another lovely additive used to give makeup its flashy colors. Well I hope you're turning some heads darlin', because carmine is the acid leftover from grinding up female bugs. To steal their coloring, the insects are immersed in hot water, steamed, or fried in an oven . . . alive.[57]

If you're a sucker for lip gloss, shampoo and moisturizing lotions—that would cover all of us—you should scour the labels for tallow, stearic acid, and squalene. Tallow is the fat from cattle, sheep, and pigs, while stearic acid, an ingredient that can come from plant sources, is often derived from the same farm animals. PETA even found some evidence that stearic acid may be extracted from euthanized dogs and cats at animal shelters.[58] That's right—Old Yeller could be living the afterlife in your body soap. Scrub-a-dub-dub. If you spot squalene on the label of your favorite lipstick or gloss, you may be rubbing a soon-to-be endangered species all over your dirty little mouth. Squalene is oil from a shark's liver. Since livers make up one-third of their body weight, there's a nasty little rumor that sharks are being hunted to supply the cosmetic industry with the goods. [59] But I didn't tell you that . . . With our oceans nearing depletion, it might be smart to leave sharks out of our makeup bags.

Other ingredients to be wary of include cetyl alcohol, FD&C colors, glycerin, hyaluronic acid, and panthenol. Any one of these guys can come from animal fat or bodily fluids, but they may also be derived from a synthetic or plant source. If you give a damn, do your homework and call the company or surf the Internet to find out. You'll feel better in the end knowing you're not slathering wildlife all over your skin. To find a list of ingredients for hundreds of beauty products, visit the EWG's Cosmetic Safety Database at cosmeticsdatabase.com.

CHAPTER 4

The Skinny: Natural Beauty

★ The Controversy Over "Organic" and "Natural" Claims

Blah, blah, blah. Companies with something to gain will tell us whatever they think we want to hear. But we're not morons. We caught on to their empty claims that we were getting 30 percent more in the bottle, our lips would be fatter and plumper in ten days, or that our purchase would save all the starving kids in Africa. *Guaranteed or our money back!*

Regardless of all the white noise, there are some terms we have come to trust; like, for example, *organic*. Hell, the word has an industry definition. Laws have been written around its use. There are chumps that sit at a desk all day making sure that corporate bastards don't just put the logo on products like a smiley face sticker. *Right?* Totally . . . for food products.

By the standards of our sophisticated (laugh out loud) food industry, the term organic is highly regulated. If that can of black beans is labeled "organic" and it isn't, somebody up in the control room is going to pay the price. In the USDA's book, claiming that your food is produced without the use of pesticides, hormones, antibiotics, or irradiation is a pretty serious claim.[60] You better be able to back it up or the USDA will take you down.

But when organic made the crossover to the beauty industry, standards fell right through the cracks. *Oopsie.* Because our shampoos and conditioners weren't made with tomatoes and lettuce, nobody knew what the hell to do. They just pointed fingers at everyone else. So rather than set down some ground rules, the people that are supposed to protect consumers just said, *Screw it.* Nobody is actually eating this stuff, so who really cares if that rose-scented body lotion is really organic or not?

Ahem. We do, idiots. We care a whole freakin' lot.

According to the Organic Monitor, health, ethical, and environmental concerns are still the three biggest things that encourage people to open their wallets. Look at that—price didn't even make the cut. Once we heard about all the crap that was in our food, we were willing to lay down our paychecks for personal care products that were natural, healthier, and didn't encourage barbaric animal testing. The problem is that nobody caught on to this faster than the manufacturers of our favorite personal care products. When they saw us flocking to organic food like white on rice, they knew that the stuff in our medicine cabinet was next. But wouldn't you know it, our government didn't. So nobody could spank these brands for using a word that wasn't clearly defined on the stuff we put *on* our bodies . . . even if it was loaded with ugly toxins.

I know you want to punch a wall right now. As consumers, we have come to expect something from the organic stamp of approval. It means it's better. It means it's made with at least 95 percent organic ingredients.[61] It's a big middle finger to the factory farm industry. It doesn't make a difference whether it's our food or our stinkin' bubble bath.

But when it comes to personal care products, "organic" still means diddly-squat. Companies can sell you a product based on the chemistry definition of organic, which means "something derived from living organisms." Guess what? This applies to anything that has ever lived. The birds, the bees, the trees—*everything.* By this definition, the toxic synthetic preservative, methylparaben, is organic

ORGANIC OR NATURAL CERTIFICATIONS

simply because it came from leaves that rotted thousands of years ago and eventually turned into oil. A liquid foundation can contain 1,4-dioxane and brag that it's organic.[62] Look it up. Nobody is regulating this. Nobody is telling manufacturers they have to stop. Organizations like the PCPC and Federal Trade Commission (FTC)—the governing body that acts as a watchdog over advertising claims—[63] are just crossing their fingers that we all shut up. Good luck on that one. A game with no rules just encourages foul play, so without any in place, fewer than 20 percent of the products on the shelves live up to their "natural" claims.[64]

I know what you are thinking right about now: *What the fuck is in my "organic" shampoo then, Kim?* Well, it could very well be pure organic ingredients, or it could be the same garbage you'd find in any bottle of shampoo. It's up to you to do some digging.

When it comes down to it, the only personal care products we can trust to meet our idea of organic are those bearing the good ole USDA organic certification. It's as simple as that. This sticker states the product is free of synthetic preservatives and petrochemicals, but more importantly, it only applies to products made of food ingredients. On the upside, we can count on the fact that anywhere from 95 to 100 percent of the food ingredients in that bottle are organic, water aside.[65] *Phew.* There is nothing wrong with washing your face with organic avocado, cinnamon, and orange extracts! But on the downside, they don't regulate products made from plant-based ingredients and/or essential oils. Since they're not food, the USDA wipes their hands clean. These products may or may not be organic, but one thing is for sure—the product won't carry the USDA seal of approval.[66]

But there are others. If the product doesn't contain the USDA organic certification and the company is waving the organic flag like it's the freakin' World Cup, you can look for a few alternative certifications. Remember, I just said others; they're not necessarily great.

ECOCERT (FRANCE, EUROPE, AND INTERNA-
TIONAL) Not the best certifying body, but I'm going
to hold my tongue since they still require a minimum
of 95 percent vegetable or natural ingredients. Of that,
it just tells you that the product was made with at least
10 percent organic content from the total of 95 percent of natural additives. Up to 5 percent of synthetic
preservatives and chemicals are allowed as long as
they aren't on EcoCert's "negative list." Some of the
ingredients on the negative list are parabens, SLS,
mineral oil, synthetic fragrance, and propylene glycol,
so there's some merit there.[67] Still, nothing says ingredients can't be washed with petrochemicals. It sounds
like it lets the weak through if you ask me, but again
it's better than no certification at all.[68]

OASIS (US AND INTERNATIONAL) A product
must contain a minimum of 90 percent organic
ingredients to gain OASIS certification. The part that
blows is that those "organic" ingredients can be
washed with sulfates during the manufacturing
process. The Oasis standard also allows the use of
synthetic preservatives, including phenoxyethanol
and ethylhexylglycerin, which would fall under the
remaining 10 percent. *Next.*[69]

NATIONAL SANITATION FOUNDATION (NSF)
(US) This is about as good as it gets when food
ingredients are not involved. The NSF standard has
a 70 percent minimum for organic ingredients
excluding water, and you can be assured that no
petrochemicals were used in the manufacturing
process. [70] If any synthetic preservatives are used,
they have to be "nature-identical." NSF is basically
the result of a compromise and handshake between
cosmetics brands and organic consumers-slash-
manufacturers when the USDA can't play a role.[71]

NATURAL PRODUCTS ASSOCIATION (NPA) (US)
NPA is really only an approval system for "natural"
ingredients, which can't be bad. Though there are no
organic requirements, the NPA doesn't put up with
any wacky organic claims, petrochemicals used to
cleanse ingredients in the manufacturing process, and
absolutely no synthetic fragrances. Not too shabby.

WHOLE FOODS PREMIUM BODY CARE SEAL (US)
The Body Care seal only plays nicely with cosmetics
that are free of all synthetic fragrances and dyes, and
doesn't allow any offensive chemicals. They don't
mess with pseudo organic claims (at least not as of
June 2011) but they do let a few artificial preservatives such as phenoxyethanol and ethylhexylglycerin
slide through. Here's the dealio—just because Whole
Foods says it's OK doesn't make it OK in my book. If
you're not down with faux preservatives, just look for
them on the label.

   If you can't locate any sort of certification on that
imaginatively marketed pump bottle, you're gonna
have to suck it up and do some label decoding. Take
a deep breath. Before you have a nervous breakdown,
I am perfectly aware that you don't know how to read
a label. Honey, I doubt Einstein would be able to read
an ingredient label on one of today's personal care
products. But there are some great investigation
tools to guide you in deciding whether you are about
to buy a credible product or a heap of hogwash. Have
some confidence.

★ The "How to Nail a Label" Handbook

RULE #1: INGREDIENTS ARE LABELED IN ORDER OF QUANTITY. Legally, all skincare products must list the ingredients in descending order of their quantity.[72] While that might mean absolutely nothing to you at this point, it's probably your best problem-solving method for one giant reason—it will tell you what ingredients really make up the bulk of the product. Typically, the top third of the ingredient list is 90 to 95 percent of the total solution, the middle is anywhere from 5 to 8 percent, and the bottom is a teeny-weeny 1 to 3 percent. Now we're getting somewhere.

If water sits at the top of the ingredient list, you're probably getting robbed. But if the product is branded with the USDA or NSF organic certification, you're in the clear—this means that water can't eat up more than 5 percent of the entire solution (since at least 95 percent of ingredients, excluding H20, have to be organic).[73] Likewise, the presence of a lot of water often means the product requires some sort of synthetic preservative (see page 126), so shift your focus down the label and see what other baloney you find.

RULE #2: INGREDIENTS USED IN CONCENTRATIONS OF 1 PERCENT OR LESS CAN BE LISTED IN ANY ORDER. Check for synthetic ingredients ... even at the end of the list. There's one little corollary that actually throws everything off, and works in favor of personal care brands. Any ingredient that is added to a product in a concentration of less than 1 percent can be listed in any order. This means you have no way of knowing what is a mere 0.3 percent and what is an entire 1 percent (the equivalent of about a teaspoon).[74]

On the same note, if you see a synthetic chemical listed in the top few ingredients, run for the hills. The truth is you don't want these ingredients in your personal care products in any way, shape, or form, but especially in the upper tier of ingredients. Some of these include: SLS or SLES, isopropyl alcohol, propylene glycol, parabens, color additives (FD&C), or artificial fragrance.

RULE #3: IF THE ACTIVE INGREDIENT IS CONSIDERED A "DRUG," IT'S LISTED FIRST REGARDLESS OF CONCENTRATION. As you probably know, the active ingredient is the one that does all the work. The irritating part is that if the active cosmetic ingredient is also classified as a drug—meaning that it can affect the function of the body by the FDA's silly guidelines—it is listed first.[75] The active ingredient may only be in a concentration of 2.5 percent and be listed first, screwing up the rule of descending order.[76] So get this straight: The active ingredient may have priority on the label, but the nastiest ingredients could be in much higher concentrations. Look for the active ingredient's percentage of concentration to see how much of the bottle may be loaded with other stuff.

RULE #4: CHECK FOR INGREDIENTS THAT ARE INDIVIDUALLY CERTIFIED ORGANIC. If that facial cleanser was made with at least 70 percent organic food ingredients, the USDA gives the green light to label it "made with organic ingredients." I'm all for this. If it's made with plant-based additives or essential oils, look for NSF certification. And if all else fails, they can still list organic ingredients individually on the back. Scan the label, baby. If it matters to you, check to see if any of those ingredients are indeed listed as organic.

SHIT LIST: ALTERNA HEMP ORGANICS
Once upon a time, Alterna Hair Care was kind enough to send me a product from their newly launched "Hemp Organics" line of shampoos and conditioners. At first, I was stoked (and not just because I love free shit). I really loved the shampoo. I lathered, rinsed, and repeated for a good few days before it hit me—I hadn't even read the back of the label yet! After just a quick ingredient check, I rocked back and forth in the shower, hyperventilating. The goddamn bottle contained butylene glycol, propylene glycol, methylparaben, propylparaben, fragrance (parfum), EDTA, TEA, PEG-20, and urea derivatives . . . just to name a few. You know how I feel about these nasties. Yet another lesson that you have to dig a little deeper before trusting "organic" buzz.

RULE #5: "DERIVED FROM" DON'T MEAN SHIT. Because fruits and vegetables sound so much better than a four-syllable chemical name, personal care brands have started to list chemicals derived from oils or produce. Let me break it down for you. Even if cocamide DEA is "derived from coconut oil," you still get a potential carcinogen[77] in the end. I don't care what natural thing it came from.

RULE #6: DON'T BE SWAYED BY GREEN-WASHING TERMS. Terms and catchphrases like "dermatologist-tested," "hypoallergenic," "gentle," "herbal," "natural," "botanical," and even "cruelty-free" are not regulated. If a company is claiming they are cruelty-free and do not test on poor little animals, then check for the PETA certification (the cute rabbit logo), or see if they are on PETA's "Don't Test" list of cruelty-free companies at PETA.org.

The Preservative Conundrum: ★
SYNTHETIC PRESERVATIVES, NATURAL ALTERNATIVES, AND WHY ANY OF THIS CRAP MATTERS

There's a lot going on behind the scenes in that daily moisturizer of yours. Without one very crucial ingredient, that baby would smell like rancid milk and be runnier than your nose during a rerun of *Steel Magnolias*.

It's called a preservative, and if there's one thing we can all make nice about and agree on, it's this: you really got to have one. What has caused quite the bitch fight in the beauty industry is what kind: synthetic or natural. You may think you know the answer to this, but don't get too cocky there, princess. In the case of preservatives, the answer isn't so black and white.

Let's start with the basics. Preservatives help stop the growth of bacteria, mold, fungus, and oxidation in products, which can cause skin irritations, make you very, very sick, or even kill you.[78] Well, that's a plus. Nobody wants her obituary to read "death by hand cream." Preservatives have become all the rage for lending an irregularly long shelf life so that big manufacturers can let them linger on store shelves. Now that's where the lines get blurred.

Like the family goldfish, everything's got a shelf life—especially your beauty products. Whether that product goes the distance or not is really dependent on whether the preservative is synthetic or natural. A synthetic preservative will make that face cream last anywhere from six months to two years (your frugal mother will likely tell you five years). With a natural preservative, however, your time together will usually be shorter. Though synthetic looks like the obvious choice right now, it's opened up its own can of worms in the past decade.

Synthetic preservatives have been used in commercial topical products for more than ninety years, ever since parabens started creeping their way into cosmetics, food, and drugs back in the 1920s. They were cheap and worked like a charm.[79] For a long, long time, the story has been that they were safe. That was until people started to question the mysterious chemicals they were rubbing all over their bodies. Though there are a dozen tongue-twisting synthetic preservatives, most of the trash talking has really been focused on the two most common culprits—parabens and phenoxyethanol.

PARABENS

The paraben family—methyl, propyl, ethyl, and butyl— has drawn attention as the most widely used preservative in the United States. Cosmetic companies fall all over this shit. They are primarily used as an antimicrobial that fights bacteria, yeast, and mold [80] in about 75 to 90 percent of personal care products. You name it, and parabens are likely making their move— sunscreens, shampoos, deodorants, lotions, toothpaste, makeup, and even condoms.[81] Actually, the only ingredient that gets more face time in cosmetics is water.

There are plenty of lenient experts that will tell you parabens are all good. Both human and animal tests have showed that the body metabolizes and gets rid of them quickly, so everyone assumed they were relatively nontoxic.[82] A CIR review in the mid-'80s stated that they were perfectly safe for use at levels up to 25 percent of the total solution.[83] Even The American Cancer Society admitted there was little evidence to show they were unsafe, and more studies would have to be done for them to think otherwise.[84] Apparently, there was no need to panic. *Psyche.*

By the early millennium, the focus had turned to questioning who the hell was behind all this research. The so-called "perfectly safe" chemicals were showing strong evidence that they messed with our hormones, acting as hormone disruptors.[85] In 2004, a UK study found they may play a role in the development of breast cancer tumors because they mess with estrogen.[86] One measly study, right? Maybe. Scientists had discovered parabens in the breast tumors of eighteen out of twenty breast cancer patients. What was even more interesting was where they suspected this contamination was coming from—absorption through the skin. According to the lead researcher on the study, the parabens were in one piece;[87] if they had been ingested through food, the body's digestive system would have broken them down. Bingo![88] Though it has never been confirmed, this finding eventually led to one big public meltdown that deodorants were causing breast cancer, since the armpit was closest to the part of the breast where the tumors were discovered.[89] Call me neurotic, but even one measly study tells me that more research is needed.

More studies followed that showed we may have all the reason in the world to freak out. In animal testing, parabens were causing the uterus to balloon.[90] Another hypothesis suggested that parabens may contribute to the early onset of puberty in adolescent girls and developmental problems with boys. [91] So much for an innocent childhood.

Despite all the evidence that supports both sides, many scientists have started to come around and admit that more research is needed. Regardless of all the he said, she said bullshit, no testing has ever been done on the long-term effects of parabens and how they impact our body's own estrogens.[92] In my eyes, it's better to be safe than sorry.

PHENOXYETHANOL

That leads us to another troublemaker in preservatives—phenoxyethanol. Though it's gained some praise as a "less-toxic" alternative to parabens, many will assure you it's hardly a better one.[93] Used in everything from bath bubbles and hair sprays to makeup and fragrance, phenoxyethanol irritates our eyes, lungs, and skin.[94]

An animal study in the Journal of the American College of Toxicology found that, like parabens, phenoxyethanol acts as a hormone disruptor and can wreak havoc on the bladder.[95] If all this isn't enough to scare you, take a good look at the EPA data: The preservative has been linked to chromosomal changes, DNA mutations, and reproductive damage in mice.[96] What more evidence do we need, people? Gimme a freakin' break.

Experts still insist that the amount of synthetic preservatives in products, typically somewhere between 0.5 and 1 percent, are not enough to do any sort of damage.[97] Let me remind you of the basic math behind that. In a 200-milliliter bottle, 1 percent is equivalent to 2 grams of concentrated, 100 percent phenoxyethanol. That is an entire teaspoon! Whether you apply it to your body all at once or are exposed in small doses for a month, the amount doesn't change. Go ahead and add it up.[98] Yep, still a teaspoon, sweetheart. Not to mention, these god-awful preservatives are found in nearly *everything*. All I have to do is brush my teeth, wash my face, shampoo and condition my hair, apply deodorant to my pits, and put on some lip gloss, and I have gotten my fair share of toxic exposure to one of these artificial preservatives. And guess what? I do this everyday. And, if I had to take a lucky guess, so do you. Wake up and smell the cancer.

Even though I've gone to town on parabens and phenoxyethanol, there are a number of other synthetic preservatives or code names that are on my shit list. I just can't really pronounce them. Some of these preservatives are urea derivatives, which can release formaldehyde and increase your risk for cancer (including DMDM-hydantoin and quarternium-15).[99]

Write these down, stick them on your fridge, host a spelling bee with them . . . whatever it takes. Just try to steer clear of any of these in your personal care products.

✖ SHIT LIST: SYNTHETIC PRESERVATIVE CODE WORDS

Parabens (Methyl-, Ethyl-, Propyl-, and Butylparaben)

Phenoxyethanol

Urea Derivatives (Imidiazolidinyl Urea (Germall 115) and Diazolidinyl Urea (Germall II)

Isothiazolones (Methylchloro- and Methyl-Isothiazolinone)

DMDM Hydantoin

Quarternium-15

Butylated Hydroxytoluene (BHT) and Butylated Hydroxyanisole (BHA)

Parahydroxybenzoic Acid (Benzyl-, Methyl-, Ethyl-, Propyl-, and Butyl-Parahydroxybenzoic Acid)

Parahydroxybenzoate (P-hydroxybenzoate)

2-Bromo-2-Nitro-Propane-1, 3-Diol (Bronopol)

Benzalkonium Chloride

NATURAL PRESERVATIVES

Consider this for a moment: Your beauty products aren't supposed to outlive your car warranty. Everything has an expiration date—your driver's license, vitamins, canned beans, and perky boobs. So it should come as no surprise that beauty products work best when used in fair time.

With more and more people raising a ruckus, many companies are phasing out parabens and other preservatives and choosing safer, more natural alternatives.

But how well do natural preservatives work? Ah, the question of the hour.

Usually the deciding ingredient is water. Yeah that stuff we're running really low on right now without a care in the world. Anytime you got water or organic (living) ingredients in a product, there is a need for a preservative. In this case, synthetic preservatives have done a bang-up job of stabilizing a formula and making it l-a-s-t, hence their popularity. Natural preservatives don't kill as wide of a range of bacteria.[100] Their shelf life is nothing to write home about, either.

But before you toss that face wash you bought at the natural health store, settle down. Natural preservatives in the form of antimicrobials and antioxidants still work by protecting oils from turning all rancid and icky. Plant-based preservatives—such as tea tree oil, thyme essential oil, rosemary extract, and vitamin E—all boast these naturally great properties.

According to Ashley Beckman, co-founder of holistic skincare line Golden Path Alchemy essential oils can make sure most products keep working their magic for about six months to a year. "Water is one of the ingredients that goes bad quickly," said Ashley. "We don't use water in our products without preserving it with alcohol (for aromatherapy sprays), glycerin, witch hazel, shea butter, organic rosemary extract or a significant amount of essential oils. This is the big reason natural creams and lotions go bad . . . they all contain water and need a strong preservative."

Ashley says that one of the most effective natural preservatives out there is rosemary oil extract. One of the newer guys is grapefruit seed extract (GSE), which is getting some good buzz for killing fungus and nasty bacteria—especially handy when you're suffering from the sniffles. GSE also helps stop oils from oxidizing. With GSE and rosemary oil extract, make sure you are getting a "clean" brand by purchasing from credible companies. Recall in the household section that GSE can be contaminated with parabens and propylene glycol.

Natural preservatives won't keep a product good for years. That's not how they work. The goal of a natural preservative is to make sure *you* last a few years longer. Any product that can sit around and collect dust in your cabinet for two years has some serious chemicals helping it out. Some companies, like Golden Path Alchemy, prefer to drop-ship directly to the buyer so they can make sure the product is not sitting around on store shelves.

Believe it or not, you play a role in all this, too. Natural products come with different care instructions. Don't ignore them. You also need to make the switch to buying products in smaller batches so you don't contract a deadly infection. I heard those aren't fun.

KEEP AWAY FROM LIGHT AND HEAT. Your natural beauty products are like a penguin. They don't do well in the heat. Push aside the soy sauce and Vegenaise and clear some room in your fridge. Unless you are taking freezing cold showers, they are better off outside of your bathroom.

USE DARK CONTAINERS OR OPAQUE PACKAGING. See-through or clear packaging allows the sun's ultraviolet rays to beam through, which spoil the product. Look for glass packaging to ensure nasty chemicals like BPA aren't leaching into your skincare and ending up in your bloodstream (glass is also reusable).

TRY TO AVOID JARS. Here's a little science lesson for you: Every time you screw off that lid, you are exposing the liquid to air. Air oxidizes natural extracts and they go bad. Tubes are better.

MAKE SURE THAT BABY IS AIRTIGHT. If you must use a jar, don't let it sit there with the lid off while you take your sweet ass time applying it on your face. You will also want to use a toothpick, spoon, or spatula to extract the amount of product you need. Keep your fingers out of the cookie jar, unless you want a bacteria infestation. Gross.

BUY (OR PREPARE) SMALL BATCHES. Newsflash: You don't need a family-size body wash. Nobody is that dirty, not even a high-priced hooker. If you are mixing up your own homemade beauty products, make them in small tubes that don't require a jacked-up shelf life.

LOOK FOR PRODUCTS THAT AREN'T WATER-BASED. Preservatives are primarily used in water-based solutions to stabilize the product. If it doesn't have water, it really doesn't require a preservative. Try and stick with makeup and beauty products that are oil-based or don't require water (lipsticks and body butters are primo examples). With these types of items, a plant extract or essential oil with antibacterial and antimicrobial properties is effective enough.

A PRESERVATIVE MÉNAGE À TROIS:
MIXING THE FAKE AND THE FRESH

Some major retailers with a conscience are combining synthetic with natural preservatives for a safer formula with a longer shelf life. Companies like Kiss My Face, Tarte, Burt's Bees, and Earth Essentials combine a wee bit of synthetic with natural preservatives such as sodium benzoate and potassium sorbate, which aren't known to trigger as many allergies or skin sensitivities.[101] Some of these products are easier to find at nationwide drugstore chains.

But do me a huge favor (it's not like I ask for much!): Be wary of companies that advertise they are "paraben-free" in huge print. Often that's a red flag. If they are flaunting it, they usually have something else to hide—like other synthetic chemicals. Do some investigating and read the label.

WELEDA BLOWS OUT ITS 90TH BIRTHDAY CANDLE

You may think this big idea of putting natural ingredients on your skin is a new fad. Hell, chances are you thought Lancôme was pure two weeks ago. Ah, the power of a "free gift with purchase."

But at Weleda, keeping it natural is business as usual. They've been giving the stink eye to chemicals for almost a century. In 2011, they celebrate ninety years of holistic beauty. That's something to be damn proud of.

The folks at Weleda were the pioneers behind one of the world's first Biodynamic® gardens. What's a garden got to do with your face wash? It should have everything to do with it. Biodynamic® farming is this novel idea of growing ingredients in a closed-loop system. From compost to fertilizer to bug control, every piece supports another. No chemicals. No hormones. It's all about keeping the soil healthy and "alive" so it will give life to healthy plants and ingredients. I dig it.

Even when the chemical revolution spit out a bunch of test tube cosmetics companies, Weleda didn't budge. Synthetic ingredients and petrochemicals weren't their style. Now while we run around crying about aluminum in our deodorant, they're just doing everything they can to not make us feel like guinea pigs. Maybe that's why they're in more than fifty countries now—and they didn't have to test on baby rabbits or drown their ingredients in formaldehyde to do it.

In light of Weleda's big ninetieth birthday, I thought, let's skip the male strippers and Champagne. Why not shoot the shit with one of the gals behind the brand instead? So we played "5 Questions" with Jennifer Barckley, director of corporate communications and education for Weleda North America.

I love that Weleda is all about supporting small farms across the globe through fair trade. What do you guys get out of this? Besides feeling good about yourselves.

Since our beginnings, our mission has been to bring health and well-being to people around the world—whether through our products or our business practices. It means we empower small famers, promote sustainability, pay a fair price for our ingredients and help communities around the world thrive. While we pay more for our ingredients, we can also ensure that we are using the highest quality ingredients.

Beyond environmental benefits, this is why we work with farmers—to help them convert from conventional to organic or Biodynamic® agriculture, or help them protect their wild plants and natural resources.

You guys are in Target now. Hallelujah. That's not just a big deal for Weleda, but for the cosmetics industry as a whole. How difficult has it been to convince larger retailers, like Target, to open up to "natural"?

Consumers are becoming more conscientious about healthy, natural products. Target approached us, and it's been a wonderful partnership. They look to us for leadership within this category, and we look to them and their customers, as we make our products ever more accessible.

A lot of cosmetics companies claim that the European Union is a bit neurotic when it comes to laying down beauty and personal care guidelines. What's Weleda's stance on this?

We have never felt that the EU safe cosmetic regulations are too stringent. Thanks to the EU, eleven hundred ingredients have been banned from thousands of personal care products sold throughout Europe. From day one—long before any regulations came into effect—we never used potentially harmful or carcinogenic ingredients. We believe that through 100 percent natural ingredients, we can bring our bodies into a place of healthy balance and beauty.

What do you think it's going to take for a bill like the Safe Cosmetics Act to pass?

It's going to take the industry, companies like ours, and consumers to stand up. While the bill has caused a controversial stir within the cosmetics industry, this bill gives us—as businesses and as consumers—an incredible opportunity to adequately raise the safety standards and guarantee that ingredients in personal care products are safe for consumers. It shouldn't matter how many products you use each day or which ones you choose. In the end, the environmental groups and businesses should work together to develop a bill that is meaningful and really works to clean up cosmetics!

Consumers, I believe, are the other very powerful piece of the equation. In the United States, we've banned just nine ingredients from use in personal care products. Compare that to the EU's list of eleven hundred. We have a lot of work to do. After all, we deserve health—for ourselves, for our environment, and for our future generations.

Okay, I know you play favorites. What Weleda products top your list?

That's a *really* tough question. I have a new favorite every month, but some all-time-can't-live-without products are: Everon Lip Balm, Salt Toothpaste, Almond Soothing Facial Oil, Pomegranate Regenerating Body Oil and of course, Weleda's Skin Food.

To shop for better skincare or learn more about Weleda, visit weleda.com.

★ A User's Guide to Essential Oils

LOOKING FOR THE PERFECT OIL

When I go to buy something, I want to get in and out of a store as fast as possible. I don't care if it's trashy lingerie, a car, or bread. Patience is not one of my best virtues.

So it was no surprise how much hair I pulled out when I was choosing essential oils. The first time I had a look at the extent of my choices, I cursed a few unnecessaries under my breath and then played a game of eeny, meeny, miny, moe. A dozen online orders later, I started to pin down which essential oils piqued my senses and which to re-gift to my mother-in-law with a kiss-ass "Thinking of You" card. (Note to self: Don't send this book to the in-laws.)

But I was going about it all wrong. My impatience got the best of me, and I never thought to ask which oils would work best for my skin, what I was using them for, or whether they were diluted with other cheap oils that weren't as good. All I knew was they smelled pretty. I'll tell you what though—it didn't take me long to catch on. I learned my lessons, and now I know the lingo.

> **Aa BITCHIONARY: ESSENTIAL OIL**
> A superconcentrated extract from plants, leaves, flowers, roots, buds, seeds, or fruit.

> **Aa BITCHIONARY: CARRIER OILS**
> A base or vegetable oil that dilutes an essential oil, named as such because it "carries" the essential oil onto the skin. A few that come to mind include: sweet almond, grapeseed, evening primrose, aloe vera, and avocado.

Buying essential oils is tricky business. Don't get excited and grab the first one you see. It doesn't work like that. You need to look for specific qualities or you could end up with a pretty scent and nothing to show for it.

Look for a natural, therapeutic-grade essential oil that hasn't been mixed with carrier oils or any other synthetic chemicals. You don't want to buy a pre-diluted oil. Your job is to dilute it. Always buy a true essential oil that doesn't share the bottle with anything foreign.

Labels with "pure essential oil" or "100% essential oil" are a good sign. But dig deeper. The term "pure" indicates that it wasn't diluted with a lesser-quality essential oil, but it doesn't mean that no chemicals were added to it. There's the rub. You need to check the label to make sure—something you're almost a professional at by now.

If the bottle says "scented oils," "aromatherapy oils," "fragrance oils," or "nature identical oil," leave it on the shelf. Those are likely cheapskate oils mixed with synthetic fragrance or substitutes. The retailer just wanted to save money, then turn around and make a quick buck off of you. Bite me.

My favorite choices are organic or ethically wildcrafted oils. That may sound like a mouthful, but I didn't ask you to memorize it. Write it down. Capeesh?

Here are a few of the best tips I can give you when shopping around for quality oils. Because if you can't learn from my mistakes, who will?

WHERE TO GET YOUR OIL ON

RULE #1: BUY OILS WITH THE BOTANICAL (LATIN) NAME ON THE LABEL. More than one essential oil can actually go by the same "common" name, though they're very different. Confusing, I know. For instance, there are many different types of eucalyptus essential oils, and each one has very different therapeutic properties. Same goes with chamomile. You could be buying Roman chamomile, German chamomile, or some other type.

RULE #2: DARK-COLORED GLASS IS YOUR BEST BET. Retailers who sell essential oils in clear glass or plastic jars usually have no clue what they are doing. Hello? This is how oils get damaged or spoiled. If your oil is shipped to you in plastic, make sure you transfer it to dark-colored glass right away.

RULE #3: LOOK FOR OILS THAT COME WITH INSTRUCTIONS. It's not a piece of Ikea furniture, but it should come with some rules. Unless you know what the hell to do with it, you just have a bottle that looks pretty.

RULE #4: AVOID RETAILERS WHO SELL ALL THEIR ESSENTIAL OILS AT THE SAME PRICE. This isn't the goddamn ninety-nine cent store. A flat rate for any and all oils is typically a good sign it's synthetic. There should be differences in price because the amount of raw materials needed to produce different oils will vary.

Don't buy essential oils from street carts or some dude with a big black trench coat. You're not buying porn, you horn dog. Seek out places and online retailers you feel comfortable buying from.

Pharmacies, department stores, cosmetic and skin-care counters, specialty stores, and major supermarkets can all carry the goods. In my experience, the best place to buy essential oils is at natural health retailers or health food stores. They usually have a knowledgeable expert on hand to answer your questions. You don't have to be trained by the FBI to tell if they know their shit.

Online retailers are a great place to buy oils. Shop around and compare before you put your credit card down. Which leads me to prices. Holy crap—can quality essential oils be pricey! Some, like lavender, tend to be a bit cheaper, but most will run you anywhere between ten and three hundred dollars depending on the quantity. (Essential oils typically come in 0.4 or 0.5 ounce sizes, but the more expensive, exotic oils come in 0.2 ounces.) Plant this in your head: Too often, cheap stands for weak or total faker. If you're buying at a discount, make sure it's a quality brand, not just a sham.

EXPERIMENTING WITH ESSENTIAL OILS

Now that you know how to choose a quality essential oil, you should get familiar with a number of ways to use them:

AS AROMATHERAPY Oils are like nature's pharmacy, and have been used for thousands of years as alternative medicine. When they are inhaled or absorbed , there is a chemical reaction in your body. The blood and sinuses circulate the fragrance to the parts of your brain that control emotions, and immune and neurological systems.

Inhaling, massaging onto your skin, or even adding pure and natural oils to a bath can change your mood, boost brain function, and even relieve pain, stress, nausea, and anxiety. We all have those days.

FOR NATURAL SKINCARE Whoever told you to keep the oils off your skin reads too many teen magazines (see page 134). Oil is not the Antichrist. It's also not to blame for the pizza face you had in high school. You can thank puberty for that. Oils are actually natural skin healers. Natural oils from plants and herbs help tone skin, treat zits, smooth wrinkles, heal scars, and give your mug that healthy glow. When you use essential oils in skincare, you can blend them with a carrier oil or add a few drops to a homemade product.

FOR FRAGRANCE Enough with the poisonous perfumes. Mix an essential oil with a carrier oil of your liking, and dab a drop of it on your wrists and neck. You'll smell orgasmic and it may just boost your mood. You can also combine essential oils to make your own scent that money just can't buy.

IN HOUSEHOLD CLEANERS One of the best things about a clean house is the way it smells. Baking soda may get the oven spotless, but an Arm & Hammer aroma isn't really what you had in mind. If you're making your own cleaner, get the fresh scent and disinfecting effects with tea tree, orange, peppermint, lemon, grapefruit, cinnamon, sandalwood, and pine oils.

But I'm going to go ahead and throw out a big caution sign before we get carried away. Most essential oils are irritants or dangerous to apply to skin undiluted. As mentioned, make sure you dilute with a carrier oil before slathering on your skin like a body lotion. Lavender and tea tree oils are a few of the skin-safe oils if applied in pure form. For a list of essential oils and complementary carrier oils based on your skin type, see hbd.com.

OILS FOR SKIN TYPES

In skincare, different strokes work for different folks. Whether you're an oily mess or are blessed with normal skin, there's an oil that works best with your body's chemistry. So use it already.

When you're whipping up your own beauty recipes, you can add these essential oils to your own cleansers and products. The new fad, coined the Oil Cleansing Method (OCM), is all about washing your face with oils. Many aestheticians and holistic beauty experts run with the mantra that "oil dissolves oil."

Here's how it works. All those heavy-duty foaming face cleansers we always thought were fighting our zits actually contribute to the cause. When harsh cleansers strip our natural oils, the body compensates by producing more. This is what causes breakouts. Natural soaps and plant-based liquid cleansers are an alternative, but many beauty gurus have said screw it altogether—*I'm washin' with oils*.

The big idea is washing your face with an unprocessed oil, such as extra-virgin olive, avocado, jojoba, castor, coconut, or almond. After you apply the oils, steam the face with a warm washcloth or towel. Then you rinse and pat dry. Easy enough. Some people follow up with a gentle cleanser, but others leave it at that. It works for almost any skin type and keeps you looking young and fresh.

Here are the best oils for each skin type:

NORMAL SKIN: Cedarwood, chamomile, geranium, jasmine, lavender, neroli, evening primrose, almond, orange, rose, rosewood, rosemary, tea tree

Carrier Oils: Apricot kernel, camellia, rosehip seed

COMBINATION SKIN: Geranium, lavender, ylang ylang, rose, rosewood, neroli, palmarosa, chamomile, sandalwood, mandarin, petitgrain, frankincense

Carrier Oils: Sweet almond, jojoba, apricot kernel, evening primrose, camellia, and hazelnut

DRY SKIN (OR AGING SKIN): Carrot seed, cedarwood, jasmine, geranium, lavender, orange, neroli, sandalwood, rosewood, rose, myrrh, patchouli, vetiver, cajeput, chamomile, ylang ylang, frankincense

Carrier Oils: Sweet almond, jojoba, avocado, wheatgerm, evening primrose, borage, apricot, peach kernel, camellia, cranberry seed, hempseed, pomegranate, and rosehip

OILY SKIN (ACNE-PRONE): Cedarwood, geranium, lavender, lemon, peppermint, cypress, patchouli, sandalwood, juniper, coriander, lime, grapefruit, rose, rosemary, eucalyptus, myrtle, neroli, thyme, palmarosa, petigrain, vetiver, mint, cajeput, niaouli, bergamot, tea tree, palmarosa, mandarin, and most citrus oils

Carrier Oils: Jojoba, grapeseed, sweet almond, carrot seed, camellia, and hazelnut

SENSITIVE SKIN: Chamomile, rose, neroli, rosewood, carrot seed, angelica, jasmine, neroli, chamomile, lavender, geranium, mandarin, petigrain, and frankincense

Carrier Oils: Sweet almond, jojoba, calendula-infused, evening primrose, and cranberry seed

KIM'S PICKS: ESSENTIAL OILS

In the spirit of not sending you on a wild goose chase, I'm opening up my skinny black book to share a few of my favorite online retailers for essential oils:

The Aromatherapy Place (auroma.com)

Simplers Botanical Company (simplers.com)

Aura Cacia (auracacia.com)

★ The Fuss Over Fragrance

Since we were old enough to wear a training bra, we've been drilled on all the things in the world that could hurt us. Driving without a seatbelt. Wearing white after Labor Day. Smoking cigarettes. But c'mon now . . . *perfume?*

But in recent years, fragrances have started to cause a real stink among consumers. As it turns out, many of the chemicals in perfumes and fragrances are as bad for you as cigarette smoke. [103] Trouble is, we have no idea what these chemicals are. This all begs a few questions: How did all this mumbo jumbo about "trade secrets" come into effect, and why doesn't J.Lo have to tell you what the hell is in her fragrance, when cosmetics are required to disclose every other ingredient hiding in a product? Yeah, shit is about to get complicated.

Let's rewind. Following a major mass poisoning and some potential health concerns, the FDA rolled out the Fair Packaging & Labeling Act in 1966 to force companies to include all ingredients on the back of their labels. But the act came with a "trade secret" exception: Companies didn't have to share any ingredients if they were part of their signature fragrance. Because a fragrance gave a company a "competitive edge" against other brands, the FDA made the decision that sharing those ingredients would affect a brand's success. [104]

Even though these busted laws were created forty years ago, they still seem to make sense to our government today. The fragrance industry itself is another one that's self-governed. The International Fragrance Association (IFRA) has more than one hundred perfume and fragrance houses from all over the world. It's their job to create a "Code of Practices" and some guidelines for members to follow. Guidelines like upholding those "trade secret" laws. [105]

To get the FDA off their backs, they created their own "nonprofit," the Research Institute for Fragrance Materials (RIFM), to test any questionable ingredients in fragrances. The "research" usually doesn't go farther than testing on human skin and poor rodents. They report their findings to the IFRA, which decides whether or not the chemical is OK to include in fragrances. [106] Hey, that sounds familiar . . . Wait, that kind of sounds like the role of the CIR and the PCPC. Ding! Ding! Ding!

There's yet another similarity to the CIR and PCPC relationship. Even when the IFRA blows the whistle on an unsafe chemical or attempts to regulate it, the fragrance houses don't have to listen. They are only expected to. But, they can still peddle the iffy ingredients to perfumers or cosmetics brands to use in their own products. Most likely, their punishment is being listed on IFRA's Web site as someone who doesn't follow the rules. Plus, the only companies the IFRA can even call out are ones that belong to their organization. Yep, that's a whopping one hundred companies. [107]

Today, we got about 3,163 possible ingredients that make up a fragrance, and 66 percent of them have never been tested for safety. [108] The IFRA has banned or put some loose restrictions on 150 of these ingredients in fragrances. [109] The only way the FDA

THE SECRET CHEMICALS IN YOUR PERFUME

even has a clue that something might be dangerous is if a fragrance producer or cosmetic brand reports it. We've been here before. What are the chances a high-and-mighty brand is going to tattle on themselves if nobody makes them? I'd say pretty slim.

This whole fiasco screams for support of new regulation. If bills like the Safe Cosmetics Act of 2010 were to go into effect, companies will no longer be able to keep secrets behind our backs. Until we see some changes industrywide, we need to be more conscious of what we're dabbing on our wrists. Read the labels, look for organic certifications that meet your standards, and avoid buying perfumes or personal care products that don't practice transparency. They're not too lazy to list what's behind their fragrance; they can always make more room on the label. They just know it's not in their best interests.

Just because Britney, Halle, J.Lo, and Miley have all slapped their name on one, doesn't mean it's safe. You think they know what's in their own perfumes? Please. It's called a licensing deal.

Because we're all kept in the dark, nobody quite knows what's in what. In 2010, the Environmental Working Group (EWG) and Campaign for Safe Cosmetics decided to test seventeen fragrance products and make sense of their labels. The results didn't smell so hot.

For each product, fourteen secret chemicals weren't listed on labels because of the convenient "trade secret" laws (thirty-eight secret chemicals were found among all seventeen brands). A dozen ingredients were potential hormone disruptors according to EWG, with an average of four in each product. Ten of the ingredients in each product can stir up allergic reactions. Oh, that's not all. There's one more punch line. The groups also found that of the ninety-one ingredients either listed on the labels or discovered in the study, only twenty-seven have been tested for safety.

Two synthetic musks—galaxolide and tonalide—kept popping up in the study, too. Both have been linked to toxicity to the endocrine system, and have been found in the umbilical cords of newborn babies. They sound more like comic book characters to me.

Soon-to-be mothers, take heed: Diethyl phthalate (DEP) also made an appearance in twelve of the seventeen products. A few sprays too many can expose the developing fetus to a potential hormone disruptor and could cause damage to their pee-pees. It's also been linked to ADD in kids. Awesome.

If you're wondering who the candidates were, and moreover, the worst offenders, I'm not keeping any trade secrets. According to EWG, American Eagle's Seventy Seven topped the list with twenty-four secret chemicals. The runners-up were Chanel Coco with eighteen; and Britney Spears Curious and Giorgio Armani Acqua Di Giò with seventeen each. Halle by Halle Berry and J. Lo Glow by Jennifer Lopez reeked of seven potential hormone disruptors each.[110]

I'd rather have BO.

▶ THE SKINNY ON SCENT

BY RACHEL LINCOLN-SARNOFF

Do you sneeze after you spritz? Does a walk through the department store leave you with a splitting headache? It's not just the prices—it's the chemicals. More than 95 percent of the chemicals used in fragrances are synthetic compounds derived from petroleum. This includes toxins that have been linked to allergic reactions, among other things.[111]

More and more people are claiming "fragrance sensitivity" is responsible for migraines, sinus attacks, and other ailments. Yet because the industry is self-regulated, there's no hard data calculating this cause and effect.

The biggest offenders are **phthalates.** Phthalates are reproductive toxins that are so prevalent in our environment; repeated studies by the Centers for Disease Control and Prevention found them in the urine of nearly every subject they tested. Unfortunately, phthalates almost always fall under the catch-all term, "fragrance," in personal care products.

Also of note are **pheromones**, or sexually attractive hormones derived from animal urine. They are occasionally added to perfumes on the theory that if the chemical reaction they cause works in animals, it will also work for us. Which makes sense if you find yourself attracted to cat piss.

The problem gets even bigger when you realize that perfume doesn't just stop at our skin: sixty percent of what goes on, goes in—to our bloodstreams, that is.[112] From there, stuff is excreted or washed down the drain, into the water system, and up the food chain. If you happen to eat fish, your dinner could contain the same chemicals as your *eau de toilette*. Or your neighbor's.

So why don't we all just switch to oh-so-natural essential oils? It all comes down to allegiance. Take me, for example. Once I graduated from the cheapo drugstore brand scents that I adored during high school and settled on a brand-name scent that I identified with, I was pretty much sold for life. First dates, job interviews, wedding day (and night)—nothing important began without the perfume-that-shall-remain-nameless touching my skin. Until I realized there was cat piss in it.

What's truly amazing is that the more we learn about this stuff, the more we realize that fragrances don't need to be expensive or contain loads of chemicals to smell gorgeous. Nor do you have to spend a fortune, drive for miles, or scour the Internet to find them. I scored sustainable scents at department stores, drugstores, beauty stores like Sephora, and online. And guess what? A lot of them are downright cheap!

Perfume and the Environment

Now before you toss out your old perfume bottle, think about recycling it. The EPA estimates that nearly 75 percent of our waste output is recyclable and/or compostable, yet we send nearly 75 percent of our trash to the landfill. Many people who religiously separate their cans and bottles from the rest of their trash stop short at recycling the containers that hold their beauty products. I don't get it. So much of it can go in the blue bin, especially those glass bottles taking up space on your bathroom counter.[113]

Besides the impact on your pretty little self, the environmental impact of buying an eco-friendly perfume should impress any consumer. Many green beauty companies are exploring different ways to proactively offset their carbon footprints—and yours. It seems like a little thing to buy a chemical-free fragrance, but each decision you make adds up to lower your carbon footprint. Buy a sustainable product and not only do you stop chemicals from going onto your body and into the ecosystem, you also support a business that is thinking outside of the box about sustainable sourcing (shrinking), developing (still shrinking), packaging (shrinking even more) and transporting (shrunk!) their products. You take a dollar from a conventional company and give it to a green company, thus tilting the economic balance in favor of sustainability-minded businesses.

Your organic *eau de toilette* buy may seem small, but stack it up with the hundreds of friends whom you talk to about what you buy.purchases you make each year and the thousands made by the Get the picture? It's like that old Faberge commercial: "She'll tell two friends, and she'll tell two friends." It all adds up.

RACHEL'S PICKS: PERFUMES

Organic perfumes created from steam-distilled plants and flowers smell amazing and you won't have cats following you down the alley trying to hump your leg. Unless you're into that. Here are a few that I love:

Pacifica (pacificaperfume.com)

A Perfume Organic (aperfumeorganic.com)

Strange Invisible Perfumes (siperfumes.com)

Rachel Lincoln Sarnoff publishes EcoStiletto.com, an online magazine dedicated to eco-friendly fashion, beauty, and lifestyle. She also founded MommyGreenest.com, an online resource for eco-friendly parenting ideas.

CHAPTER 5

The Skinny: Personal Care Products

★ Put a Plug In It:
TAMPONS

Nobody likes being on the rag. Period. It takes every ounce of energy not to blow up at the cable guy or cry our eyes out during a Hallmark commercial. And not even the most expensive pair of Spanx could hold back our bloated guts.

But just because we're pissed off at the world doesn't mean we should take it out on our vaginas. Yet we do—every time we stick one of those synthetic plastic plugs up there to block a heavy flow.

Traditional tampons are made of a chemical-laden fiber called rayon. You'll never hear Tampax leak this, but rayon doesn't just pop up in nature. The process of turning it from a wood pulp into a soft fiber creates dioxins, cancer-causing toxins that linger in teeny amounts in tampons and pillage the environment.[114]

TOXINS IN OUR HOO-HAS

First a little about your vajayjay: It is the most absorbent part of the body.[115] Do you want "trace" amounts of dioxins making contact with your delicate flower? Um, I'll pass. And think about how many tampons we use over the course of our lifetimes: The more than 70 percent of menstruating chicks in America who use tampons bulldoze through as many as sixteen thousand before menopause.[116] In my eyes, there are no safe levels of dioxins, honey. None. Zilch. Zero.

Dioxins aren't something we should be introducing to our lady bits, let alone our reproductive system. They are a serious party crasher. People exposed to high levels may be at risk for a wrecked immune system, an increased risk of pelvic inflammatory disease (PID), and it could reduce the chances of getting knocked up.[117] Plus, they are linked to endometriosis, a painful disease in which uterine tissue grows outside the uterus.[118]

But rayon doesn't deserve all the dioxin-unleashing credit in this vagina monologue. For those of you choose the cotton variety, you can also find dioxins in all-cotton tampons and pads courtesy of bleach and pesticides.

Feminine hygiene makers bleach the hell out of tampons and pads with chloride bleaches. Not because they get off on the fumes, but because the FDA requires them to in order to get rid of bacteria, lignans, and waxes left over from farming. While the bleaches are not as harsh as they once were—or so we're told—dioxins are still detected in tampons.[119]

And then there's conventional cotton farming. If you haven't forgotten, cotton calls for a buttload of chemicals in the fields. The USDA says that U.S. cotton farmers dump about fifty-five million pounds of pesticides into cotton fields every year.[120] Unfortunately, these commercial pesticides also produce dioxins. It's just a big dioxin party and we're all invited! In 2005, the FDA Office of Women's Health proved that dioxins don't play favorites, when they found detectable levels of dioxins in seven different brands

♥ KIM'S PICKS: TAMPONS

Seventh Generation Chlorine-Free Organic
Tampons (seventhgeneration.com)

Natracare Certified Organic All-Cotton
Tampons (natracare.com)

Organic Essentials Certified Organic Cotton
Tampons (dwellsmart.com)

of tampons, including at least one all-cotton one.[121]

While I could rattle on about dioxins and pesticides all day, tampons have other ways of causing discomfort. Anyone recall the Toxic Shock Syndrome (TSS) scare of the late 1970s? A rare and potentially fatal disease caused by toxic bacteria, TSS claimed 813 cases and 38 deaths at its peak in 1980.[122] Luckily the disease has laid low in recent years, but the reason for the decline is debatable. Some say it's simply because we lightened up and started avoiding super-absorbency tampons, which are caked with chemicals to boost their absorbency. But tampon makers have also removed three of the four most toxic ingredients—polyester, carboxymethyl-cellulose, and polyacrylate rayon—believed to promote the TSS toxin.[123] No matter which way you stick it, highly absorbent rayon is still widely used.

Another problem is deodorized tampons, which are splashed with perfume. This one is beyond me. Ladies, you have your period. You are bleeding. Your uteran walls are breaking down. A little fragrance may distract you from the fact that your hoo-ha smells, but it's increasing your risk of infection. The perfumes in traditional tampons can alter the balance of good bacteria in the vagina that keeps yeast in check. H-e-l-l-o yeast infections.[124] Plain and simple, using fewer commercial tampons means less itching, burning, and finding stuff you don't like in your underwear.

This doesn't mean you have to revert to cloth diapers. You just need to use your brain before you snag the first box of tampons on the grocery shelf.

Choose organic cotton tampons that are fragrance-free and whitened without chlorine bleach. Stand up for your vagina and go dioxin-free. Rayon-free tampons reduce the risk of TSS, and the organic versions will lessen your exposure to chemical pesticides and fertilizers used on traditional cotton.

THE TAMPON-FREE REVOLUTION

Some of you would rather get daily pap smears during happy hour than wear a tampon. There is a whole army of you, and I salute. With the rise of environmental and health concerns, there are some pretty cool alternatives designed for our monthly curse. Here are just a few reasons tampons and throwaway pads aren't a fit for everyone.

TAMPONS ARE AN ENVIRONMENTAL HEADACHE.

We dump nearly twenty billion disposable tampons and pads every year in this country alone (to say nothing of the dioxins they unleash in nature).[125] No one is suggesting you reuse, but that is a hair-raising number. The plastic applicators can take anywhere from three hundred to five hundred years to break down in a landfill,[126] and birds regularly choke to death by swallowing them.[127]

TAMPONS HAVE LITTLE RESPECT FOR YOUR LADY PARTS. The tissue inside your vagina is extremely delicate. Tampons' only agenda is to act like the Hoover Dam and stop the flow. In the meantime, they can cut, pinch, and scrape vaginal walls, sometimes causing arterial lacerations. It hurts just to read that. Rayon fibers in tampons and small fibers from cardboard applicators can crawl up into these tiny cuts and put you at risk for infection, too.[128] That is no way to treat your womanhood.

B BITCHWORTHY:
Do you have a standing date with your plumber once a month? Stop flushing your tampons down the toilet! Disposable pads and tampons are the culprit in nine out of ten plumbing emergencies. I hope you at least buy the guy a drink.

TAMPON AND TRADITIONAL SANITARY NAPKIN ALTERNATIVES

REUSABLE MENSTRUAL CUPS   At first, these reminded me of a plunger. Honestly, not the best first impression. Once I got over the oddity of putting a cup into my, well, you know, I could see the appeal. You basically insert the cup and it collects blood rather than absorbing it, with a "pull-tab" to empty it with ease. There are a handful of options on the market. The DivaCup offers a reusable cup made of medical-grade silicone (divacup.com). The Keeper offers a silicone and a latex-free option (The Keeper Mooncup) for those with an unfortunate latex allergy (thekeeper.com).

DISPOSABLE MENSTRUAL CUPS   If you like the idea of a cup but don't see reusing it in your future, Instead, Softcup makes a disposable version that can be kept in during *any* activity—like sex and riding the mechanical bull. For the absentminded, it can be left in for up to twelve hours. These can be a bitch to find at supermarkets or drugstores, so buy online. *Visit softcup.com.*

Brusha, Brusha, Brusha: ★
TOXINS IN YOUR TOOTHPASTE

There is some crazy shit going down in that mouth of yours. Straight up *crazy*. It's probably nothing your dentist can see or warn you about. Actually, between you and me, they probably would tell you it's a bunch of gibberish. I'm just going to leave the toothbrush in your hand and let you make the call.

So, here's the dealio—your everyday toothpaste is chock-full of chemicals and artificial additives that are better off in the engine of your car than your mouth. A handful of them—SLS, SLES, propylene glycol, triclosan—you may not even be able to find on the label. They all have different strengths. Some can build up in your body fat and damage your liver and kidneys.[129] Others can give you mouth ulcers (a fancy name for canker sores).[130] And another is pretty mild. It can just mess with your DNA, weaken your bones, and make you dumber.[131]

What really floors me is that your mouth isn't just absorbent. The mucus membranes inside your flytrap have a special knack for absorbing 90 percent of what they make contact with. Once absorbed, they offer a one-way ticket to the blood, brain, and other cells in the body.[132]

So let me tell you what you don't want your mouth absorbing. Brush up on a few of the major players in your toothpaste, and figure out which ones you don't want in there.

THE FLUORIDE DISPUTE

Yes, I'm gonna go there. I'm gonna talk about fluoride and make a solid case for why it shouldn't be in your toothpaste. For my dentist and dental hygienist readers, feel free to curse my name right now.

In its most basic form, fluoride is a poison [insert skull and crossbones here]. It's a neurotoxic chemical that can also be tumorigenic—meaning it can cause tumors when swallowed.[133] It gets uglier. Before its foray into our toothpaste, it was actually used as a rat poison and an insecticide—that was discontinued after it started to kill plants. Small detail.[134]

The FDA even requires toothpaste brands that contain fluoride to carry the following poison warning: *If you accidentally swallow more than used for brushing, seek professional help or contact a poison control center immediately.*[135]

Now I may not be chugging fluoride like it's Hefeweizen, but most of us brush our teeth every day, two to three times a day. Well, hopefully. You'd have to be pretty damn talented not to swallow *any*. When you also take into account that fluoride is added to our water supply—I know, it's Looneyville— it looks like we're getting a double dose of a toxin that accumulates in the body.[136] All camps seem to agree that healthy kidneys can only get rid of about 50 percent of our daily fluoride intake.[137] So the other half just keeps piling up in our kidneys, thyroid, heart, liver, and lungs. Oh, I almost forgot—and in our bones and teeth.[138] Forgive me.

The damage all this fluoride exposure seems to cause can be both apparent and hidden. Even in lower doses, it can promote a condition called fluorosis, which makes itself known through yellow, discolored teeth. [139] Yes, your "whitening" toothpaste could indeed be turning your smile yellow. Oh, all the irony. Fluoride also damages your gums by slowing down the enzymes that help your gums repair themselves in a timely manner—a little piece of information from the late Dr. John Yiamouyiannis, who just happened to be the world's authority on fluoride.[140] Over time, it can also ruin your teeth by making them too hard and brittle.[141]

Your chompers aren't the only thing fluoride can turn brittle. The toxin seems to have the same effect on our bones. Call me crazy, but we kind of need those. Some studies show that chronic exposure to fluoride may cause arthritis, bone fractures, and possibly even osteosarcoma, a rare type of blood cancer that targets kids.[142]

Still many dentists swear that fluoride is critical in preventing cavities in kids, since younger children have softer tooth enamel that makes it more vulnerable to decay. The best solution is to be diligent about educating your kid on brushing and spitting. Experts recommend using no more than a pea-size amount and supervising any child under six to make sure there's no swallowing business going on. As for adults, maybe not so much. Natural toothpastes use ingredients like xylitol to kill the bacteria that causes decay and fight cavities. Though it sounds scary, xylitol is a natural sugar from fruits and veggies that doesn't contribute to tooth decay. Big girls don't need no stinkin' fluoride.

B **BITCHWORTHY: FLUORIDE FILTERS**
You can kick your toothpaste to the curb, but getting fluoride out of your water will require effort. Before you swear off water for a life of Red Bull, look into getting a water distiller, alumina defluoridation system, or reverse osmosis system that filters out fluoride. Trust me, they are easier to find than they sound. Don't look at your Brita or Pur filter for help. All those water filter pitchers that fit snugly in your fridge are useless against fluoride.

ANTIBACTERIALS

Your mouth has a lot of bacteria swimming around. Like, a lot. There are more than one hundred million bacteria in every milliliter of saliva in your kisser.[143] It's not all bad bacteria, but conventional toothpaste makers often add triclosan to the mix to kill everything you got. Triclosan may knock down your immune system and could harm your liver, lungs, and kidneys,[144] but I'm talking about a little chemical reaction that it jumpstarts in your mouth. There are reports that when triclosan is added to chlorine in tap water, it can create chloroform—the same stuff that leads to cancer and can knock people unconscious by just breathing it.[145] Who knew our mouths were a test tube? That would be the people making your toothpaste.

FOAMING AGENTS

To get a good lather going, conventional toothpaste brands like to call on sodium laureth sulfate (SLS) or sodium lauryl ether sulfate (SLES) for a soft, foamy texture. Both SLS and SLES cause microscopic tears in your oral tissues that lead to painful canker sores.[146] The sulfates are also known to swell up gums, which can lead to gum receding.[147] Don't listen to the jargon on the back of boxes that sway you into thinking SLS is "derived from coconut oil" or maybe "palm kernel oil." It may have come from natural sources, but it's far from natural. To produce the chemical, the coconut oil is reacted with an atom and molecule in a complicated process that leaves the end result unstable and aggressive.[148]

ARTIFICIAL SUGARS

Many of us could brush our teeth all day long just for that fresh, minty breath. That isn't mint you're tasting, girlfriend. It's coal tar. Saccharin tastes great, causes cancer, and it's in our toothpaste! Personal care brands add artificial sugars like saccharin to toothpaste to give it that sweet flavor. On top of that sweet flavor, it may also cause allergic reactions, asthma, headaches, and irritation to the gums and oral tissue.[149] Sweet!

FOOD DYES

Our toothpaste is full of pretty colors. Red, white, blue, green, yellow—whatever the hell they can squeeze into that four-ounce tube. As fun as it looks when it spits out swirls on your toothbrush, it's just good ole petroleum and coal tar at heart.[150] The synthetic dyes such as FD&C Blue 1, Red 3, Red 33, Red 40, and Yellow 10 Lake all live up to their controversy. Some have been banned from cosmetics, others are not approved for anything that goes near our eyes, but apparently they are fine in our mouths.[151] Spit, please.

MOISTURIZER

To keep your toothpaste from drying out, you'll often find propylene glycol and PEG hiding out in the tube. The glycol duo also acts as penetration enhancers to help other ingredients get through.[152] As if one of the most absorbent parts of your body needed some assistance in soaking up the bad chemicals.

In antifreeze, propylene glycol comes with a warning label to avoid skin contact due to potential complications linked to brain, kidney, and liver damage. Really?[153] So it can't touch your skin but we're told it's perfectly safe for your mouth in small quantities? Posing similar concerns, PEG can be contaminated with ethylene oxide and 1,4-dioxane—both of which are linked to the big "C."[154]

NATURAL TOOTHPASTES

Pay attention when buying "natural" toothpastes. Some of the brands you'll find in the aisles of a natural health retailer still contain some of the icky ingredients we just covered. It's up to you to decide which ingredients you don't want in your mouth.

Aside from xylitol, some of the cleaner, natural ingredients to look for are zinc citrate, a mineral that helps control the calcification of plaque into tartar.[155] Natural silica, which actually comes from sand, helps give your mouth a good cleansing, and encourages pearly whites without abrasives or bleaching ingredients.

KIM'S PICKS: TOOTHPASTE

Desert Essence Natural Tea Tree Oil and Neem Toothpaste (desertessence.com)

Jason PowerSmile All-Natural Whitening Toothpaste (jasoncosmetics.com)

Weleda Toothpaste (usa.weleda.com)

WANTED: WHITE CHOMPERS

Keeping your chompers white, bright, and shiny can be a pain in the ass. Over time, overexposure to fluoride, lack of calcium, certain medications, and medical conditions can cause stains or discolor teeth from the inside out, making them look yellower than a can of Mountain Dew. Add our everyday dirty habits like soft drinks and staining beverages (coffee, tea, and wine) and the natural process of aging can make the enamel vulnerable to ugly stains. While professional dental whitening can cost a month's paycheck, your pantry may be the answer. Save some moolah and get the job done with some of these home remedies.

Strawberries: This fresh and yummy fruit contains malic acid, which acts as a natural astringent. Apply strawberries directly to your teeth or create a paste with 1 crushed strawberry and 1/2 teaspoon baking soda. Leave on for about 5 minutes (no longer) and brush thoroughly with toothpaste to remove the mixture. A little floss will help get rid of the strawberry seeds. Crossing my fingers you own some floss.

Baking soda: Once or twice a month, mix a little baking soda with water and dip your toothbrush in the solution. Lightly brush your teeth with the baking soda mixture, spit, and rinse thoroughly when done. This one freshens your breath, too.

Orange and lemon peels: Orange and lemon juice are well recognized for their cleaning properties. Cut a wedge of a lemon or orange peel, and rub the inside of the peel against your teeth for about fifteen minutes before rinsing.

Important Tips

Rinse. It's *muy importante* to rinse after applying strawberries and citrus peels because of the citric acid. Prolonged acid exposure can decay the enamel on your teeth.

Use sparingly. Don't go overboard. Since citric acid can strip your teeth of calcium, you do not want to use as a regular whitening method. Start with once a week to see how sensitive you are.

Get professional advice. All teeth weren't created equal. If you're concerned about natural remedies, check with a holistic practitioner or your dentist to make sure they won't do any harm to your teeth.

★ Sweat the Small Stuff:
THE STINK AROUND DEODORANTS AND ANTIPERSPIRANTS

Try going one day without deodorant and see if you can live with pits au naturel. My bet is that deodorant will quickly become your desert-island item. (You know the question: "If you were stranded on a desert island and could only take one item . . . ") I know you answered extra-volume mascara. But you really meant deodorant. It doesn't matter if you're the sole survivor and will never see another sign of life again. The answer is still deodorant.

Even if it's tough to understand how so much stank and sweat can come out of one girl, sweating is a natural part of life. Actually, it's vital. Sweating is like our body's air conditioner. It cools us down. If we didn't do it, we'd be one hot, *dead* mess.

Together, deodorants and antiperspirants separate us from European backpackers, but they each work in pretty different ways. While both address body odor, deodorants tackle the bacteria under the pit that cause offensive odors, and then douse it with artificial perfumes to hide the evidence. But antiperspirants go another route. They tell the body to stop sweating altogether (recall that your body needs to sweat to chill out). Put aside their differences though, and both have something very much in common—chemicals. Yes ma'am. Those time-honored deodorants and antiperspirants on the store shelves are using more than so-called Teen Spirit to get you smelling like a rose garden.

Antiperspirants are so harsh on the body that they are classified as an over-the-counter drug by the FDA. To spell it out for you, that means they chemically alter the way the body functions.[156] Take a big whiff of that: Our deodorants are right up there with Viagra.

THE JUNGLE UNDER YOUR ARMS

It's pretty tough to find deodorants that don't contain antiperspirants, though they are out there. But that's beside the point. The point is to get familiar with some of these chemicals so you can start taking your pits elsewhere.

ALUMINUM SALTS Now what would aluminum be doing in your antiperspirant? Good question. It works closely with the natural salts in your body to create a tiny gel that plugs up the sweat glands.[157] But as studies are now showing, this isn't such a hot idea.

Breast Cancer: No, I'm not implying that deodorant causes breast cancer. Not exactly. I am saying there's something fishy going on there. Aluminum compounds have been shown to act as hormone disruptors,[158] which throw off normal balances of hormones like, say, estrogen. This kind of hormonal imbalance has been linked to breast cancer tumors. If I may jump to conclusions, we're applying these aluminum compounds pretty darn close to our boobies. I'm just saying . . . [159]

Alzheimer's Disease: There have been a lot of rumors going around about how aluminum in deodorants can get into our bloodstream and find its way to our brains. A public health report released by the World Health Organization found that autopsies of patients with Alzheimer's had high concentrations of aluminum in their brains.[160] Think about it: Aluminum is a neurotoxin that is capable of crossing the barrier to our thinking cap.[161] This is something you may want to remember.

PROPYLENE GLYCOL A form of mineral oil, propylene glycol wears several hats in deodorants. It helps keeps your underarms (and the deodorant) moist and acts as a liaison between other ingredients to keep them working together. Outside of your deodorant, you can also find it in industrial antifreeze, and automatic brake and hydraulic fluid. Well, isn't that comforting?

TRICLOSAN You know it doesn't belong in your antibacterial hand soaps, so why would it be OK in your deodorant? It's not. The EPA actually classifies triclosan as a pesticide, and it can be contaminated with cancer-causing dioxins during manufacturing.[162] Conventional deodorant makers use it because it destroys the bacteria that give us bad BO. Triclosan is another one of those pesky hormone disruptors, which, when used in tandem with aluminum,[163] could potentially make our hormones go haywire.

TALC This superfine powder used to enhance absorbency and deodorize has been linked to ovarian cancer.[164] It can also cause both mild and chronic lung irritation, so my advice is to stay away from aerosol or spray deodorants.[165]

ETHANOL (ETHYL ALCOHOL) Celebrated as the biofuel of the future, ethanol is often found in deodorants as a penetration enhancer for other ingredients.[166] In the case of your deodorant, "other" ingredients being a mess of toxic chemicals. Ethanol can also irritate skin, eyes, and the lungs. Best not to apply something to your underarms that powers our vehicles.

> **KIM'S PICKS: DEODORANTS**
> I'm not going to lie to your face. It took me a solid six months—OK, I'm already lying . . . *a year*—to make the transition to natural deodorants. Without all the chemicals, the natural brands really don't stop your body from doing what it wants to do. But unless you're training for the next Ironman, your body's chemistry will start to mesh with the plant oils. Give it a few weeks. Test out these vegan, chemical-free deodorants that will make you feel a bit closer to nature, and farther from brain damage.
>
> **Erbaviva Lemon Sage Organic Deodorant** (erbaviva.com)
>
> **Crystal Body Deodorant** (thecrystal.com)
>
> **Terressentials Fragrance-Free Super Protection Deodorant** (terressentials.com)

★ Lather, Rinse, Repeat:
SHAMPOOS AND CONDITIONERS

You've got a whole mess of hair on that head. Each one of us is packing about 100,000 strands (unless you're a blonde, and then somehow you're blessed with 50 percent more). As alive as it looks when you're flipping it around like a tease, it's dead. But it's a good kind of dead—dead cells made of keratin that give it that tough, coarse texture. Since it's RIP, something needs to keep it healthy or it will *look* lifeless, too. That something is sebum.

Sebum is the stuff that protects our scalps from infection, fights off chemicals, and maybe when it has a minute, makes our hair big and shiny so we make all our friends insanely jealous. Not too much to ask. The problem is that detergents, synthetic preservatives, and petroleum derivatives in your everyday shampoo are notorious for stripping away this sebum. When sebum is MIA, our scalp sits there violated and naked for chemical nasties to penetrate. Not a good look for you or your poor scalp.

SULFATES AND YOUR SCALP

The worst of the shampoo ingredients are SLS and SLES—the chemicals that make your shampoo foam up in your palm. Their main gig is to pick up the dirt so it can be rinsed out. During the process that SLS undergoes to lose its abrasive edge, it may also produce 1,4-dioxane—another cancerous suspect that won't pop up on the label. Do me a favor. Stop massaging that gunk into your scalp—1,4-dioxane can do a number on your eyes, strip your scalp of essential oils, and attack your lungs.[167] The part that really blows my mind is that the sulfates are known to corrode and stunt hair growth.[168] What the fuck is it doing in 95 percent of shampoos?!

Other god-awful detergents in the bottle include DEA, MEA, ammonium laureth sulfate, and PEG. Not just a drop either. Think for a minute about that lesson I taught you earlier on how to read a label. Here it is: all ingredients are listed in order of volume. Most of those ingredients I just listed sit at the top. Grab your calculator. That means these industrial poisons take up nearly one-third of your shampoo.[169]

Then to wrap it up, they have to add some preservative to make sure that economy-size shampoo can fart around on the shelves for half a year. Methyl- and propyl-parabens are usually their first choice. But if they're feeling a little randy, they may add DMDM hydantoin to that toxic trap. It's a science experiment in your shower.

PLANT EXTRACTS USUALLY ONLY TAKE UP 1 PERCENT

You don't need a high school diploma to figure out what makes greedy companies tick. We've gone over this. Even the organic posers will say that their products are made with pure ingredients. Please tell me you're even slightly curious what "made with" means. "Made with" could mean anywhere between 1 and 100 percent of that product. But I'll take the fun out of guessing—plant extracts usually don't add up to more than 1 percent. One stinkin' percent. What really matters is the bulk of the bottle. The whole enchilada. They're not going to get a pat on the back for adding a few essential oils and herbs when it's weighed down by toxic crap that accumulates in our bodies. Not from me at least.

LET YOUR SCALP GET USED TO THE NEW YOU

Commercial shampoo and conditioner junkies, brace yourselves. With natural suds, you're not going to get a great lather in your palm. Actually, it may even feel like you need more shampoo to get it real clean. Your hair may not feel as clean for the first week or so. Keep at it. Don't be a pussy and put the Tigi Big Sexy Hair back in the shower. Your scalp just needs to get used to your new natural ways. Put it through hair rehab. It's addicted to chemicals and you need to wean it off.

CONDITIONERS

Now that you know a little bit about hair, hopefully you're smart enough to figure out that all those sweet chemicals, vitamins, and minerals are not going to bring your hair back to life. Even if the bottle promises it will. You can soak it in holy water, and it's not going to rise from the grave.

What you need is a good conditioner to replenish those natural oils and coat the hair follicles with plant-based silicones and waxes, and essential oils. That will arouse and stiffen the hair shaft so it makes your mane look alive (man, that sounded dirty). You don't need chemicals to arouse anything.

KIM'S PICKS:
SHAMPOOS AND CONDITIONERS

Amazon Beauty Rahua Shampoo and
    Conditioner (rahua.com)

Giovanni Smooth as Silk Deep Moisture
    Shampoo and Conditioner
    (giovannicosmetics.com)

Sukihair Clean Balance Shampoo
    (futurenatural.com)

Glory Locks Hair Cream
    (mountofolivesoap.com)

THE MANE THING:

ALEXANDRA SPUNT AND SIOBHAN O'CONNOR, AUTHORS OF *NO MORE DIRTY LOOKS*, SHARE THEIR PATH TO CLEANER HAIR

Every woman's path to clean cosmetics starts with an aha moment, and ours was precipitated by a hair fiasco: the Brazilian blowout. At the time, the treatment was being touted as a revolutionary new hair therapy. All the celebrities were doing it, and the stylists at our favorite salon sold us on its virtues. They promised this "keratin" would strengthen our hair with protein. And so, cheerful guinea pigs that we were, we made appointments.

If the choking fumes didn't tip us off, the protective goggles probably should have. But it was only two months later, when our hair was flat and broken with fly-aways, that we discovered our tresses (and our lungs) had been exposed to a serious dose of formaldehyde. Aha, indeed.

So began our search for clean cosmetics. We catalogued our findings in our book, *No More Dirty Looks*, and on our Web site, nomoredirtylooks.com, informing readers about the unsafe or untested ingredients used in everyday cosmetics. But we also wanted to make it fun, so we spent a year trying the very best products, treatments, and DIY recipes. Even though we were shocked by some of the things we learned, we also discovered that going clean actually made us look better. Our hair was more hydrated, shinier, and suppler. Our skin cleared up and calmed down. And our body barely needed any products at all to feel smooth and hydrated.

While the path to clean cosmetics can be daunting for some, we have some tips to help you on your way. The main thing is the mane thing: Start with your hair. It's where we began our clean journey, and here's why: Who hasn't cut, dyed, straightened, or fried her hair at some point? We love to experiment with our manes, and most of us begin messing with what the gods gave us in our early teens. So, all you need to do is commit to changing the hair products you use every day: your shampoo, conditioner, and leave-ins. We promise you will be rewarded for your efforts.

Understand that the more you use, the more you need. Something magical happened when we stopped washing with harsh, foaming shampoos, silicone- and fragrance-laden conditioners, and handfuls of leave-ins:

Our hair started to behave for the first time since our teens.

Change your shampoo. When you use a truly clean shampoo, it won't lather like you're used to, but your scalp will adjust to the gentler regimen and reward you with more manageable hair. These days, Siobhan just uses a clean shampoo and conditioner and *nothing* else—her hair no longer needs to be tamed by the leave-ins it once did.

If you're really feeling brave—and this works especially well for women with coarse and curly hair—you can ditch your shampoo altogether. That's what Alexandra tried, and she was so pleased with the experiment that she never went back.

Use oils on your hair. We're all hard-wired to squirm when we see lots of oil, thinking it will make us feel sticky or dirty or, worse, break us out. But skin- and hair-friendly oils will do no such thing if you use them properly. Coconut oil is especially good at penetrating the hair. It makes for a wonderful hair mask, to put on for 20 minutes before you shampoo. Look for oil-rich conditioners with shea butter, olive oil, coconut oil, or jojoba.

Seek out a clean salon, or scale back your visits. As you've learned, one of the most effective ways to choose your products is by reading ingredient labels. Unfortunately, that's not a luxury you're afforded at the salon—most stylists don't even know what's in the treatments they're exposed to *every day*.

If you can't give up your hair dye, we totally understand. But we do encourage you to reduce the number of times you're visiting the salon every year, and we beg you not to go if you're pregnant. As our Brazilians taught us, salons can be pretty toxic places.

The good news is that clean, or at least *cleaner* salons are popping up in cities far and wide. None of us want to give up the pampering ritual a visit to the hairdresser offers, and as long as we demand a nontoxic experience, the market will follow us.

Follow Alexandra and Siobhan on their blog at nomoredirtylooks.com.

★ The Guilty Glow:
SELF-TANNERS

We all have that friend who's always tan. Rain or shine. Winter or summer. Seattle or Cabo San Lucas. It's like the chick has a reflector on her steering wheel.

But we're on to her. No matter how many times she claims that bronze is in her blood, her skin don't lie. She has fake 'n bake written all over her.

Luckily, we no longer need an entire bottle of baby oil to get some color. Tanning beds, sunless misting booths, and self-tanners in a bottle have changed the lives of millions of pasty chicks who used to hide under a towel at the pool.

That's all good and great. But are all of these tanning shenanigans safe? It depends. What's your poison?

TANNING BEDS

The most obvious overdose is ultraviolet rays from a tanning bed. Oompa-Loompa is not a good look for anybody. No matter how much the underage knockout behind the counter wants to convince you that indoor tanning boosts vitamin D, they're just trying to sell you a tanning package, honey. And an overpriced bottle of lotion chock-full of chemicals.

What they probably won't sell you on is the fact that people who use tanning beds may have a 75 percent higher risk of getting skin cancer. Soak that in: 75 percent. That doesn't leave many, well, percents.[170] It's awesome that we're checking our boobs for lumps in the shower, but skin cancer is actually the most common form of cancer in America.[171]

While a few weekends in Daytona could easily increase your risk, your frequent visits to the "bed" are putting you at a much greater risk. The good thing is we have other options. We don't have to fry four times a week in a bed on UVA steroids to put our paleness behind us. The solution: take a bronzer shower.

SUNLESS TANNING BOOTHS AND SOLUTIONS

It might just be one of the greatest inventions ever made. You pop in, you pop out, and voilà! You look like you just got back from a Mexican cruise. Who cares if you're feeling claustrophobic and smell offensive?

The active ingredient found in sunless and spray tanning solutions is called dihydroxyacetone (DHA). It is a pretty nontoxic ingredient that comes from plant sources such as sugar cane and beets, or from glycerin. Let me be clear, DHA is not a dye. It works by reacting with the amino acids in your dead skin cells to leave you with a deep, dark tan. The FDA oversees and approves DHA as a color additive in cosmetics, but only when applied externally. Translation: Do not apply anywhere near your eyes, lips, or any orifice on your body. If our eyes, lips, and hoo-has are exposed to the tanning solution, then it loses its seal of approval. They also make it pretty darn clear that it shouldn't be inhaled. Case closed.

The problem is that only a select few of us have enough brains to take any of these precautions when we jump into the spray machine. All we care about is getting that tan, and fast. But if you actually look around, tanning salons *should* provide you with optional eye goggles and face (mouth) mask. As for your *other* orifices . . . wear underwear, hussy. I know you think you know what you're doing, but if the FDA says we shouldn't inhale it, then I would wear a helmet in that booth.

There are a few other kinks in spray tanning. Though it is considered safe—that is, when it's not inhaled, swallowed, or sprayed in your eyeball—DHA is not the chemical you have to worry about. No ma'am. It's all the other chemicals in the bottle. Recall from your cool handbook on "How to Nail a Label" (see page 122) that you shouldn't trust a product based on its active ingredient? Now you can apply that. DHA may be the additive at work in sunless tanning solutions, but some of the other

AT-HOME SUNLESS TANNERS AND BRONZERS

nasty ingredients you may find are dimethyl ether, (di)propylene glycol, phenoxyethanol, parabens, and EDTA.[172] Oh, did I spoil your tan? Like I care . . .

As an alternative, look for salons that carry solutions made with no parabens, synthetic preservatives, fragrance, alcohol, or oils. Companies like the Australian-based SunFX offer such natural solutions at salons across the world (sunfx.com). And, yes, they do some significant business in the United States. You don't need to go Down Under to get your healthy tan on.

Another option is seeking out a solution that has gained USDA organic certification. Though DHA itself can't be certified as an organic ingredient under the standards of the USDA's National Organic Program (NOP), the rest of the ingredients can be. A company in St. Petersburg, Florida called Biddiscombe makes a tanning cocktail that contains 95 percent certified-organic ingredients. The other 5 percent is natural, including the color additives.

So here's a thought: Do some research. But don't just call your local tanning salon and ask them what is in their tanning solutions, then take their word for it. Many of them don't know and will just start rambling off some pitch about their great selection of lotions. Ask them what brands they use for sunless tanning spray and do your own research.

If you can't locate a SunFX or other certified-organic solution, limit your spray tanning habit. Practice a little restraint. Notice I'm not saying ban sunless tanning spray-downs from your life like you did meat. There is a time and a place. In the meantime, there's always at-home sunless tanning lotions. Finally, something my wallet will approve of.

A tan in a bottle. What's not to love? You can do it from home. You won't smell like your internal organs are burning alive. You don't need to stand in a dark chamber holding your breath for forty-five seconds like an Olympic swimmer.

Oh, I can think of a few things not to love. They're called 1,4-dioxane, parabens, synthetic fragrances, and oxybenzone. On top of that, some companies test on animals, or offer products that contain beeswax, lanolin, and ceramides from animal sources. Like almost everything else sitting on the drugstore shelf, self-tanners are nothing golden.

After years of trying every at-home formula under the sun, I found a few that work really well without the chemicals and allergic reactions. A tan chick with hives is really not hot.

KIM'S PICKS: SELF-TANNERS

Chocolate Sun Absolute Sun Sunless Tanning Cream (spiritbeautylounge.com)

Swissclinical Self-Tanner (swissclinicalusa.com)

Caribbean Solutions Beach Colours Natural Self-Tanner (caribbean-sol.com)

★ Smoke Screen:
SUNSCREENS

Screw kindergarten. All we ever really needed to know we learned from three letters: SPF. We heard ya loud and clear, Doc. The numbers after those letters better be real flippin' high. The sun's gonna turn us into little raisins and the only thing that will save us is slathering on the white stuff. Got ya.

Then we found out that everything we thought we knew was . . . wrong. First the Tooth Fairy, then the Easter Bunny. Was the ocean just a big swimming pool? Was our sunscreen not really protecting us from harm, after all?

The rumor is true—some sunscreens are banging us up more than they're doing any good. Research is unveiling that the brands we've worshipped for sun protection for more than thirty years aren't only causing major health problems, but they're letting the wrong rays in. And what about those three telling letters? Yeah, it turns out that the SPF doesn't tell us jack shit. That's right, Virginia—there's no Santa Claus, either.

HORMONE IMPERSONATORS IN OUR SUNSCREEN

All this crazy talk around sun*scream* is news to everyone, not just consumers. The interrogation started years back with one of the most popular chemicals in sunscreen, benzophenone-3, or oxybenzone. Studies were showing that it was yet another one of those lousy hormone disruptors that accumulated in the body.[173] Though it's been all the rage for absorbing ultraviolet rays to protect us against skin cancer, oxybenzone mimics estrogen, which screws up the body's responses and boosts cancerous cells.[174] When it reacts with UV light, it can also produce free radicals, which are also known to cause cancer.[175] Since the whole damn point is for oxybenzone to react with UV light and absorb those rays, something was very wrong. Trading one cancer for another isn't exactly what we had in mind.

This all hits even closer to home when we realize that everyone is rubbing it on. Oxybenzone is found in more than 60 percent of beach and sport sunscreens. When the side effects of the chemical's game of hormonal Pac-Man became news, the Centers for Disease Control and Prevention decided to find out just how big a problem we had on our hands. Go figure. It showed up in the pee-pee of 97 percent of Americans tested.[176]

VITAMIN A . . . *A FOE?*

With that said, we kind of expect this trouble from a man-made chemical. We sure as hell don't expect it from a vitamin. Scratch that, too. The FDA is now saying that a form of vitamin A called retinyl palmitate—an ingredient hiding in 41 percent of sunscreens to stop our skin from aging [177]—is a photo-carcinogenic. In simple terms, our skin and vitamin A go through some funky chemical changes in the presence of UV rays that may cause cancer. You heard me correctly: The FDA is concerned. If they pulled their heads out of their asses long enough to question it, that's all the evidence I need.

THE SPF HOAX

The SPF debacle is an entirely different issue, but it's one that sunscreen makers have tried to keep under wraps for a long, long time. In short, the SPF tells us to what degree a sunscreen will protect our skin from the direct rays of the sun. We've always relied on those two numbers that follow it to guide us in our level of sun protection. But it doesn't tell us what we think it does. The SPF only refers to UVB rays. Those are the rays that cause sunburn and play the biggest role in malignant melanoma skin cancer, which is the more serious of skin cancers caused by the cells that produce your pigment.[178] No doubt, they are bad with a capital "B." But the number tells us diddly-squat about those other UV rays—the "A" team. Rest assured, they are there and no less dangerous. Since the earth's ozone layer absorbs most UVB rays, about 90 to 99 percent of the harmful rays that actually hit us are UVA rays.[179] Guess what? These rays cause skin cancer, too. They also dig more deeply into the skin to make our skin age prematurely.[180] For a girl who likes the sun, it's important to look for broad-spectrum sunscreens that protect against both UVA and UVB rays, but you won't find it in the SPF. What a shame.

The SPF controversy doesn't stop there. The new marketing scam is focused on those sky-high SPF claims—SPF 50, 75, 80 . . . and on up. The concern is that these lofty numbers fill consumers with a false sense of security that they can bake in the sun longer. Remember that the SPF disregards UVA rays so there's your first problem. Secondly, we only apply about a quarter of what is instructed on the label—likely the only bit of information on that label we should follow. Applying such small amounts would take an SPF 100 down to a 3.2, and an SPF 30 down to a 2.3.[181] A bottle of Crisco might offer more protection at that point.

THE FDA GIVES IT FOUR STARS

Advocacy groups have gone after the FDA to put tighter restrictions on sunscreens since 1978. At the time this book went to press, these restrictions included laying down some rules on UVA protection levels and SPF labels higher than fifty.[182] With these rules, sunscreen makers are required to scale their products with a UVA-protection "four-star" system—zero meaning it sucks and four meaning it offers great protection. Even this has its weakness since manufacturers wouldn't be forced to offer any UVA protection; they would just have to throw down zero stars.[183] The hope is that transparency will force these companies to start offering UVA protection to keep up with the competition. Once the FDA makes the rating system mandatory, companies will have a year to comply, which doesn't put any kind of federally regulated sunscreens on the shelves until the winter of 2012 at the earliest. Story of our lives.

Truth be told, we could all wise up ourselves. There is no doubt that ten minutes a day of unprotected sun exposure is good for us—it's a solid source of vitamin D, which protects against heart disease. But you could get ten minutes walking the dog or grabbing lunch. For all you broads who walk slow, checking the mail will get you all the vitamin D you need. But that doesn't mean you should dab on a dime-size amount of sunscreen for a whole day at the beach. Snap out of it, doll face. There's nothing healthy about that kind of exposure. Skin cancer is the most common form of cancer in this country. Take note: About 90 percent of non-melanoma skin cancers— the more common and thankfully, cureable, if treated early—are associated with sun exposure.[184] You need to wear sunscreen or you are going to have much bigger issues than a pasty face. You could also be taking some other precautions, like say, wearing a hat, popping up an umbrella, or wearing a tank top over your skanky bikini. Now there's a bright idea.

TAKE YOUR PICK: SUNSCREENS THAT MEET TOUGH STANDARDS

The best sunscreens on the market contain minerals such as zinc oxide and titanium dioxide in nanoparticle form. As active ingredients in sunscreens, they are praised for their stability and for blocking cancer-causing rays without the pale white look that only hot college lifeguards can pull off. Though some research suggests these tiny particles may be able to penetrate the body in ways larger particles can't, in cream formulations, they appear to be safe since they are not inhaled.

Another option is sunscreens that contain chemicals such as oxybenzone or 4-MBC, in lieu of nanoparticles. The issue with these sunscreens is they have a weaker stability under UV rays and may mess with your body's hormones. Even the best of the chemical sunscreens offer a maximum protection of 3 percent of UVA rays, which doesn't cut it in my book.[185] If you decide to go this route, look for avobenzone as the active ingredient and avoid the more dangerous chemicals, oxybenzone or 4-MBC.

To guide us all in choosing the most efficient sunscreens with the least health impacts, every year the Environmental Working Group (EWG) rolls out an annual Best Sunscreen Guide. It lists the healthiest leading sunscreens on the market, including both mineral and non-mineral options. As far as sunscreens go, it's one of the most reliable databases you will find. I was not, however, fully satisfied with their coveted list, so I created a companion checklist that you will find below. Yes I am anal, and you are welcome. *Visit ewg.org to find the best sunscreen for you.*

KIM'S PICKS: SUNSCREENS

Caribbean Solutions Natural Biodegradable SolGuard SPF 25 (caribbean-sol.com)

Elemental Herbs Sunscreen Sport SPF 22, Tinted. (elementalherbs.com)

Goddess Garden Natural Sunscreen SPF 30 (goddessgarden.com)

KIM'S SUNSCREEN CHECKLIST

☑ **DOES IT OFFER PROTECTION AGAINST UVA AND UVB RAYS?** Look for broad-spectrum sunscreens that go to work against both types of cancer-causing rays. Remember that SPF is not a be-all and end-all.

☑ **WHAT OTHER CHEMICALS ARE HIDING IN THERE?** You know what to do. Read the label to see how many other synthetic ingredients are in the bottle. Some of EWG's top-rated sunscreens contained dimethicone, alumina compounds, propylene glycol, alcohols, and harsh preservatives such as parabens and phenoxyethanol. Beeswax hung out in a few, as well. As usual, the fewer toxic chemicals or animal by-products, the better. *Obviously.*

☑ **IS IT WATERPROOF?** Almost all of the best sunscreens on EWG's list weren't waterproof. So if you go with one of the waterproof formulas and spend a lot of time in the water, wise up and apply every forty-five minutes to two hours, or after you get out of the water, for the best coverage.

B BITCHWORTHY:
Every year, about four to six thousand tons of sunscreen slides off our bodies and into the oceans. This doesn't only pollute the oceans with chemicals but it's killing our coral reefs. The four ingredients to blame? Parabens, cinnamate, benzophenone, and camphor.[186] Yet another reason to ditch the Coppertone and use natural sunblocks with as few chemicals as possible.

★ Nail Thank You:
NAIL POLISHES

There's a good reason your nail polish smells like your high school biology class. A disturbing 70 percent of that Fire Engine Red is packed with chemical solvents.[187] Just take a whiff, polish junkie. Like I have to ask you twice . . .

The three big red flags in your everyday nail polish—dibutyl phthalate (DBP), toluene, and formaldehyde—aren't just suspected to be hazardous.[188] Actually, there's no question they're hazardous. Extended exposure to the "toxic trio" is raising a fair share of eyebrows. Studies are showing that nail salon workers have shorter attention spans, trouble processing, breathing problems,[189] and there is a concern they may face a higher risk of getting breast cancer.[190]

THE TOXIC TRIO:
PHTHALATES, TOLUENE,
AND FORMALDEHYDE

For you nail biters, DBP is added to polish to give it that soft flexibility so your nails don't feel like paperweights. It also adds shine and prevents chipping. Sounds like they nailed it with that one, right? Not so much. DBP has been linked to cancer in lab animals and to birth defects for those of you considering having kids. It is a phthalate, people. It may be doing funky stuff to our reproductive systems and messing with our kidneys, liver, and lungs.[191]

Toluene is responsible for that smooth finish and lasting color. You can also thank it for potentially causing damage to your central nervous system,

annoying headaches, dizziness, nausea, and feeling tired for no reason. Your body also absorbs it easily, so it's just ready and waiting.[192]

And, what would a good, cheap product be without formaldehyde? Well, safer, for starters. Formaldehyde acts as a preservative that hardens and strengthens nails. The good news? It can irritate your eyes, nose, and throat on contact.[193] Yes, that's the good news. The bad news? It's a known carcinogen that the Environmental Defense Scorecard names one of the world's most hazardous compounds to both the environment and our health.[194] In some cases, formaldehyde won't be on the label, either. It may fall under urea derivatives like imidazolidinyl urea, which releases formaldehyde.[195]

The knock-down, drag-out fight to get all this shit out of our nail polish has been going on for years. In 2006, the Campaign for Safe Cosmetics went after the leading salon brand, OPI Products Inc., to pressure them into using safer chemicals. At the time, the EWG ranked OPI as one of the most toxic products in its cosmetic database. No big surprise, OPI was already reformulating for the European market to meet strict EU standards, yet the nail polish leaders weren't willing to bend for Americans. Funny what some picketing, demonstrations, and angry letters will do. OPI eventually caved and removed the entire toxic trio from their line of polishes. Orly and Sally Hansen did the same shortly after.[196] Now you can chew on your nails with a few less worries.

Big brands are biting the bullet and omitting the worst stuff, but the safest thing you can do is practice some BYOP during your next touch up. Bring Your Own Polish. It's better for you, the girl who does your nails, and the air we all breathe.

Look at you—saving the world, one nail salon at a time.

SHIT LIST:
OTHER NAIL JUNKIES

The toxic trio doesn't deserve all the credit. There are plenty of other chemicals that are more fit for industrial buildings than our hands. Check the back of the label to make sure none of these are laying low.

ACETONE This one has a familiar ring. Acetone works really well in removing the chipped crap from your nails. That would be dandy if it didn't also pollute indoor air and irritate your eyes, nose, and throat. Breathe enough of it in and it can make you feel drunk off your ass. The most ridiculous part is that acetone actually promotes nail peeling and splitting, brittleness, and skin rashes on the fingers and hands. Because it's strong enough to remove polish quickly and efficiently, manufacturers just look at its benefits.

BENZOPHENONE-1 A likely hormone disruptor found in nail polishes to brighten colors and prevent degradation from sunlight. Severe allergic reactions such as hives have prompted the CIR to take a second look at this chemical.[197]

ETHYL LACTATE This stuff is derived from lactic acid, a syrupy liquid found in the blood and muscle tissues of animals.[198] Yum!

XYLENE Added to nail products as a fragrance and solvent, this one sure screws up your lungs. Take a big whiff—xylene can be toxic when inhaled and is being investigated for possibly causing cancer. Verdict is still out.[199]

KIM'S PICKS: NAIL POLISHES SANS THE "BIG 3"

It's not just that you stick your dirty fingers in your mouth. You also wash your lady parts, rub your eyes, and scratch your ass with those fingers. Take it from me: You don't want to coat them with chemicals that cause cancer and mess with your reproductive system.

While "natural" nail polishes can still contain naughty chemicals, here are a few of the most innocent. To save yourself a lot of wasted time researching ingredients that may conceal animal by-products, look for polishes that pride themselves on being vegan.

Acquarella (acquarellapolish.com)

Zoya (zoya.com)

SpaRitual (skinstore.com)

CHAPTER 6

The Skinny: Makeup and Skincare

★ The Bitch's Bag of Tricks:

A VEGAN BEAUTY MAKEOVER

All this talk of chemicals and animal fat in your medicine cabinet is a lot to swallow. I'm with you. It wasn't long ago that I thought: the stronger a beauty product, the better. Shit, if it could degrease a car engine, just imagine what it could do to my "premature" wrinkles. I was a dumb blonde.

Then it all clicked. I didn't wake up one morning and go, "Dude, I had a dream that my lipstick is giving me cancer." No, it clicked because someone was ballsy enough to question society and talk about it. Then someone else did. Then someone else opened her mouth. It's a good thing women like to talk.

It's natural to assume that there is some higher power running the show making sure we're all safe. But sorry honey, our government trumps God here on the ground. And they're not doing anything but stomping on bills created to keep us safe.

But don't throw in the towel and tell yourself that if cancer is going to get you anyway, you might as well have good hair. There are plenty of products on the market these days that won't make you feel like a crunchy hippie, and the results are similar, if not the same. By buying these products, you'll show our useless government that we're not going to wait around for them to do something. Um, we're women. We don't like to wait.

The following products and brands are what I find right about the cosmetic industry. I use them myself, or a girlfriend uses them, or they come with the highest recommendations. No hard sell. No endorsements. No advertising dollars (I wish). These are just healthier and safer products that are competitive with any damn product behind the luxury beauty counter.

You'll find that I don't include every beauty category, because that would drive me freakin' crazy. I really just focused on my regimen. All in all, this section will speak to safer, more natural, vegan alternatives to toxic beauty products, and why you should care. Because I hope that if you are reading this, you do.

Now rinse. Lather. Scrub. Brush. Apply. Repeat. Do your body a huge favor. The payback will be sweet.

THE SKINNY: INCI STANDARDS

Just when you think you have the art of reading labels down pat, you see it: *Prunus Amygdalus Dulcis Oil*. Beg your pardon? Prunu . . . what? Are you effin' kidding me?! That isn't even English. That's right, babe. It's Latin—and all it really means is sweet almond oil.

In an effort to be honest with American consumers, some brands have taken the initiative to meet the tough standards laid down by the European Union. The EU's labeling standards—International Nomenclature for Cosmetic Ingredients (INCI)—requires all personal care brands to fully disclose *all* of the ingredients on the packaging according to their Latin names. The point is to create a level playing field and encourage a common understanding for consumers. All companies that sell personal care products in Europe and Canada have no choice but to adhere to INCI standards. But only the responsible ones have decided to offer that same respect to American consumers, even though our government doesn't make them.

Jennifer Barckley, director of corporate communications at Weleda USA, gave us a few tips on how to nail an INCI label:

READ BETWEEN THE PARENTHESES. You don't have to learn Latin, honey. Next to the multilingual name, the common English name is usually there in parentheses. For instance, sweet almond oil would be listed as: *Prunus Amygdalus Dulcis (Sweet Almond) Oil*. If you're not sure if an ingredient is natural, here's another clue: a scientific name will be followed by "oil" or "flower extract," or similar.

FRAGRANCE (PARFUM) CAN MEAN SYNTHETIC OR NATURAL. This one can be misleading, so let's fix that pronto. By EU law, all fragrances must be listed as "fragrance" or "parfum," regardless of whether they are synthetic or natural (such as essential oils). But the EU rulebook goes further. The company must also list the individual fragrance components—think of them as little ingredients within ingredients—listed on an ingredient label as a fragrance with an asterisk (see sample label). After all, they don't want you thinking they're using the artificial garbage.

Any fragrance ingredient known to cause an allergy has to be disclosed. For those of you with bad allergies, INCI might be your saving grace. There are twenty-six fragrances that the European Union believes to "cause allergies in sensitive individuals." For these, rather than tell you the common name of the fragrance, such as "rose oil," the company has to list the individual components that may cause the allergies. In this case, it's geraniol. How's that for transparency?

INGREDIENTS ARE LISTED IN ORDER OF QUANTITY. Similar to FDA standards, all ingredients have to be listed in order of quantity in the product, with the highest at the top.

NOT ALL INGREDIENTS HAVE A FANCY LATIN NAME. You'll still find common terms like propylene glycol, sodium laureth sulfate, dimethicone, methylparaben, and more. No Latin name can make them any less harmful.

It would be impossible to list all of the Latin names. There are more than seventeen thousand in the INCI system, and it keeps growing. To get a complete breakdown of each ingredient, visit Specialchem4cosmetics.com.

FACIAL CLEANSERS

I don't care how blessed you think you are, every girl needs to wash her face. All that crap you apply on your mug every morning is just part of what's on there. You're also wearing smog, dust, smoke, sweat, chemicals, dead cells, and excess oil like you paid for it at the beauty counter. And are you paying for it. Have you taken a look in the mirror lately? Whiteheads, blackheads, dryness, acne, wrinkles, and pores the size of craters. Don't kid yourself.

You don't need much to get rid of the daily grime that sits on the surface. Something gentle will do. But no, you use an industrial potion to get it clean. Congratulations. You're the reason cosmetic companies continue to spend billions in advertising every year. Because it works.

All that shit you are washing your face with is stripping it of the bad and the good. The penetration enhancers and foamy agents, preservatives, acids, and mystery fragrance all overdo it. When you add up all the different products you are trained to use, you have a mess of chemicals all competing against one another on your face like a game of dodge ball. So the products don't work as well. That's not all. Some of the stuff marketed on the bottle to fight troubled skin actually needs to sit on your face for some time to work its magic. But you're washing it right off because you're lazy.

The key is to keep it simple. Wash your face with a gentle cleanser that won't rob your face of its natural pH balance. What you need is a 100 percent plant-based soap or cleanser that won't screw with the acid mantle—the top layer of skin—and leave all the other layers open for intrusion.

Soap bars get a lot of heat for clogging pores, but there's a reason behind that nonsense. Facial soaps can be made of lard and tallow—animal fat from cows, sheep, or pigs. Gag me. The fat can clog pores and damage skin. Plenty of soap makers will tell you that the lard is chemically altered during processing, which makes it healthy to use. Let me tell you what it's "altered" with: caustic soda or lye. Sounds real safe for your skin.[200]

If you prefer liquid cleansers, look for pure or cold-pressed oils—sunflower, sesame, coconut, almond, and

WHAT'S THE DEAL WITH TONERS?

jojoba are great for cleansing—and organic herbal extracts such as sage, geranium, rosemary, or chamomile. Liquid cleansers typically call for harsher preservatives to keep them from spoiling in two weeks, so look for mild preservatives such as sodium benzoate, potassium sorbate, and glycine. Again, make sure you also stay away from artificial fragrance in both soap bars and liquid cleansers. Sometimes it's blended into natural soaps, which defeats the whole purpose.

Toners are swell at soothing irritated skin and adding extra moisture. But, alas, the big brands are still a part of the chemical conspiracy. Many of them are loaded with alcohol—isopropyl alcohol and ethyl alcohol being some of the prime poisons—which dries out and irritates skin. Other ingredients animal lovers should pass on are lactic acid and squalene, unless they come from a vegetable. Look for natural spritz toners with distilled or mineral water, and floral extracts. Other calming ingredients are rose water, witch hazel, calendula, green tea, and lavender. You can even spray over makeup for that sexed-up, dewy complexion.

KIM'S PICKS: FACIAL CLEANSERS

Terra Firma Cosmetics Face the Day Cleanser (terrafirmacosmetics.com)

OSEA Ocean Cleanser (oseaskin.com)

Suki Sensitive Cleansing Bar (sukiskincare.com)

KIM'S PICKS: TONERS

L'Uvalla Certified-Organic Eucalyptus Toner (luvalla.com)

Dr. Alkaitis Organic Herbal Toner (alkaitis.com)

BITCHWORTHY: ARCONA LOS ANGELES

OK, I'll admit it—I'm lucky to live in a city like Los Angeles. With a concentration of more green-conscious consumers, especially in Santa Monica and Venice, we can find the crème de la crème of natural skincare practically anywhere. If it weren't for the annoying traffic and outta hand rent, I'd have little to bitch about.

One of my favorites is Arcona Los Angeles, a truly natural skincare collection and holistic spa. You rarely run across such a luxurious brand that uses strictly plant-based ingredients. Everything is cosmeceutical-grade and cold-pressed so they deliver the most bang. (Plus, they give the most bomb facials.)

It's tough to pick my favorites, but I am slightly addicted to the Arcona Triad Pads. The all-in-one, cleansing-toning-moisturizing pads are made from cranberry extract and a rice milk base. They are great for a quick refresh after a jog, and a must-have in your carry-on bag (airport-security approved). Sometimes, I open the jar just for a ten-second aromatherapy fix. Hey, we all have our vices.

Arcona Triad Pads (45 pads); $30. Visit arcona.com.

THREE COMMON MYTHS IN SKINCARE:
THE GALS BEHIND GOLDEN PATH
ALCHEMY TALK ABOUT BEAUTY GIBBERISH

From the minute we were old enough to wipe our own asses, people have been putting bogus ideas into our heads. *More expensive makeup works better. Switch up your shampoo every couple weeks or your hair will look blah.* Yeah, yeah, yeah. I can't even count how many Avon reps have tried to schmooze me into buying their entire three-step program because the products are more effective as a "team." Is that right? Your words reek of commission, honey. Run along now.

Ashley Beckman and Minka Robinson Stevens—co-founders of Golden Path Alchemy—are equally sick of the beauty game of telephone. Some of the hype holds merit. But some of it is complete bullshit.

In their early twenties, the BFFs quit using their favorite products cold turkey when they realized what was in the bottles. They started to make their own in DIY fashion, and the enterprise eventually became Golden Path Alchemy. The herbal skincare line follows one big rule: If you put it on your body, it should be good enough to eat—literally. The girls grow some of their own raw materials on their organic farm in Montecito, California, and are crusaders against chemical junk in our products.

Once they got over the scare of the actual ingredients, it was clear how many other misconceptions about skincare were on the streets. So they thought it would be nice to set the record straight. How could I say no?

• **MYTH #1: Acne is caused by oily skin.** Acne is a complicated condition. It is influenced by many factors and these can vary greatly from person to person. Acne can be caused by hormonal fluctuations, birth control pills and other medications, candida, a congested liver or kidneys, allergies (wheat, gluten, dairy, corn, and soy are the top offenders), processed foods, and of course, stress. It is also important to know where your breakouts occur. In traditional Chinese medicine, this can help diagnose where the imbalance is coming from.

Oily skin is often a symptom that the skin is actually dry and dehydrated. The sebaceous glands—the guys that regulate how much oil is produced—often secrete oil to balance the skin. This usually occurs after years and years of using products that strip the skin of its natural oils. Do you remember that tight, stretched feeling you got after using an astringent toner full of alcohol, or a drying cream (benzoyl peroxide) for zits? They could have actually been contributing to your problem. If you have acne, it's about time you nourish and balance the skin so it glows. Which leads us to Myth #2 . . .

• **MYTH #2: Lotions and creams are the best moisturizers for the skin.** Oil-based serums deliver moisture to different layers of the skin without preservatives or added ingredients. The most common nourishing oils include: jojoba, sweet almond, avocado, sea buckthorn, pumpkin seed, rosehip, borage, macadamia nut, sesame, and coconut. These oils address specific concerns and deeply nourish the skin without clogging pores. Oils are cleansing to the skin and help balance it even if you are prone to acne. They regulate the skin's natural sebum production while keeping the skin looking fresh, healthy, and radiant. Ditch the petrochemicals and preservatives and go back to nature. Use cold-pressed organic oils and your skin will thank you.

FACIAL MOISTURIZERS AND ANTI-AGING SERUMS

Whether your skin produces enough oil to gas up a car, or is drier than the Sahara, moisturizers help soothe and protect it from bacteria and oxidants. Oxidants are what make you look like a senior citizen when you're thirty years old. Now you know why AARP has been stalking you to join.

Just to give you an idea of what is going on, you lose around one pint of water every day through your pores. Moisturizers help pull in and trap some of that water in the epidermis, so you don't look like an old hag. The more water that sits in that upper layer of skin, the fewer wrinkles you'll have and the longer you'll be able to convince yourself you don't need Botox. Moisturizers also work with your skin's natural hydrators (aka sebum) to make sure its protective barrier doesn't lose its mojo.

Unfortunately, most moisturizers are also loaded with chemicals. They will still trap water in, but they also trap debris, bacteria, dead skin cells, dirt, smog, sweat, and sebum under a thick film.[201] That is why your skin goes buck wild and you have to wear its revenge in public. A little tip if I will: Wear a paper bag. It will look a lot better.

Aside from the inflammation, imagine all those chemicals building up in your organs. You do apply that special cream at least once, likely twice, each day. In *one* year, that's anywhere between 365 and 750 applications. Now think about how many years you've been rubbing it in . . . Yeah, that hurts.

• **MYTH #3: The quality of your skin is no reflection of what is going on inside your body.** Everyone has heard the expression the eyes are the mirror of the soul. Well to us, the skin is a mirror of the health of the body. The skin is our largest organ and it is a direct reflection of what is going on inside. One of the functions of our skin is to eliminate toxins through sweating. Acne and hyper-pigmentation can often point to a body that has been exposed to many toxins (environmental or ingested), and hormonal fluctuations (PMS, pregnancy, birth control pills). In Chinese medicine, the face is mapped out and different areas represent different organs. For example, acne that occurs around the mouth can be associated with imbalances in the stomach or digestive system.

To get yourself some of Golden Path Alchemy's handmade herbal skincare remedies, check out goldenpathalchemy.com.

KIM'S PICKS: FACIAL MOISTURIZERS/ ANTI-AGING SERUMS

Luminos Hydrating Moisturizer by Keys Soap (keys-soap.com)

Josie Maran 100 Percent Organic Argan Oil (josiemarancosmetics.com)

Jenulence Alpha Lipoic Acid Antioxidant Serum (jenulence.com)

FACIAL MASKS

Our faces are covered in dead cells. Your body is in charge of sloughing off all this weathered skin so your mug doesn't look like cracked plaster when you smile. But, for whatever reason, this skin can get stubborn. When that happens, it forms a dry and crusty layer that starts to crack, peel, and clog up your pores. Your skin looks dull. You get beastly zits. Your makeup looks out of whack. And your boyfriend starts saying things like, "I think you're beautiful no matter what."

Too often, we try to fix the problem by dousing our faces in moisturizer, which can't break through the dead, dull layer of misery to treat the skin underneath. Or we react by exfoliating the crap out of our faces until our skin feels like a baby's ass. But even though we want to get rid of the lizard skin pronto, heavy-duty exfoliators are like sandpaper, leaving tiny tears in the skin. You think this is helping? Wise up. These tears aggravate acne and open your face up to bacteria and infection. The gritty scrubbing action also pulls and loosens skin so it gets all saggy. Another great way to age ungracefully.

What you need to do is stop the insanity and start using facial masks (and gentle exfoliators) as prevention. Daily cleansing alone gets rid of the surface debris. Still, a good, healthy facial mask every few days—maybe with some mild exfoliating action—can get rid of the junk underneath the surface. Facial masks help nudge dead cells on their way by dissolving the crusty layer, flushing out toxins, and unclogging your pores. Once you release the surface pressure, moisturizers and toners can get down deep to do what they're supposed to do—make you smokin' hot.

If you're running to the phone to book an appointment at the spa, I haven't taught you shit. While I appreciate a good pampering on occasion, spas are infamous for more intensive scrubbing and extractions that open up your pores. Sure, it's great for them to breathe. But not when they're smothered under a mask chock-full of petrochemicals, sulfates, fragrance, dyes, and preservatives.

Get real. You can mask it up from home. Hydrating masks clean deep down and add moisture to ward off wrinkles. Clay-based or mud masks are better for those with oily skin or acne trouble. The clay and mud variety actually draw blood to the surface for that special glow.

> **KIM'S PICKS: FACIAL MASKS**
>
> Dr. Alkaitis Organic Cellular Repair Mask (alkaitis.com)
>
> Arcona Wine Hydrating Mask (arcona.com)
>
> Gourmet Body Treats Chocolate Facial Mask (gourmetbodytreats.com)

> **KIM'S TIP:**
> After a good face mask or exfoliation, grab the moisturizer and go to town. The face is a sensitive flower and can dry out. Dryness= wrinkles. Save your money for a new walk-in closet, not a face-lift at forty.

FACE IT : EASY-TO-FIND INGREDIENTS FOR AT-HOME FACIALS

It's not that tough, ladies. You don't need to resort to chemical warfare to get rid of that volcano erupting on your chin. Same goes for dead, dry skin and those dark bags under your eyes. (Quit stalking ex-boyfriends on Facebook until five o' clock in the morning, and you won't look so hellish in the first place.)

All you need to do is step into your kitchen. Yeah, that place where you keep your pots and pans. There are plenty of ingredients sitting right in front of you that work doubletime on your face. And you don't have to be a natural in the kitchen to prepare these recipes—just smart enough to follow directions. Grab your lemons, and let's do this.

MAKE IT YOURSELF: PANTRY FACIALS

OILY SKIN + BLACKHEADS

What You Need: Tomatoes, Lemons, and Oatmeal

Why: Tomatoes have antioxidant qualities that can prevent skin damage and help tighten those large pores you were cursed with. If you're prone to breakouts, they also stop acne before it starts. Jesus, I sound like a damn Clearasil commercial.

Ingredients: 1 tomato, 1 tablespoon lemon juice, 2 tablespoons uncooked oatmeal

How: Peel the tomato and mash it in a bowl. Combine the tomato, lemon juice, and oatmeal in a blender and purée until blended. Apply mask to freshly cleansed skin and leave on for 15 minutes. Wash off with warm water. Pat dry.

Quick Tip: If tomatoes aren't your thang, replace with strawberries. The sweet fruit is a natural astringent.

EXFOLIATE

What You Need: Papaya and Pineapples

Why: Papaya and pineapple juice contain enzymes that soften and heal damaged skin while exfoliating. They also reduce age spots and fine lines so you can finally look your age.

Ingredients: 1 tablespoon pineapple juice and 1 tablespoon papaya juice OR 1 slice ripe pineapple and 1 slice green papaya

How : Massage the juice or fruit slices onto your face. Let it dry completely, leaving the juices on your face for about 10 minutes. (It will feel sticky!) Rinse with warm water. Pat dry.

ACNE AND BREAKOUTS

What You Need: Green Tea and Rice Flour

Why: Rice flour is awesome for treating blemishes, wrinkles, and discoloration. Green tea is full of antioxidants, helps reduce inflammation, and has a natural astringent that soothes and heals skin. A great mask to recover from an all-nighter.

Ingredients: Brewed green tea, 4 tablespoons rice flour

How: Brew a pot of green tea and let cool (leave in fridge if in a rush). Mix 3 tablespoons of the brewed green tea with the rice flour. The mixture should be smooth, but not watery. Add more tea if it's too thick. Apply the mask to your face and leave on for 15 minutes. Rinse off with water while rubbing the mask to exfoliate your skin.

> **B** **BITCHWORTHY:**
> Use a cotton ball to apply lemon or grapefruit juice for added cleansing, exfoliating, and brightening.

DRY SKIN

What You Need: Avocado and Carrots

Why: Avocados are high in vitamins A B, D, and E, and contain more potassium than a banana, which moisturizes and makes the skin smooth. Carrots have antioxidants and vitamin A to repair skin that's beat. If you're all red and splotchy, carrots also calm redness and inflammation.

Ingredients: ½ ripe avocado, 1 carrot, 1 tablespoon olive oil

How: Boil the carrot until soft and then mash. Purée the carrot with the ripe avocado and olive oil in a blender for a smooth consistency. Apply to face. Leave on for 20 minutes. Rinse with warm water. Pat dry.

FOUNDATION/CONCEALER

Some of you girls can't leave the house without full stage makeup. Gotta cover up any skin crimes or someone might realize you don't crawl out of bed a Perfect Ten every morning. Now wouldn't that be disastrous?

While tinted moisturizers sound nice in theory, most of you have more than a freckle to hide. A tint isn't going to do much for under-eye circles, discoloration, inflammation, and wrinkles. So instead, you hide all the evidence with mineral oils, waxes, silicones, parabens, and formaldehyde. Might as well slap some Vaseline on there, too. This junk may cover up the damage, but it's clogging up your pores and inviting skin problems to continue making your life a living hell.

Even worse is when you cake makeup on a zit that you went to town on the night before. It's an open wound, sweet cheeks. So not cool. Tiny tears in the skin just invite petrochemicals and toxins in to commit even more skin offenses. And think about how long cover-up sits on your face. You're not just putting it on and washing it off. These chemicals are lingering for upwards of thirteen hours, letting your skin devour them.

The snag is that it can be tough to find a good match. Most vegan foundations and concealers are a bitch to find in stores—online is where it's at. The best suggestion I can give you is to find an online retailer that offers a return policy or guarantee, and buy a few shades that are possible matches for your skin tone. Return the ones that make you look ridiculous.

What to Look For: When you're looking for a healthier foundation or concealer, there are a few things to sleep on. Do you wear a sunscreen under your makeup? Yes or no. If you're dumb enough to go commando, look for something with a sunscreen (titanium dioxide, zinc oxide, or a combo). Next look at the color— is it tinted by FD&C colors or carmine? Sick. Don't put your face through that. Speaking of dead bugs, was that product tested on any animals? Don't just take their word for it. Seek out the PETA cruelty-free Leaping Bunny logo. Beeswax, collagen, and cholesterol from animals are also common in foundations. Look for a cover-up that uses natural dyes and pigments from fruits, plants, vegetables, minerals, or algae. The best foundations are made primarily with herbal extracts and plant oils such as shea butter, jojoba oil, and almond oil.

**KIM'S PICKS:
FOUNDATION/CONCEALER**

Beauty Wise Corrective Liquid Foundation
(holisticbeauty.net)

Suncoat Natural Liquid Foundation
(suncoatproducts.com)

Gabriel Powder Concealer
(gabrielcosmeticsinc.com)

TO INHALE OR NOT TO INHALE: THE LOWDOWN ON MINERAL MAKEUP

Mineral makeup couldn't have come into our lives at a better time. We were looking for something more natural, and here it was—just simple ingredients and pigments derived from the earth. But its shit still stinks.

No regulations govern the labeling of mineral makeup and there is no definition for what in the world it means. So companies take that as permission to use their imagination. With no boss around, they are mixing so-called earth-derived ingredients with synthetic chemicals and slapping the "mineral" on the label.[202] Another shocker. These "natural" products can carry another ingredient that may be "derived from the earth," but, vegan or not, we'd be sick to want it on our faces. Dead beetles (aka carmine) are very popular road kill in mineral makeup. Carmine has also been shown to cause allergic contact facial dermatitis. [203]

NANOPARTICLES

The biggest debate is over micronized powder, or nanoparticles, in mineral makeup. Nanoparticles are tiny, itty-bitty particles about one-thousandth the thickness of a strand of human hair. In a cream or liquid form, like that of sunscreen, these nanoparticles may not be as hazardous as you think. It's not loose in the air for you to inhale, but in dust form, have mercy. These particles are inhaled and then go after our lungs.[204] One of the most potent minerals, titanium dioxide is a possible carcinogen. Other less melodramatic minerals are zinc oxide, mica, and bismuth oxychloride.

HANDLING MINERALS WITH CARE

Enough with all the bashing. Mineral makeup also has its fair share of benefits, too. It's less likely to cause allergic reactions, and can be free of most chemicals. The goal is to get one that is as "pure" as possible.

GO FOR LIQUID MINERAL MAKEUP. To rid yourself of the fears of inhaling tiny chemicals, consider liquid mineral foundations, bronzers, concealers, and eye shadows. Since they're not airborne, they are tougher to breathe in.

AVOID THE SYNTHETICS. If you love mineral makeup, warts and all, look for products without all the toxic by-products such as talc, parabens, synthetic dyes, carmine, and FD&C colors. You can't have it all, though. Most mineral loose powders contain either titanium dioxide, zinc oxide, mica, or bismuth oxychloride. My best suggestion is to steer clear of the potentially cancer-causing titanium dioxide, and opt for the latter three.

SKIP THE NANOS. There are plenty of studies and research to be done before we know the true effects of nanoparticles. If you want to play it safer, look for non-nano minerals that are larger than one hundred nanometers.

KIM'S PICKS: MINERAL MAKEUP

Sevi Eco Vegan Bodycare (ecosevi.com)

Earth's Beauty (earthsbeauty.com)

Monave (monave.com)

Erth Minerals Warm Bronzer (lushbrush.com)

BLUSH

Why deal with being pale when we can breathe instant life into our cheekbones and T-zones? Pucker those lips like a goldfish, and ta da! You look like you have a 105-degree fever.

Blush has spoiled us silly. And I'm all for being spoiled. Just not when it involves lead, arsenic, tons of artificial dyes, and other toxic waste.[205] Cream or powder, blush is one of the worst offenders in our makeup bags. In loose powder blushes, that rosy hue may be made from talc, which can be contaminated with asbestos—a set of toxic minerals that have been banned in the European Union, New Zealand, and Australia for suspicious links to ovarian and lung cancer.[206] But not in the United States! Trace amounts can still be found in your everyday consumer product. The EPA tried to ban asbestos in 1989, but the ruling was overturned two years later.[207]

Creams are no better. Aluminum starch octenylsuccinate (ASO) is a thickening and anti-caking agent in both whipped and powder blushes that have activists flipping out. The aluminum may poison the nervous system and organs. There's also some genuine concern it's polluted with heavy metals. ASO earns a big fat "9" on the Environmental Working Group's scale of hazardous chemicals, with the worst being a "10."[208]

What to Look For: Vegan blushes in cream form with fruit or natural pigments. When possible, avoid synthetic FD&C color additives and carmine. If you're having trouble finding powder or cream vegan blushes without nano minerals, my best suggestion is to opt for iron oxides rather than titanium dioxide.

> ### KIM'S PICKS: BLUSHES
> **Coastal Classic Creations Blushes**
> (coastalclassiccreations.com)
>
> **Rejuva Minerals Organic Botanicals**
> (rejuvaminerals.com)

EYE MAKEUP: EYE SHADOW/ EYE LINER/MASCARA

Go ahead and cake some more gunk on those eyelids. Aside from your cooch, your eyelids have the thinnest skin on the entire body.[209] What do you think that paper-thin skin is capable of absorbing? Some cuckoo shit, I tell ya.

It's the same obnoxious story as your blushes and mineral makeup. Eye shadows and liner can be made with lead, arsenic,[210] talc, FD&C colors,[211] carmine, and oxides. Carmine has been shown to cause allergic contact dermatitis on the eyelids and face.[212] Nothing says "window to the soul" like a bright red rash. Eye shadows may also flaunt the same notorious ingredients that can produce 1,4-dioxane and release formaldehyde.[213]

As for your batty lashes, contrary to what you may think, they weren't made solely to get you out of speeding tickets. They're there to keep the wrong stuff out—sweat, debris, dust, the usual. But, unfortunately for you, your eyelashes aren't smart enough to know the difference between dust and the popular foreign invaders in your mascara—lyral,[214] rayon, paraffin,[215] wax thickeners, dyes,[216] and nerve-damaging preservatives.[217]

We seem to forget that our eyes have a key function, and being target practice for carcinogens isn't one of them. They are there to spread tears and other juices on the eyeball to keep it moist. When you paint makeup all over your lids and lashes like it's Halloween, some of that crap is destined to find its way in. When it doesn't get flushed out, you end up with funky eye infections you used to get when you were a kid, including conjunctivitis (aka pink eye) and styes. Only you're a grown woman now and didn't contract it on the playground. Another common condition is blepharitis. Quit trying to sound it out. All you need to know is it leads to blurred vision, itchiness, redness, out-of-control tearing, and light sensitivity. It also makes your eyes burn and swell like a water balloon.[218] Open your goddamn eyes. You see the world with these two holes in your head. Putting a dozen toxic chemicals on your lids is about as smart as a blind dude driving a school bus.

What to Look For: Cruelty-free shadows with natural ingredients and pigments in lieu of synthetic dyes. A few of my favorite brands come in crushed minerals with zero nanoparticles. As for clean, vegan mascaras, I'm not going to lie: It's not easy to find one that packs a punch. It's not exactly Voluminous, if you know what I mean. You may have to settle for one chemical or another, but the goal is to get as pure as possible. Some of my favorite brands are chock-full of vitamins and herbal extracts, and made with kaolin clay and earth pigments.

KIM'S PICKS:
EYE SHADOWS/LINERS/MASCARAS

No Miss All Natural Vegan Eye Shadows
(nomiss.com)

Coastal Classic Creations Eye Shadows
(coastalclassiccreations.com)

Erth Minerals Eye Shadows (lushbrush.com)

Suncoat Natural Mascara
(suncoatproducts.com)

ZuZu Luxe Mascara (gabrielcosmetics.com)

METAL IN MY LIPSTICK

Maybe it's just me, or maybe it's Maybelline, but there are some things that shouldn't be near our lips. Filet mignon. Diet Coke. Sweet'N Low. But *lead?* That seems more like a bogus urban legend.

Back in 2003, an e-mail hoax claimed that you could test for "cancer-causing" lead in lipstick by just scratching it with a 24K gold ring. If the lipstick turned black, you had a winner. How fun. But after a while, the verdict was in: This urban legend was false.

Fast forward to 2007, and suddenly the status of the lipstick challenge had changed. Now it read: *mostly false.* What the hell did "mostly" mean? Exactly what we were hoping it didn't mean. The Campaign for Safe Cosmetics had decided to do a bit of its own detective work, and sent thirty-three popular brands of lipstick to the lab. "Mostly," as it turns out, was a compliment.[219] Sixty-one percent of the lipsticks contained the heavy metal, including some of the biggest names in beauty, such as L'Oreal's Colour Riche, and Cover Girl's Incredifull. Price didn't matter. Not a trace of lead was found in Wet 'n Wild's cheapo tube. But it did pop up in Dior's pricey $24 red stain.[220] The same company that makes a perfume called "Poison." Shocking.

After that, the FDA finally lifted a finger and decided to do some testing themselves. They found lead in every sample of lipstick they tested, at levels four freakin' times higher than what the first study revealed. Screw lip service. We were getting lead service.

As you probably know by now, lead is out to kill you. It is a known neurotoxin[221] and carcinogen that is poisonous in all forms. Experts say it is the most hazardous of all the heavy metals because it accumulates in the body with some pretty nasty side effects. To name a few, you got muscle weakness, numbness, depression, brain damage, coma, and death.[222] Studies have even linked lead to a lowered IQ. Expectant mothers and kids see the worst of it, since the brain is still developing.[223] Not to mention it's been linked to miscarriage and infertility.[224] Small detail.

A slew of industry peeps jumped on their soapbox to dismiss public concerns as a joke, claiming that lead was present in such "miniscule amounts that it has no adverse effects on consumers."[225] Doctors have agreed, citing that the FDA approves and allows trace levels of heavy metals—including lead—in lipsticks as color additives, so we need to calm down.[226] My question is: *Are you sure you want to be name-dropping the FDA to support your case? The same guys who allow levels of lead in candy?*[227] Get back to me when you have some real support.

Despite all the baloney that it's barely even there in lipstick, get this shit: The EWG estimates that we eat about nine pounds of lipstick over the course of our lifetime. As in nine *somebody hand me a goddamn Xanax* pounds.[228]

The notion that lead is something we don't want near our bodies is not revolutionary. Lead was banned in paint in the late 1970s,[229] then in gasoline almost twenty years later.[230] The European Union has banned it in cosmetics. The Canadians? Hold on a minute. Yep, banned in cosmetics there, too.[231] California tried to ban it in 2008; it passed the state senate but didn't stand a chance against industry lobbying. But in the United States, it's still a-okay.[232]

So let me get this straight. We ban lead in paint and gasoline, and apparently, every other country on this planet seems to know it's straight up the work of the devil. Yet the most powerful country in the world can't accept that maybe it's not safe to slather all over our lips? Looks like the decision makers in this country have been wearing too much lipstick.

Whether we're wearing it or painting our bedrooms with it, there really is no safe level of lead exposure. No safe level has been identified by the EPA.[233] Ever. The only levels we have to go by are the levels of lead allowed in candy—and that just feels flat-out wrong.

We can read labels until our lips turn red, but we won't find lead as an ingredient. Why? Well, because beauty companies are only required to list the intended ingredients.[234] Companies claim lead is not added "intentionally," since it is found in color pigments that are considered harmless.[235] Great cover-up.

There is something we can do, though. We can scream like lunatics that this is not cool and tell everyone to pass it on. I find that always works in my favor. We can also write these companies and tell them that while we'd be delighted to get lead poisoning, it won't look too good with this season's eye shadows. Or we can buy cleaner brands. I vote for all three.

A little surfing on the Internet will lead you to plenty of brands that haven't tested positive for lead, but I did some further research. Half of these brands—even Tarte cosmetics, one of the proud wearers of Sephora's "Naturally Sephora" seal—didn't contain lead but the rest of the ingredients were nothing to brag about. Read my lips: phenoxyethanol, titanium oxide, a handful of synthetic dyes, and PEG.[236] I'll pass.

To top it all off, you will find that most lipsticks contain beeswax, carmine, and lanolin—big vegan caution signs. So I did the work for you. Here are a few animal-friendly, lead-free brands that have become my go-to for a nice pucker.

KIM'S PICKS: LIPSTICKS

ZuZu Luxe Lipstick (store.veganessentials.com)

Organic Rosehip Lipstick (naturallysafe.com.au)

Ecco Bella Flowercolor Lipstick (ecobella.com)

PUT ON A FRESH FACE:

JESSA BLADES SHOWS YOU
HOW TO PLAY NICELY
(WITH MAKEUP)

Jessa Blades used to be on the "other" side, working for the big cosmetic brands, before she defected to the "good guy" camp. As the founder of Blades Natural Beauty, she no longer questions what she's putting on women's faces. Ain't that a sweet feeling. With an impressive roster of clients in New York City, Jessa can easily be credited with pushing natural into the mainstream market. She also pays it forward by educating women on the importance of what they put on their bodies through personal makeup lessons and shopping consultations. A true *Skinny Bitch* herself, Jessa was nice enough to offer a few insider secrets.

Use foundation just where you need it. Foundation and concealer don't need to feel like a mask. I like to use a cream concealer or foundation and focus it under the eyes, around the nose, and on the chin; then blend it out toward the sides of the face. After you have applied it to the areas that need it most, you might find that you don't actually need as much product as you thought you did. Loose powder is great for setting the foundation and can sometimes give a more natural look. But pressed powder is much more convenient for travel.

Use mascara to frame the face. Mascara is one of my favorite ways to frame and wake up the face without using too much makeup. After you coat both the top and bottom lashes, make sure to use a wand to separate the lashes to avoid clumping. My favorite trick? Take an old mascara tube headed for the trash. Take out the wand and wash it in some soap, let it dry, and voilà! You have your very own mascara brush to use for combing out your lashes.

Use lip liner as a base color. I like to use liner as a base for adding more color and helping lipstick last longer. Moisturize the lips with a natural liner and let that sink in. Then add the liner to your whole lip, and add your lipstick. This is also helpful because natural lipstick won't last eighteen hours without the usual synthetic ingredients. A natural liner will help it bind to the lips. Liners can also add a lot more choices to your lip color options. If you fill your lips in with a red liner and then top with a clear gloss, you have a light red wash of color on your lips. Or you could fill in with the red, and then put a dark purple lipstick. The red base warms up a purple lipstick and makes it more dynamic and versatile. You double the amount of color options by just adding one or two lip liners to your makeup bag.

Don't be afraid of bronzer. Most everyone looks better with a warm, healthy glow. Be sure to find one without shimmer or glitter. And keep on the brown side; stay away from orange ones. Apply it to the high planes of your face where you normally get the most sun—the cheeks, forehead, and nose. Then blend all of those spots together.

Make your own rules. Makeup is about looking like the best version of yourself. Imagine what you look like on vacation: you have been outside, you are well hydrated, happy, and healthy. I like to show people how to use makeup to bring that glow back—and have fun with it!

Get to know Jessa and check out her blog at bladesnaturalbeauty.com.

★ Confessions of a Makeup Hoarder:
SHELFLIFE OF NATURAL MAKEUP

Sometimes we just have to throw in the towel. Call it quits. Admit to ourselves that while it felt real freakin' good, it's just not working out anymore. Don't let the door hit you in the ass.

But it's really hard to do with our makeup. If that bronzer's not covered in fuzzy mold spores, then why shouldn't it still give us that healthy glow? A glow, maybe. But healthy? Good try.

Makeup isn't meant to grow old with you. It's not even meant to last from bikini to trench coat season. Use it for a few months, then be thankful for the time you had together.

This is especially true with more natural and cruelty-free cosmetics. Because natural makeup doesn't traditionally contain all the harmful synthetic shit or animal by-products that extend the shelf life, it needs to be tossed out with the trash sooner than usual. The alternative is not pretty. Makeup past its expiration date can cause dangerous infections and skin irritations that can be painful and, even worse, make you look like a troll.

Think about your foundation and powder for a second. Bacteria or yeast can build up in makeup that is past its heyday, leading to a slight disorder called perioral dermatitis—little red bumps that form a rash around your eyes, mouth, and nose. It's itchy, uncomfortable, and makes you look like a 13-year-old with a bad case of cystic acne. And you thought your Clearasil days were behind you.

And who woulda thunk: You don't need to knock boots with a few random dudes to contract herpes. Even if you don't see signs of puss-filled cold sores, people can harbor a strain of the sexually contracted disease on their lips. The virus can be transmitted through lipsticks, lip gloss, or balms, so next time someone asks you to share, politely decline. As for in-store testers, don't get me started. I speak my peace.

Generally, the lifespan of organic makeup is three to six months, but there are many factors that play a role. Ask a cosmetic professional at the makeup counter, check the back of the label, or call the company to be sure how much time you have.

PAO: PERIOD AFTER OPENING

You really don't have to take a guess as to when your makeup is dunzo. Look for the PAO or "Period After Opening" symbol on the label, front of the package, or on the bottom of the product. It looks like a preschool drawing of a jar with the lid off, and will include a number and symbol inside the open jar. Hint: that's the shelf life. In other words, this is how long you got with that product from the day you open it.

Let's practice, shall we? If you find a shampoo you are crazy about, and it says "12 M," this implies it is safe to use for twelve months, or one year, from the day you pop the lid off.

The PAO symbol isn't found on all cosmetics, but it's a growing trend. Since the European Union is required to include such labeling on beauty products with a shelf life of thirty months or more,[237] you will find it on all products made by international companies.

MAKING IT LAST

Though you have to trust your gut when you think some-thing in your makeup bag has gone to a better place, there are some general rules. Sometimes you just have to let go. Honey, it's makeup. You can get through this.

TIP #1: DON'T HOLD ON TO EYE MAKEUP AND MASCARA FOR MORE THAN A SEASON. Mascara actually has the shortest lifespan and is highly vulnerable to bad bacteria. Your eye shadows and liquid eyeliners are not far behind. Experts say to toss them every three months, and never, ever share with friends. Clumpy and dried-out mascara is a good sign that its time is up, even if it's only been a month.

TIP #2: PUT YOUR LIQUID FOUNDATION IN THE REFRIGERATOR. It's typically time to kiss liquid foundation goodbye after three months, but to rack up a longer shelf life, store it in the fridge. It keeps the product from separating and can double its lifespan.

TIP #3: SHAVE PENCILS. For eyeliner and lip liner pencils, just sharpen off the top every one to two weeks to reduce bacteria build-up.

TIP #4: GO WITH THE SMELL TEST. The first sign that your makeup has gone to a better place is when it starts to smell funny. By funny, I mean *strange*. At that point, it is beyond salvation. Just part ways and move on.

TIP #5: TOSS YOUR MAKEUP BAG (OR GIVE IT A GOOD CLEANING). I don't give a damn if Anna Wintour signed your makeup bag during New York Fashion Week, get a new one every six months. That pouch is prime breeding ground for bacteria. If you're too attached, the far more intensive route is to scrub the inside with an old toothbrush and a chem-ical-free laundry or dish detergent. Let it dry for a few hours and spritz the interior with a natural antibac-terial spray before putting your makeup back in. Sidenote: You can also toss in the washing machine if the label gives the OK.

TIP #6: APPLY MAKEUP WITH A COSMETIC SPONGE, APPLICATOR, OR COTTON SWAB. Don't use your dirty fingers to get makeup out of a tube or whatever snazzy container it came in. Washing your hands is no excuse. This is how bac-teria make the rounds. A little birdie once told me to scrape the foundation off with a brush or applicator and then put on your finger to apply to your face. Aestheticians also suggest tossing your makeup sponges every week.

★ Cosmetic Tools for Animal Lovers

Your makeup bag could be a petting zoo. Sure, it may not seem like the most obvious place for a farm animal, but chances are it's singing *ee-i-ee-i-oh*, sweetheart.

It might come as a rude awakening, but conventional cosmetic brushes are made from animal hair, particularly the tails or coats of horses, squirrels, minks, goats,[238] rabbits, and sables.[239] Don't let anybody tell you it's just hair—the hair is a by-product of mindless animal cruelty. Farmers aren't just pulling out the scissors and giving animals haircuts like Little Bo Beep. Goats and sheep are shorn by careless workers for their hair. Mink and sable are raised in fur farms, where they are beaten, drowned, electrocuted, and skinned alive. Squirrels are trapped and killed for their coats.[240] It's a sick circle of life.

If fur coats aren't your thing, makeup brushes from Old MacDonald's farm probably aren't either. There are plenty of conscious companies that offer 100 percent synthetic bristles, and don't believe in animal testing or exploiting animals. It works out for your skin and health, too. Animal hairbrushes can be crawling with dead skin cells and bacteria.

Make sure you invest in companies you know you can trust. If they claim they are "vegan" or "cruelty-free," look for PETA's cruelty-free Leaping Bunny logo. You can always cruise their database at PETA.org for companies who are doing the right thing.

While I'm not one to smile on products made from petroleum, synthetic taklon fiber bristles are your only option if you don't want to powder your face with a dead squirrel. You can also find brushes made from recyclable or biodegradable materials, such as aluminum or bamboo handles. Not to throw another wrench into the works, but keep in mind that "natural" bristles don't stand for plant-based; it often means silk, goat hair, or a mixture of both. Double-check with the company or see if you can find any details on the package.

♥ KIM'S PICKS: MAKEUP BRUSHES

For a cruelty-free mug, check out these options:

EcoTools (parispresents.com)

Branded J. (brandedjcollections.com)

Aveda (aveda.com)

The Body Shop (thebodyshop-usa.com)

CLEANING MAKEUP BRUSHES

Ask yourself the last time you cleaned your makeup brushes. If you're pleading the fifth, listen up. Most experts recommend washing them once a week. Yes, a week. Would you go more than a week without washing your hair? I sure hope not. If you are too busy to avoid a Staph infection, suck it up and clean them before you go to bed so they can dry overnight.

Follow these steps to ensure they get extra clean, and not just waterlogged.

Step 1: Soak in a solution of castile soap and apply a dab of conditioner for an extra-soft feel for 2 minutes (some people use olive oil or tea tree oil instead of conditioner). Give them a good swirl to watch the makeup lift from the brushes. Do not leave them hangin' for any more than 5 minutes.

Step 2: Squeeze a nickel-sized drop of castile soap and a teaspoon of water in the palm of your hand (preferably distilled water). Then swish the brushes, one by one, in the solution, rinsing and repeating until you don't see any signs of makeup. When they look as clean as a whistle, give them a final rinse in warm water.

Step 3: Squeeze any water out and let them dry on a towel. Fluff them a few times to make sure they don't get too stiff while drying. Do not, I repeat, *do not* use a blow dryer to dry them quicker; it just makes the bristles coarse and brittle.

Part III: Your Style

Your mama lied to you. There are plenty of monsters hiding in your closet. Don't be a chicken—open those doors and take a good look. They're called your clothes, and you think you look so damn cute in them.

Oh, I'm sorry. Are these not the monsters you had in mind? My, isn't that unfortunate.

Every day, we walk out of the house with the weight of the world on our backs. From the cotton T-shirts and jackets, to jeans and shoes, to handbags and purses, we're talking about an industry that is cruel to animals, our bodies, and that great, big world.

The apparel and footwear industries present so many dilemmas for the conscious shopper: sourcing, transportation, brutal chemical processing, waste and pollution, animal cruelty, unfair labor practices, even marketing bunk (yes, the clothing industry is jumping on the "organic" and "natural" train, too).

COTTON ... *AGAIN*

If you live in comfortable tees and jeans like me, you're a part of the ugly cotton cycle. It's a massive business. Cotton meets almost half of the world's textile needs.[1] That would be splendid if it wasn't also the most toxic crop on the planet.[2] Every year, cotton fields ask for more than $2 billion worth of hazardous fertilizers, pesticides, and insecticides.[3] It also promotes child labor in some countries[4] and sucks up a wicked amount of water. Water that could, hey, I don't know, maybe go to the almost one billion people in the world who have no clean drinking water.[5] Just a thought.

Synthetic fabrics like polyester and nylon don't fare much better. They're both made from petroleum (though some polyester is now made from recycled plastic bags). Plus, they require some pretty intensive chemicals to get hangar-ready.

THE CLOSET THAT MOOOOS AND OINKS

Turns out we're not just putting farm animals in our mouths. We're wearing them, too. Fur, leather, wool, silk, and down are all popular materials in a fashionista's wardrobe. The animals in our clothes, shoes, and handbags aren't just a by-product of the food industry, either. Many of them are killed solely for the purpose of making you look good in those boots on Friday night.[6] Face it, there's little difference between eating it and wearing it.

Choosing not to wear animals ain't just a "thang" against cruelty. It's also something for environmentalists to think about. Since livestock and poultry production accounts for 51 percent of greenhouse gas emissions, kicking animals out of your closet can shrink your carbon footprint. Just ask Natalie Portman, Alicia Silverstone, Pamela Anderson, Ellen DeGeneres, and Jenny McCarthy.[7] A meat- and dairy-free lifestyle isn't restricted to their plates. They wear it well, too.

THE WASTEFUL
MANUFACTURING PROCESS

Petroleum, cows, and pesticides are not even the half of it. Textiles go through a hellish cycle to get them ready for the storefront: bleaching, drying, straightening, stain and wrinkle resistance, deodorizers, shrink reduction, fireproofing, [deep breath] and mothproofing. Not done yet. Then manufacturers add detergents, disinfectants, resins, and deadly chemicals to finish them off. Do you really think that none of these residues stick to your clothing and rub off on your skin? Sit there and play stupid if you like.

Experts have found that clothes imported from other countries are often embedded with disinfectants. Meaning, it's in their chemical makeup.[8] Well, guess what? Ninety-freakin' percent of America's clothing comes from somewhere else.[9] It may be grown here, but then we ship it overseas to get dyed, bleached, and prepped, just for it to be sent back to us. I know we're extremely efficient. The international safety standards when shipping into the United States are not what we would call "up to par." One study found that only 53 percent of the garments exported from China to other countries met safety health standards. It gets a little uglier, though. When they tested the threads, they found formaldehyde at levels nine hundred times more than the levels known to affect humans.[10] Nine times, I could handle. But nine hundred? Holy shit.

Throughout this chapter, we're going to have a heart-to-heart about all of these fashion emergencies. But first, some transparency. The apparel and footwear industries are still working out the kinks. It can still be hairy to find animal-friendly threads that don't call on synthetic fabrics. And vice versa. Some of the most eco-friendly alternatives are made with wool. You're going to have to make some tough choices here and you may have to decide between being cruelty-free or environmentally friendly. I'm not gonna judge.

Cost is another factor. Since eco fabrics are more costly to produce, you will pay accordingly. Say farewell to cheap mall shops and shoe outlets. However, you will find fake fur alternatives at these run-of-the-mill stores if you go cruelty-free.

That said, being a more conscious chick doesn't have to cost you much at all. Thrift shops, vintage stores, and clothing swaps are all the new rage. Everybody's doing it. I will also give you some tips on upcycling—taking something you're bored with and making it into something awesome—so you can save your money for the tables in Vegas.

Now, who's ready to play dress up?

THE SHIT LIST

The Worst Fabrics and Materials in Your Closet

BLEACH

Apparel manufacturers don't just use bleach to get your clothes disturbingly white. Bleach is also used to get rid of waxes, bacteria, and natural colors that would otherwise make the final product look funky. Fabricators often bleach the hell out of traditional cotton and other natural fibers with nasties such as sodium hypochlorite (chlorine bleach).[11]

Bleach is nuts. Even in the smallest amounts, it irritates and burns skin, and damages tissues. Sodium hypochlorite is the one with the worst cred. It's a known mutagen.[12] Do you know what that means? It has superhuman abilities to alter your DNA and living cells.[13] This, kids, is how you get cancer and other life-threatening diseases.[14]

Bleach makers may try to convince you that bleach doesn't *contain* dioxins.[15] That may be. But they sure do release them into the environment during the manufacturing process.[16] These toxic by-products end up in groundwater, soil, and the food chain. When it's in our food chain, it works its way back up to us. Don't you doubt it. Chlorine also plays a big part in acid rain, and the depletion of our ozone layer and global warming.[17]

COTTON

We're all for saving a buck in this country, and cotton is cheap. But the price on the tag is only half of what you're really paying. When you put down your money for the average "100 percent" cotton tee, you're really only getting about 73 percent cotton. The other 27 percent is pesticides and cancer-causing residues.[18] Once this cotton goes into production to make you those tighty-whities or baby tee, it has to be bleached and doused in chemicals to get rid of the harmful gunk.[19] Think about how nicotine patches work. You stick them on your arm and your skin inhales the active chemicals to pass to your bloodstream. This isn't any different. Your skin is eating that chemical shit right up.

FABRIC DYES

Most of the dyes in our threads come from petroleum or coal. You don't say? These dyes can be packed with all sorts of chemicals including caustic soda, heavy metals, formaldehyde (no shit?), dioxins,[20] and acids.[21] Artificial dyes are doted on for making colors last longer, but exposure to them has also been linked to headaches, rashes, diarrhea, muscle pain, dizziness, fatigue, and difficulty breathing.[22]

Here's where that whole natural and synthetic debate comes into play. Natural dyes can be made from plant-based materials. But they can also come from carmine.[23] Yep, the crushed dead bugs can be lingering in your miniskirt, too. Natural dyes or "dye-free" are the best alternatives, but not so easy to find. You'll find that even the most conscious of denim makers are still having trouble finding nontoxic dyes that get you that baby blue hue.

FLAME RETARDANTS

Manufacturers are *real* concerned about our kids. So concerned they add flame retardants to clothes to make sure they don't go up in flames. The manufacturers don't really have a choice. Federal regulations require that any item of children's sleepwear be flame-resistant, but how they get them fireproof is up to them.

There is a gang of flame retardants on the market used in clothing. PBDEs have been linked to lower IQ in kids,[24] while proban, a toxic fireproof coating for cotton, stays effective in clothing material for more than thirty-five washes. Nomex is a flame-resistant fiber that was introduced by none other than Dupont.[25] Wool, on the other hand, is naturally fire resistant but it's a product of animal cruelty.

Your best bet is to go with 100 percent organic fabrics. By definition, they can't contain any toxins or chemicals.

FORMALDEHYDE RESIN

We meet again, formaldehyde. (Don't you wish you could just "de-friend" this mo-fo on Facebook?! Jeez!) Clothing manufacturers use this, then they use it again, then one more time to make sure we never have to take care of our clothes. It's mixed with urea—yes, animal piss—to make clothing wrinkle-, mildew- and stain-resistant, water-proof, anti-static, and free of odors.[26] Studies have found that even after two washes, the levels of formaldehyde don't fade at all.[27] It's some persistent stuff.

Wearing something bathed in formaldehyde can easily find its way under your skin. It causes contact dermatitis, which is like living with one big rash.[28] The major issue is that formaldehyde can "sensitize" people, so even the slightest exposure to the cracked-out chemical can encourage allergic reactions. Symptoms include nausea and headaches. Oh, and before I forget, it causes cancer. The end.[29]

PERFLUORINATED CARBONS (PFCs)

PFCs are used to make clothes stain resistant. The most notorious PFC is perfluorooctanoic acid (PFOA). It's the controversial chemical used to make nonstick cookware that has seen the inside of the courtroom on multiple occasions.[30] The biggest manufacturers have agreed to start phasing PFCs out of cookware, but what about your clothes? Nah. In animal studies, they have caused liver, pancreatic, testicular, and breast tumors.[31] Hey, here's a bright idea: Quit spilling coffee on yourself, ya klutz. Then you wouldn't need a stain repellant.

RAYON

Rayon comes from wood pulp that undergoes an intense process to convert it to artificial fiber. The cellulose is dipped in harsh solvents like sodium hydroxide, then treated with carbon disulfide, then soaked again in the solvent. Only 50 percent of the chemical is recovered during the process, and the rest chills out in the environment.[32]

SYNTHETIC FABRICS: POLYESTER, NYLON, AND ACRYLIC

Polyester may have been more popular in your mama's closet, but it's still making the rounds. Probably because it's cheap. And let's be honest, we are fickle consumers so cheap is good. Polyester also lasts a long time, and resists mold and mildew. While everything sounds peachy, polyester is a form of plastic derived from petroleum. It requires a shitload of energy to produce—about twice as much as cotton for virgin polyester and 65 percent more for recycled polyester.[33]

If you're a fan of polyester, look for polyester made from recycled plastics or used clothes. It still consumes some energy and chemicals in the "recycling" process, but I'd rather you wear recycled polyester than leather, honey. You can also hit up thrift stores, and then you're really closing the loop.

Other petroleum-based materials that get a lot of play in our closets are nylon and acrylic. Nylon calls on a handful of toxic chemicals during production, which release nitrous oxide into the atmosphere.[34] Plus, there is no system in place to recycle it, so it just sits in the landfills for generations.[35] Acrylic fabrics don't fare much better—they come from polycrylonitriles, which are suspected to be carcinogenic.

The Vegan Taboos:
CRUELTY FABRICS AND MATERIALS

You would look so much hotter in something that didn't formerly breathe. Or something that didn't get beat down for our fashion no-nos. Get a clue. If you had some real style, you'd be digging through the vintage racks and wearing something with timeless class. Your leather motorcycle jacket just screams *crass*.

Just in case you're not familiar with the dead animals in your closet, here are a few of the materials you shouldn't throw your cash at.

DOWN

To revisit, down feathers are plucked inhumanely from the breasts of ducks and geese while they are still alive to preserve the quality of the feathers. Birds go through this torture not once, not twice, but three to five times during their life. Once they've been plucked to death, we send them off to be slaughtered for their meat.

Down Alternatives: Down is expensive, woman. Pocket that stash, and look for synthetic down and polyester fill.

FUR

Every year, the fur industry alone slaughters and kills more than fifty million animals for fashion.[36] Raccoons, dogs, foxes, mink, and chinchillas are all part of the trade. That's a lot of suffering for you to look good in a coat that wasn't even cool in the '80s. *Skinny Bitch* readers may recall that there are actually fur factory farms. Animals suffer in cages, and then to make sure the coat doesn't get soaked in blood, fur traders use cruel methods such as gassing, anal electrocution, and neck-breaking to get what they need. Does this sound like a nice way to live? Um, no.

Millions of other wild animals are also trapped in nature using steel-jaw and body-crushing traps, and wire neck snares. Hunters will wait for days to claim their catch. Not because they were busy making cookies with the wifey, but just so the animal is dehydrated, hungry, and scared enough to be beaten to death without a fight.

These traps can't really tell the difference between a fox and an endangered species, either. It just traps them, puts the animal through a mess of suffering, and then they die. Endangered or not, this is flat-out wrong. In China and other Asian nations, companion animals are used for clothing, accessories, and trinkets. We're talking stolen pets, strays, and domestic animals put through the unthinkable for shit we're gonna get bored of by next season.

SEALS

Seals fall under the fur category, but I thought they deserved to be singled out. More than 300,000 seals are hunted in Canada every year for their soft fur. The Canadian's little annual game of hide-and-seek is the largest slaughter of marine animals on earth. We don't need seal products. It's just a sadistic hobby for ruthless men with small egos (Little Man's Syndrome!). The seals—many just a few weeks old—are shot or beaten to death with a club, and sometimes skinned alive for the sake of style.[37]

Fur Alternatives: It's cheesy as hell, but if you must flaunt fur, buy the fake stuff. Nobody is going to know the difference. Fake furs come in acrylic and polyester fabrics.

LEATHER

The leather industry makes a killing off of us. Every year, more than one billion animals are slaughtered solely for their skins and hides.[38]

Most of the leather products in the United States come from cows. When cows aren't looking too hot, farmers may decide that they are too weak or sick for people to eat. So, they let them starve with no water or care until they drop off. If they refuse to die, then they're slaughtered, and sometimes skinned alive. Farm animals such as calves and lambs are often inhumanely killed solely for more "superior" leather products. Like what . . . wallets?

Leather casts a much wider net than the barn. The skins of horses, sheep, goats, and pigs are used as a byproduct of meat slaughter. More exotic species that are hunted and killed solely for their skins include zebras, bison, water buffalo, boars, kangaroos, elephants, sharks, dolphins, seals, walruses, frogs, turtles, crocodiles, lizards, and snakes. How's that for style? Nearly the entire animal kingdom is being sacrificed for our superficial needs.

If you think the family dog or cat doesn't fall under this category, then you're sadly mistaken. It's a sick and twisted industry. Hundreds of thousands of dogs and cats are traded in Europe every year, with two million bludgeoned in China to meet the demand. Since manufacturers try to keep this under wraps, leather and fur products are often intentionally mislabeled. In other words, you won't find "Made from Genuine Dog." In France, cats are stolen from people's homes in an underground operation! A few years ago, a police raid on a dog and cat tannery in the country found fifteen hundred skins, which were used to make baby shoes.[39] All you need to remember is this: when you buy leather products, you have no idea where they may be coming from. The farm or the doghouse. Got it?

Leather Alternatives: Score fashions made with natural or manmade fibers such as organic cotton, hemp, linen, and synthetic microfibers.

SILK

As exotic as it seems, silk is about as low on the food chain as they come. Silk is what you get when the caterpillar of the silk moth spins a cocoon. Each worm can spin up to 1.5 miles of continuous silk thread. You probably watched a silk worm do this in kindergarten. What your teacher failed to mention is that silkworms are steamed, baked, or boiled alive because the silk threads are cut short and rendered useless if the caterpillar eats its way out of its cocoon naturally. By cooking them alive, we get a "continuous" spool of thread and the cocoons are easier to unravel. Does that sound pleasant to you?[40]

Silk Alternatives: Try and fight me on this one, but bamboo fabric feels an awful lot like silk. You have to watch your back because bamboo can undergo some harsh chemical processing that pretty much renders its environmental reputation null and void. Be on the lookout for bamboo linen, which is more "green," or do some digging for Tencel (or lyocell), which is also made from wood pulp but undergoes a much more eco-sound production process than bamboo (see page 192).

Other fill-ins for silk are milkweed seed-pod fibers and silk-cotton tree filaments. If you're a bit more lenient, look for peace silk. Eco designers are gaga over it, and it's gaining popularity on the vegan circuit. Instead of torturing the caterpillars, they basically sit back and wait for the moth to emerge from the cocoon. The moth goes on with its life, and the broken filaments of silk it leaves behind are collected and spun into yarn. It's not one "continuous" strand of silk, but nobody's getting burned alive.[41] What a concept.

WOOL

To revisit, sheep, angora rabbits, and cashmere and mohair goats all endure sad, lonely, and unbearable lives for the wool off their backs. Farmers cram them into tight living quarters, and cut their balls or horns off with no anesthesia. Animals can be sheared painfully close to the skin, stripping them of any protection from infection, parasites, or extreme temperatures. Sheep get extra special treatment thanks to the traditions of tail docking or mulesing, where skin is cut out of their asses to keep the flies off.

Wool Alternatives: Look for lightweight materials in recycled polyester, organic cotton, or acrylic. Some of these are harsher on their environment, but until we find better eco-friendly alternatives, save a sheep (or a rabbit, or goat . . .).

CHAPTER 7

The Skinny:
The Sustainable
Wardrobe

★ The Eco-Vegan Staples:

ITEMS EVERY GIRL HAS GOT TO HAVE

It's not like your shopping days are over. You just have to put in a little more effort when you care about what's hanging in your closet. No more running to the mall every paycheck, grabbing a handful of size mediums, and throwing down your credit card like you're being timed. That's just flat-out irresponsible. Did you expect me to tell you that you look smashing in pesticides and road kill? I don't talk out of my ass.

To get my closet in order, I look to my friend and stylist, Monica Schweiger. When I started out as a vegan and conscious shopper, I had no idea what to wear before I met Monica. But she whipped me right into shape and before long I could buy a pair of shoes without her supervision. (Full disclosure: I had no choice. She got sick of holding my hand when we went shopping.)

Monica is a fly chick. A stylist to the stars and major household brands, she's built her lookbook on vintage classics and earth-friendly pieces instead of trends. Not that there's never a place for a trend, but you got to have the basics first. Here are her top five picks for everyday pieces that every broad has got to have. For more picks, visit www.healthybitchdaily.com.

MONICA SCHWEIGER'S ECO-FASHION ESSENTIALS

ORGANIC COTTON TEES AND TANKS There are so many companies that offer clean, comfy cotton and sexy tees. The silhouettes and colors now are endless—you're not going to be stuck with a boxy beige tee. I love Alternative Apparel. While I'm writing this, I am wearing the softest dove grey oversized crop top. Loomstate, American Apparel, and even large companies like the Gap and Banana Republic now offer organic selections from time to time.

A GREAT VINTAGE TRENCH COAT A trench is a classic piece that will never go out of style. Think about it, Burberry has been selling the same classic trench for ages (with a few updates and tweaks, of course). But a good trench is a good trench. It's waterproof, khaki, and belted. I have one of my mom's from the late sixties and I never get sick of hearing the compliments! Where to look? Your local thrift store, Goodwill, or resale store (Buffalo Exchange, Crossroads, etc.).

If you want a really chic vintage one, check out vintage Web sites such as Chicandyoushallfind.com. What comes around goes around.

ORGANIC COTTON, SOY, OR BAMBOO UNDIES With all those toxins out in the world, lets start this eco-clothing revolution at the bottom (no pun intended) and get you some sexy, pesticide-free panties and bras. With companies such as American Apparel, Patagonia, Eberjey, Only Hearts, Hanky Panky and Stella McCartney rocking the organic innerwear wave, you're bound to find something sexy enough for you.

Bamboo Textiles: ★
THE HARD FACTS

A LITTLE BLACK DRESS (LBD) We all need one, and these days you can have your choice of earth- and animal-friendly fabrics—hemp, organic cotton, and bamboo jersey. There are so many out there but Loomstate, PI Organics, Beau Soleil, and ecoSkin are some great places to start.

ECO WORKOUT WEAR If you squeeze in a workout a few times a week, you need to have some eco-friendly activewear. The traditional stuff is made with pesticide-ridden cotton. Look for soy, hemp, and bamboo fabrics from Gaiam, Lululemon, Patagonia, and Be Present.

For more on Monica, check her out at monicaschweiger.com.

WHERE TO FIND: ECO STAPLES
Alternative Apparel/ alternativeapparel.com
American Apparel/ americanapparel.com
Banana Republic/ bananarepublic.gap.com
Beau Soleil/ shopbeausoleil.com
Eberjey/ eberjey.com
ecoSkin/ ecoskincollections.com
Gaiam/ gaiam.com
Gap/ gap.com
Hanky Panky/ hankypanky.com
Loomstate/ loomstate.org
Lululemon/ lululemon.com
Only Hearts/ onlyhearts.com
Patagonia/ patagonia.com
PI Organic/ shop.piorganic.com
Stella McCartney/ stellamccartney.com

It didn't take much for bamboo to start growing on us. Once we learned that the joy ride was over for our forests, we were ready to root for anything that claimed to press the reverse button. When bamboo was pushed into the spotlight with a few facts to back up its sustainable qualities, we didn't have to hear another word. Bamboo had us at hello.

But the love affair has unraveled just a bit. Bamboo fabric is not quite everything it appeared to be. You know, it's complicated. So environmentalists are calling bullshit, and now everyone's running in circles waiting for someone to tell them what to do.

So, were we bamboozled? Like I said, it's complicated. There's the good bamboo and the bad bamboo. As long as you know the difference.

THE DEFENSE

Bamboo is a woodsy grass that grows really fast and is ready to be harvested after just four years.[42] Compare that to an oak tree, which can take up to 120 years to reach maturity. Once it's chopped down, bamboo doesn't need to be replanted because its roots sprout new shoots that can grow a yard or more a day. The wonder grass also doesn't require pesticides or fertilizers, and requires little water or energy to grow.

That's the bamboo plant in its natural state. It's when manufacturers get their hands on it that bamboo loses its squeaky clean image.

THE PROSECUTION

There are two ways to process bamboo for fabrics: mechanically or chemically. The mechanical method isn't used as often because it's pricey and requires some hefty labor. But you best believe it's better for the earth and our health. The woodsy parts of the bamboo shoots are crushed, then natural enzymes break it down into mush so the fibers can be smoothed out and spun into yarn.[43] This is also how flax and hemp are made into linen fabric. So the industry uses some common sense and labels bamboo fabric derived from this method "bamboo linen." Bamboo linen is truly green. Ecofabulous. A stand-up bitch. Can do no wrong.

The alternative is to use chemicals to process bamboo. This, ladies, is where shit gets complicated. In a nutshell, the bamboo stalks are "cooked" in some serious chemical solvents such as sodium hydroxide and carbon disulfide. They like to call this hoighty-toighty process "hydrolysis alkalization combined with multi-phase bleaching."[44] Read: *You're looking at rayon . . . not bamboo.* This process ain't sustainable. It ain't green. It's just contributing to global warming and allergic reactions.

Both caustic soda and carbon disulfide suck big time. Even the lowest levels of carbon disulfide trigger headaches, nerve damage, and exhaustion (it's also been known to cause brain damage among workers in rayon manufacturing plants). Sodium hydroxide, or caustic soda, irritates our eyes and skin. You can also find it in Drano.[45] Yay for that.

Some newer bamboo manufacturers are still taking the chemical route to save a buck, but are turning to the lyocell process. Ooohhh, what's that? Lyocell is a cellulose fiber, like bamboo and rayon, that comes from wood pulp. The process of converting the pulp into fiber has been dubbed the lyocell "process," but the actual product you get in the end has been named Tencel (the spiffy patent name). This process uses an amine oxide, hydrogen peroxide, and alcohol to do the same job. This seems to get more cred because it's a closed-loop system. That means 99.5 percent of the chemicals used are trapped and recycled to make more fiber (the remaining half percent escapes into the environment).[46]

With bamboo's cover completely blown, more chemical processes that are gentler on the earth are being introduced. They may also use chemicals, but they incorporate closed-loop systems and milder solvents.

Here's a quick recap: Bamboo can be made into fabric in two ways—mechanically or chemically. The mechanical process is great. As for the various chemical processes, one can bite me, the other one earns a B+ for improvement, and the jury is still out.

HOW TO GET SUSTAINABLE BAMBOO

By now, you are familiar with the false claims brands can make. They will slap just about anything on the package if it's even partly true. Well, brace yourself—the companies selling bamboo makers are big talkers, too. Here are a few tips to make sure you're buying quality bamboo and not supporting fakers.

LOOK FOR CERTIFICATION FROM AN INDEPENDENT AND RELIABLE SOURCE. Bamboo producers that gain certification have to follow some rules to prove the production processes are safe for consumers and the enviroment. Don't trust just any certification. The good ones are Soil Association, SKAL's EKO certification, and KRAV. Oeko-Tex is another trusty certification, but it only says the end product is healthy—it doesn't look at the manufacturing process.

If a company trumpets their "ISO 9000" or "ISO 14000" creds, it doesn't mean squat. They're just cool industry tools, but ISO (short for International Organization for Standardization) has no way of knowing whether companies meet their goals.[47]

LOOK FOR BAMBOO LINEN. Bamboo linen is found more often in bed sheets and towels, but it's also used for higher-quality fabrics and dresses. Remember, "linen" is better because it's less taxing on us and our surroundings.

WHEN BAMBOO IS MIXED WITH COTTON, BUY "CERTIFIED-ORGANIC" COTTON. To give a garment a nice sturdy texture, many clothing designers mix bamboo with cotton (somewhere around 30 percent cotton). If there's any cotton in it, make sure it's certified organic. You don't want to wear pesticides to work.

AVOID "RAYON MADE FROM BAMBOO." Bamboo that undergoes harsh chemical processing is basically "rayon." True, bamboo still saves virgin trees from being cut down no matter the process. We all love trees. But rayon made from bamboo still releases toxic junk into the air, loses its antimicrobial properties, and is no longer biodegradable.

The FTC has started calling out companies that claim their product is "100% bamboo," "made in an environmentally friendly manner," "naturally antimicrobial," or "biodegradable," when it's really not. Those companies are being pushed to label their products "rayon made from bamboo" so we don't have to take a lucky guess.[48]

WHY BAMBOO IS THE BOMB

Enough with the negative. There are a handful of reasons to love bamboo fabric when it isn't put through the wringer. Before you get on your soapbox and ramble on that rayon has some of these natural qualities, too, let me remind you that rayon comes from virgin woods.

Soft like a baby's bum. Bamboo is softer than cotton and has a silk-like texture. Even more reason for you to let the silk worms be free.

Doesn't aggravate allergies. Bamboo won't trigger skin sensitivities or dermatitis. Some people experience minor allergies with bamboo, but that's usually when it's been dunked repeatedly in chemicals.[49]

Keeps you cool and warm. Bamboo adapts to it surroundings to regulate your body temperature. You stay cool in the summer and toasty in the winter.

Sucks up moisture. For those of you who sweat like a pig, there are teeny micro-holes in bamboo that absorb moisture and allow the material to breathe better. Actually, bamboo fibers are four times as absorbent as cotton.

Naturally fights bacteria. Bamboo has built-in antimicrobials called *kun*. These stop bacteria growth that causes odors so you won't smell like a plumber.

★ A Denim Disaster

As far as I'm concerned, jeans were the greatest invention ever. Screw the telephone. I'd rather communicate through paper cups than live without denim. All seven pairs. My work jeans. My mommy jeans. My painting-slash-gardening jeans. My "It-should-be-illegal-to-look-this-hot" jeans. And the "I-shouldn't-have-eaten-the-whole-buffet" jeans.

But what about the "I'm-an-asshole-for-putting-the-planet-through-hell" jeans? C'mon, that's all we wear.

Most women own at least eight pairs of jeans (I did until I got rid of my "no-wonder-they-were-on-sale" jeans). Though it pains me to say it, this addiction to denim is really doing a number on the earth.

IT'S STILL THE FABRIC OF OUR LIVES

Your jeans are made of cotton. We've been through this. Cotton is the most pesticide-intensive crop in the world. Not strawberries . . . your T-shirt. These pesticides pollute our air, groundwater, and soil, affecting our health and killing off wildlife.

DENIM'S DEEP THIRST

And let's not forget about all that water. Just a single pair of jeans guzzles about 6,800 liters of the stuff we drink. What a coincidence! That's exactly how much water it takes a day to support the average American's lifestyle. But that's not a fair comparison since we think water is an endless commodity in this goddamn country. In other parts of the world, some people don't even have access to enough clean water to meet their basic needs. The United Nations says that's a *minimum* of 50 liters on a daily basis. Most countries are lucky to get 20 liters.[50]

THE DENIM BLUES

How do you think your jeans get that iconic blue? Most companies—even the ones with the "organic" tag—use a synthetic dye called *indigo* to get the blue color. Indigo comes from petroleum. To transform the actual color into a dye requires some aggressive toxins, including hydrogen cyanide and heavy metals.[51] These chemicals pollute the air and groundwater all around denim factories. Take Tehuacan, Mexico, one of the largest producers of denim. Tehuacan's once beautiful canals and hot springs are now stained a bright, artificial blue thanks to denim dyes.

GENETICALLY MODIFIED (GM) COTTON SEEDS

Genetically modified seeds (GMs) are another big can of worms. Almost 70 percent of cottonseeds in the United States are modified to scare off bugs.[52] GM seeds were praised for a while because cotton farmers didn't have to soak fields with as many pesticides. Indeed, the seeds were going to war against pests. A victory? Not so much. For a while China was using a GM seed courtesy of the jerks at Monsanto that produced a pesticide that warded off bollworms. Everything was hunky-dory for a while because cotton farmers were spraying fewer toxins. Well, eventually nature did what it's best at, and mirid bugs—who are magically resistant to the Monsanto cottonseed—took over like nobody's business. Mirid bugs are not fun. They feed on more than two hundred varieties of fruit, vegetable, and grain crops.[53]

THE DENIM DEFINITION OF ORGANIC

I'm not telling you to stop wearing jeans. I would rather die. It doesn't matter if you're fat, skinny, have a huge ass, or long legs. There are plenty of organic denim lines on the market making more conscious jeans. Even corporate giants such as Levi's, Gap, AG, and Seven For All Mankind. And guess what? They fit just as well.

As with any purchase though, you do want to make sure you're not getting duped by wild organic claims. Here are a few things to consider before you buy another pair of baby blues.

TRY TO GO WITH CERTIFIED-ORGANIC DENIM BRANDS THAT USE LESS HARSH CHEMICAL PROCESSING, AND NATURAL DYES AND FINISHES. Just because it rocks the organic label doesn't mean it's saving the planet with every pair of skinny jeans. The USDA certified-organic label on a pair of jeans simply states they've been produced without synthetic pesticides on cotton fields. It says nada about the manufacturing process. An "organic" pair of jeans could still be processed with destructive dyes, bleaches, and finishes.

It's more work, but try to go with organic brands that use plant-based dyes, natural or few-to-no finishing agents (formaldehyde being a common one to seal in color), and no harsh bleaches. Up front, know that it's tough to find a denim line that is completely innocent. But if you're dead set on all-sustainable jeans all around, they are out there.

Currently, there's really only one certifying body for organic threads that looks at the whole cycle—from how it was grown, to safe working conditions, to which dyes and bleaches are used, to air- and water-quality standards. It's called the Global Organic Textile Standard (GOTS) and they're not screwing around. These guys just launched in 2006, so it will take some time for companies to start wearing the GOTS logo of approval.[54] ROMP, a British fashion house that gained some American cred when it invaded Los Angeles, is one demin brand that rocks the GOTS certification.

BE WARY OF "MADE WITH" ORGANIC COTTON. "Made with" is a cop-out—it could be as little as 3 percent organic cotton.[55] So uncool.

AVOID "DISTRESSED" DENIM UNLESS THERE'S A NATURAL EXPLANATION. I was guilty of this sin. For some reason, I prefer jeans that look as if they've been worn since the Dark Ages. Silly me. A lot of heavy labor goes into the worn look so popular in weathered or acid-washed jeans. (Hello? The eighties called and they want their jeans back.) To make them look old, factory workers repeatedly wash them in industrial bleach and then grind them with volcanic pumice stone. The stone has to be mined and shipped from all over the world, which translates into a colossal carbon footprint. After they're done, most companies just throw the pumice stone like careless bastards into the local river or water supply. The chemical bleach blasting isn't so nice on the environment or factory air-quality conditions either.[56]

CONSIDER BUYING ORGANIC COTTON DENIM THAT IS GROWN AND MADE IN THE USA. There's another dirty secret. The USDA requires that all imported raw fiber be sprayed with fumigants before being shipped over so foreign bugs don't make it into this country. It doesn't matter—organic or not. If the jeans have already been spun into fabric, you're all good. But if it's raw "organic" cotton coming to America to be made into jeans, there's a problem. Those dirty jeans could still be labeled "organically grown cotton."

THINK ABOUT BUYING USED. Believe me, buying a new pair of jeans gives me that warm and fuzzy feeling, too. But it's still inviting something new into your closet that is utterly wasteful. Think about hitting up the thrift store, Goodwill, or a local consignment shop first. Even if there is nothing eco about those jeans, they have already done their damage. You're just making sure they don't end up in a landfill. And, let's be real, they will look "worn."

ECO-DENIM GUIDE

Eco jeans are a dime a dozen nowadays. Do expect to put out some more cash for organic jeans, but remember how loud your purchase speaks. Some stand-up brands are Loomstate, Howie's Organic Denim, DelForte Denim, Rawganique, and even Levi's Eco label uses 100 percent organic cotton with zero chemicals in the production process. The celebrities are doing it, too. Rock star Bono and his wife, Ali Hewson, launched Edun to support sustainable business in Africa (only part of the line is organic). Another company I'm slightly infatuated with, UJeans Eco Jeans, allows you to customize jeans based on your measurements. They use only natural dyes and washes—no chlorine bleach or formaldehyde—and source fair-trade organic cotton. So, take your pick. Visit www.healthybitchdaily.com for a few more of my favorite denim lines.

B BITCHWORTHY: GOOD SOCIETY ECO JEANS

While I'm a big fan of buying jeans "Made in the USA," I got to give it up for those denim companies trying to make things better for a family in a poor country. Good Society Eco Jeans is one such brand that sources their all-organic cotton from indie farmers in India and ensures they are paid a fair wage. Calling themselves a "movement" with a dot org to back it up, the company donates proceeds to help Nepalese women and children get out of human sex trafficking. Plus, their jeans are the bee's knees. *Visit Goodsociety.org.*

KIM'S TIP:

If trying to find a denim brand that uses low-impact dyes is making you want to poke your eyes out, go dark. Darker-colored denim usually requires fewer chemicals, since it doesn't need to be bleached to a pulp.

B BITCHWORTHY: PRESERVING YOUR JEANS

Reduce the impact of your jeans by just washing them less. You won't look like a slob. As long as you didn't spill coffee or BBQ sauce everywhere, wear them a few times before throwing them in the wash. Then air dry. If they start to smell a bit in between washes, toss them in the freezer for a few hours. This will kill the bacteria responsible for the odor and use less energy in the process.

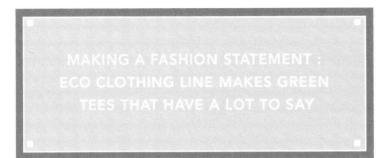

MAKING A FASHION STATEMENT :
ECO CLOTHING LINE MAKES GREEN
TEES THAT HAVE A LOT TO SAY

Sisters Alison Stanich Power and Jennifer Stanich Banmiller were at the top of their careers when they both decided that "green" fashion wasn't cutting it stylewise. Frankly, they thought it was ugly. Hideous. Like, why would anybody even wear it unless it was a paid endorsement? Though the girls weren't what you'd call "familiar" with the apparel industry, they knew they could do a better job.

At first, the big idea was to create a collection of hip tees, tanks, and accessories with socially conscious messages, made of eco-friendly and organic fabrics and manufactured in the United States. Today, their line, A Lot To Say, is made entirely of recycled polyethylene terephthalate (PET) bottles and uses a revolutionary no-water dye process. In comparison to typical T-shirt production, their system reduces water pollution by 91 percent and carbon emissions by 79 percent.[57] Every tee, tank, scarf, umbrella, and even pillowcase makes it very clear that the person behind it has something to say. Whether that message is about fueling your car, taking shorter showers, recycling, loving yourself, or remembering to breathe—you are making yourself heard.

The question is . . .will these two broads ever shut up? Yeah, good luck with that.

OK, ladies. Tell us about your big aha moment that led to the launch of ALTS.

We both, separately and on different coasts, saw this "eco" tee being touted in a big fashion mag being worn by an equally big celebrity. We immediately got on the phone and our conversation went something like this: *Did you see that ugly tee so and so had on? And what's with the message? Is it even English? Plus, it's not even actually eco if you look at how it's made. And did you see what they're charging? Ridiculous.* Ditto. Ditto. Ditto. Then the lightbulb went off: We can do better, much better. Hopefully, we are.

"Green" may have been a whole new world for you girls, but you're kicking ass. You've adopted no-water dyes, fabric made from recycled PET . . . and so on. What were your "non-negotiables" when it came to the production process?

Really, we weren't willing to settle for any part of the production or manufacturing process that would ever make us guilty of being a part of that greenwashing mentality that spurred us to start this journey in the first place. More simply put, we didn't ever want to be called disingenuous. We knew we could do it right and still make it right.

To shop the A Lot to Say collection, visit shop.alottosay.com. A portion of all proceeds go to support a number of charities and environmental causes.

You're giving the environment some sex appeal with some of these tees. What was behind that? (P.S. I like it.)

We are big, big believers that eco should not equal granola. And sometimes in our truly defining moments we ask ourselves, "Would Heather Locklear rock this?"

I know it was important for you to do everything in the USA, to help boost the economy and create jobs. You also saw the issues with sweatshop labor. How big of a problem is this in other countries?

Huge. Sweatshop labor is happening all over the world: Bangladesh, Costa Rica, Dominican Republic, Haiti, Honduras, Indonesia, and Vietnam. People—oftentimes children—make as little as 13 cents an hour and work up to seventy-hour workweeks. Plus, they are exposed to horrible, harmful toxic environments, as well as verbal and sexual abuse. We don't have the solution to this huge and inhumane problem. But we do know that even if we can't control the big picture, we absolutely can control the choices we make.

What questions should consumers always ask before buying something for their closet?

Can this item, like Shirley MacLaine, come back in another life, but still look as hot as Heather Locklear in this one? (If you haven't figured it out by now, we're a little obsessed with HL.) In other words, can it be recycled or upcycled.

But this is about more than tees and tanks. You girls are helping push a movement. Many women out there have "a lot to say" and don't know what the hell they can do or where to start. What's the best advice—and most uncheesy—you can give them?

We hope this isn't cheesy, because we really believe it's true. Find someone who'll listen and it doesn't matter who. A good friend, your local barista, a really good blogging community, your mailman, yoga teacher, cube mate, husband, veterinarian, whomever. Then say whatever it is you need to say. Get a dialogue going. Ruffle some feathers. Open some minds. Just put it out there and watch things change.

    Our manifesto: "If you think something, say it. If you believe something, say it. If you want something, say it. Because saying it creates new awareness. Awareness sparks new behavior. And new behavior inspires us all to be better."

★ Don't Freeze Your Buns Off :

BRAVE THE COLDER TEMPERATURES IN COMPASSIONATE COATS AND SWEATERS

A warm, stylish sweater or winter coat can be a tough find when you're a vegan who just happens to give a damn about our global crisis. Almost every piece of outerwear is made of merino wool, cashmere, or leather. If you find one that isn't misery-friendly, you see it on the tag: "100% vinyl." Just peachy. Yet another winter spent pretending I can pull off gym sweats with boots.

Your choices are limited. But that doesn't mean you're getting clubbed by the fashion police. Look at the bright side: You may have to look a little harder, but it also means you won't have the same jacket as every other fake at the office. That's a plus.

I have preached like a nun that most synthetic materials—especially the ones with petroleum ties—are a sin. I hold to that. But if you insist on wearing exotic faux fur and fake leather jackets like a biker chick, you may have to make a purchase that's not so hot for the environment. In the war against animal cruelty, sometimes a girl's gotta do what a girl's gotta do.

To keep you honest, I've laid out some of my cold-weather favorites, and some of your alternatives.

KNIT SWEATERS AND CARDIGANS

By the looks of it, animals make for a real nice sweater. Or a mean one. Wool, cashmere, and silk are all cold, cruel comforts when it gets chilly.

Alpaca isn't any better. You hear that? That's me cracking the vegan whip. The alpaca is a small llama from South America whose fleece has started to make an appearance in our clothing. They are like huge stuffed animals and should only be taken advantage of for cuddling. Don't support their demise in your sweater collection. Your choices are not that limited.

And take a good look at your cardigan—lightweight sweaters really favor the silk. It takes around three thousand silkworms to produce just one measly pound of that fabric on your back. Peace silk, or cruelty-free silk, has become popular in clothing, but some vegans are still against it because it's a by-product of an animal. It really depends on how strict your standards are. More and more, you will find it used in sweaters, dresses, scarves, and lightweight jackets.

Other alternatives for sweaters are hemp, 100 percent organic cotton, canvas, bamboo, and even soy. I find the classiest and easiest to find are hemp and organic cotton. Hemp feels lightweight and lets your body breathe. It also dries pretty quickly, and gets softer every time you wear and wash it.

> **KIM'S PICKS: SWEATERS**
> Loomstate (loomstate.org)
> Indigenous (indigenousdesigns.com)

JACKETS, COATS, AND BLAZERS

For blazers and jackets, it's all about wool, leather, and suede. But not only do leather and suede come from the skin of a dead animal—I'll never get sick of telling you that—the production of leather requires heavy metals and deadly chemicals to tan the hides. Your alternatives tend to be grim—cheap, manmade materials such as PVC (vinyl), nylon, acrylic, and rayon.

Leather Alternatives: If you're a hard-ass and need to let everyone know it, look for "pleather" made from polyurethane, or PU, rather than PVC. Both are plastics—hence the "p" in pleather—but PVC contains chlorine and leaches dioxins and heavy metals when it's processed. Its buddy, polyurethane, is definitely no model citizen, but it's a greener choice because it's already soft and flexible. It doesn't call for oodles of hazardous solvents and waste to get it soft like PVC and real leather do.[58]

As for comfort, PVC doesn't offer any breathing room. It feels like you're wearing a parka. It's also a pain in the ass to clean. Polyurethane is more airy and washable for all those cross-country bike trips you think you're taking. Ride like the wind, honey.

There are more sustainable alternatives than pleather, but they are rarely used. Cork leather—made from the bark of a cork tree—is growing in popularity. But, holy crap, is it expensive! (Designer label DDC Lab was one of the first to debut it as a leather coat. It would *only* cost you $2,400.) Other more natural faux leather materials on the down-low are ocean leather, which is made from kelp, and vegetan. The latter is an artificial microfiber that was mainly designed to help offset all those leather hides we're zipping through.

You can find faux leather jackets made from PU at traditional retailers such as Nordstrom, Macy's, GUESS, Urban Outfitters, Forever 21, and JCPenny. If you like to shop online, check out Alternativeapparel.com and Zappos.com.

B BITCHWORTHY: REKNIT

No matter how much attention you give that delicate sweater, eventually it's going to wear out. Instead of saying goodbye (which can be painful), send it to ReKnit. Started by a mama's boy who felt like putting his mom to work, ReKnit reuses the yarn from your old sweater and upcycles it (OK—she knits it) into something new you can use, like a matching scarf and hat. Because he only has one mom, the orders are limited to thirty per month. *Visit rekn.it.*

KIM'S PICKS: FAUX LEATHER JACKETS

Burlington Coat Factory (burlingtoncoatfactory.com)

AStars (alpinestars.com)

Recycled Materials: Cozy winter coats and form-fitting jackets that are wool-free are more my style. Leave the acrylic and vinyl for the teenagers. You're a woman with class. Look for wool-like coats and heavy jackets in organic cotton or recycled materials. Brands with a conscience—such as Nau, Elroy, and prAna—all offer a solid selection of jackets made from organic cotton or recycled polyester fabrics. Mama like. Nau uses a fabric that combines polyester waste using a closed-loop system. If for any reason you're over it in a few years—which I so highly doubt—it can be recycled again to make another coat.

KIM'S PICKS: JACKETS AND COATS

Nau (nau.com)

Elroy (shopelroy.com)

PrAna (prana.com)

B BITCHWORTHY: VAUTE COUTURE

Think "vegan style" is too lowbrow for your tastes? Come down off that pedestal (I can see up your nose). Once you check out Leanne Mai-ly Hilgart's line, Vaute Couture, you'll ask her to keep your credit card on file. Leanne has been making a statement since the fifth grade with puff-painted tees that read, "Spay and Neuter, Save the Dogs." Today, the fashion model-turned-designer melds both eco and compassion with high-fashion pea coats, bulky sweaters, oversized bomber jackets, upcycled windbreakers, and sheer tanks with cruelty-free messages. It didn't take long for her to win over media critics and celebrity fans like Alicia Silverstone, Ginnifer Goodwin, Emily Deschanel, and even Oprah. You go girl. *Visit vautecouture.com.*

FAUX FURS

Faux furs walk the same fine line as pleather. I'm not going to knock your style if you like fake fur. I want to. But I'm going to keep my mouth shut. If you mean to give off the impression that you killed one hundred chinchillas for your pleasure, then I'd much rather you use go with a faux fur than a real one. The problem with these fakers is they're made from acrylic and polyester. There is really no way of getting around it. To make just three fur coats, we're talking about one gallon of oil.[59] Just try to find one made from recycled materials. I triple-dog dare you.

B BITCHWORTHY: FAUX FUR

Imposter (imposter4animals.com)

Fabulous-Furs (fabulousfurs.com)

★ Dirty Laundry:
THE SILENT KILLERS IN OUR LAUNDRY DETERGENT

You can run that spin cycle until your head spins, but you're still going to end up with a dirty load of laundry. Your clothes may smell like fresh linen but they reek of problems.

The amount of energy and petroleum that goes into pumping our washers and dryers is a part of it. For the love of fabric softener, we do about 1,100 loads of laundry a second in this god-forsaken country! But that's not nearly as filthy as the smack we're pumping into our oceans, groundwater, lakes, rivers, and soil. It goes by the name of detergent. And there's nothing it's deterring but our health and wildlife populations.

Laundry detergent is like most other toxic household products, except in this case, we're also wearing it all day long. Chlorine bleach, brighteners, ethanolamines, naphthas, EDTA, phosphates, SLS, and fragrance are just a few of the offenders in your laundry room.[60] Did they teach you any of that in Chemistry 101? Somehow I doubt it.

DIRT AND GRIME ELIMINATORS

Some of these toxins—linear alkylate sulfonate (LAS) and alkylphenol ethoxylates (APEs)—are surfactants used to magically reduce the surface tension of water so that it can mix with grease and grime and carry it away.[61] I'm not saying they don't work. All I'm saying is we should probably find something safer. LAS produces benzene and carcinogens during the manufacturing process and are slow to biodegrade.[62] APEs are much tamer—they're merely hormone disruptors. The chemicals imitate estrogen and have been shown to speed up the growth of cancer cells and even feminize male fish.[63] Considering we dump almost eight thousand pounds of this bunk in the Mississippi River every day, this is a slight concern.[64] Nobody wins.

PHOSPHATES

Phosphates in detergents help soften water and make sure the dirt that surfactants pick up doesn't settle back onto clothes. In theory, they're not that bad. Phosphates are essential to plant and animal life . . . when they occur naturally in the ecosystem. But our cheap laundry detergents dump more phosphates into the environment than it can handle, suffocating and killing fish and wildlife.[65] They've caused so much trouble in the environment that many brands have started to phase them out. Their replacements? EDTA and phenols. The latter are banned in Europe and are toxic to your central nervous system.[66] And EDTA ends up in our oceans and ecosystem, where it can actually free up heavy metals, like mercury, trapped in underwater sediments. Once heavy metals are loose, they re-enter the food chain and end up in the stuff we eat.[67]

OPTIMAL BRIGHTENERS

Have you ever wondered how that detergent gets your clothes looking so white? Optimal brighteners. They are a group of fluorescent chemicals that trick the naked eye into thinking they're whiter. Brighteners don't clean clothes better; they just make us see things that aren't really there.[68] They are actually designed to leave residues on clothes, so they can keep fooling us into thinking those panties are white as hell. Well, enjoy blinding people because these chemicals rub off onto skin and cause allergic reactions that look an awful lot like a bad sunburn.[69] To stay away from the artificial "glow," read your labels very closely because they can be listed as optical bleaches, whitening agents, or fluorescent lightening agents.

CLEAN LAUNDRY:
A HEALTHIER SPIN CYCLE

There is no need to bang your head against the washer like a two-year-old. Your ties with Tide were less than perfect. Who knows, you might just discover a side of clean you never knew existed if you quit being so stubborn. Hold on, is that a smile? Now, that's the spirit.

Before we get to some of the safer brands, here are a few tips for choosing a detergent that's better for your health and the ecosystem. You should know by now to avoid synthetic dyes and fragrances and support companies who believe in full ingredient disclosure. Even if one or two additives are questionable, at least you know they were open enough to let you know what other ingredients are in the bottle. That goes a long way.

LOOK FOR PLANT-BASED SURFACTANTS. Look for biodegradable, plant-derived cleaning agents that act as natural grime eliminators; coconut, palm, or vegetable oil are good choices. Method Home, Biokleen, Caldrea, Citra-Solv, Ecover, and Seventh Generation have all adopted natural surfactants.

Some companies will use part synthetic and part natural materials; as long as the laundry product you're looking at meets some of the other requirements, they are still better than petrochemicals. Plus, some synthetic ingredients are biodegradable and don't ravage the environment. If you have allergies or sensitive skin, I always recommend doing some research on any suspicious ingredients prior to buying the product.

> **KIM'S TIP:**
> Many brands sell unscented detergents. Take it home and add a dozen drops of essential oils into each load to make them smell good.

CHOOSE PRODUCTS THAT ARE FREE OF PHOSPHATES AND OPTICAL BRIGHTENERS. These are the two worst culprits in your laundry detergent. If it contains phosphates or optical brighteners, it doesn't deserve your laundry. And if ingredients aren't listed, chances are there is something to hide.

THINK BEFORE YOU WASH

GET IT WHITE WITH OXYGEN BLEACH (AKA HYDROGEN PEROXIDE). Avoid chlorine bleach (sodium hypochlorite) at all costs, and instead, pour in a cup of oxygen bleach or hydrogen peroxide (3 percent solution). This disinfectant biodegrades, fights odors, removes stains, and brightens colors and whites. It also actually helps soften the water to add some horsepower to your detergent. If you use powdered oxygen bleach, dissolve in water before adding to clothes. Obviously, don't toss in with your colors. It might not do a thing, but it can discolor them.

BITCHWORTHY: TREATING STAINS
When using natural detergents, it's best to treat stains before they set in. Treat the stain with some hydrogen peroxide and let sit for 10 minutes, then toss in the washer. If it's being stubborn, scrub it a bit with an old toothbrush. Peroxide even gets blood stains out of clothes! If peroxide freaks you out, try distilled white vinegar. Because I'm full of ideas, you can also rub some vegetable glycerin into a new or old stain and let it pre-soak for about 30 minutes prior to washing. Wash in cold water since hot water sets stains.

KIM'S PICKS: LAUNDRY DETERGENTS
Biokleen Free and Clear Laundry Liquid (biokleenhome.com)
Seventh Generation Natural Laundry Liquid (seventhgeneration.com)

Before you throw a few loads in the wash, ask yourself if it can wait. If you live in an urban area and have to make a trip to the Laundromat, you probably are more frugal when it comes to laundry time. But for all of you with a washer and dryer down the hall, quit taking advantage of the convenience (right after you count your damn blessings). Here are a few things to consider next time you go to throw in a few pairs of socks.

DO LESS LAUNDRY. Save energy and water by not washing clothes as much. The average household does more than 400 loads a year, and wastes about 13,500 gallons of water.[70] Just thinking of it makes me tired. Wait until you can fill the washer-dryer up before you schedule laundry time. They run more efficiently when they're at capacity.

USE COLD WATER. Your washer wastes 99 percent of the energy it consumes just to heat up the water.[71] Quit being so set in your ways and start washing with cold. Cold water also helps remove stains and puts less wear and tear on your wardrobe.

TRY LINE DRYING. Dry your clothes on a clothesline or even hang them over the back porch in the sun. You can also buy drying racks at home stores that fit easily anywhere indoors. Visit Urbanclotheslines.com for dozens of options. If you have to use the dryer, make sure the lint trap is cleaned out before each load. When it's blocked, it requires more energy to dry a load.

DRY CLEANING

Step away from the "Dry Clean Only" tag. You're not paying for quality. All you're signing up for is a truckload of useless plastic cling and an annual bill of about $1,500. If you're lucky, maybe they'll even throw in a headache and an upset stomach.

More than 85 percent of dry cleaners still use perchloroethylene, a poisonous solvent more commonly known in cleaner lingo as "perc." Perc has been linked to some serious health issues in dry cleaner employees, including miscarriage, infertility, and a handful of cancers.[72] When you're exposed to it, perc accumulates in your fatty tissues and breast milk, and there are concerns it could cause liver and kidney damage. Don't you doubt it; if you're bringing home threads from the cleaners, you are exposed to it. The EPA has found that freshly dry cleaned clothes emit perc into your home.[73]

The earth doesn't like it too much either. Cleaners are supposed to take some special precautions to make sure it doesn't get out into the environment, but if only it were that simple. A shit-ton of it leaks out of pipes and machinery, and ends up polluting the air we breathe.[74] All the toxic perc that doesn't end up in our air seeps into our drinking water, oceans, rivers, lakes, and soil where it kills plants.[75]

Perc also happens to fall under the category of persistent organic pollutants, or POPs, which means it can jump coasts and countries by catching a ride in the atmosphere.[76] That means the toxic effects of your pressed and pleated dress pants can end up in China.

There are some safer dry cleaning alternatives. I listed them in order of best results.

CARBON DIOXIDE DRY CLEANING It's as simple as it sounds. Instead of using perc, cleaners use CO_2 to get clothes clean and pressed. No additional CO_2 is created in the process, while much of it is actually recycled. CO_2 dry cleaning is more expensive so not widely available, but it's the best option in my book. To find one in your area, visit Findco2.com.

GREENEARTH CLEANING A cleaner solution to dry cleaning, GreenEarth uses liquid silicone, or D5, instead of toxic solvents. Apparently, it's much safer and less harsh on clothes, but one study says otherwise. D5 was found to cause cancer in rats. The EPA hasn't looked into it yet, and the Silicones Environmental Health and Safety Council say that's bonkers. But the verdict is still out.[77]

WET CLEANING This professional system is available at some dry cleaners, especially in metropolitan areas. Rather than use perc, they get your clothes superclean with water, nontoxic biodegradable solvents, and conditioners. Your threads are then ironed and pressed with safer equipment. Before you drop 'n go, call the cleaners and ask what chemicals they use. Do a little background check first. Some use trichloroethylene, which is similar to perc, to pretreat clothes.

HAND WASH If a label reads "Dry Clean Only," that could just mean not to put it through the ringer in the washer and dryer. Get off your ass and use your hands. Make sure to use a gentle, nontoxic detergent and lay it down flat to air dry. My little trick is to lay a thin damp towel over the item when it's dry, and iron over the towel. This keeps it safe from the direct heat of the iron, but uses steam to get the pressed look.

CHAPTER 8
The Skinny: Accessories

★ Walking the Walk:
A VEGAN SHOE GUIDE

The last time it was adorable to wear animals on our feet was when we were also sporting pigtails. That's because they were fuzzy slippers, girlfriend, and we were five years old. We were just too young to see the irony.

Now that we're old enough to cross the street without holding mommy's hand, the animals on our feet aren't so precious. That's because they are real—real dead. They went through a lot of trouble to end up on our feet.

You probably don't even think twice about it. Shoe and apparel manufacturers have been brilliant at keeping us so disconnected from our products and their sources. Court us with labels that say "Made with Genuine Leather," and we think *quality*. Not a calf getting his throat slit. When in fact, pound for pound, leather is a slaughterhouse's most profitable product—not meat.[78] It gets even sicker. Much of the leather in this country is from India and China.[79] In China, there are very few laws around animal rights, so those tan leather boots could be coming from somebody's dog. As in, ruff-ruff.

The environment suffers from all this animal exploitation, too. Animal skins are supposed to be inherently biodegradable. But if that leather jacket started to biodegrade while you were wearing it, it might not look too good for the company who sold it to you. Refund, please. To prevent biodegradation, they use a fair share of deadly chemicals. Some of the more common are formaldehyde, aniline, chromium, arsenic, chlorophenols, and cyanide-based dyes.[80] Chlorophenols are what you get when you add chlorine to phenol, a compound that comes from benzene.[81] Not good. These sulfides, acids, and sludge sneak out of tanneries and pose some serious threats to our health and nature.[82] It's a fact. A study from the Centers for Disease Control even found that the incidence of leukemia among residents near one tannery was five times greater than the rest of the United States.[83]

REBECCA MINK'S SHOE FETISH

It goes without saying, we need more vegan shoes. Especially cute ones. If you're a vegan with style, you know where I'm coming from. I'd wear those silly animal slippers before stepping out in public in half of the cruelty-free shoes out there.

Enter SoCal native and vegan shoe goddess-slash-designer, Rebecca Mink. Rebecca's Italian-made shoe line, Mink Shoes, is her solution to weaning the fashion world off of leather or any other animal materials. Back in 2000, she jumped on a plane to Italy, shoe sketches in hand, looking for someone who would make them. The response was not cool. Sixteen factories refused to even think about manufacturing a shoe that didn't make barnyard noises. Then Rebecca met Marco Gambassi. Marco's family had been shoe cobblers for generations, and he saw vegan shoes as a challenge.

Three years later, Rebecca had some shoes to sell, fabricated from materials such as reclaimed wood, denim, rubber, linen, faux fur, cork, and organic fabrics. "It is *not* difficult to find materials to make quality shoes from," said Rebecca. "But it is difficult to change the mentality that shoes don't have to be made from animal products." She has named every style in honor of the animal kingdom—Mink, Chimpanzee, Lemure, Coyote, Raccoon to throw out a few. (I'm nuts for her gray velvet "Kitten" flats with leopard print lining.) The blond bombshell even ships her chic heels and footwear in a reusable shoebox with recycled paper and handles. I just want to spank her she's so damn savvy.

With the new environmental push, Rebecca is also hoping that designers and shoemakers stop using as many animal products to lower their impact. Whatever gets us there. "It takes twenty times more energy to produce a leather pelt as it does to make a synthetic material or non-animal product," she says.

Though Mink Shoes is now a hot item—especially on the celebrity circuit—Rebecca welcomes competition. She'd like to see more vegan shoe brands. Why? Because she has a heart, people. The whole reason she got into this damn business was to stop ruthless animal cruelty. She says that everything is starting to change. Factories are reaching out wanting to help make her product even more sustainable, and there are more vegan material options. Department stores are ordering because of consumer demand. That would be *you*. Nike, Timberland, Columbia, New Balance, and even Payless are making vegan shoe options.

"The entire shoe industry is adapting. If a shoe company does not do something to make their shoes more sustainable, they are now asked why. The customer is educated and wants to buy a product they feel good about."

Visit www.healthybitchdaily.com for more vegan shoe shopping tips next time you think those Screw Me pumps in the storefront window are calling your name. They're calling every girl's name with a wallet, sugar.

THE ANATOMY OF
A VEGAN SHOE

It looks like shoe designers are finally starting to get creative with what they use to decorate our feet. Just for shits and giggles, Rebecca clued me in on what unconventional materials are making their way into vegan shoe designs for a lighter footprint:

"UPPER," OR OUTER MATERIALS: Look for organic cotton, organic cotton velvet, bio ultra suede, organic linen, organic canvas, recycled materials, recycled hardware, cotton satin, organically dyed denim, and organic paints. "Upcycled" materials such as plastic bottles, cassette tapes, and glass are great, too. Reclaimed materials help out in more ways than one: They save animals and lighten your carbon footprint.

SOLES AND HEELS: Look for corn plastic, biodegradable plastics, titanium, wood (from sustainable sources), eco cork, and rubber.

GLUES: Look for non-animal glues made from plant-based or water-based solvents.

EXTRA CREDIT—SHIPPING MATERIALS: Ask if they use boxes or bags made from 100 percent recycled material and soy-based inks.

Um, what are you waiting for? Your feet want some Mink action. Check out minkshoes.com to get you a pair.

VEGAN SHOE GUIDE

Be willing to ask some questions when you're on the hunt for cruelty-free shoes. You can't just click your heels together and have them magically appear. Though that would be super. You have to watch out for the shoes that reel you in with a man-made upper; when you turn them upside down you might find a problem . . . leather. If it means anything to you, ask questions. That is why shoe stores hire people—to wait on you hand and foot.

If you want to save valuable time, below are some of the brands I always turn to when I need to style out my feet with something cruelty-free. Keep in mind that some of these brands also carry non-vegan shoe lines, so you have to narrow your search.

Neuaura Shoes (neuaurashoes.com)
Beyond Skin (beyondskin.co.uk)
Stella McCartney (stellamccartney.com)
Madden Girl (mooshoes.com)
Olsenhaus (olsenhaus.com)
Saucony Originals Jazz Low Pro Vegan
   (saucony.com)
Footzyrolls (footzyrolls.com)
TOMS Shoes (toms.com)

ECOISTA 101:
QUIT TREATING STYLE LIKE YOUR LATEST FLING

We buy. And we buy. Then we buy some more. But retail therapy will only make you feel better about getting dumped for, like, five minutes. Then you realize you're stuck with a pair of white leggings that you can't wear until after Easter. Poor you.

"We need to change the way we think about buying clothes," says Rachel Lincoln Sarnoff, founder and editor of EcoStiletto.com. Like me, Rachel is so over seeing people waste their money to create more waste. "Just say no to disposable fashion made from cheap and unsustainable fabrics, and think about creating a long-term relationship with your closet! Avoid hook-ups and one-night stands—think about clothing purchases as things that you want to live with for a long, long time. That doesn't mean wearing things that are out of style. It simply means being more conscious of what we buy—and working with what we've got."

As up as she is now on her environmental facts, Rachel was once clueless. A journalist by trade, the woman was writing for top fashion magazines for more then ten years about little black dresses and why python was the new leopard print. Then while she was preggo with her third child, she got involved with Healthy Child, Healthy World—an organization that educates consumers on the environment's effect on our kids' health. All this talk about pesticides in cotton and upcycling got her thinking that maybe—just maybe—she was all wrong about fashion. She got to work brushing up on her stuff, and now takes the green message mainstream as an eco-spokesperson for leading fashion and beauty publications, blogs, and entertainment shows. Through her own online magazines—EcoStiletto.com and MommyGreenest.com—Rachel is educating the fashion-hungry and mamas alike to get with the picture. Seriously, do you really need a few dozen baby bibs? Don't just throw a baby shower to see how much you can fit in one crib.

So you get it. Rachel likes putting band-aids all over the planet. It's real cute and all, but that's not why I went to her. I wanted this stylish know-it-all to tell us where she shops. Every time I see her, she looks like she just had lunch with Anna Wintour. I want some of that. I want to look like that. Rachel, Rachel, Rachel!

Without further ado, here are a few of Rachel's favorite sustainable go-tos for girls who like to shop:

Dalia MacPhee Evening Gowns (daliaonline.com)

Nicole Bridger Basics (nicolebridger.com)

Milk and Honey Shoes (milkandhoneyshoes.com)

★ Arm Candy:
VEGAN PURSES AND HANDBAGS

Every girl is entitled to a good purse . . . or three. Just because you've chosen not to sling around leather on your arm doesn't mean you have to go handbag-less. Ditch the fake Chanel and "Goach" purses too while you're at it. Vegan or not, that's just a flat-out fashion don't.

Nowadays, cruelty-free bags aren't just for those with a heart. The more women like you realized that genuine leather wasn't the statement you wanted to make, the more designers saw a market with their name on it. You can't blame them. Any run-of-the-mill designer can make a leather bag that sells. But there are so many more materials to play with when you're not treating animals like commodities—recycled plastic bottles, organic cotton, hemp, bamboo, vintage fabrics such as brocades or taffeta, microfibers, straw, pleather, faux fur, and more. Clutch or handbag, day or night—I have found plenty of vegan arm candy that looks straight off the pages of *Vogue* (Shhh, but some of them are). You can maintain your image and the fashion police won't bother you either. Besides, they're way too busy with the girls in the see-thru leggings whose bare asses are hanging out.

HELL IN A HANDBAG

Whether you're a vegan looking to expand your options or just interested in losing the leather addiction, here are a few things to take into consideration:

LOVE THE LEATHER AND EXPECT THE PLEATHER. As with jackets, you do hit an environmental conundrum. If you like the leather look—which many of us do—it's tough to avoid pleather. For an everyday bag, they're actually the most reasonable in terms of price and efficiency. Again, look for bags and clutches made from polyurethane (PU) because it's considered much safer for both your body and home. As long as you buy a bag that matches the better part of your wardrobe, it should last you a while. If you keep that purse around for a year, then swap it with a friend or donate it to a secondhand store, that makes it an even better buy. One more thing before I bag on PVC . . . if you're going pleather, think about buying secondhand. You'll save a buck and it's better for the environment.

REALLY, REALLY TRY TO AVOID PVC. While it's not easy to do, steer clear of faux handbags made from PVC. The hazardous plastic seems to be a part of a major lead epidemic. When the Center for Environmental Health (CEH) tested purses made from PVC at one hundred different retailers, they found scary levels of lead. Some were one hundred times higher than the "safe levels" set for kid's toys![84] You're bringing that lead into your home and letting it invade your closet when you flaunt PVC on your arm. Let's just say a few of those purses didn't contain lead. Kudos to them. Instead, they were

contaminated with chlorine, phthalates, and VOCs. Hear that? VOCs don't just offgas from your god-damn walls and furniture. They're just as happy emanating from your purse, too.[85]

LOOK FOR PURSES MADE FROM RECYCLED BOTTLES. Let me start by saying that a bag made from recycled bottles or containers doesn't have to look like plastic bottles. No, honey. Nobody expects you to hit the clubs with your driver's license in a clutch made of juice boxes. I'd rather sit home and watch old western movies than go to dinner with a handbag made of upcycled Capri Suns. Actually recycled bottles can achieve any look the designer or manufacturer really wants. Just ask Matt & Nat. The vegan handbag and accessory brand uses plastic bottles to create faux suede and nylon linings that look just like the real thing. Believe it.

LESS IS MORE. I'm not going to tell you how many purses you should have. If I did, I'd be calling myself out. But for your sanity and to limit clutter, stick with neutral colors. You waste half of your day trying to find debit cards, your ID, birth control, and lipstick when you switch purses like a crazy person. A woman's purse is already like the Bermuda Triangle. Don't make yourself even more scatterbrained.

NATURAL DOESN'T MEAN NATURAL LOOKING. I'm not kidding when I tell you that bags made of recycled or natural materials don't have to be homely. You will come across the most stylish bags made with organic hemp and cotton corduroy, natural rubber, vintage zippers and embellishments, and reclaimed car upholstery—the latter being the work of Kim White, one of Monica Schweiger's vintage handbag designer favorites (see page 191). Think roadster style like Steve McQueen with a touch of your mom's closet.

> **KIM'S PICKS:**
> **HANDBAGS, PURSES, AND CLUTCHES**
> Matt & Nat (mattandnat.com)
> Parapette (parapette.com)
> Big Buddha (ebigbuddha.com)
> Vegan Queen (veganqueen.com)

Acknowledgments

I want to thank my literary agent Laura Dail for believing in me, and having the tenacity to get things done. I appreciate you always being on top of everything. To everyone at Running Press who played a part in this book, especially Chris Navratil, Jennifer Kasius, Craig Herman, Seta Zink, and Joshua McDonnell. Your hard work and dedication is unwavering, and deeply appreciated.

Thank you to the amazing team who created such beauty in the photography for this book—Photographer Katrine Naleid, your eye for beauty is impeccable. Katrine's amazing assistant Stephen Austin Welch, and my son's favorite of the crew Chad Walker the digital technician. Stylist and interior designer Sarah Rosenhaus, who helped make everything look so spectacular. Rebecca Mink for the use of your beautiful shoes, and Stephane Barnouin for the incredible furniture you designed that ended up in almost every photo.

A big thank you to Dr. Cathy Green. My son visited you so often you practically became a family friend. You are such a kind and compassionate doctor, which makes all the difference when my little one is sick. You inspired me to dig deeper to uncover a healthier life for Jack. Andrea Adams, you have opened my eyes to so many things in life and I am grateful for your guidance and wisdom. Elizabeth Bryan, you are heaven sent my friend. I thank you for your strength, compassion and friendship.

To all my fabulous contributors: Emily Kroll, Dianne Kraus, Danny Seo, Sarah Backhouse, Sara Snow, Jill Pollack, Stacy Malkan, Ashley Beckman, Minka Robinson, Jennifer Barckley, Jenefer Palmer, Rachel Lincoln-Sarnoff, Alexandra Spunt, Siobhan O'Connor, Jessa Blades, Monica Schweiger, Alison Stanich Power, Jennifer Stanich Banmiller, Leanne Mai-ly Hilgart, and Rebecca Mink. You all have a piece of this book, and I thank you for your knowledge. Each of you is inspiring a movement to create a healthier place for the next generation.

Julie C. May, thank you so much for your friendship, and for taking the reigns of Healthybitchdaily.com and making magic happen.

You are greatly appreciated and I love you dearly.

Stacy Snavely, meeting you at Mothers Beach that February day was simply meant to be. I am very lucky to have you in my life; your kindness and love are beyond generous.

Jesse Sarr, we are cut from the same cloth, my Pisces friend. I treasure our friendship and feel blessed to have you in my life.

To my dear friend Carly Harrill, I am deeply grateful for your hard work, dedication, and creativity. Thank you doesn't quite express my gratitude for the constant help you provide in my life. I would be lost without you.

To my BFF Keesha Whitehurst Fredricksen, I am eternally grateful to have you as my best friend and sister. I could not function properly without your support. You are my rock.

To my family Jeri, Chrissy, Amanda, Melissa, Alex, and Eliott, and the Bessettes: John, Pat, Peter and Danny. I love you all so much.

To my parents; Rob and Linda, all my love as always. Thank you for being my parents. I wouldn't be here if it weren't for you, Momushka.

To my son Jack, you were the inspiration for this book, and it all started while you were growing in my tummy. I wanted you to have a healthy life from the start, which led me to this journey. You inspire me to be a better person and work through my issues so I don't pass anything too annoying on to you. I have learned so much from you and I am honored to be your mommy. You are a brilliant, funny, sweet boy, and I look forward to a lifetime of happiness with you.

To my husband Stephane, my love, you are always patiently waiting for me to finish a book. I thank you from the bottom of my heart for being so supportive in what I do. Words cannot express how thankful I am that you are always there for me, no matter what. Thank you for your love. Thank you for Jack. Thank you for giving me the freedom to be who I am. I love you.

SOURCES CONSULTED

"A Good Home Water Filter Will Protect You From Drinking Human Feces, Chlorine, Lead, Pesticides, and Prescription Drugs." Waterfilterresearch.com, accessed Oct 3 2010. waterfilterresearch.com

"A Lot To Say Eco T-Shirt Line: The Revolution." Alototsay.com, accessed Nov 23 2010. shop.alottosay.com/pages/why-our-tees-are-the-ultimate-environmental-wear

"About Chemicals & Fertilizers." Landscape-planet.com, accessed Aug 2 2010. www.landscapeplanet.com/maintenance-2.htm

"About phthalates-history." Phthalate-free.de, accessed Aug 3 2010. www.phthalate-free.de/history.htm

"About Phthalates."Ourstolenfuture.org, last modified Nov 2006. Accessed July 28 2010. www.ourstolenfuture.org/newscience/oncompounds/phthalates/phthalates.htm

"About the Breast Cancer Fund." Breast-cancerfund.org, accessed March 29 2011. www.breastcancerfund.org/about/

"Absolutely Scandalous." Animalaid.org.uk, Apr 2005. Accessed Feb 27 2011. secure.wsa.u-et.com/www.animalaid.org.uk/lwc/fashion.htm

"Active Ingredients." Sephora.com, accessed Feb 22 2011. www.sephora.com/browse/product.jhtml?id=P190038#moreInfo

Adams, Jill U. "FDA is reviewing the use of antibacterial products containing triclosan." Los Angeles Times, April 19 2010. Accessed Sept 3 2010. articles.latimes.com/2010/apr/19/health/la-he-closer-20100419-20

Adams, Kristen. "Paraben Preservatives and Cosmetics: Controversy and Alternatives." Ecomall.com, accessed Sept 18 2010. www.ecomall/greenshopping/cosmetic.htm

Adams, Mike. "Warning: Toxic Chemical Triclosan Can Turn Your Toothpast Into Chloroform." Naturalnews.com, Feb 13 2006. Accessed Feb 18 2011. www.naturalnews.com/017804.html

Agarwal, Sandeep. "Vintage Denim-At What Cost To Environment?" Denimsandjeans.com, Nov 18 2009. Accessed Aug 17 2010. www.denimsandjeans.com/denim/manufacturing-process/vintage-denim-at-what-cost-to-environment/

"Air Purifier Glossary." Rabbitair.com, accessed Sept 3 2010. www.rabbitair.com/air-purifier-glossary.aspx

"Allergic Contact Dermatitis From Carmine: Case Report." Medscape.com, accessed July 22 2010. www.medscape.com/viewarticle/717745_2

Alleyne, Richard. "Household cleaners may double risk of breast cancer." Telegraph.co.uk, July 2010. Accessed Sept 10 2010. www.telegraph.co.uk/health/healthnews/7837863/Household-cleaners-may-double-risk-of-breast-cancer.html

"Aluminum Starch Octenylsuccinate." Cosmeticsdatabase.com, accessed Oct 2 2010. www.cosmeticsdatabase.com/ingredient.php?ingred06=700326

"American Cancer Society on Parabens: Should I Be Concerned About Parabens in Antiperspirants?" Vashonorgaics.com, accessed Feb 24 2011. www.vashonorganics.com/education_center/american-cancer-society-on-parabens

"An Introduction to Indoor Air Quality (IAQ) Carbon Monoxide." Epa.gov, updated March 2 2011. Accessed Sept 20 2010. www.epa.gov/iaq/co.html#Health-Effects-Associated-with-Carbon-Monoxide

"An Introduction to Indoor Air Quality (IAQ): Formaldehyde." Epa.gov, accessed Sept 4 2010. www.epa.gov/iaq/formalde.html#HealthEffects

"An Introduction to Indoor Air Quality (IAQ): Volatile Organic Compounds (VOCs)." Epa.gov, Updated Nov 29 2010. Accessed Aug 3 2010. www.epa.gov/iaq/voc.html

"An Overview of the State of the World's Fresh and Marine Waters." Unep.org. Accessed Feb 24 2011. www.unep.org/dewa/vitalwater/article186.html

"American Cancer Society on Parabens: Should I Be Concerned About Parabens in Antiperspirants?" Vashonorgaics.com, accessed March 1 2011. www.vashonorganics.com/education_center/american-cancer-society-on-parabens

Anisman-Reiner, Victoria. "Aluminum in Deodorant: Toxic Ingredients in Antiperspirant, Brain Health, and Alzheimer's." Suite101.com, Feb 22 2008. Accessed Dec 2 2010. www.suite101.com/content/aluminum-in-deodorant-a45498

Anisman-Reiner, Victoria. "Toxic Toothpaste Inactive Ingredients: Hidden chemicals in your family's toothpaste may harm teeth & health." Suite101.com, Apr 25 2009. Accessed Feb 23 2011. www.suite101.com/content/toxic-toothpaste-inactive-ingredients-a112476

"Antibacterial Products." Greeninbklyn.com, accessed March 29 2011. greeninbklyn.com/1033/antibacterial-products/

"Are Leading Brand Laundry Detergents Environmentally Friendly?" Laundry-alternative.com, accessed Nov 1 2010. www.laundry-alternative.com/detergentsinfo.htm

"Are Leading Brand Laundry Detergents Environmentally Friendly?" Laundry-alternative.com, accessed Nov 13 2010. www.laundry-alternative.com/detergentsinfo.htm

"Are our Gulf Oil Spill Problems Over...or Just Beginning?" Sixwise.com, accessed July 15 2010. www.sixwise.com/Newsletters/2010/August/25/Gulf-Oil-Spill-Secret-Deceptions.htm

"Are You And Your Children Safe?" Cleaning-pro.com, accessed Sept 27 2010. www.cleaningpro.com/toxic.cfm

"Asbestos." En.wikipedia.org, last modified March 8 2011. Accessed Sept 17 2010. en.wikipedia.org/wiki/Asbestos

Ashton, Karen and Elizabeth Salter Green. *The Toxic Consumer:*

Living Healthy in a Hazardous World, New York/London: Sterling, 2008.

"Avon Beyond Color Radiant Lifting Eyeshadow." Cosmeticsdatabase.com, updated June 28 2010. Accessed March 29 2011. www.cosmeticsdatabase.com/product/331251/Avon_BEYOND+Color_Radiant_Lifting_Eyeshadow/

Ballad, Tricia. "Is Flame-Resistant Clothing Safe For Children?" livestrong.com, accessed Feb 27 2011. www.livestrong.com/article/257714-is-flame-resistant-clothing-safe-for-children

"Bamboo: Facts behind the fiber." Organicclothing.blogs.com, accessed March 30 2011. organicclothing.blogs.com/my_weblog/2007/09/bamboo-facts-be.html

"Bans on BPA gain traction." Stateline.org, March 4 2010. Accessed July 25 2010. www.stateline.org/live/details/story?contentId=465907

Barley, Lisa. "If cows wore shoes...they'd wear these. The newest vegan shoes are fun comfy, stylish and affordable. Hard to believe, huh?" Vegetarian Times, posted on findarticles.com, June 2005, accessed Feb 27 2011. findarticles.com/p/articles/mi_m0820/is_332/ai_n13734234/

Barron, Jon. "Antibacterial Soaps, Triclosan, and You." Healthiertalk.com, May 18, 2010. Accessed March 27 2011. www.healthiertalk.com/antibacterial-soaps triclosan-and-you-1806

"Beauty Basics: Expiration Dates." Wholeliving.com, accessed Oct 27 2010. www.wholeliving.com/article/beauty-basics-expiration-dates

"Beauty Secrets: Phthalates." Ewg.org, accessed Sept 26 2010. www.ewg.org/node/8168

"Beauty Secrets: The Dangers of Phthalates: Industry Spin vs Fact." Ewg.org, accessed Aug 1 2010. www.ewg.org/node/8174

"Beauty Industry Secrets Investigated." Aolhealth.com, Nov 9 2009. Accessed Nov 22 2010. www.aolhealth.com/2009/11/09/beauty-industry-secrets-investigated/

"Beauty Product Danger." Natureprofarms.com, accessed March 16 2011. www.natureprofarms.com/page.html

"Bees and honey." Vegansociety.com, accessed Aug 29 2010. www.vegansociety.com/resources/animals/bees-and-honey.aspx

"Bedding." Greenyour.com, accessed Aug 27 2010. www.greenyour.com/home/bedroom/bedding

"Benzene." En.wikipedia.orf, last modified March 9 2011. Accessed Jan 27 2011. en.wikipedia.org/wiki/Benzene
"Benzophenone-1." Cosmeticdatabase.com, accessed Feb 26 2011. www.cosmeticdatabase.com/ingredient.php?ingred06=700685

"Biodegradability." En.wiktionary.org, last modified Oct 21 2010. Accessed July 20 2010. en.wiktionary.org/wiki/biodegradability

"Biodegradable Plastic Bags." Biodegradable-plasticbags.org, accessed Sept 27 2010. www.biodegradableplasticbags.org/

Bird, Katie. "Safe Cosmetics Act introduced in House of Representatives." Cosmeticdesign.com, July 22 2010. Accessed Nov 3 2010. www.cosmeticsdesign.com/Market-Trends/Safe-Cosmetics-Act-introduced-in-House-of-Representatives

"Bisphenol A. Quickview." U.S Environmental Protection Agency, updated march 7 2011. Accessed Sept 2 2010. cfpub.epa.gov/ncea/iris/index.cfm?fuseaction=iris.showQuickView&substance_nmbr=0356

Blair, L.Ac, Katie. "Choosing the right (non-poisonous) candles for your home." Allthingsnaturalstore.com, accessed July 12 2010. www.allthingsnaturalstore.com/candles%20article.htm

Blair, Katie. "Why Organic Cotton." Allthingsnaturalstore.com, accessed March 27 2011. www.allthingsnaturalstore.com/why%20organic%20cotton%20article.htm

"Bleach." Everything2.com, March 14 2005. Accessed July 17 2010. everything2.com/user/allseeingeye/writeups/Bleach

"Bleach and the Environment." Factsaboutbleach.com, accessed Jan 2 2011. www.factsaboutbleach.com/bleach_and_the_environment.html

"Bleach." How Products Are Made Volume 2, Madehow.com, accessed Feb 26 2011. www.madehow.com/Volume-2/Bleach.html

"Blepharitis." En.wikipedia.org, updated Feb 13 2011. Accessed March 25 2011. en.wikipedia.org/wiki/Blepharitis

"Blush Potentially Containing: Lead." Cosmeticsdatabase.com, accessed Nov 27 2010. www.cosmeticsdatabase.com/browse.php?category=blush&impurity=726334

Bocco, Diana. "How Much Garbage Does a Person Create in One Year?" Wisegeek.com, last modified Feb 22 2011. Accessed March 30 2011. www.wisegeek.com/how-much-garbage-does-a-person-create-in-one-year.htm

"Bottled Water: Pure Drink or Pure Hype?" Nrdc.org, accessed Oct 15 2010. www.nrdc.org/water/drinking/bw/exesum.asp

"BPA and Phthalates...Should you "Purge" your plastics?" Autismspot.com, Aug 30 2010. Accessed Sept 27 2010. www.autismspot.com/blog/BPA-and-Phthalates...should-you-"purge"-your-plastics

Breyer, Melissa. "Air Fresheners: Easy Greening." Care2.com, accessed Sept 2 2010. www.care2.com/greenliving/air-fresheners-easy-greening.html

Breyer, Melissa. "Parabens: Easy Greening." Care2.com, Jan 20 2007. Accessed March 30 2011. www.care2.com/greenliving/parabens-easy-greening.html#

Bristow, Sydney. "Green and Clean Kitchen Sponges." Apartmenttherapy.com, July 3 2008. Accessed July 8 2010. www.apartmenttherapy.com/la/cleaning/green-and-clean-kitchen-sponges-055172

Bronner, David. "A 5 Star Comparison & Ranking of US & European "Organic", "Made with", and "Natural" Personal Care Standards." Organicconsumers.org, accessed Jan 17 2011. www.organicconsumers.org/bodycare/drb_compare.cfm

"Buy Organic Cotton Jeans." Greenyour.com, accessed Nov 23 2010. www.greenyour.com/body/clothing/jeans/tips/buy-organic-cotton-jeans

Butterworth, Trevor. "Is The EPA About To Shut Down Urban Renewal Across The U.S.?" Forbes.com, Sept 15 2010. Accessed Oct 16 2010. blogs.forbes.com/trevorbutterworth/2010/09/15/is-the-epa-about-to-shut-down-urban-renewal-across-the-u-s/

Cadena, Christine. "Oral Health: Do You Know What'you're your Toothpaste?" Associatedcontent.com, accessed Feb 27 2011. www.associatedcontent.com/article/294740/oral_health_do_you_know_what_is_in.html?cat=69

"California's phthalates ban now in effect." Saferstates.com, Jan 5 2009. Accessed Aug 1 2010. www.saferstates.com/2009/01/californias-pht.html

"Can I recycle My Straw? Top 12 Recycling FAQs Answered Once and For All." Ecostiletto.com, May 3 2010. Accessed Feb 25 2011. www.ecostiletto.com/index.php?/GoodLife/comments/can_i_recycle_my_straw_burning_recycling_faqs_answered_once_and_for_al

"Cancer." Cosmeticdatabase.org, accessed March 30 2011. cosmeticsdatabase.org/ingredient.php?ingred06=702285#cancer

"Candles and the environment." Greenlivingtips.com, first published Feb 2007, updated March 2009. Accessed Sept 1 2010. www.greenlivingtips.com/articles/78/1/Candle-choices.html

"Carcinogenesis Bioessay of Bisphenol A." U.S Department of Health and Human Services, March 1982. Accessed Jan 28 2011. ntp.niehs.nih.gov/ntp/htdocs/LT_rpts/tr215.pdf

"Care What You Wear: Facts on Cotton & Clothing Production. Cotton: Facts Behind the Fiber (Part One)." Organicconsumers.org, July 29 2007. Accessed Feb 27 2011. www.organicconsumers.org/articles/article_6347.cfm

"Cargo Blu_Ray Mascara." Cosmeticdatabase.com, updated Oct 1 2009. Accessed Oct 29 2010. www.cosmeticdatabase.com/product/170234/CARGO_blu==ray_Mascara/

"Cars, Trucks, Air Pollution and Health." Nutramed.com, Updated March 2011. Accessed March 3 2011. www.nutramed.com/environment/cars.htm

Case, David. "The Real Story Behind Bisphenol-A." Watonics.org, Jan 16 2001. Accessed March 26 2011. - watoxics.org/news/pressroom/press-clips/the-real-story-behind-bisphenol-a

Ceruti, Silke. "Toothpaste-What's in it, and What You Should Know." Ezinearticles.com, accessed Sept 22 2010. ezinearticles.com/?Toothpaste—-whats-in-it-and-what-you-should-know&id=4235998

"Ceteareth-12: Cosmetic Toxin Data." Natural-skincare-authority.com, accessed 18 2010. www.natural-skincare-authority.com/ceteareth-12.html

Chadderdon, Lisa J. "Do You Know What's in that Paint You Put on your Walls?" Greenfeet.net, accessed Aug 25 2010. greenfeet.net/newsletter/whatsinpaint.shtml

"Charity: Water." Charitywater.org, accessed March 30 2011. www.charitywater.org/

Chavis, Jason C. "What is Phenoxyethanol." Wisegeek.com, last modified Jan 26 2011. Accessed March 30 2011. www.wisegeek.com/what-is-phenoxyethanol.htm

"Chemical Encyclopedia: (2,4-dichlorophenoxy) acetic acid." Healthychild.org, accessed Aug 26 2010. healthychild.org/issues/chemical-pop/polybrominated_dipheyl_ethers/

Chemical Encyclopedia: Toluene." Healthychild.org, accessed Sept 3, 2010. healthychild.org/issues/chemical-pop/toluene/

"Childhood Lead Poisoning Publication." Centers for Disease Control and Prevention, cdc.gov, updated March 3 2011. Accessed March 29 2011. www.cdc.gov/nceh/lead/publications/

Chinn, Lisa. "FDA Lead Regulations." Ehow.com, updated Aug 23 2010. Accessed Sept 27 2010. www.ehow.com/list_6860729_fda-lead-regulations.html

"Chlorophenols Other Than Pentachlorophenol." International Programme on Chemical Safety, Inchem.org, accessed Feb 28 2011. www.inchem.org/documents/ehc/ehc/ehc093.htm

"Choose life over death, Kindness over killing." Veganpeace.com, accessed Sept 4 2010. www.veganpeace.com/veganism/compassion.htm

"Choose Natural Nail Polish." Greenyour.com, accessed March 30 2011. www.greenyour.com/body/cosmetics/nail-care/tips/choose-natural-nail-polish

Clarren, Rebecca. "Not-so-green-jeans: Organic cotton is a leap ahead for the garment industry—not so the toxic dyes and finishing agents used in trendy eco-jeans." The Good Life posted on Salon.com, Jan 7 2008. Accessed March 29 2011. www.salon.com/life/good_life/2008/01/07/organic_jeans

"Coal Tar Hair Dyes: hair care cautions." Hairfinder.com, accessed March 29 2011. www.hairfinder.com/info/coaltardyes.htm

"Coal Tar Dyes." Davidsuzuki.org, accessed Feb 25 2011. www.davidsuzuki.org/issues/health/science/toxics/chemicals-in-your-cosmetics—-coal-tar-dyes/

"Cocamide DEA." Cosmeticdatabase.com, accessed Aug 2 2010. www.cosmeticsdatabase.com/ingredient.php?ingred06=701516

Cockcroft, Lucy. "Cosmetics giants agree to stop using shark oil." Telegraph online, Jan 30 2008, accessed Aug 1 2010. www.telegraph.co.uk/news/uknews/3323530/Cosmetics-giant-agree-to-stop-using-shark-oil.html

Coleman, Brenna. "The Benefits of Organic Cotton and Natural Latex Mattresses." Suite101.com, March 2 2010. Accessed June 2 2010. www.suite101.com/content/all-natural-green-mattresses-a208526

"Common household toxics and the products they're found in; Formaldehyde in the Home." Elc.org.uk, accessed Jan 2 2011. www.elc.org.uk/pages/envirohome.htm

"Compounds in non-stick cookware may be associated with elevated cholesterol in children and teens." Sciencedaily.com, Sept 7 2010. Accessed Oct 8 2010. www.sciencedaily.com/releases/2010/09/100906203040.htm

"Comprehensive Rules For Ecological And Socially responsible Textile Production." Global-standard.org, accessed Jan 1 2011. www.global-standard.org/

"Confidential Business Information." Epa.gov, updated Feb 10 2011. Accessed Oct 2 2010. www.epa.gov/oppt/tsca8e/pubs/confidential-businessinformation.html

"Congress Set to Reform Law on Personal Care Product Safety." Environmental-leader.com, July 22 2010. Accessed Feb 27 2011. www.environmentalleader.com/2010/-7/22/congress-set-to-reform-law-on-personal-care-product-safety/

"Consumers union and organic consumers association file federal trade commission petition urging action on deceptive 'organic' labeling practices of personal care products." Consumersunion.org, accessed Oct 22 2010. www.consumersunion.org/pub/core_product_safety/016027.html www.consumersunion.org/pdf/FTC-petition-0310.pdf

Corkil, Katherine. "Is Fragrance the Poison Dose." Personalcaretruth.com, Sept 28, 2010. Accessed Jan 22 2011. personalcaretruth.com/2010/09/is-fragrance-the-poison-dose/

"Cosmetics Bill Seeks Full Ingredient Disclosure, FDA Oversight." Greenbiz.com, July 22 2010. Accessed Feb 22 2011. www.greenbiz.com/news/2010/07/22/cosmetics-bill-seeks-full-ingredient-disclosure-fda-oversight

"Cosmetic Ingredient Review." Sourcewatch.org, accessed Sept 22 2010. www.sourcewatch.org/index.php?title=Cosmetic_Ingredient-Review

"Cosmetic Labeling Label Claims." The U.S Food and Drug Administration, Fda.gov, accessed July 17 2010. www.fda.gov/cosmetics/cosmeticlabelinglabelclaims/cosmeticlabelingmanuel/ucm126444.htm#clgl4

"Cosmetics Safety 'Virtually Unregulated' by fed law." Ewg.org, accessed Feb 22 2011. www.ewg.org/node/26544

"Cotton and the Environment." Ota.com, updated Feb 17 2011. Accessed Oct 1 2010. www.ota.com/organic/organic/environment/cotton_environment.html

"Cover Girl Exact Eyelights Mascara Black Sapphire 710." Cosmeticdatabase.com, June 18 2009. Accessed March 28 2011. cosmeticdatabase.com/Product/313360/CoverGirl_Exact_Eyelights_Mascara_Black_Sapphire_710_Blue_Eyes/

"Covergirl Fantastic Lash Curved Brush Mascara, Very Black 835."

Cosmeticdatabase.com, updated March 15 2009. Accessed Feb 22 2011. www.cosmeticdatabase.com/product/164942/CoverGirl_Fantastic_Lash_Curved_Brush_Mascara_Very_Black_835/

Crawford, S. "What Are The Different Types Of Water Based Adhesives." Wisegeek.com, accessed Feb 22 2011. wisegeek.com/what-are-the-different-types-of-water-based-adhesive.htm

"Cruelty Free Makeup Brushes." Animalfreezone.co.uk, accessed Feb 25 2011. animalfreezone.co.uk/cruelty-free-make-up-brushes.html

Dadd, Debra Lynn. "What is the difference between petroleum distillates and petrochemicals? Is one more toxic than the other?" Healthychild.org, accessed Sept 18 2010. healthychild.org/live-healthy/faq/petroleum_distillates_vs._petrochemicals

"Dangers of PEG Compounds in Cosmetics. Women at Increased Breast Cancer Risk?" Healthy-communications.com, accessed Aug 18 2010. www.healthy-communications.com/8polyethyleneglycol.htm

Das, Dr. Subrata. "Bamboo-21st century eco fiber: Application in towel sector." Fibre2fashion.com, accessed July 19 2010. www.fibre2fashion.com/industry-article/3/269/bamboo-21st-century-eco-fiber-application-in-towel-sector1.asp

Davis, Sammy. "Trust these 6 Green Beauty Product Labels." Thedailygreen.com, accessed July 12 2010. www.thedailygreen.com/living-green/natural-beauty-cosmetics/natural-beauty-product-labels

Decker, Susan, Jack Kaskey. 3M, DPont Settle Patent Fight over Coating Process for Teflon." Bloomberg.com, Dec 17 2010. Accessed Aug 3 2010. www.bloomberg.com/news/2010-12-17/3m-dupont-settle-patent-fight-over-coating-process-for-teflon.html

Deforestation: If We Don't Take Action, It Won't be an Issue Much Longer." Dougieg.com, accessed March 4 2011. www.dougieg.com/no_denial/deforestation.html

"Dental Systematic Health Hazards in your Toothpaste." Healingnaturally.com, accessed July 15 2010. www.healingnaturally.com/dental-systematic-health-hazards-toothpaste.html

Dudley PhD, Susan, Salwa Nassar, BA, Emily Hartman, BA. "Tampon Safety." Center4research.org, revised July 2009. Accessed Feb 24 2011. www.center4research.org/2010/04/tampon-safety/

Denison, Richard. "EPA IG Report: New Chemicals Program fails to assure protection." Edf.org, updated Feb 20 2010. Accessed March 29 2011. blogs.edf.org/naanotechnology/2010/02/20/epa-ig-report-new-chemicals-programs-fails-to-assure-protection/

"Deodorant." En.wikipedia.org, updated Mar 8 2011. Accessed March 29 2011. en.wikipedia.org/wiki/Deodorant

"Do You Use Products with Sodium Lauryl Sulfate (SLS)?" Antiagingchoices.com, revised July 17 2010. antiagingchoices.com/harmful_ingredients/sodium_lauryl_sulfate.htm

"Does fluoride accumulate in the body?" Poisonflouride.com, accessed Feb 22 2011. www.poisonflouride.com/pfpc/html/accumu-late_.html

"Don't Pucker up: Lead in Lipstick. From the Department Store to the Drugstore: Lead on Your Lips." Abcnews.go.com, Oct 12 2007. Accessed Oct 23 2010. abcnews.go.com/GMA/story?id=3722013

"Dry cleaning." En.wikipedia.org, last modified March 11 2011. Accessed Feb 26 2011. en.wikipedia.org/wiki/Dry_Cleaning

Dunn, Collin. "Get the Scoop on Green Wood Furniture: Find furniture that's healthy for you and your home." Planetgreen.discovery.com, April 22 2008. Accessed July 19 2010. planetgreen.discovery.com/home-garden/find-eco-friendly-wood-furniture-for-health.html

Dunn, Collin. "Haute Green Sneak Peek. Organic Cotton Upholstery by Mod Green Pod." Treehugger.com, accessed Aug 2 2010. www.treehugger.com/files/2006/05/organic_cotton_4.php

"Dust Mites: Everything you might not want to know!" Ehso.com, accessed Oct 1 2010. www.ehso.com/ehshome/dustmites.php

Dwornick, Lorie. "Chemical Warfare Agents and Toxic Waste Disquised as Household Cleaning Products." Rense.com, accessed Aug 2 2010. www.rense.com/general19/chemical.htm

"Easily Lead." Snopes.com, updated Nov 12 2008. Accessed March 29 2011. www.snopes.com/medical/toxins/lipstick.asp

"Eco-Friendly Wood Furniture: Go Green with Your Home Décor." Greenprofs.com, accessed Aug 2 2010. greenprofs.com/eco-friendly-wood-furniture-go-green-with-your-home-décor/

"Educate Yourself." Thehomebottega.com, accessed July 10 2010. thehomebottega.com/productinformation.aspx

"8 Cosmetic Chemical Offenses." Greenlivingideas.com, May 20 2008. Accessed March 28 2011. greenlivingideas.com/topics/fashion-and-beauty/cosmetics/8-cosmetic-chemical-offenses

"8 Household Cleaning Agents to Avoid: Detox your home by avoiding these chemical culprits." Life.gaiam.com, accessed Sept 2 2010. life.gaiam.com/gaiam/p/MopCloset-MakeoverGetthechemicalsout.html

Ellin, Abby. "Skin Deep-A Simple Smooch or a Toxic Smack?" New York Times online, May 27 2009. Accessed March 28 2011. www.nytimes.com/2009/05/28/fashion/28skin.html?_r=1

"Endocrine Disruptors." Nrdc.org, revised Nov 25 1998. Accessed Sept 4 2010. www.nrdc.org/healthy/effects/qendoc.asp

"Endocrine disruptors." En.wikipedia.org, last modified March 4 2011. Accessed Sept 2 2010. en.wikipedia.org/wiki/Endocrine_disruptors

"EPA Settles PFOA Case against DuPont for Largest Environmental Administration Penalty in Agency History." Epa.gov, Dec 14 2005. Accessed Sept 4 2010. yosemite.epa.gov/opa/admpress.nsf/68b5f2d54f3eefd28525701500517fbf/fdcb2f665cac66bb852570d7005d6665!opendocument

"EPA Takes Final Step in Phaseout of Leaded Gasoline." Epa.gov, Jan 29 1996. Accessed Feb 21 2011. www.epa.gov/history/topics/lead/02.htm

Epstein, Sam. "Talcum Powder: The Hidden Dangers." Drfranklipman.com, accessed Feb 21 2011.
www.drfranklipman.com/talcum-powder-the-hidden-dangers/

Epstein, Samuel S. "The Danger of Toxic Consumer Products, Fragrances." Thehuffingtonpost.com, July 7 2010. Accessed Feb 22 2011.
www.huffingtonpost.com/samuel-s-epstein/toxic-chemicals_b_625648.html

"European Laws." Safecosmetics.org, accessed Feb 22 2011.
www.safecosmetics.org/article.php?id=346

"EU Ban on Animal Testing Comes into Force Today." Cosmeticdesign-europe.com
www.cosmeticdesign-europe.com/Formulation-Science/EU-ban-on-animal-testing-comes-into-force-today

"EWG Scorecard on Bottled Water." Energycommerce.house.gov, July 2009. Accessed Feb 24 2011.
democrats.energycommerce.house.gov/Press_111/20090708/ewgscorecard.pdf

"Eyelid." En.wikipedia.org, last modified March 10 2011. Accessed March 28 2011.
en.wikipedia.org/wiki/Eyelid

"Facts About Plastic Bottles." Earth911.com, accessed Aug 26 2010.
www.earth911.com/recycling/plastic/plastic-bottles/facts-about-plastic-bottles

"Facts about the Fur Trade." Infurmation.com, accessed March 28 2011.
www.infurmation.com/facts.php

"Facts to Know and How You Can Help." Illinois.edu, accessed Jan 22 2011.
www.campusrec.illinois.edu/gogreen/facts.html

"FAQ: The Compact for Safe Cosmetics." Safecosmetics.org, accessed Feb 20 2011.
www.safecosmetics.org/article.php?id=284

Faria, Alison. "What is Blush?" Wisegeek.com. Nov 17 2010. Accessed March 28 2011.
www.wisegeek.com/what-is-blush.htm

Farley, Dixie. "Dangers of Lead Still Longer." Allergybuyersclub.com, accessed Oct 1 2010.
www.allergybuyersclub.com/learning/articles/tfh/leadlingers.html

"FDA Regulations." Safecosmetics.com, accessed Feb 23 2011.
www.safecosmetics.org/section.php?id=75

"Federal Hazardous Substances Act." Consumer Product Safety Commission, updated March 16 2005. Accessed Feb 22 2011.
www.cpsc.gov/businfo/pppa/pppa09.pdf

Ferlow, Klaus. "Cosmetics to Die For." Stanson.org, updated Oct 21 2010. Accessed Oct 3 2010.
stanson.org/articles/wellbeing/health/Cosmetics-To-Die-For.html

"Few Sunscreens Win Green Rating." Ewg.org, May 24 2010. Accessed Sept 16 2010.
www.ewg.org/2010sunscreen/full-report/

"15 Ingredients in Cosmetics You Should Know About." Forensicsciencetechnician.org, accessed July 28 2010.
www.forensicsciencetechnician.org/15-ingredients-in-cosmetics-you-should-know-about/

"Finding the best sunscreen: You know the drill: when the sun's rays are fierce, duck and cover." Ewg.org, accessed Feb 26 2011.
ewg.org/sunscreens-Get-Flunking-Grade-for-UVA-Protection

"Flame Retardant in Furniture Causes Concern." NYtimes.com, Jan 30 2002. Accessed Aug 2 2010.
www.nytimes.com/2002/01/30/us/flame-retardant-in-furniture-causes-concern.html

Fletcher, Lisa. "Lead Found in Women's Handbags. ABC News Exclusive: Retailers Agree to Test Purses for Lead Levels." ABC World News, abcnews.go.com, Jan 22 2010. Accessed March 28 2011.
abcnews.go.com/wn/lead-found-womens-handbags/story?id=9638944

"Fluorinated tap water and bottled water unsafe for infants, children, adults, and elderly." Examiner.com, accessed Sept 24 2011.
www.examiner.com/water-in-minneapolis/flourinated-water-tap-water-and-bottled-water-unsafe-for-infants-children-adults-and-elderly

"Formaldehyde." En.wikipedia.org, modified March 4 2011. Accessed March 4 2011.
en.wikipedia.org/wiki/Formaldehyde

"Formaldehyde and Cancer Risk." National Cancer Center, Cancer.gov, reviewed Nov 15 2010. Accessed Dec 1 2010.
www.cancer.gov/cancertopics/factsheet/Risk/formaldehyde

"Formaldehyde: It's not just for embalming anymore." Home-ec101.com, accessed Jan 28 2011.
www.home-ec101.com/formaldehyde-its-not-just-for-embalming-anymore/

"Formaldehyde Releasers in Everyday Products." Ecomall.com, accessed Jan 24 2011.
www.ecomall.com/greenshopping/formaldehyde.htm

"Four Chemicals That You Definitely Do Not Want in Your Moisturizer." Scribd.com, accessed Jan 2 2011.
www.scribd.com/doc/10047125/Four-Chemicals-That-You-Definitely-Do-Not-Want-in-Your-Moisturizer

"Frederick vom Saal: BPA in Bodies of 90% of Americans." Earthsky.org, Oct 11 2010. Accessed Aug 3 2010.
earthsky.org/health/frederick-vom-saal-bpa-harmful-to-humans-in-extremely-small-amounts

"Frequently asked questions: Toluene." Aromaticsonline.net, Sept 24 2010.
www.aromaticsonline.net/faq-toluene.html

"FTC Blows The Whistle On Bamboo-Based Textiles' Green Claims." Sincerelysustainable.com, Aug 14 2009. Accessed Feb 25 2011.
www.sincerelysustainable.com/products/clothing/ftc-blows-the-whistle-on-bamboo-based-textiles-green-claims

Gabriel, Julie. *The Green Beauty Guide*. Deerfield Beach, FL: Health Communications, Inc, 2008.

Gavigan, Christopher. "Beware of Lead in Christmas trees and Lights." Webmd.com, Nov 25 2009. Accessed Aug 1 2010. blogs.wedmd.com/health-ehome/2009/11/

Gerstein, Julie. "The Truth About Natural Toothpaste." Thedailygreen.com, accessed Feb 24 2011. thedailygreen.com/living-green/natural-toothpaste-ingredients-0307

"Getting the lead out." Snopes.com, updated Dec 31 2005. Accessed Oct 3 2010. www.snopes.com/inboxer/household/leadwick.asp

Gibson, M.D, Lawrence E. "Is it true that lipstick contains lead?" Mayoclinic.com, accessed Feb 21 2011. www.mayoclinic.com/health/lead-in-lipstick/AN01618

"Glossary." Raic.org, last modified Oct 15 2008. Accessed Sept 10 2010. www.raic.org/2030wiki/index.php?title=Glossary

Gonzalez, Samantha. "Get a Greener Clean: Hazards and Eco-Friendly Cleaning Options." Natural-products.suite101.com, March 2 2010. Accessed Sept 3 2010. natural-products.suite101.com/article.cfm/get-a-greener-clean

Gore-Tex." En.wikipedia.org, last modified Feb 15 2011. Accessed Aug 23 2010. www.en.wikipedia.org/wiki/Gore-Tex

Graham, Janis. "4 Summer Health Hazards and how to keep them from spoiling your warm-weather fun." Redbookmag.com, accessed Feb 24 2011. www.redbookmag.com/health-wellness/advice/summer-health-yl

"'Greener' stain-resistant coatings developed; avoid PFOA." Innovations-report.com, Aug 30 2005. Accessed Feb 23 2011. www.innovations-report.com/html/reports/life_sciences/report-48402.html

"Grime Fighters: How to take care of kitchen sponges." Revolutionhealth.com, updated Nov 30 2007. Accessed Oct 2 2010. www.revolutionhealth.com/healthy-living/natural-health/natural-home/health-hazards/sponge

"Green Dry Cleaning." Treehugger.com, June 1 2005. Accessed Jan 24 2011. www.treehugger.com/files/2005/06/green_dry_clean.php

"Greenwashing." En.wikipedia.org, last modified March 1 2011. Accessed Sept 25 2010. en.wikipedia.org/wiki/Greenwashing

Greer, Beth. "Chemicals in household cleaners may pollute indoor air." SFGate.com, July 19 2006. Accessed Aug 2 2010. articles.sfgate.com/2006-07-19/home-and-garden/17304606_1_cleaning-products-hazardous-chemical-endocrine-disrupting

"Guide to less toxic products: Cosmetics and Personal Care." Lesstoxicguide.ca, accessed Aug 3 2010. www.lesstoxicguide.ca/index.asp?fetch=personal

Gutierrez, David. "Chemicals in Soap Can Harm Children." Naturalnews.com, Feb 3 2011. Accessed Feb 25 2011. www.naturalnews.com/031192_soap_chemicals.html

Gunzelmann, Doug. "Plastic Bottle Facts Make Your Think Before You Drink." Greenupgrader.com, Aug 23 2008. Accessed Oct 1 2010. greenupgrader.com/3258/plastic-bottle-facts-make-you-think-before-you-drink/

Gutierrez, David. "Pests invade GM cotton crops in China." Naturalnews.com, Sept 26 2010. Accessed Jan 23 2011. www.naturalnews.com/029855_GM_crops_pests.html

Halliday, Sandy. "Alarming Toxic Chemicals in Sunscreen." Thedetoxspecialist.com, June 10 2009. Accessed Feb 12 2011. thedetoxspecialist.com/blog/detox/toxic-chemicals-in-sunscreens

Hautner, Wenonah. "Key Hand Sanitizer Ingredient May Cause More Harm Than Good." Institute for Policy Studies, Ips-dc.org, Feb 7, 2011. Accessed March 27 2011. www.ips-dc.org/articles/key_hand_sanitizer_ingredient_may_cause_more_harm_than_good

"Have you ever counted how many cosmetics or personal care products you use in a day? Chances are it's nearly 10." Cosmeticdatabase.com, accessed Feb 24 2011. www.cosmeticdatabase.com/research/whythismatters.php

Haynes, Fiona. "Is Non-Stick Cookware Safe? Is PFOA present in nonstick pans?" Lowfatcooking.about.com, accessed Aug 3 2010. lowfatcooking.about.com/od/healthandfitness/a/nonstickpans.htm

"Health Effects of Low-Level Exposure to Formaldehyde." Journal of Occupational and Environmental Medicine. December 1983. Volume 25 Issue 12. Accessed Aug 17 2010. journals.lww.com/joem/Abstract/1983/12000/Health_Effects_of_Low_Level_Exposure_to.13.aspx

"Health News: SLS." Webed.com, accessed July 7 2010. www.webed.com/healthnews/sls.htm

"Healthy furniture is the future in a green home." Greenlifesmartlife.com, March 12 2010. Accessed July 20 2010. greenlifesmartlife.wordpress.com/2010/03/12/healthy-furniture/

"Healthy Low VOC Interior and Exterior Sealers." Greenbuildingsupply.com, accessed Aug 27 2010. www.greenbuildingsupply.com/Public/Non-ToxicFinishes/Sealers/index.cfm

Heilprin, John. "Dupont sued over Teflon." Usatoday.com, posted July 19 2005. Accessed Sept 2 2010. www.usatoday.com/money/industries/manufacturing/2005-07-19-teflon_x.htm

Helmenstine, Anne Marie, ph.D. "Flame Retardant People: Health Effects of PBDE Absorption." Chemistry.about.com, accessed July 1, 2010. chemistry.about.com/cs/medical/a/aa102603a.htm

Henderson, Georgie. 'Hypoallergenic Properties of Bamboo Flooring." Suite101.com, Jul 12 2010. Accessed Oct 25 2010. www.suite101.com/content/hypoallergenic-properties-of-bamboo-flooring-a260623

Herbst, Helen. "How to green your garb. From shopping to washing, from drying to dry cleaning, let MNN show you how to green your sleeves." Mnn.com, Nov 26 2008. Accessed Aug 18 2010. www.mnn.com/lifestyle/responsible-living/stories/how-to-green-your-garb

"Hormone Disruptors and Women's Health: Reasons for Concern." Healthandenvironment.org, accessed Feb 20 2011. www.healthandenvironment.org/?module=uploads&func=download&fileId=550

"Hormone Mimics (Endocrine Disruptors): They're in Our Food. Should We Worry?" Consumer Reports, posted on Mindfully.org, June 1998. Accessed July 3 2010. www.mindfully.org/Pesticide/Hormone-Mimics-In-Food-htm

Hornick, Betsy, Eric Yarnell. "Alternative Treatments for Cancer." Discovery Health, Health.howstuffworks.com, accessed Feb 21 2011. health.howstuffworks.com/wellness/natural-medicine/alternative/alternative-treatments-for-cancer-ga5.htm

Houlihan, Jane. "Cosmetics with Banned and Unsafe Ingredients." Ewg.org, Sept 2007. Accessed Sept 17 2010. www.ewg.org/unsafecosmetics

Houlihan, Jane, Kris Thayer, Jennifer Klein. "EWG finds heated Teflon pans can turn toxic faster than DePont claims." Ewg.org, May 2003. Accessed Aug 23 2010. www.ewg.org/reports/toxicteflon

Houlihan, Jane, Sonya Lunder, Anila Jacob. "Timeline: BPA From Invention to Phase-Out." Ewg.org, April 2008, updated Dec 2010. Accessed Oct 4 2010. www.ewg.org/reports/bpatimeline

"Household Products Containing Petroleum Distillates and other Hydrocarbons; advance Notice of Proposed Rulemaking; Request for comments and information. " Cpsc.gov, Feb 26 1997. Accessed June 27 2010. www.cpsc.gov/businfo/frnotices/fr97/frpet-dis.html

"Household Products Database." Whatsin-products.com, accessed July 27 2010. whatsinproducts.com/msds.php?brandId=6990

"Household Products Labeling Act." Womensvoices.org, accessed Aug 18 2010. www.womensvoices.org/our-work-safe-cleaning-products/impact-laws/household-products-labeling-act/

"How Can Natural Skin Care Products Make a Difference." Grouped.biz, Sept 7 2010. Accessed Oct 13 2010. grouped.biz/2010/09/how-can-natural-skin-care-products-make-a-difference-2/

"How Eco-Friendly Is Bamboo." Life.gaiam.com, accessed Oct 2 2010. life.gaiam.com/gaiam/p/How-EcoFriendly-is-Bamboo.html

"How Green Are Plastic and Wire Coat Hangers." Foxnews.com, posted on Stevenkotler.com, Jan 1 2009. Accessed Aug 18 2010. www.stevenkotler.com/node/106

"How to Know What is in Household Cleaners." Ehow.com, accessed Aug 2 2010. www.ehow.com/how_5054062_household-cleaners.html

"How Recycling can Help Stop Global Warming." Help-stop-global-warming.com, accessed Sept 14 2010. www.help-stop-global-warming.com/global-warming-recycling.html

"How to Shop for Eco-Friendly Clothes-Part 2: Try TENCEL or Lyocell." Biggreenpurse.com, Jan 23 2011. Accessed Feb 26 2011. blog.biggreenpurse.com/biggreenpurse/toxic-chemicals/

"How To Use Essential Oils Efficiently." Floracopeia.com, accessed Jan 28 2011. www.floracopeia.com/content/uncategorized/how-to-use-essential-oils-safely

"How Toxic Are Your Household Cleaning Supplies?" Organicconsumers.org, accessed Sept 26 2010. www.organicconsumers.org/articles/article_279.cfm

"How Worried Should We Be About Everyday Chemicals." Shine.yahoo.com, June 8 2010. Accessed Sept 3 2010. shine.yahoo.com/channel/parenting/how-worried-should-we-be-about-everyday-chemicals-1676855

Huff, Ethan A. "More states move to ban BPA even while FDA does nothing." Naturalnews.com, May 7 2010. Accessed March 28 2011. www.naturalnews.com/028738_BPA_plastics.html

"IMIDAZOLIDINYL-UREA: Cosmetic Toxin Data." Natural-skincare-authority.com, accessed Feb 21 2011. www.natural-skincare-authority.com/IMIDAZOLIDINYL-UREA.html

"Imported Kids Apparels from China-Are they Toxic?" Fibre2fashion.com, June 5 2009. Accessed Jan 21 2011. www.fibre2fashion.com/industry-article/20/1930/imported-kids-apparels-from-china-are-they-toxic1.asp

"Impurities of Concern in Personal Care Products (As of Dec 2006)." Cosmeticdatabase.com, accessed Dec 2 2010. www.cosmeticsdatabase.com/research/impurities.php

"Include Low Level BPA Studies." Environmental Health News, June 14 2010. Accessed Aug 27 2010. www.thedailyclimate.info/ehs/blog/studies-showing-safe-levels-harm-are-missing

"Increase Fuel Mileage on a Car." Mindfully.org, accessed July 2 2010. www.mindfully.org/Sustainability/Magazine-Environmental-impacts.html

"Indoor Plants Found to Release Volatile Organic Compounds." Sciencedaily.com, Sept 6 2009. Accessed Sept 2 2010. www.sciencedaily.com/releases/2009/09/090903163949.htm

"Indoor Water Use in the United States." United States Environmental Protection Agency, Epa.gov. Accessed Jan 23 2011. www.epa.gov/WaterSense/pubs/indoor.html

"Ingredients in Makeup and Cosmetics that are Dangerous." Healthfoodemporium.com, accessed March 27 2011. www.healthfoodemporium.com/index_dangerous-ingredients.php

"International Study Finds No Safe Level of Lead in Children's Blood." Cincinnatichildrens.org, July 6 2005. Accessed July 28 2010. www.cincinnatichildrens.org/about/news/release/2005/7-lead.htm

"Is bottled water healthier or safer than tap?" Mnn.com, Oct 23 2008. Accessed Oct 3 2010. www.mnn.com/lifestyle/health-wellbeing/questions/is-bottled-water-healthier-or-safer-than-tap

"Is it a Cosmetic, a Drug, or Both? (or is it Soap?)" The U.S Food and Drug Administration, Gov.gov, July 8 2002. Accessed Feb 20 2011. www.fda.gov/cosmetics/guidancecomplianceregulatoryinformation/ucm074201.htm

"Is Perfume Pollution as Harmful as Cigarette Smoke?" Shine.yahoo.com, May 14 2009. Accessed Feb 21 2011. shine.yahoo.com/channel/beauty/is-perfume-pollution-as-harmful-as-cigarette-smoke-462329

"Is rayon bad for the environment?" Greenanswers.com, accessed Feb 23 2011. greenanswers.com/q/20527/products-shopping/manufacturing-materials/rayon-bad-environment

"Is Sodium Lauryl sulfate Safe?" Amomsblog.wordpress.com, July 2 2010. Accessed July 27 2010. amomsblog.wordpress.com/2010/07/02/is-sodium-lauryl-sulfate-safe/

"Is There a Squirrel in Your Makeup Bag?" Peta.org, accessed Feb 23 2011. www.peta.org/living/beauty-and-personal-care/synthetic-make-up-brushes.aspx

"1,4-dioxane." Safecosmetics.org, accessed Oct 1 2010. www.safecosmetics.org/article.php?id=288

Johneen, Manning. "Beauty Product Ingredients to Avoid." Suite101.com, accessed Jan 24 2011. www.suite101.com/content/beauty-product-ingredients-to-avoid-a79295

Joyce, Shawn Dell. "Hidden Danger of Phthalates." Paramus Post, March 8 2010. Accessed June 28 2010. www.paramuspost.com/article.php/201003080729337

Juniper, Tony. "Greenhouse effects:dishwasher tablets. Consumers need to take action themselves as cleaning agents for dishwashers often have a high phosphate content." The Sunday Times, timesonline.co.uk, accessed Oct 2 2010. www.timesonline.co.uk/tol/news/environment/article7008837.ece

Kahn, Michael. "Antibacterial wipes can spread superbugs: study." Reuters.com, June 2 2008. Accessed July 16 2010. www.reuters.com/article/iduSL0383329520080603

Kassem, Noreen. "Allergens and Toxins in Laundry Detergents. Synthetic Ingredients That Are Harmful to People and the Environment." Suite101.com, Mar 21 2010. Accessed Sept 13 2010. www.suite101.com/content/allergens-and-toxins-in-laundry-detergents-a21637

Kayne, R. Edited by Niki Foster."Is Teflon Dangerous?" Wisegeek.com, last modified Feb 24 2011. Accessed Sept 1 2010. www.wisegeek.com/is-teflon-dangerous.htm

Keim, Brandon. "Antibiotics Breed Superbugs Faster Than Expected." Wired.com, Feb 11 2010. Accessed March 28 2011. www.wired.com/wiredscience/2010/02/mutagen-antibiotics/

"Kid-safe Chemicals are now within our reach." Ewg.org, accessed Sept 1 2010. www.ewg.org/kid-safe-chemicals-act-blog/kid-safe-chemicals-act/

Koch, Wendy. "U.S. law requires less formaldehyde in wood products." USAtoday.com, July 19 2010. Accessed Aug 26 2010. content.usatoday.com/communities/greenhouse/post/2010/07/law-wood-less-formaldehyde/1

Kowski, Paul Kret, Marian Keeler, Kirsten Ritchie, Andrew Mangan. "Navigating the flooring Thicket: Find the Greenest Way to Meet Your Needs." Greenhomeguide.com, Sept 3 2009. Accessed July 27 2010. greenhomeguide.com/know-how/article/navigating-the-flooring-thicket-find-the-greenest-way-to-meet-your-needs

"Label Search Results." Greenerchoices.org, accessed July 27 2010. www.greenerchoices.org/eco-labels/label.cfm?LabelID=275&searchType=ProductArea&searchValue=Kitchen%20%26%20Bathroom%20Cleaners&refpage=productArea&refqstr=ProductCategoryID%3D328%26ProductAreaID%3D329

Lacroix, Lynda. "Eco-Friendly Handbags and Footwear- Surprising Facts About Leather and PVC." Ezinearticles.com, accessed Sept 2 2010. ezinearticles.com/?Eco-Friendly-Handbags-and-Footwear—-Surprising-Facts-About-Leather-and-PVC&id=3778505

Larkman, Michael. "Eco-friendly Bamboo: The hard facts behind the fiber." Curl Magazine, Curl.co.nz, Sept 14 2010. Accessed Jan 12 2011. www.curl.co.nz/2010/09/14/eco-friendly-bamboo-the-hard-facts-behind-the-fiber/

"Laundry Supplies: The Problems With Conventional." Ecoeveryday.com, accessed March 29 2011. www.ecoeveryday.com/the-facts.html

"Lead Acetate." Cosmeticsdatabase.com, Dec 12 2005. Accessed July 14 2010. www.cosmeticsdatabase.com/ingredients/703511/LEAD_ACETATE/

"Lead in Lipstick." Safecosmetics.org, accessed Feb 23 2011. www.safecosmetics.org/article.php?id=223

"Lead Poisoning." En.Wikipedia.org, last modified March 2 2011. Accessed Oct 3 2010. en.wikipedia.org/wiki/Lead_poisoning

"Leather." Idausa.org, accessed Jan 23 2011. www.idausa.org/facts/leatherfacts.html

"Leather: Animals Abused and Killed for Their Skins." Peta2.com, accessed Feb 22 2011. peta2.com/takecharge/t_factsheet_leather.asp

Lee, Xiao-Pen, Keizo Sato. "Toluene, benzene, xylene, and styrene." Springerlink.com, accessed Sept 1 2010. www.springerlink.com/content/mv1h582077p1h939/

Lewis, Truman. "Wal-Mart Bans BPA, Other Retailers Likely to Follow: Studies link the chemical to possible hormonal changes." Consumeraffairs.com, April 12 2008. Accessed Sept 28 2010. www.consumeraffairs.com/news04/2008/04/bpa.html

Lincoln-Sarnoff, Rachel. "Queen of Green: Cruelty Free Fashion Designers." Shoestringmag.com, March 26 2010. Accessed Sept 2 2010. www.shoestringmag.com/shopping/queen-green-cruelty-free-fashion

"Lips Against Lead-Free Lipstick From Terra Firma, Lavera, Suki and Jane Iredale." Ecostiletto.com, March 29 2009. Accessed Jan 23 2011. www.ecostiletto.com/index.php?/Beauty/comments/lips_against_lead-worthy_lipstick_from_terra_firma_lavera_suki_and_physica/

Loux, Renee. Easy Green Living: The Ultimate Guide to Simple, Eco-friendly Choices for You and your Home. New York: Rodale, 2008.

Lovattsmith, David. "Deadly facts about chemical-based household cleaners." Helium.com, Aug 30 2007. Accessed Aug 29 2010. www.helium.com/items/566373-deadly-facts-about-chemical-based-household-cleaners

"Lyral." Cosmeticdatabase.com, accessed Aug 2 2010. cosmeticdatabase.com/ingredient.php?ingred06=703649

M, Rex. "Dangers Hidden in Your Mattress." Sustainlane.com, Dec 29 2009. Accessed Sept 15 2010. www.sustainlane.com/reviews/dangers-hidden-in-your-mattress/KFYA2ZFB-DAVDN888JC9F1TUP98YO

McGilton, Jennifer. "Can Aluminum Pass the Blood Brain Barrier?" Biology.arizona.edu, Nov 1997. Accessed July 23 2010. student.biology.arizona.edu/ad/bbb.html

McKay, Michele. "Is Your Sunscreen Killing Coral?" Downtoearth.org, accessed Jan 23 2011. www.downtoearth.org/environment/ocean/your-sunscreen-killing-coral

McNally, Misty. "6 Ways to Manage Paint Leftovers." Naturalhomemagazine.com, July/Aug 2005. Accessed Sept 25 2010. www.naturalhomemagazine.com/Suggestions-for-your-Green-Home/6-ways-to-Manage-Paint-leftovers.aspx

"Make Up 101: Organic Schmorganic: The Truth About Organic Makeup." Collegecandy.com, Jan 15 2009, accessed Aug 22 2010. collegecandy.com/2009/01/15/makeup-101-organic-shmorganic-the-truth-about-organic-makeup/

Malan, Stacy. Not Another Pretty Face, BC, Canada: New Society Publishers, 2007.
"Managing Insomnia." Womenfitness.net, accessed Aug 27 2010. www.womenfitness.net/managing_insomnia.htm

Mangano, Frank. "The 5 Dangerous Chemicals In Our Homes." Naturalhealthontheweb.com, accessed Sept 24 2010. www.naturalhealthontheweb.com/chemicals/in-home.htm

Manning, Jennifer. "Looking Good, Feeling Bad; or, What's the problem with Perc (Percholorethylene)?" Environmentalchemistry.com, March 7 2006. Accessed Aug 3 2010. environmentalchemistry.com/yogi/environmental/200603percholorethylene-pt2.html

Mariec, Jean. "The Safe Chemicals Act: Fifteen Burning Questions and Fifteen Quenching Answers." Safetec.net, July 26 2010. Accessed Sept 1 2010. www.safetec.net/blog/2010/07/safe-chemicals-act-q-and-a.html

"Maryland is 5th state to ban BPA." Enviroblog.org, April 28 2010. Accessed Aug 3 2010. www.enviroblog.org/2010/04/maryland-bans-bpa-in-some-childrens-products.html

Mason, Donita. "The Healing Properties of Grapefruit Seed Extract." Examiner.com, Oct 9 2009. Accessed Sept 2 2010. www.examiner.com/alternative-pet-health-in-salt-lake-city/the-healing-properties-of-grapefruit-seed-extract?render=print

Masters, Coco. "How "fresh" is Air Fresheners." Time.com, Sept 24 2007. Accessed Oct 17 2010. www.time.com/time/health/article/0,8599,1664954,00.html

"Material Safety Data." Trconsultinggroup.com, April 1 2000. Accessed March 26 2011. www.trconsultinggroup.com/safety/msds/toluene.pdf

"Material Safety Data Sheet: Vitamin D Internal Standard Stock." Esainc.com, accessed March 27 2011. www.esainc.com/docs/spool/MSDS-062_Vitamin_D_Internal_Std_Stock.pdf

Maurer, Jacob. "Green Laundry Detergent Packs Mean Less Waste." Associatedcontent.com, Oct 8 2010. Accessed Jan 2 2011. www.associatedcontent.com/article/5875428/green_laundry_detergent_packs_mean.html?cat=57

"MedlinePlus: trusted Health Information for You." Food and Drug Administration, Jan 19 2011. Nlm.nih.gov, accessed Oct 22 2010. www.nlm.nih.gov/medlineplus/cosmetics.html

Meier, Eric. "Restricted and Endangered Wood Species." Wood-database.com, accessed Sept 20 2010. www.wood-database.com/wood-articles/restricted-and-endangered-wood-species/

Merchant, Brian. "How Fast Does Bamboo Grow? And why does it matter." Planetgreen.discovery.com, April 23 2009. Accessed Sept 3 2010. planetgreen.discovery.com/tv/go-for-the-green/green-brain-bamboo-grow.html

"Method for bleaching raw cotton and cotton textiles." Freepatentsonline.com, accessed Aug 27 2010. www.freepatentsonline.com/3990843.html

"Method for creating higher grade products from lower grade lumber." Freepatentsonline.com, accessed Aug 27 2010. www.freepatentsonline.com/6358352.html

Miller, G. Wayne, and Peter B. Lord. "Fatal Foam: It's just about everywhere." The Providence Journal. Provo.com, Sept 28 2003. Accessed June 3 2010. www.projo.com/sharedcontent/east/foam/partone.htmlNothing

"Mineral Makeup Dangers." Chemicaloftheday.squarespace.com, Apr 7 2010. Accessed Jan 29 2011. chemicaloftheday.squarespace.com/most-controversial/2010/4/7/mineral-makeup-dangers.html?currentPage=2

Mittelstaedt, Martin. "Coming to terms with perils of non-stick products." Theglobeandmail.com, published May 29 2006, last updated April 5 2009. Accessed Aug 2 2010. www.theglobeandmail.com/life/coming-to-terms-with-perils-of-non-stick-products/article826433/

Mok, Kimberly. "Buy Green: Tampons. From organic cotton to sea sponges to reusable cups, these five feminine products are easy on your body and the earth." Planetgreen.discovery.com, June 8 2009. Accessed Sept 24 2010. planetgreen.discovery.com/buying-guides/buy-green-tampons.html

Morrissey, Ed. "The good news that went unreported on air quality." March 15 2010. Accessed Nov. 3, 2010. hotair.com/archives/2010/03/15/the-good-news-that-went-unreported-on-air-quality

"Most Bottled Water Brands Don't Disclose Information About Source, Purity and Contaminates." Ewg.org, July 8 2009. Accessed Oct 4 2010. www.ewg.org/health/report/BottledWater/Bottled-Water-Scorecard/NewsRelease

"MSDA Toluene: Cosmetic Toxin Data." Natural-skincare-authority.com, accessed Aug 25 2010. www.natural-skincare-authority.com/msds-toluene.html

Mueller, Jennifer. "chemicals in Home Cleaning Products Revealed: Manufacturers to Disclose Ingredients in Detergents and Soaps." Greenliving.suite101.com, Sept 24 2001. Accessed Aug 27 2010. greenliving.suite101.com/article.cfm/chemical_ingredients_to_be_revealed_in_2010

"Nail Products and Salons." Safecosmetics.org, accessed Sept 26 2010. www.safecosmetics.org/article.php?id=224&printsafe=1

"Nanomaterials and hormone disruptors in sunscreens." Ewg.org, accessed Sept 3 2010. www.ewg.org/2010sunscreen/full-report/nanomaterials-and-hormone-disruptors-in-sunscreens

"NASA Study House Plants Clean Air." Zone10.com, accessed Aug 26 2010. www.zone10.com/nasa-study-house-plants-clean-air.html

"Nasal Polyps, Asthma, Allergies & Sinusitis." Achooallergy.com, originally published in the Feb 2008 Allergy Journal Report. Accessed Oct 2 2010. www.achooallergy.com/nasal-polyps.asp

Natural Home Magazine, July/August 2010 Issue, page 87

"Natural Organic Cosmetics." Health-report.co.uk, accessed Feb 23 2011. www.health-report.co.uk/natural_organic_cosmetics.htm

"Nail Products and Salons." Safecosmetics.org, accessed March 29 2011. www.safecosmetics.org/article.php?id=224&printsafe=1

"Natural Products." Natural-products.suite101.com, accessed June 27 2010. natural-products.suite101.com/article.cfm/how-to-green-with-organic-pest-control

"Natural Skincare: The Dangers of Phenoxyethanol." Organicpoteke.com, accessed Jan 3 2011. www.organicapoteke.com/blog/2010/06/natural-skin-care-the-dangers-of-phenoxyethanol/

"Natural vs Synthetic." Purrfumery.com, accessed July 3 2010. www.purrfumery.com/store/HTML_pages/natural.html

"Natural vs. Synthetic Fabric Dyes." Livejournal.com, accessed Jan 2 2011. community.livejournal.com/naturalliving/5542139.html

Nazaroff, William W, Beverly K. Coleman, Hugo Destaillats, Alfred T. Hodgson, De-Ling Liu, Melissa M. Lunden, Brett C. Singer, and Charles J. Weschler. "Indoor Air Chemistry: Cleaning Agents, Ozone and Toxic Air Contaminats." Arb.ca.gov, updated Apr 2006. Accessed Aug 2 2010. www.arb.ca.gov/research/apr/past/01-336_a.pdf

Nemeth, Alexa. "More Safe to Eat Off Toilet Seat Than Office Desk." Foodsafetynews.com, July 22 2010. Accessed Sept 25 2010. www.foodsafetynews.com/2010/07/according-to-the-germ-busting-microbiologist/

"Neutrogena Soft Color Blush for Cheeks, Plum Perfect 80." Cosmeticsdatabase.com, updated March 24 2008. Accessed Feb 23 2011. www.cosmeticsdatabase.com/product/23954/Neutrogena_soft_color_blush_for_cheeks_plum_perfect_80/

"New Light Shed on Health Dangers of Nanoparticles by Michigan State Research." Medicalnewstoday.com, Feb 21 2006. Accessed March 27 2011. www.medicalnewstoday.com/articles/38063.php

"Not So Sexy: Chemicals in perfume and Cologne." Ewg.org, May 2010. Accessed July 23 2010. www.ewg.org/notsosexy

"Not So Sexy: The Health Risks of Secret Chemicals in Fragrance." Ewg.org, accessed Feb 24 2011. www.ewg.org/files/SafeCosmetics_FragranceRpt.pdf

O'Connor, Siobhan and Alexandra Spunt, *No More Dirty Looks*. New York: DeCapo Press, 2010.

O'Connor, Siobhan. "Ten ways to avoid gender bending chemicals." Good.is, May 27 2010. Accessed June 28 2010. www.good.is/post/ten-ways-to-avoid-gender-bending-chemicals/

O'Conner, Siobhan. "What's Going on With O.B Tampons?" Nomoredirtylooks.com, Dec 23 2010. Accessed Feb 25 2011. nomoredirtylooks.com/tag/tampons/

"Occupational Safety and Health Guideline for Chlorine." Osha.gov, accessed Sept 26 2010. www.osha.gov/SLTC/healthguidelines/chlorine/recognition.html

"100 Toxic Ingredients used in Skincare, Makeup, Haircare, and Fragrances." Narratethenatural.wordpress.com, Mar 25 2009. Accessed Feb 28 2011. narratethenatural.wordpress.com/2009/03/25/100-toxic-ingredients-used-in-skin-care-makeup-hair-care-and-fragrances/

"Optical Brightener." En.wikipedia.org, last modified March 3 2011. Accessed March 28 2011. en.wikipedia.org/wiki/Optical_brightener

Oram, Brian. "What are phosphates?" Water-research.net, accessed Oct 2 2010. www.water-research.net/Watershed/phosphates.htm

"Organic Mattress Guide: Helping the Environment in Your Sleep." Bestbedguide.com, accessed Sept 4 2010. www.bestbedguide.com/organic-mattresses/

"Organic Standards for Different Products." Naturalproductsmarketplace.com, Apr 1 2010. Accessed Jan 2 2011. www.naturalproductsmarketplace.com/articles/2010/03/organic-standards-for-different-products.aspx

"Organic." Wordnet Search. Wordnetweb.princeton.edu, accessed August 25 2010 wordnetweb.princeton.edu/perl/webwn?s=organic

"Outgassing." En.wikipedia.org, Updated Jan 3 2011. Accessed August 5 2010. en.wikipedia.org/wiki/Off_gassing

Ozaki, Hiroaki. "Volatile Organic Compounds." Apec-vc.or.jp, accessed Sept 5 2010. www.apec-vc.or.jp/e/modules/tinyd01/index.php?id=28

"PABA." Cosmeticdatabase.com, accessed Jan 2 2011. www.cosmeticdatabase.com/ingredient/704390/PABA/

"Paint." Greenyour.com, accessed June 2 2010. www.greenyour.com/home/home-improvement/paint/tips/choose-natural-paints

Patterson, Suzanne. "Controversial Ingredients in Cosmetics." Creativeartistryfx.com, accessed July 2 2010. www.creativeartistryfx.com/controversial%20ingredients%20in%20cosmetics.pdf

Payne, Craig. "Misleading "Natural" Claims." Naturalcosmeticnews.com, Feb 4 2010. Accessed Aug 28 2010. www.naturalcosmeticnews.com/misleading-claims/misleading-natural-claims/

"PEG-32." Cosmeticdatabase.com, accessed July 24 2010. www.cosmeticsdatabase.com/ingredient.php?ingred06=704582

"Perchloroethylene." Healthychild.org, accessed Oct 2 2010. healthychild.org/issues/chemical-pop/perchloroethylene/

"Perfluorooctanoic Acid." En.Eikipedia.org, modified Feb 16 2011. Accessed Sept 2 2010. en.wikipedia.org/wiki/Perfluorooctanoic_acid

"Perfluorinated Compounds (PFCs)", Pollutioninpeople.org, accessed October 2 2010. pollutioninpeople.org/toxics/pfcs

"PET (#1) Plastic May Leach Endocrine Disruptors." Thesoftlandingbaby.com, Dec 9 2009. Accessed March 25 2011. thesoftlandingbaby.com/2009/12/09/pet-1-plastic-may-leach-endocrine-disruptors/

"Peta's Shopping Guide to Compassionate Clothing: Introduction." Peta.org, accessed June 27 2010. www.peta.org/living/fashion/cruelty-free-clothing-guide-introduction.aspx

"Petroleum Distillate in your lip gloss and furniture polish shown to cause tissue disease!" Sixwise.com, accessed July 26 2010. www.sixwise.com/newsletters/05/03/08/petroleum-distillate-in-your-lip-gloss-and-furniture-polish-shown-to-cause-tissue-disease.htm

"PFCs: Global Contaminants: DuPont's Spin About PFOA." Ewg.org, April 2003. Accessed Sept 4 2010. www.ewg.org/node/21776

"PFCs—-The Stain-Resistant Teflon Chemicals." Cleanandhealthyme.org, accessed Sept 2 2010. www.cleanandhealthyme.org/BodyofEvidence Report/TheChemicals/PFCsStainResistan TeflonChemicals/tabid/98/Default.aspx

"Phthalates." Ewg.org, accessed Aug 27 2010. www.ewg.org/chemindex/term/480

"Phthalates." Web.colby.edu, accessed Oct 1 2010. web.colby.edu/cleanmakeup/meet-the-ingredients/endocrine-disruptors/

"Phenoxyethanol: Preservative with Dirty Past." Thegreenbeautyguide.com, Nov 9 2008. Accessed Oct 1 2010. thegreenbeautyguide.com/?p=169

Phenoxyethanol." Wisegeek.com, last modifies Jan 26 2011. Accessed March 27 2011. www.wisegeek.com/what-is-phenoxyethanol.htm

Philpott, Tom. "Canada Bans BPA. Why haven't we?" Grist.org, Aug 27 2010. Accessed Oct 1 2010. www.grist.org/article/food-canada-bans-BPA-why-havent-we/

"Pigments." Sigmaaldrich.com, accessed July 26 2010. www.sigmaaldrich.com/analytical-chromatography/air-monitoring/applications/paints-and-coatings/pigments.html

"Pitcher faqs." Brita.com, accessed March 28 2011. www.brita.com/support/faq/pitcher.faq/

"Plastic Bottle Facts." Nubiusorganics.com, accessed July 28 2010. www.nubiusorganics.com/PlasticBottleFacts.aspx

Platt, Teresa. "Plastic Bags on Our Backs." Furcommission.com, March 14 2008, revised Dec 17 2008. Accessed Sept 4 2010. www.furcommission.com/resource/perspect999ce.htm

Porter, Stephanie. "Toxic Tampons." Alive.com, accessed Oct 2 2010. www.alive.com/print_version.php?chosen_topic_id=948&site_id=3

"Public Health Statement for Polybrominated Diphenyl Ethers (PBDEs)." Agency for Toxic Substances and Disease Registry. Atsdr.com, Sept 2004, updated March 3 2011. Accessed Oct 2 2010. www.atsdr.cdc.gov/phs/phs.asp?id=899&tid=183

"Pressed Wood." En.Wikipedia.org, modified March 14 2009. Accessed Aug 3 2010. en.wikipedia.org/wiki/Pressed_wood

"Pressed Wood Products." Doityourself.com, accessed Aug 2 2010. www.doityourself.com/stry/pressed-wood-products

"Product Safety." Dow.com, accessed Aug 28 2010. www.dow.com/productsafety/overview/glossary2.htm

"Propylene Glycol, Alcohol." Natural-health-information-centre.com, accessed Oct 2 2010. www.natural-health-information-centre.com/propylene-glycol.html

Provey, Joe. "How to Dispose of Leftover Paint." Diylife.com, Oct 1 2010. Accessed Oct 25 2010. www.diylife.com/2010/10/01/dispose-of-leftover-paint/

"Put a Ban On It." Simplynorwex.wordpress.com, Feb 4 2011. Accessed March 26 2011. simplynorwex.wordpress.com/2011/02/04/put-a-ban-on-it/

"Question 23: Does fluoride inhibit the activity of enzymes in humans." Fluoridedebate.com, accessed Jan 23 2011. www.flouridedebate.com/question23.html

"Quotes about Toluene from the world's top natural health/natural living authors." Naturalpedia.com, accessed March 27 2011. www.naturalpedia.com/TOLUENE.html

"Recession Gardens: 10 Easy Herbs & Vegetables You Can Grow at Home to Save Money." Steadfastfinances.com, accessed Sept 1 2010. steadfastfinances.com/blog/2009/03/20/recession-gardens-10-easy-herbs-vegetables-you-can-grow-at-home-to-save-money/

"Reclaim Your Mailbox." 41pounds.org, accessed July 27 2010. www.41pounds.org/?gclid=cjkw1ewy9qMFCQs_bAodrzb00w

"Reducing Your Exposure: Avoiding Hormone Disruptors." Wsn.org, accessed Aug 20 2010. www.wsn.org/cbe/hormone.html

Reinhart, Kevin Ann. "What Makes Clothing Fire Retardant?" Ehow.com, June 14 2010. Accessed Sept 1 2010. www.ehow.com/about_6625651_clothing-fire-retardant_.html

"Reproductive Health and Fertility Problems." Saferchemicals.org, updated Nov 2010. Accessed Feb 2 2011. healthreport.saferchemicals.org/reproductive.html

Richter, Morgan. "Real Fur Vs. Faux." Ehow.com, accessed Oct 1 2010. www.ehow.com/about_5412875_real-fur-vs-faux.html

Root, Jessica. "60,000 Plastic Bags Are Being Used This Second: Help Slow it Down." Planetgreen.discovery.com, Apr 16 2009. Accessed July 27 2010. planetgreen.discovery.com/home-garden/plastic-bag-facts.html

Rubin, Rita. "Estrogen may join carcinogen list. Talc also under consideration; benefits don't play into decision." Mindfully.org, from USA Today, Dec 8 2000. Accessed Sept 27 2010. www.mindfully.org/Health/Estrogen-Carcinogen-List.htm

Ryan, Eric and Adam Lowry. *Squeaky Green: The Method Guide to Detoxing your Home.* San Francisco: Chronicle Books, 2008

"Safety and Health Topics: Ethylene Glycol." Osha.gov. U.S Department of Labor, updated Nov 12 04. Accessed July 10 2010. www.osha.gov/dts/chemicalsampling/data/CH_240404.html

Sainio EL, Jolanki R, Hakala E, Kanerva L. "Metals and Arsenic in Eye Shadows." National Center for Biotechnology Information; National Institute of Health. Ncbi.nlm.nih.gov, accessed Aug 27 2010. www.ncbi.nlm.nih.gov/pubmed/10644018

Saloman, Laurie. "Are Scented Candles Dangerous to Your Health." Qualityhealth.com, accessed July 26 2010. www.qualityhealth.com/allergies-articles/scented-candles-dangerous-your-health

Sarasohn, Eliza and Sonia Weiss. *The Complete Idiot's Guide to Organic Living.* New York: Penguin Group, 2009.

Shapiro, Mark. *Exposed: The Toxic Chemistry of Everyday Products And What's at Stake for American Power.* Vermont: Chelsea Green Publishing, 2007.

Schneider, Andrew. "Study: Many Sunscreens May Be Accelerating Cancer." Aolnews.com, May 24 2010. Accessed Sept 26 2010. www.aolnews.com/health/article/study-many-sunscreens-may-be-accelerating-cancer/19488158

"Scotchgard Strikes back." Ourstolenfuture.org, accessed Oct 1 2010. www.ourstolenfuture.org/NewScience/oncompounds/PFOS/2001-04pfosproblems.htm

Shahan, Zachary. "70% of Human DNA Same as Sea Sponges." Planetsave.com, Aug 10 2010. Accessed Oct 3 2010. planetsave.com/2010/08/10/70-of-human-dna-same-as-sea-sponges/

Shannon, Elaine. "Does BPA Cause Infertility." Ewg.org, June 26 2009. Accessed July 25 2010. www.ewg.org/kid-safe-chemicals-act-blog/2009/06/yale-scientists-discover-how-bpa-causes-infertility/

Shapley, Dan. "FDA Tests Find Lead in Lipstick." Thedailygreen.com, Sept 1 2009. Accessed Sept 27 2010. www.thedailygreen.com/environmental-news/latest/lead-lipstick-47072702.

Sharmani. "Is Water an Organic Skin Care Ingredient?" Pharmacymix.com, Oct 28 2009. Accessed Aug 3 2010. blog.pharmacymix.com/is-water-an-organic-skin-care-ingredient

"Shedding Some Light on Optical Brighteners." Seventhgeneration.com, accessed Aug 2 2010. www.seventhgeneration.com/no-glow

Sherman, Cathy. "Do You Know What Toxic Chemicals Lurk in Your Clothing?" Organicconsumers.org, March 10 2008. Accessed Sept 26 2010. www.organicconsumers.org/articles/article_10830.cfm

"Silk Series: Peace Silk." Trueup.net, accessed Aug 26 2010. www.trueup.net/fabric-study/silk-series-peace-silk/

Sinha, V.R, Maninder Pal Kaur. "Permeation Enhancers for Transdermal Drug Delivery." University Institute of Pharmaceutical Sciences, Panjab University. Laserandskin.com.au, accessed March 27 2011. www.laserandskin.com.au/pdf/penetration-3.pdf

"Skin Cancer Facts." Skincancer.org, accessed Sept 26 2010. www.skincancer.org/skin-cancer-facts/

Skinner, Geoffrey. "How "Green" is your Gear? The Environmental Impact of Nylon." Trailcenter.org, Spring 2000. Accessed Sept 3 2010. www.trailcenter.org/newsletter/2000/spring2000/spring2000-06.htm

Smith, Gary. "Wool is Cruel." Elephantjournal.com, Jan 4 2010. Accessed July 7 2010. elephantjournal.com/2010/01/pulling-the-woll-over-our-eyes-gary-smith/

Smith, S.E. "What Are Parabens." Wisegeek.com, last modified Dec 22 2010. Accessed Aug 26 2010. www.wisegeek.com/what-are-parabens.htm

"Sodium Lauryl Sulfate (SLS) and Sodium Laureth Sulfate (SLES). The Killers in your bathroom." Natural-health-information-centre.com, accessed July 1 2010. www.natural-health-information-centre.com/sodium-lauryl-sulfate.html

"Soy-Based Glues for Wood Products." Azom.com, Sept 30 2010. Accessed Oct 5 2010. www.azom.com/news.asp?NewsID=24676

Sparacino, Alyssa. "Melanoma Risk Upwards of 75 Percent Higher with Tanning Bed Use." Aolhealth.com, May 27 2010. Accessed July 24 2010. www.aolhealth.com/2010/05/27/use-of-tanning-beds-can-quadruple-melanoma-risk

"State Legislation." Safecosmetics.com, accessed Sept 28 2010. www.safecosmetics.org/article.php?id=345

"States Push EPA, Congress To Curb Business Confidentiality Claims for Chemicals." New York Times online, March 1 2010. Accessed Aug 26 2010. www.nytimes.com/gwire/2010/03/01/01greenwire-states-push-epa-congress-to-curb-business-conf-35359.html?pagewanted=2

Stefanson, Sarah. "Animal Derivatives in Cosmetics: Uncover the Sources of Ingredients in Your Grooming Products." Suite101.com, Sept 11 2008, accessed Jan 2 2011. www.suite101.com/content/animal-derivatives-in-cosmetics-a68316

Sternberg, Steve. "To head off allergies, expose your kids to pet and dirt early. Really." USA Today, March 19 2006. Accessed Sept 27 2010. www.usatoday.com/news/health/2006-03-19-allergies-cover_x.htm

Stevie, Eileen. "Clutter and Disorganization-Can you afford it?" Carytimes.com, March 2 2009. Accessed Oct 1 2010. www.carytimes.com/bm/life/getorganized/clutter-and-disorganization-can-you-afford-it.shtml

"Stop Forced and Child Labour in the Cotton Industry of Uzbekistan: Frequently Asked Questions." Cottoncampaign.org, accessed Sept 4 2010. www.cottoncampaign.org/frequently-asked-questions/

"Sun Protection and Sunscreens." University of Iowa Health Care, Uihealthcare.com, last reviewed 2005. Accessed Oct 2 2010. www.uihealthcare.com/topics/skinhealth/sunprotection.html

Swain, D. "Aromatherapy Candles Can Be Dangerous to Your Health." Associatedcontent.com, May 22 2007. Accessed Oct 24 2010. www.associatedcontent.com/article/252928/aromatherapy_candles_can_be_dangerous.html?cat=5

"Synthetic Clothing-Friend or Foe?" Strocel.com, Sept 24 2010. Accessed Oct 2 2010. www.strocel.com/synthetic-clothing-friend-or-foe/comment-page-1/#comment-59495

"Synthetic Dyes: A look at Environmental & Human Risks." Greencotton.wordpress.com, June 18 2008. Accessed Sept 3 2010. greencotton.wordpress.com/2008/06/18/synthetic-dyes-a-look-at-the-good-the-bad-and-the-ugly/

Tarr Kent, Linda. "Sprat Tanning Ingredients." Livestrong.com, Jan 1 2010. Accessed Aug 1 2010. www.livestrong.com/article/69273-spray-tanning-ingredients/

"Testing Cosmetics and Household Products on Animals." Scribd.com, accessed Aug 27 2010. www.scribd.com/doc/36187299/Animal-Tests-and-Household-Products

"Textile Chemicals." Teonline.com, accessed July 26 2010. www.teonline.com/knowledge-centre/textile-chemicals.html

Thatcher, Christina. "Are latex beds prone to mold?" Ehow.com, updated Nov 17 2010. Accessed Oct 6 2010. www.ehow.com/facts_7510291_latex-beds-prone-mold.html

"The Bisphenol-A Debate-Truly Toxic or Money Making Ploy?" Ezinemarl.com, accessed Feb 23 2011. education.ezinemark.com/the-bisphenol-a-debate-truly-or-money-making-ploy-4d3bedbab38.html

"The Dangers of BPA." Thegreenestdollar.com, accessed Jan 3 2011. www.thegreenestdollar.com/2009/03/the-dangers-of-bpa/

"The Dangers of Cadmium." Globalhealingcenter.com, accessed June 20 2010. www.globalhealingcenter.com/dangers-of-cadmium.html

The Dangers of Nanoparticles in Sunscreen." Thegreenists.com, Aug 16 2007. Accessed Sept 3 2010. thegreenists.com/beauty/nanoparticles-in-sunscreen/329

"The Difference Between Linoleum and Vinyl Flooring." Doityourself.com, accessed Sept 2 2010. www.doityourself.com/stry/the-difference-between-linoleum-and-vinyl-flooring#ixzz-zOxjTwsVxO

"The Dirty Truth about Washing Your Hands." Livescience.com, March 11 2005. Accessed Oct 1 2010. www.livescience.com/6895-dirty-truth-washing-hands.html

"The Disappearing Rain Forests." Raintree.com, updated March 20 2010. Accessed July 10 2010. www.rain-tree.com/facts.htm

"The Environmental and Climate Costs of Using Virgin Materials." Learner.org, accessed Oct 1 2010. www.learner.org/interactions/garbage/solid-waste.html

"The Feminist Debate: Menstrual Products." Mooncupsandkeepers.com, accessed Aug 24 2010. www.mooncupsandkeppers.com/article_feminist.html

"The Global Antibacterials Market: R&D Pipelines, Market Analysis and Competitive Landscape." Arrowheadpublishers.com, Aug 2007. Accessed Sept 1 2010. www.arrowheadpublishers.com/infectious-disease/59-the-global-antibacterialsl

"The Health and Environmental Problems with Clothes Dyes." Natural-environment.com, accessed Jan 23 2011 www.natural-environment.com/blog/2008/04/07/the-health-and-environmental-problems-with-clothes-dyes/

"The Health Dangers of Phenols Found in Common Household Cleaners." Shop.sixwise.com, accessed Sept 2 2010. https://shop.sixwise.com/index.asp?PageAction=Custom&ID=73

"The Trash Vortex." Greenpeace.org, accessed Sept 24 2010. www.greenpeace.org/international/en/campaigns/oceans/pollution/trash-vortex/

"The Ugly Side of Cosmetics: makeup and body care products have been linked to allergic reactions, birth defects, and even cancer. Here's what you need to know." Greenamericatoday.org, May/June 2005, accessed Aug 24 2010. www.greenamericatoday.org/pubs/realgreen/articles/cosmetics.cfm

"There are thousands of harmful petrochemicals that we come into contact with daily. Here is a list of the petrochemicals that are most common." Thomkosquarespace.com, accessed Sept 5 2010. thomko.squarespace.com/harmful-petro-chemicals/

Thomas, Justin. "The Best Water Filters of 2010." Metaefficieant.com, Feb 17 2010. Accessed Aug 29 2010. www.metaefficient.com/water-filters/best-water-filters.html

"Time Magazine Lists Flouride as "Environmental Toxin." Blacklistednews.com, Apr 15 2010. Accessed Jan 24 2011. www.blacklistednews.com/?news_id=8281

"Tip 3: Avoid fire retardants." Ewg.org, accessed June 5 2010. www.ewg.org/files/EWG-PBDEguide.pdf

"Toothpaste: Hazardous to dental and bodily health?" Healingteethnaturally.com, accessed Jan 2 2011. www.healingteethnaturally.com/dental-systemic-health-hazards-toothpaste.html

"ToxFAQs for Benzene." Atsdr.cdc.gov, updated March 3 2011. Accessed Sept 8 2010. www.atsdr.cdc.gov/toxfaqs/tf.asp?id=38&tid=14

ToxFAQs for Sodium Hydroxide (NaOH)." Atsdr.cdc.gov, April 2002. Accessed Oct 3 2010. www.atsdr.cdc.gov/toxfaqs/tf.asp?id=248&tid=45

"ToxFAQs for Trichloroethylene (TCE)." Atsdr.cdc.gov, July 2003. Accessed Aug 2 2010. www.atsdr.cdc.gov/toxfaqs/tf.asp?id=172&tid+30

"Toxic Beauty Product Ingredients." Beauty-critic.net, accessed Oct 2 2010. www.beautycritic.net/toxic-beauty-product-ingredients

"Toxic Chemicals Found in Laundry Soaps and Air Fresheners." Livescience.com, June 24 2008. Accessed Aug 27 2010. www.livescience.com/health/080724-toxic-laundry.html

Trail, Gail. "Un-Fantastic Plastic: Choose the Best Containers for Growing Fruits and Vegetables." Naturalhomemagazine.com, May/June 2010. Accessed Sept 2 2010. www.naturalhomemagazine.com/tips/un-fantastic-plastic-choosing-the-best-containers-for-growing-fruits-and-vegetables.aspx

Tremblay Jr, K.R, M.P Vogel. "Improving Air Quality in Your Home." Colorado State University. Ext.cocostate.edu, July 2006, updated May 12 2010. Accessed Aug 28 2010. www.ext.colostate.edu/pubs/consumer/09938.html

"Triclosan." Beyondpesticides.org, accessed Aug 28 2010. www.beyondpesticides.org/antibacterial/triclosan.htm

"Triclosan in Antibacterial Soaps May Actually Be Bad For You." Neatorama.com, April 10 2010. Accessed Sept 1 2010. www.neatorama.com/2010/04/10/triclosan-in-antibacterial-soaps-may-actually-be-bad-for-you/

"Turning the Page: Environmental Impacts of the Magazine Industry, Recommendations for Improvement." Mindfully.org, June 1 2010. Accessed April 2 2011. www.mindfully.org/Sustainability/Magazine-Environmental-impacts.htm

"12,050 Fabrics." Greensage.com, accessed Feb 23 2011. www.greensage.com/SLCP-fabric.htm

"279,332 Beauty Salons: Companies in the U.S" Manta.com, accessed Feb 24 2011. www.manta.com/mb_35_B30E7000_000/beauty_shops

"Twist Eco-Friendly Sponges Product Review." Thegreenestdollar.com, accessed Aug 2 2010. www.thegreenestdollar.com/2009/04/twist-eco-friendly-kitchen-sponges-product

Ultra Dawn Original Ingredients." Pg.com, accessed Sept 1 2010. www.pg.com/productsafety/ingredients/household_care/dish_washing/Dawn/Ultra_Dawn_Original.pdf

"Unacceptable Ingredients: The Chemicals to Avoid." Healthy-communications.com, accessed Aug 2 2010. www.healthy-communication.com/ingredientstoavoid.html

Uricchio, Marylynn. "The ugly side of beauty, some cosmetics can be toxic." Pittsburg Post-Gazette online, July 20 2010. Accessed Sept 23 2010. www.post-gazette.com/pg/10201/1073854-314.stm

"U.S. EPA Targets Cancerous Dyes, Toxic Detergent Chemicals." Greenbiz.com, Aug 19 2010. Accessed Sept 27 2010. www.greenbiz.com/news/2010/08/19/us-epa-targets-cancerous-dyes-toxic-detergent-chemicals

"U.S. Scented Candles Study." Lead.org.au, last updated Jan 25 2010. Accessed Aug 25 2010. www.lead.org.au/lanv7n4/L74-9.html

"U.S: Unwanted Imports: Goods deemed toxic elsewhere shipped to U.S." Associated Press, Corpwatch.org, Oct 15 2006. Accessed Aug 3 2010. www.corpwatch.org/article.php?id=14169

"Use an eco-friendly bath sponge or brush." Greenyour.com, accessed Sept 2 2010. www.greenyour.com/body/personal-care/body-cleansers/tips/use-an-eco-friendly-bath-sponge-or-brush

"Use-and-Toss Plastic Bottle Facts." Reuseit.com, accessed Sept 3 2010. www.reuseit.com/learn-more/top-facts/plastic-bottle-facts

Uydess, Steve. "The HHW Dilemma: Lots of Waste, Nobody to Collect." Earth911.com, July 20 2009. Accessed September 5 2010. earth911.com/news/2009/07/20/the-hhw-dilemma-lots-of-waste-nobody-to-collect/

"Vegan Fashion=Compassionate Threads." Happycow.net, accessed Oct 2 2010. www.happycow.net/vegan_fashion.html

"Vegan or Animal Cruelty Free Makeup Brushes=Good Karma." Greenorganics.com.au, Feb 5 2009. Accessed Sept 1 2010. www.greenorganics.com.au/organic-natural-skin-care-products/vegan-or-animal-cruelty-free-makeup-brushes-good-karma

"Vocs: Perils of Paint."Healthyhouseinstitute.com, Updated Feb 28 2011. Accessed July 29, 2010. www.healthyhouseinstitute.com/a_731-Perils_of_Paint

"Volatile Organic Compound." Mimi.hu, accessed Oct 25 2010. en.mimi.hu/environment/volatile_organic_compound.html

"WakeUP and Smell the Formaldehyde." Organicclothing.com, accessed Aug 23 2010. organicclothing.blogs.com/my_weblog/2006/04/wakeup_and_smel.html

Ward, Deborah. "The Candle Making Manual." Naturesgardencandles.com, accessed Sept 2 2010. www.naturesgardencandles.com/mas_assets/pdf/manual.pdf

Ward, Logan. "The Nervous Mom's Guide to Germs." Parents.com, accessed Aug 24 2010. www.parents.com/baby/health/sick-baby/guide-to-germs/

Washam, Cynthia. "Legislation: California Enacts Safe Cosmetics Act." National Institute of Health, Ncbi.nln.nih.gov, last updated July 2006. Accessed Oct 1 2010. ncbi.nlm.nih.gov/pmc/articles/PMC/1513294/

"Water pollution caused by cosmetic chemicals, cleaning supplies and plastics: Triclosan." Ewg.org, accessed Sept 1 2010. www.ewg.org/node/21840

Wedgood, Tamasin. "Health Hazards of Chlorine Bleach." Ehow.com, July 19 2010. Accessed Aug 17 2010. www.ehow.com/list_6747555_health-hazards-chlorine-bleach.htm

West, Larry. "First U.S Ban on BPA Begins Today." Environment.about.com, Jan 1 2010. Accessed Aug 3 2010. environment.about.com/b/2010/01/01/first-u-s-ban-on-bpa-begins-today.htm

"What Are Alternative Menstrual Products." Thewikifire.org, last modified Dec 7 2007. Accessed Aug 25 2010. www.thewikifire.org/index.php?title=Alternative_menstrual_products

"What are Clothing Fabric Dyes Made Of?" Fibers.com, accessed Sept 24 2010. www.fibers.com/blog/what-are-clothing-fabric—dyes-made-of/

"What Are Endocrine Disruptors?" Epa.gov, last updated April 22 2010. Accessed Sept 26 2010. www.epa.gov/endo/pubs/edspoverview/whatare.htm

"What is BPA? Most sunscreens come free of PABA now to avoid allergic reactions. Here's what you need to know about PABA-free sunscreens." Thedailygreen.com, July 8 2010, accessed Sept 2 2010. www.thedailygreen.com/environmental-news/latest/Paba-sunscreen-ingredients

"What is Butyl Cellosolve And why Should I Avoid it." Thegoodhuman.com, accessed Oct 21 2010. www.thegoodhuman.com/2007/10/18/what-is-butyl-cellosolve-and-why-you-should-avoid-it

"What Does the "Organic" Label Really Mean?" United States Department of Agriculture, Usda.fda.gov, accessed Oct 2 2010. usda.fda.com/articles/organic.htm

"What makes Greencradle's cribs & furnishings different?" Greencradle.com, accessed July 10 2010. www.greencradle.com/ProductDetails.asp?ProductCode=PR-1639-Artisan-Maple-Crib

"What makes polyurethane (PE) or polypropylene (PP) or PET more sustainable?" Cr4globalspec.com, April 22 2007. cr4.globalspec.com/thread/7239/what-makes-polyurethane-PE-or-polypropylene-PP-or-PET-more-sustainable

"What percentage of people are affected by insomnia." Chacha.com, May 24 2010. Accessed July 10 2010. www.chacha.com/question/what-percentage-of-people-are-affected-by-insomnia

"What to Consider when Buying Furniture." Healthychild.org, March 29 2007. Accessed Sept 4 2010. healthychild.org/blog/comments/furniture/#ixzz13VyOqVMP

"What Women Should Know Before Buying Tampons." Ecomall.com, accessed Nov 23 2010. www.ecomall.com/greenshopping/tamp1.htm

Whittaker, Margaret H, Elizabeth Engimann, Imogen Sambrook. "Eco-labels: Environmental Marketing in the BeautyIndustry." Gcimagazine.com, Aug 11 2009. Accessed July 25 2010. www.gcimagazine.com/marketstrends/segments/natural/52976687.html

"White Spirit." En.Wikipedia.org, modified Jan 18 2011. Accessed Sept 5 2010. en.wikipedia.org/wiki/White_spirit

"Why Indoor Air Quality is Essential for Good Health." Vitaweb.org, Oct 15 2010. Accessed Sept 2 2010. www.vitaweb.org/environmental-health/why-indoor-air-quality-is-essential-for-good-health.htm

"Why Is Recycling Important?" Ilacsd.org, accessed Sept 23 2010. www.ilacsd.org/recycle/r_why.php

"Why Recycle." Headwatersrecycle.com, accessed Sept 3 2010. www.headwatersrecycle.com/why.html

"Why Your Microwave Popcorn May be Toxic." Fitsugar.com, Oct 17 2008. Accessed Sept 25 2010. www.fitsugar.com/Why-Your-Microwave-Popcorn-May-Yoxic-2337532

Wilcox, Christie. "Plastic Troubles: Brominated Flame Retardants (PBDEs)." Nutritionwonderland.com, Sept 3 2009. Accessed Aug 16 2010. nutritionwonderland.com/2009/09/plastic-troubles-brominated-flame-retardants-pbde/

Winter, Ruth. *A Consumer's Dictionary of Cosmetic Ingredients.* New York: Three Rivera Press, 2009.

Woods, Jeannie. "About Lard Soap." Ezinearticles.com, Feb 18 2010. Accessed Nov 23 2011. ezinearticles.com/?About-Lard-Soap&id=3783202

Woody, Tasha. "Paint Colors That Sell- 7 Tips to Choosing Colors Buyers Will Love." Ezinearticles.com, Feb 2 2009. Accessed July 26 2010. ezinearticles.com/?Paint-Colors-That-Sell—-7-Tips-to-Choosing-Colors-Buyers-Will-Love&id=1950139

Yiamouyiannis, Dr. John. Flouride: The Aging Factor (2nd Edition) Health Action Press 1986 Flouride Action Network, posted on Flouridealert.org, accessed Feb 25 2011. www.fluoridealert.org/aging-factor.htm

York, Sarah. "HEPA Vacuum Cleaning." Ehow.com, accessed Oct 3 2010. www.ehow.com/way_5417881_hepa-vacuum-cleaning.html

Zandonella, Catherine, M.P.H. "Chemical Culprits: PBDEs and other Flame Retardants." Simplesteps.org, Aug 16, 2010. Accessed Sept 5 2010. www.simplesteps.org/articles/chemical-culprits-pbdes-and-other-flame-retardants

Zhang, Jane. "FDA Questions Use of Antibacterial Soaps." Mindfully.org, Oct 18 2005. Accessed July 2 2010. www.mindfully.org/Health/2005/Antibacterial-Soaps-FDA18oct05.htm

"Zinc Citrate." Livestrong.com, accessed Jan 24 2011. www.livestrong.com/zinc-citrate/

ENDNOTES

Part 1

[1] "Cars, Trucks, Air Pollution and Health." Nutramed.com

[2] Morrissey. "The good news that went unreported on air quality." Hotair.com

[3] "How Worried Should We Be About Everyday Chemicals?" Shine.yahoo.com

[4] Uydess. "The HHW Dilemma: Lots of Waste, Nobody to Collect." Earth911.com

[5] "Why Indoor Air Quality is Essential for Good Health." Vitaweb.org

[6] "Are You And Your Children Safe?" Cleaningpro.com

[7] "Organic." Wordnet search. Wordnetweb.princeton.edu

[8] "An Introduction to Indoor Air Quality (IAQ): Volatile Organic Compounds (VOCs)." Epa.gov

[9] "Outgassing." En.wikipedia.org

[10] "Volatile Organic Compound." Mimi.hu

[11] "Vocs: Perils of Paint." Healthyhouseinstitute.com

[12] "Volatile Organic Compounds (VOCs): Definitions." Toxics.usgs.gov

[13] Ozaki. "Volatile Organic Compounds." Apec-vc.or.jp

[14] "Endocrine Disruptors." Nrdc.org

[15] "Reducing Your Exposure: Avoiding Hormone Disruptors." Wsn.org

[16] "Phthalates." Web.colby.edu

[17] "Perfluorinated Compounds (PFCs)," Pollutioninpeople.org

[18] "There are thousands of harmful petrochemicals that we come into contact with daily. Here is a list of the petrochemicals that are most common." Thomkosquarespace.com

[19] "ToxFAQs for Benzene." Atsdr.cdc.gov

[20] Frederick vom Saal "BPA in Bodies of 90% of Americans." Earthsky.org

[21] "The Dangers of BPA." Thegreenestdollar.com

[22] "Are Our Gulf Oil Spill Problems Over...or Just Beginning?" Sixwise.com

[23] "What is Butyl Cellosolve And why Should I Avoid It." Thegoodhuman.com

[24] "Unacceptable Ingredients: The Chemicals to Avoid." Healthy-communications.com

[25] Wedgood. "Health Hazards of Chlorine Bleach." Ehow.com

[26] "Occupational Safety and Health Guideline for Chlorine." Osha.gov

[27] "Guide to Less Toxic Products: Cosmetics and Personal Care." Lesstoxicguide.ca

[28] Winter. *A Consumer's Dictionary of Cosmetic Ingredients*, 375

[29] "Formaldehyde." En.wikipedia.org

[30] "Health Effects of Low-Level Exposure to Formaldehyde." Journals.lww.com

[31] "There are thousands of harmful petrochemicals that we come into contact with daily. Here is a list of the petrochemicals that are most common." Thomko.squarespace.com.

[32] "Safety and Health Topics: Ethylene Glycol." Osha.gov

[33] Helmenstine, "Flame Retardant People: Health Effects of PBDE Absorption." Chemistry.about.com

[34] "Tip 3: Avoid fire retardants." Ewg.org.

[35] "Household Products Containing Petroleum Distillates and Other Hydrocarbons; Advance Notice of Proposed Rulemaking; Request for Comments and Information. " Cpsc.gov

[36] "Petroleum Distillate In Your Lip Gloss and Furniture Polish Shown to Cause Tissue Disease!" Sixwise.com

[37] Dadd. "What is the Difference Between Petroleum Distillates and Petrochemicals? Is One More Toxic Than the Other?" Healthychild.org

[38] "The Health Dangers of Phenols Found in Common Household Cleaners." Shop.sixwise.com

[39] Oram. "What are phosphates?" Waterresearch.net

[40] Loux, *Easy Green Living*, 240

[41] Joyce. "Hidden Dangers of Phthalates." Paramuspost.com

[42] "Perfluorooctanoic Acid." En.Eikipedia.org

[43] "ToxFAQs for Sodium Hydroxide (NaOH)." Atsdr.cdc.gov

[44] "Is Sodium Lauryl Sulfate Safe?" Amomsblog.wordpress.com

[45] "Unacceptable Ingredients: The Chemicals to Avoid." Healthy-communications.com

[46] "1,4-dioxane." Safecosmetics.org

[47] "Sodium Lauryl Sulfate (SLS) and Sodium Laureth Sulfate (SLES). The Killers in your bathroom." Natural-health-information-centre.com

[48] "Frequently asked questions: Toluene." Aromaticsonline.net

[49] "Chemical Encyclopedia: Toluene." Healthychild.org

[50] "MSDA Toluene: Cosmetic Toxin Data." Natural-skincare-authority.com

[51] Chemical Encyclopeida: Toluene." Healthychild.org

[52] "ToxFAQs for Trichloroethylene (TCE)." Atsdr.cdc.gov

[53] Smith. "Wool is Cruel." Elephantjournal.com

[54] "Choose Life Over Death, Kindness Over Killing." Veganpeace.com

[55] "Vegan Fashion=Compassionate Threads." Happycow.net

[56] "Flame Retardant in Furniture Causes Concern." NYtimes.com

[57] Miller and Lord. "Fatal Foam: It's just about everywhere." THE PROVIDENCE JOURNAL, Projo.com

[58] "What to Consider When Buying Furniture." Healthychild.org

[59] Zandonella. "Chemical Culprits: PBDEs and Other Flame Retardants." Simplesteps.org

[60] Wilcox. "Plastic Troubles: Brominated Flame Retardants (PBDEs)." Nutritionwonderland.com

[61] "Chemical Encyclopedia: (2,4-dichlorophenoxy) acetic acid." Healthychild.org

[62] Zandonella. "Chemical Culprits: PBDEs and Other Flame Retardants." Simplesteps.org

[63] "U.S. EPA Targets Cancerous Dyes, Toxic Detergent Chemicals." Greenbiz.com

[64] "What to Consider When Buying Furniture." Healthychild.org

[65] "PFCs: Global Contaminants: DuPont's Spin About PFOA." Ewg.org

[66] Ryan and Lowry, *Squeeky Green*, 73

[67] "Dust Mites: Everything you might not want to know!" Ehso.com

[68] "Nasal Polyps, Asthma, Allergies & Sinusitis." Achooallergy.com

[69] "Pressed Wood." En.Wikipedia.org

[70] "Pressed Wood Products." Doityourself.com

[71] Dunn. "Get the Scoop on Green Wood Furniture: Find furniture that's healthy for you and your home." Planetgreen.discovery.com

[72] "An Introduction to Indoor Air Quality (IAQ): Formaldehyde." Epa.gov

[73] "Formaldehyde and Cancer Risk." National Cancer Center, Cancer.gov

[74] "Air Purifier Glossary." Rabbitair.com

[75] "An Introduction to Indoor Air Quality (IAQ): Formaldehyde." Epa.gov

[76] "U.S: Unwanted Imports: Goods deemed toxic elsewhere shipped to U.S." Associated Press, Corpwatch.org

[77] "What makes Greencradle's cribs & furnishings different?" Greencradle.com

[78] "Formaldehyde and Cancer Risk." National Cancer Center, Cancer.gov

[79, 80] "Healthy Low VOC Interior and Exterior Sealers." Greenbuildingsupply.com

[81] "The Disappearing Rain Forests." Raintree.com

[82] "Deforestation: If We Don't Take Action, It Won't Be an Issue Much Longer." Dougieg.com

[83] Gavigan. "Beware of Lead in Christmas Trees and Lights." Webmd.com

[84] "Soy-Based Glues for Wood Products." Azom.com

[85] Crawford. "What are the Different Types of Water-Based Adhesive?" Wisegeek.com

[86] "What is FSC-US?" Fscus.org

[87] Sarasohn and Weiss. *The Complete Idiot's Guide to Organic Living*, 35

[88] "Method for creating higher grade products from lower grade lumber." Freepatentsonline.com

[89] Crawford. "What Are The Different Types Of Water- Based Adhesives." Wisegeek.com

[90] Meier. "Restricted and Endangered Wood Species." Wood-database.com

[91] "Eco-Friendly Wood Furniture: Go Green with Your Home Décor." Greenprofs.com

[92] "Healthy Furniture is the Future in a Green Home." Greenlifesmartlife.com

[93] Dunn, Collin. "Haute Green Sneak Peek. Organic Cotton Upholstery by Mod Green Pod." Treehugger.com

[94] "How Eco-Friendly Is Bamboo?" Life.gaiam.com

[95] Merchant. "How Fast Does Bamboo Grow? And why does it matter?" Planetgreen.discovery.com

[96] Chadderdon. "Do You Know What's in that Paint You Put on your Walls?" Greenfeet.net

[97] Ibid.

[98] "White Spirit." En.Wikipedia.org

[99] Chadderdon. "Do You Know What's in that Paint You Put on your Walls?" Greenfeet.net

[100] McNally. "6 Ways to Manage Paint Leftovers." Naturalhomemagazine.com

[101] Provey. "How to Dispose of Leftover Paint." Diylife.com

[102] Shannon. "Does BPA Cause Infertility." Ewg.org

[103] "Pigments." Sigmaaldrich.com

[104] "The Dangers of Cadmium." Globalhealingcenter.com

[105] "International Study Finds No Safe Level of Lead in Children's Blood." Cincinnatichildrens.org

[106] Farley, Dixie. "Dangers of Lead Still Longer." Allergybuyersclub.com

107 Chadderdon. "Do You Know What's in that Paint You Put on your Walls?" Greenfeet.net

108 Ibid

109 "Paint." Greenyour.com

110 Woody, Tasha. "Paint Colors That Sell—7 Tips to Choosing Colors Buyers Will Love." Ezinearticles.com

111 "Glossary." Raic.org

112 Kowski, Paul Kret, Marian Keeler, Kirsten Ritchie, Andrew Mangan. "Navigating the Flooring Thicket: Find the Greenest Way to Meet Your Needs." Greenhomeguide.com

113 "Lead Poisoning." En.Wikipedia.org

114 Kowski, Paul Kret, Marian Keeler, Kirsten Ritchie, Andrew Mangan. "Navigating the Flooring Thicket: Find the Greenest Way to Meet Your Needs." Greenhomeguide.com, Sept 3 2009. Accessed July 27 2010.

115 Ibid.

116 "Formaldehyde and Cancer Risk." National Cancer Center, Cancer.gov

117 Winter. A Consumer's Dictionary of Cosmetic Ingredients, 244

118 Lee, Xiao-Pen, Keizo Sato. "Toluene, benzene, xylene, and styrene." Springerlink.com

119 www.airbrains.org/CARPETresources.htm

120 "Dust Mites: Everything you might not want to know!" Ehso.com

121 "The Difference Between Linoleum and Vinyl Flooring." Doityourself.com

122 "What percentage of people are affected by insomnia." Chacha.com

123 "Managing Insomnia." Womenfitness.net

124 "Cotton and the Environment." Ota.com

125 "Method for bleaching raw cotton and cotton textiles." Freepatentsonline.com

126 "Chlorine Monoxide." En.wikipedia.org

127 Loux. Easy Green Living, 273

128 "How to Shop for Eco-Friendly Clothes-Part 2: Try TENCEL or Lyocell." Biggreenpurse.com

129 "Cotton and the Environment." Ota.com

130 Coleman, Brenna. "The Benefits of Organic Cotton and Natural Latex Mattresses." Suite101.com

131 "Bedding." Greenyour.com

132 Loux. Easy Green Living, 273

133 Ibid., 270

134 Ibid., 280

135 "Peta's Shopping Guide to Compassionate Clothing: Introduction." Peta.org

136 Thatcher. "Are latex beds prone to mold?" Ehow.com

137 M, Rex. "Dangers Hidden in Your Mattress." Sustainlane.com

138 "Public Health Statement for Polybrominated Diphenyl Ethers (PBDEs)." Agency for Toxic Substances and Disease Registry. Atsdr.com

139 "Organic Mattress Guide: Helping the Environment in Your Sleep." Best-bedguide.com

140 Tremblay Jr, Vogel. "Improving Air Quality in Your Home." Colorado State University. Ext.cocostate.edu

141 "PFCs: Global Contaminants: DuPont's Spin About PFOA." Ewg.org

142 "Gore-Tex." En.wikipedia.org

143 "PFCs—-The Stain-Resistant Teflon Chemicals." Cleanandhealthyme.org

144 "Scotchgard Strikes back." Ourstolenfuture.org

145 Mittelstaedt. "Coming to terms with perils of non-stick products." Theglobeandmail.com

146 Haynes. "Is Nonstick Cookware Safe? Is PFOA present in nonstick pans?" Low-fatcooking.about.com

147 "Perflurooctanoic Acid." En.wikipedia.org

148 Kayne. "Is Teflon Dangerous?" Wisegeek.com

149 Heilprin, John. "DuPont sued over Teflon." Usatoday.com

150 Mittelstaedt. "Coming to terms with perils of non-stick products." Theglobeandmail.com

151 Houlihan, Thayer, Klein. "EWG finds heated Teflon pans can turn toxic faster than DuPont claims." Ewg.org

152 Haynes. "Is Nonstick Cookware Safe? Is PFOA present in nonstick pans?" Low-fatcooking.about.com

153 Ibid.

154 "EPA Settles PFOA Case against DuPont for Largest Environmental Administration Penalty in Agency History." Epa.gov

155 Decker, Kaskey. 3M, DuPont Settle Patent Fight over Coating Process for Teflon." Bloomberg.com

156 Haynes. "Is Nonstick Cookware Safe? Is PFOA present in nonstick pans?" Low-fatcooking.about.com

157 "Compounds in non-stick cookware may be associated with elevated cholesterol in children and teens." Sciencedaily.com

158 Mittelstaedt, Martin. "Coming to terms with perils of non-stick products." Theglobeandmail.com

159 "PFCs: Global Contaminants: DuPont's Spin About PFOA." Ewg.org

160 "PFCs—The Stain-Resistant Teflon Chemicals." Cleanandhealthyme.org

161 "Scotchgard Strikes Back." Ourstolen-future.org

162 "Meet Perfluorooctanoic Acid." Saferchemicals.org

163 "Why Your Microwave Popcorn May be Toxic." Fitsugar.com

164 "Educate Yourself." Thehomebot-tega.com

165 Swain, D. "Aromatherapy Candles Can Be Dangerous to Your Health." Associat-edcontent.com

166 "U.S. Scented Candles Study." Lead.org.au.

167 Ibid.

168 Ibid.

169 "Lead Poisoning." En.Wikipedia.org

170 Ibid.

171 "An Introduction to Indoor Air Quality (IAQ) Carbon Monoxide." Epa.gov

172 Loux. *Easy Green Living*, 337

173 Saloman. "Are Scented Candles Dangerous to Your Health?" Quality-health.com

174 "Biodegradability." En.wiktionary.org

175 "Candles and the environment." Green-livingtips.com

176 Ward. "The Candle Making Manual." Naturesgardencandles.com.

177 Blair, L.Ac. "Choosing the right (non-poisonous) candles for your home." Allthingsnaturalstore.com

178 Blair Lac. "Choosing the right (non-poisonous) candles for your home." Allthingsnaturalstore.com

179 "Getting the lead out." Snopes.com

180 "Bees and honey." Vegansociety.com

190 Breyer. "Air Fresheners: Easy Greening." Care2.com

191 Dwornick. "Chemical Warfare Agents and Toxic Waste Disguised as Household Cleaning Products." Rense.com

192 "Toxic Chemicals Found in Laundry Soaps and Air Fresheners." Live-science.com

193 Alleyne. "Household cleaners may double risk of breast cancer." Tele-graph.co.uk

194 Breyer. "Air Fresheners: Easy Greening." Care2.com

195 Nazaroff, Coleman, Destaillats, Hodgson, Liu, Lunden, Singer, and Weschler. "Indoor Air Chemistry: Cleaning Agents, Ozone and Toxic Air Contaminats."

196 O'Connor. "Ten ways to avoid gender bending chemicals." Good.is

197 "Reducing Your Exposure: Avoiding Hormone Disruptors." Wsn.org

198 "What Are Endocrine Disruptors?" Epa.gov

199 Masters. "How "fresh" is Air Fresheners" Time.com

200 "NASA Study House Plants Clean Air." Zone10.com

201 Ibid.

202 "Indoor Plants Found to Release Volatile Organic Compounds." Sci-encedaily.com

203 Andrews, Ph.D, Wiles. "Off the Books: Industry's Secret Chemicals." Ewg.org

204 "Confidential Business Information." Epa.gov

205 Andrews, Ph.D, Wiles. "Off the Books: Industry's Secret Chemicals." Ewg.org

206 "How Worried Should We Be About Everyday Chemicals?" Shine.yahoo.com

207 Andrews, Ph.D, Wiles. "Off the Books: Industry's Secret Chemicals." Ewg.org

208 "States Push EPA, Congress To Curb Business Confidentiality Claims for Chemicals." NYTimes.com

209 Andrews, Ph.D, Wiles. "Off the Books: Industry's Secret Chemicals." Ewg.org

210 Denison. "EPA IG Report: New Chemicals Program fails to assure protection." Edf.org

211 "States Push EPA, Congress To Curb Business Confidentiality Claims for Chemicals." NYtimes.com

212 "EPA Settles PFOA Case against DuPont for Largest Environmental Administration Penalty in Agency History." Epa.gov

213 "Household Products Labeling Act." Womensvoices.org

214 Mariec. "The Safe Chemicals Act: Fifteen Burning Questions and Fifteen Quenching Answers." Safetec.net

215 "Kid-safe Chemicals Are Now Within Our Reach." Ewg.org

216 Ibid.

217 Mueller. "Chemicals in Home Cleaning Products Revealed: Manufacturers to Disclose Ingredients in Detergents and Soaps." Greenliving.suite101.com

218 "8 Household Cleaning Agents to Avoid: Detox your home by avoiding these chemical culprits." Life.gaiam.com

219 Alleyne. "Household cleaners may double risk of breast cancer." Tele-graph.co.uk

220 Lovattsmith. "Deadly facts about chemical-based household cleaners." Helium.com

221 Gonzalez."Get a Greener Clean: Hazards and Eco-Friendly Cleaning Options." Natural-products.suite101.com

222 "Greenwashing." En.wikipedia.org

223 "Testing Cosmetics and Household Products on Animals." Scribd.com

224 "Quotes about Toluene from the world's top natural health/natural living authors." Naturalpedia.com

225 "Material Safety Data." Trconsulting-group.com

226 "How to Know What is in Household Cleaners." Ehow.com

227 "Federal Hazardous Substances Act." Consumer Product Safety Commission

228 Ibid.

229 Payne, Craig. "Misleading "Natural" Claims." Naturalcosmeticnews.com

230 "How Toxic Are Your Household Cleaning Supplies?" Organic-consumers.org

231 Greer. "Chemicals in household cleaners may pollute indoor air." Sfgate.com

232 Gunzelmann. "Plastic Bottle Facts Make You Think Before You Drink." Greenupgrader.com

233 "Label Search Results." Greener-choices.org

234 "Ultra Dawn Original Ingredients." Pg.com

235 Mason. "The Healing Properties of Grapefruit Seed Extract." Examiner.com

236 Zhang. "FDA Questions Use of Antibacterial Soaps." Mindfully.org

237 Ward, Logan. "The Nervous Mom's Guide to Germs." Parents.com

238 "The Global Antibacterials Market: R&D Pipelines, Market Analysis and Competitive Landscape." Arrowhead-publishers.com

239 Zhang. "FDA Questions Use of Antibacterial Soaps." Mindfully.org

240 Adams. "FDA is reviewing the use of antibacterial products containing triclosan." LATimes.com

241 Keim, Brandon. "Antibiotics Breed Superbugs Faster Than Expected." Wired.com

242 Kahn. "Antibacterial wipes can spread superbugs: study." Reuters.com

243 Adams. "FDA is reviewing the use of antibacterial products containing triclosan." LATimes.com

244 "Triclosan in Antibacterial Soaps May Actually Be Bad For You." Neatorama.com

245 "Antibacterial Products." Greenin-bklyn.com

246 "Put a Ban On It." Simplynorwex.word-press.com

247 "Triclosan." Beyondpesticides.org

248 "The Dirty Truth about Washing Your Hands." Livescience.com

249 Sternberg. "To head off allergies, expose your kids to pet and dirt early. Really." USAToday.com

250 "Twist Eco-Friendly Sponges Product Review." Thegreenestdollar.com

251 "Grime Fighters: How to take care of kitchen sponges." Revolutionhealth.com

252 Nemeth, Alexa. "More Safe to Eat Off Toilet Seat Than Office Desk." Foodsafe-tynews.com

253 "Use an eco-friendly bath sponge or brush." Greenyour.com

254 Bristow, Sydney. "Green and Clean Kitchen Sponges." Apartmenttherapy.com

255 Shahan, Zachary. "70% of Human DNA Same as Sea Sponges." Planetsave.com

256 York, Sarah. "HEPA Vacuum Cleaning." Ehow.com

257 Masterson, Kathleen. "The History of Plastic: From Billiards to Bibs." Npr.org

258 "Facts to Know and How You Can Help." Illinois.edu

259 "Use-and-Toss Plastic Bottle Facts." Reuseit.com

260 Gunzelmann. "Plastic Bottle Facts Make You Think Before You Drink." Greenupgrader.com

261 "Why Recycle?" Headwatersrecycle.com

262 Gunzelmann. "Plastic Bottle Facts Make Your Think Before You Drink." Greenupgrader.com

263 "Use-and-Toss Plastic Bottle Facts." Reuseit.com

264 "The Trash Vortex." Greenpeace.org

265 Walsh, Brian. "The Truth About Plastic." Time.com

266 Platt, Teresa. "Plastic Bags on Our Backs." Furcommission.com

267 Huff. "More states move to ban BPA even while FDA does nothing." Natural-news.com

268 Andrews, Ph.D, Wiles. "Off the Books: Industry's Secret Chemicals." Ewg.org

269 Houlihan, Lunder, Jacob. "Timeline: BPA From Invention to Phase-Out." Ewg.org

270 "Carcinogenesis Bioessay of Bisphenol A." U.S Department of Health and Human Services Ntp.niehs.nih.gov

271 Philpott. "Canada Bans BPA. Why haven't we?" Grist.org

272 Huff. "More states move to ban BPA even when FDA does nothing." Natural-news.com

273 Philpott. "Canada Bans BPA. Why haven't we?" Grist.org

274 "Bisphenol A. Quickview." U.S Environmental Protection Agency. Epa.com

275 Houlihan, Lunder, Jacob. "Timeline: BPA From Invention to Phase-Out." Ewg.org

276 Philpott. "Canada Bans BPA. Why haven't we?" Grist.org

277 West. "First U.S Ban on BPA Begins Today." Environment.about.com

278 "Bans on BPA gain traction." Stateline.org

279 "Maryland is 5th state to ban BPA." Enviroblog.org

280 "Bans on BPA gain traction." Stateline.org

281 Lewis. "Wal-Mart Bans BPA, Other Retailers Likely to Follow: Studies link the chemical to possible hormonal changes." Consumeraffairs.com

282 "The Bisphenol-A Debate—Truly Toxic or Money Making Ploy?" Ezinemarl.com

283 Case, David. "The Real Story Behind Bisphenol-A." Watonics.org

284 "Beauty Secrets: Phthalates." Ewg.org

285 "About phthalates—history." Phthalate-free.de

286 "Phthalates." Ewg.org

287 "About Phthalates."Ourstolenfuture.org

288 "Beauty Secrets: Phthalates." Ewg.org

289 Joyce. "Hidden Danger of Phthalates." Paramuspost.com

290 "About Phthalates."Ourstolenfuture.org

291 "Reproductive Health and Fertility Problems." Saferchemicals.org

292 Mangano. "The 5 Dangerous Chemicals In Our Homes." Naturalhealthontheweb.com

293 "Beauty Secrets: The Dangers of Phthalates: Industry Spin vs Fact." Ewg.org

294 "Phthalates." Ewg.org

295 "California's phthalates ban now in effect." Saferstates.com

296 Masterson. "The History of Plastic: From Billiards to Bibs." Npr.org

297 "About Phthalates." Ourstolenfuture.org

298 Loux. *Easy Green Living*, 122

299 "BPA and Phthalates...Should you "Purge" your plastics?" Autismspot.com

300 "Bottled Water: Pure Drink or Pure Hype?" Nrdc.org

301 "Facts About Plastic Bottles." Earth911.com

302 Gunzelmann. "Plastic Bottle Facts Make Your Think Before You Drink." Greenupgrader.com

303 "Is bottled water healthier or safer than tap?" Mnn.com

304 "Plastic Bottle Facts." Nubiusorganics.com

305 "Most Bottled Water Brands Don't Disclose Information About Source, Purity and Contaminates." Ewg.org

306 "Bottled Water: Pure Drink or Pure Hype?" Nrdc.org

307 Ibid

308 "Is bottled water healthier or safer than tap?" Mnn.com

309 "EWG Scorecard on Bottled Water." Energycommerce.house.gov

310 "PET (#1) Plastic May Leach Endocrine Disruptors." Thesoftlandingbaby.com

311 Ibid

312 Thomas. "The Best Water Filters of 2010." Metaefficieant.com

313 "Water Purifier Reviews: What to look for in an online review." Allwaterpurification.com

314 "Pitcher faqs." Brita.com

315 "How To Choose A Water Filter or Purifier." Rei.com

316 Root. "60,000 Plastic Bags are Being Used This Second: Help Slow it Down." Planetgreen.discovery.com

317 "Plastic Bag Ban Fizzles Again in California Amid Heavy Lobbying.What Do You Think?" LosAngelesTimes.com

318 "Campaign Against the Plastic Plague Background Info." Earthresource.org

319 Root. "60,000 Plastic Bags Are Being Used This Second: Help Slow it Down." Planetgreen.discovery.com

320 "Paper vs Plastic- The Shopping Bag Debate." Greenfeet.com

321 "Planet Earth's New Nemesis." News.bbc.co.uk

322 West. "Paper, Plastic, or Something Better?" About.com, accessed Mar 8 2011

323 Root, Jessica. "60,000 Plastic Bags are Being Used This Second: Help Slow it Down." Planetgreen.discovery.com

324 "Paper vs Plastic- The Shopping Bag Debate." Greenfeet.com

325 Weiss. "Plague of Plastic Chokes the Seas." *Los Angeles Times*, last updated Aug 2 2006. Accessed March 1 2011

326 Boyle. "25-foot Turtle Stumps for Plastic Bag Ban." Huffingtonpost.com

327 "Paper or plastic-What's the greener choice?" Msnbc.msn.com

328 "The Environmental Benefits of Using Reusable Bags." Squidoo.com

329 "Biodegradable Plastic Bags." Biodegradableplasticbags.org

330 Stevie. "Clutter and Disorganization-Can you afford it?" Carytimes.com

331 "Reclaim Your Mailbox." 41pounds.org

332 "Turning the Page: Environmental Impacts of the Magazine Industry, Recommendations for Improvement." Mindfully.org

333 "Increase Fuel Mileage on a Car." Wikihow.com

334 "Recession Gardens: 10 Easy Herbs & Vegetables You Can Grow at Home to Save Money." Steadfastfinances.com

335 "About Chemicals & Fertilizers." Landscapeplanet.com

336 "An Overview of the State of the World's Fresh and Marine Waters." Unep.org.

337 "Indoor Water Use in the United States." United States Environmental Protection Agency, Epa.gov.

338 Ibid.

339 "Natural Products." Naturalproducts.suite101.com

340 "Household Products Database." Whatsinproducts.com

341 Trail. "Un-Fantastic Plastic: Choose the Best Containers for Growing Fruits and Vegetables." Naturalhomemagazine.com

342 Bocco. "How Much Garbage Does a Person Create in One Year?" Wisegeek.com

343 "The Environmental and Climate Costs of Using Virgin Materials." Ecomii.com

344 Butterworth, Trevor. "Is The EPA About To Shut Down Urban Renewal Across The U.S.?" Forbes.com

345 "The Environmental and Climate Costs of Using Virgin Materials." Ecomii.com

346 "Why Is Recycling Important?" Ilacsd.org

347 "How Recycling can Help Stop Global Warming." Help-stop-global-warming.com

Part 2

1 "279,332 Beauty Salons: Companies in the U.S." Manta.com

2 "Cosmetics Safety 'Virtually Unregulated' by fed law." Ewg.org

3 Manning. "Beauty Product Ingredients to Avoid." Suite101.com

4 Schapiro. *Exposed: The Toxic Chemistry of Everyday Products and What's at Stake for American Power*, 27

5 "Have you ever counted how many cosmetics or personal care products you use in a day? Chances are it's nearly 10." Cosmeticdatabase.com

6 Gabriel, *The Green Beauty Guide*, 5

7 Ibid.

8 FDA Regulations." Safecosmetics.com

9 Gabriel, *The Green Beauty Guide*, 12

10 Ferlow. "Cosmetics to Die For." Stanson.org

11 "About the Breast Cancer Fund." Breastcancerfund.org

12 Malkan, *Not Just Another Pretty Face*, 56

13 "Impurities of Concern in Personal Care Products (As of Dec 2006)." Cosmeticdatabase.com

14 "European Laws." Safecosmetics.com

15 Schapiro, *Exposed: The Toxic Chemistry of Everyday Products and What's at Stake for American Power*, 23

16 "EU Ban on Animal Testing Comes into Force Today." Cosmeticdesign-europe.com

17 "European Laws." Safecosmetics.org

18 Schapiro, *Exposed: The Toxic Chemistry of Everyday Products and What's at Stake for American Power*, 25

19 "Congress Set to Reform Law on Personal Care Product Safety." Environmentalleader.com

20 "Cosmetic Ingredient Review." Sourcewatch.org

21 Uricchio. "The ugly side of beauty, some cosmetics can be toxic." *Pittsburg Post-Gazette*

22 Washam. "Legislation: California Enacts Safe Cosmetics Act." National Institute of Health, Ncbi.nln.nih.gov

23 Schapiro, *Exposed: The Toxic Chemistry of Everyday Products and What's at Stake for American Power*, 28

24 "Coal Tar Hair Dyes: hair care cautions." Hairfinder.com

25 "State Legislation." Safecosmetics.com

26 Malan, *Not Another Pretty Face*, 61

27 "The Ugly Side of Cosmetics: makeup and body care products have been linked to allergic reactions, birth defects, and even cancer. Here's what you need to know."

28 "Have you ever counted how many cosmetics or personal care products you use in a day? Chances are it's nearly 10." Cosmeticdatabase.com

29 Houlihan. "Cosmetics with Banned and Unsafe Ingredients." Ewg.org

30 "State Legislation." Safecosmetics.org

31 "Cosmetics Bill Seeks Full Ingredient Disclosure, FDA Oversight." Greenbiz.com

32 "The Compact for Safe Cosmetics." Safecosmetics.org

33 "FAQ: The Compact for Safe Cosmetics." Safecosmetics.org

34 Schapiro, *Exposed: The Toxic Chemistry of Everyday Products and What's at Stake for American Power,* 34

35 Bird. "Safe Cosmetics Act introduced in House of Representatives." Cosmeticdesign.com

36 "Ceteareth-12: Cosmetic Toxin Data." Natural-skincare-authority.com

37 Winter, *A Consumer's Dictionary of Cosmetic Ingredients,* 142

38 Ibid.

39 O'Connor, Siobhan and Alexandra Spunt. *No More Dirty Looks,* 39

40 Winter. *A Consumer's Dictionary of Cosmetic Ingredients,* 159

41 Ibid. 292

42 "IMIDAZOLIDINYL-UREA: Cosmetic Toxin Data." Natural-skincare-authority.com

43 Winter. *A Consumer's Dictionary of Cosmetic Ingredients,* 297

44 Ibid. 324

45 "New Light Shed on Health Dangers of Nanoparticles by Michigan State Research." Medicalnewstoday.com

46 Winter. *A Consumer's Dictionary of Cosmetic Ingredients,* 407

47 "Coal Tar Dyes." Davidsuzuki.org

48 Winter. *A Consumer's Dictionary of Cosmetic Ingredients,* 407-408

49 Ibid

50 "What is BPA? Most sunscreens come free of PABA now to avoid allergic reactions. Here's what you need to know about PABA-free sunscreens." Thedailygreen.com

51 "PABA." Cosmeticdatabase.com

52 Winter. *A Consumer's Dictionary of Cosmetic Ingredients,* 393

53 "Beauty Product Danger." Natureprofarms.com

54 "Ingredients in Makeup and Cosmetics that are Dangerous." Healthfoodemporium.com

55 "8 Cosmetic Chemical Offenses." Greenlivingideas.com

56 "Ingredients in Makeup and Cosmetics that are Dangerous." Healthfoodemporium.com

57 "Dangers of PEG Compounds in Cosmetics. Women at Increased Breast Cancer Risk?" Healthy-communications.com

58 Winter. *A Consumer's Dictionary of Cosmetic Ingredients,* 160

59 Stefanson. "Animal Derivatives in Cosmetics: Uncover the Sources of Ingredients in Your Grooming Products." Suite101.com

60 Cockcroft. "Cosmetics giants agree to stop using shark oil." Telegraph.co.uk

61 "What Does the "Organic" Label Really Mean?" United States Department of Agriculture. Usda.fda.gov

62 Ibid.

63 "Make Up 101: Organic Schmorganic: The Truth About Organic Makeup." Collegecandy.com

64 "Consumers union and organic consumers association file federal trade commission petition urging action on deceptive 'organic' labeling practices of personal care products." Consumersunion.org

65 Whittaker, Engimann, Sambrook. "Ecolabels: Environmental Marketing in the Beauty Industry." Gcimagazine.com

66 "Organic Standards for Different Products." Naturalproductsmarketplace.com

67 Davis."Trust these 6 Green Beauty Product Labels." Thedailygreen.com

68 Sharmani. "Is Water an Organic Skin Care Ingredient?" Pharmacymix.com

69 Bronner. "A 5 Star Comparison & Ranking of US & European "Organic," "Made with", and "Natural" Personal Care Standards". Organicconsumers.org

70 Ibid.

71 Ibid.

72 Ibid.

73 "Natural Organic Cosmetics." Healthreport.co.uk

74 Davis. "Trust these 6 Green Beauty Product Labels." Thedailygreen.com

75 "Beauty Industry Secrets Investigated." Aolhealth.com

76 "Is it a Cosmetic, a Drug, or Both? (or is it Soap?)" The U.S. Food and Drug Administration. FDA.gov

77 "MedlinePlus: Trusted Health Information for You." U.S. Food and Drug Administration, Jan 19 2011. Nlm.nih.gov

78 "Cocamide DEA." Cosmeticdatabase.com

79 Patterson. "Controversial Ingredients in Cosmetics." Creativeartistryfx.com

80 Ibid.

81 Breyer, Melissa. "Parabens: Easy Greening." Care2.com

82 Ashton and Green. *The Toxic Consumer: Living Healthy in a Hazardous World,* 69

83 Ibid. 67

84 Gabriel. *The Green Beauty Guide,* 28

85 "American Cancer Society on Parabens: Should I Be Concerned About Parabens in Antiperspirants?" Vashonorgaics.com

86 Adams. "Paraben Preservatives and Cosmetics: Controversy and Alternatives." Ecomall.com

87 Breyer. "Parabens: Easy Greening." Care2.com

88 Ibid.

89 Ashton and Green. *The Toxic Consumer: Living Healthy in a Hazardous World*, 69

90 Ibid. 68

91 Gabriel. *The Green Beauty Guide*, 28

92 Adams. "Paraben Preservatives and Cosmetics: Controversy and Alternatives." Ecomall.com

93 Gabriel. *The Green Beauty Guide*, 28

94 Chavis, Jason C. "What is Phenoxyethanol?" Wisegeek.com

95 O'Connor and Spunt. *No More Dirty Looks*, 49

96 "Natural Skincare: The Dangers of Phenoxyethanol." Organicpoteke.com

97 "Phenoxyethanol: Preservative with Dirty Past." Thegreenbeautyguide.com

98 Smith. "What Are Parabens?" Wisegeek.com

99 "Phenoxyethanol: Preservative with Dirty Past." Thegreenbeautyguide.com

100 Gabriel. *The Green Beauty Guide*, 29

101 Pamphlet: "How to Use Preservatives in Cosmetics" by Somerset Cosmetic Company. www.makingcosmetics.com

102 Gabriel. *The Green Beauty Guide*, 27

103 "How To Use Essential Oils Efficiently." Floracopeia.com

104 "Is Perfume Pollution as Harmful as Cigarette Smoke?" Shine.yahoo.com

105 "Cosmetic Labeling Label Claims." The U.S Food and Drug Administration. Fda.gov

106 Epstein."The Danger of Toxic Consumer Products, Fragrances." Thehuffingtonpost.com

107 Ibid.

108 Corkil. "Is Fragrance the Poison Dose." Personalcaretruth.com

109 "Not So Sexy: Chemicals in Perfume and Cologne?" Ewg.org

110 "Not So Sexy: The Health Risks of Secret Chemicals in Fragrance." Ewg.org

111 "Not So Sexy: Chemicals in Perfume and Cologne." Ewg.org

112 "Natural vs Synthetic." Purrfumery.com

113 "How Can Natural Skin Care Products Make a Difference?" Grouped.biz

114 "Can I Recycle My Straw? Top 12 Recycling FAQs Answered Once and For All." Ecostiletto.com

115 Dudley PhD, Nassar, BA, and Hartman, BA. "Tampon Safety." Center4research.org

116 "What Are Alternative Menstrual Products." Thewikifire.org

117 Dudley PhD, Nassar, BA, and Hartman, BA. "Tampon Safety." Center4research.org

118 Porter. "Toxic Tampons." Alive.com

119 "What Women Should Know Before Buying Tampons." Ecomall.com

120 Porter. "Toxic Tampons." Alive.com

121 O'Conner. "What's Going on With O.B Tampons?" Nomoredirtylooks.com

122 Dudley PhD, Nassar, BA, and Hartman, BA. "Tampon Safety." Center4research.org

123 Ibid.

124 "What Women Should Know Before Buying Tampons." Ecomall.com

125 Graham. "4 Summer Health Hazards. And how to keep them from spoiling your warm-weather fun." Redbookmag.com

126 Mok. "Buy Green: Tampons. From organic cotton to sea sponges to reusable cups, these five feminine products are easy on your body and the earth." Planetgreen.discovery.com

127 "The Feminist Debate: Menstrual Products." Mooncupsandkeepers.com

128 "What Women Should Know Before Buying Tampons." Ecomall.com

129 Ibid.

130 "Toothpaste: Hazardous to dental and bodily health?" Healingteethnaturally.com

131 Anisman-Reiner. "Toxic Toothpaste Inactive Ingredients: Hidden chemicals in your family's toothpaste may harm teeth and health." Suite101.com

132 "Time Magazine Lists Flouride as "Environmental Toxin." Blacklistednews.com

133 Anisman-Reiner. "Toxic Toothpaste Inactive Ingredients: Hidden chemicals in your family's toothpaste may harm teeth & health." Suite101.com

134 "Time Magazine Lists Fluoride as "Environmental Toxin." Blacklistednews.com

135 Loux. *Easy Green Living*, 206

136 "Time Magazine Lists Fluoride as "Environmental Toxin." Blacklistednews.com

137 "Does fluoride accumulate in the body?" Poisonfluoride.com

138 "Does fluoride accumulate in the body?" Ipn.at

139 "Question 23: Does fluoride inhibit the activity of enzymes in humans?" Fluoridedebate.com

140 Loux. *Easy Green Living*, 206

141 Yiamouyiannis. *Fluoride: The Aging Factor*, posted on Fluoridealert.org

142 "Toothpaste: Hazardous to dental and bodily health?" Healingteethnaturally.com

143 "Fluorinated tap water and bottled water unsafe for infants, children, adults, and elderly." Examiner.com

144 Arnold. "Mouth Bacteria: It's a Jungle in There." Brighthub.com

145 "Toothpaste: Hazardous to dental and bodily health?" Healingteethnaturally.com

146 Adams. "Warning: Toxic Chemical Triclosan Can Turn Your Toothpaste Into Chloroform." Naturalnews.com

147 Gerstein."The Truth About Natural Toothpaste." Thedailygreen.com

148 "Toothpaste: Hazardous to dental and bodily health?" Healingteethnaturally.com

149 "Health News: SLS." Webed.com

150 Anisman-Reiner. "Toxic Toothpaste Inactive Ingredients: Hidden chemicals in your family's toothpaste may harm teeth & health." Suite101.com

151 Ibid.

152 Loux. *Easy Green Living*, 207

153 Ceruti, Silke. "Toothpaste—What's in it, and What You Should Know." Ezinearticles.com

154 Cadena. "Oral Health: Do You Know What is in Your Toothpaste?" Associatedcontent.com

155 "PEG-32." Cosmeticdatabase.com

156 "Zinc Citrate." Livestrong.com

157 "PEG-32." Cosmeticdatabase.com

158 "Deodorant." En.wikipedia.org

159 "100 Toxic Ingredients used in Skincare, Makeup, Haircare, and Fragrances." Narratethenatural.wordpress.com

160 "Hormone Disruptors and Women's Health: Reasons for Concern." Healthandenvironment.org

161 Anisman-Reiner. "Aluminum in Deodorant: Toxic Ingredients in Antiperspirant, Brain Health, and Alzheimer's." Suite101.com

162 McGilton, Jennifer. "Can Aluminum Pass the Blood Brain Barrier?" Biology.arizona.edu

163 Loux. *Easy Green Living*, 212

164 "Water pollution caused by cosmetic chemicals, cleaning supplies and plastics: Triclosan." Ewg.org

165 Rubin. "Estrogen may join carcinogen list. Talc also under consideration; benefits don't play into decision." Mindfully.org, from USA Today

166 Epstein."Talcum Powder: The Hidden Dangers." Drfranklipman.com

167 Sinha, V.R, and Maninder Pal Kaur. "Permeation Enhancers for Transdermal Drug Delivery." University Institute of Pharmaceutical Sciences, Panjab University. Laserandskin.com.au

168 "Material Safety Data Sheet: Vitamin D Internal Standard Stock." Esainc.com

169 Halliday. "Alarming Toxic Chemicals in Sunscreen." Thedetoxspecialist.com

170 "Do You Use Products with Sodium Lauryl Sulfate (SLS)?" Antiagingchoices.com

171 Ibid.

172 Sparacino. "Melanoma Risk Upwards of 75 Percent Higher with Tanning Bed Use." Aolhealth.com

173 "Skin Cancer Facts." Skincancer.org

174 Tarr. "Sprat Tanning Ingredients." Livestrong.com

175 "Hormone Mimics (Endocrine Disruptors): They're in Our Food. Should We Worry?" Consumer Reports, posted on Mindfully.org

176 Halliday. "Alarming Toxic Chemicals in Sunscreen." Thedetoxspecialist.com

177 "Few Sunscreens Win Green Rating." Ewg.org

178 Sparacino. "Melanoma Risk Upwards of 75 Percent Higher with Tanning Bed Use." Aolhealth.com

179 "Sun Protection and Sunscreens." University of Iowa Health Care. Uihealthcare.com

180 "Finding the best sunscreen: You know the drill: when the sun's rays are fierce, duck and cover." Ewg.org

181 "Sun Protection and Sunscreens." University of Iowa Health Care. Uihealthcare.com

182 Schneider. "Study: Many Sunscreens May Be Accelerating Cancer." Aolnews.com

183 Ibid.

184 "Finding the best sunscreen: You know the drill: When the sun's rays are fierce, duck and cover." Ewg.org

185 "Skin Cancer Facts." Skincancer.org

186 "Nanomaterials and hormone disruptors in sunscreens." Ewg.org

187 McKay. "Is Your Sunscreen Killing Coral?" Downtoearth.org

188 "Suncoat-water-based nail polish." Suncoatproducts.com

189 "Choose natural nail polish." Greenyour.com

190 "Nail Products and Salons." Safecosmetics.org

191 "Breast Cancer Risk Profile of Vietnamese Nail Salon Workers." California Breast Cancer Research Program. Cbcrp.org

192 "Choose natural nail polish." Greenyour.com

193 Ibid

194 "Nail Products and Salons." Safecosmetics.org

195 "Common household toxics and the products they're found in; Formaldehyde in the Home." Elc.org.uk

196 "Formaldehyde Releasers in Everyday Products." Ecomall.com

197 "Nail Products and Salons." Safecosmetics.org

198 "Benzophenone-1." Cosmeticdatabase.com

199 Winter. *A Consumer's Dictionary of Cosmetic Ingredients*, 318

200 "Choose natural nail polish." Greenyour.com

201 Winter. *A Consumer's Dictionary of Cosmetic Ingredients*, 551

202 Woods. "About Lard Soap." Ezinearticles.com

203 "Four Chemicals That You Definitely Do Not Want in Your Moisturizer." Scribd.com

204 "Mineral Makeup Dangers." Chemicaloftheday.squarespace.com

205 "Allergic Contact Dermatitis From Carmine: Case Report." Medscape.com

206 "Mineral Makeup Dangers." Chemicaloftheday.squarespace.com

207 "Blush Potentially Containing: Lead." Cosmeticsdatabase.com

208 Faria. "What is Blush?" Wisegeek.com

209 "Asbestos." En.wikipedia.org

210 "Aluminum Starch Octenylsuccinate." Cosmeticsdatabase.com

211 "Eyelid." En.wikipedia.org

212 Sainio EL, Jolanki R, Hakala E, and Kanerva L. "Metals and Arsenic in Eye Shadows." National Center for Biotechnology Information; National Institute of Health. Ncbi.nlm.nih.gov

213 "Toxic Beauty Product Ingredients." Beautycritic.net

214 "Allergic Contact Dermatitis From Carmine: Case Report." Medscape.com

215 "Avon Beyond Color Radiant Lifting Eyeshadow." Cosmeticsdatabase.com

216 "Lyral." Cosmeticdatabase.com

217 "Covergirl Fantastic Lash Curved Brush Mascara, Very Black 835." Cosmeticdatabase.com

218 "Cover Girl Exact Eyelights Mascara Black Sapphire 710." Cosmeticdatabase.com

219 "Cargo Blu_Ray Mascara." Cosmeticdatabase.com

220 "Blepharitis." En.wikipedia.org

221 "Lead in Lipstick." Safecosmetics.org

222 Ellin, Abby. "Skin Deep—A Simple Smooch or a Toxic Smack?" NYTimes.com

223 "Lead Acetate." Cosmeticsdatabase.com

224 Winter. *A Consumer's Dictionary of Cosmetic Ingredients*, 324

225 Shapley, Dan. "FDA Tests Find Lead in Lipstick." Thedailygreen.com

226 "Don't Pucker up: Lead in Lipstick. From the Department Store to the Drugstore: Lead on Your Lips." Abcnews.go.com

227 "Easily Lead." Snopes.com

228 Gibson, M.D. "Is it true that lipstick contains lead?" Mayoclinic.com

229 Chinn, Lisa. "FDA Lead Regulations." Ehow.com

230 "Lips Against Lead-Free Lipstick From Terra Firma, Lavera, Suki and Jane Iredale." Ecostiletto.com

231 Shapley. "FDA Tests Find Lead in Lipstick." Thedailygreen.com

232 "EPA Takes Final Step in Phaseout of Leaded Gasoline." Epa.gov

233 "Lead Acetate." Cosmeticsdatabase.com

234 "Lead in Lipstick." Safecosmetics.org

235 "Childhood Lead Poisoning Publication." Centers for Disease Control and Prevention. CDC.gov

236 Ellin. "Skin Deep—A Simple Smooch or a Toxic Smack?" NYTimes.com

237 "Don't Pucker up: Lead in Lipstick. From the Department Store to the Drugstore: Lead on Your Lips." Abcnews.go.com

238 "Active Ingredients." Sephora.com

239 "Beauty Basics: Expiration Dates." Wholeliving.com

240 "Is There a Squirrel in Your Makeup Bag?" Peta.org

241 "12050 Fabrics." Greensage.com

242 Blair. "Why Organic Cotton: Do I really need organic cotton?" Allthingsnaturalstore.com

243 "Buy Organic Cotton Jeans." Greenyour.com

244 "Stop Forced and Child Labour in the Cotton Industry of Uzbekistan: Frequently Asked Questions." Cottoncampaign.org

Part 3

1 "Charity: Water." Charitywater.org

2 "Vegan Fashion=Compassionate Threads." Happycow.net

3 Lincoln-Sarnoff. "Queen of Green: Cruelty Free Fashion Designers." Shoestringmag.com

4 Sherman."Do You Know What Toxic Chemicals Lurk in Your Clothing?" Organicconsumers.org

5 "How Green Are Plastic and Wire Coat Hangers." Foxnews.com, posted on Stevenkotler.com

6 "Imported Kids Apparel from China—Are they Toxic? Fibre2fashion.com

7 "Textile Chemicals." Teonline.com

8 "Bleach." Everything2.com

9 "Product Safety." Dow.com

10 Hornick and Yarnell. "Alternative Treatments for Cancer." Health.howstuffworks.com

11 "Bleach and the Environment." Factsaboutbleach.com

12 "Bleach." How Products Are Made Volume 2, Madehow.com

13 www.mcspotlight.org/media/reports/wenchlorine.html

14 Blair. "Choosing the right (non-poisonous) candles for your home." Allthingsnaturalstore.com

15 Blair, Katie. "Why Organic Cotton." Allthingsnaturalstore.com

16 "Synthetic Dyes: A look at Environmental and Human Risks." Greencotton.wordpress.com

17 "Natural vs. Synthetic Fabric Dyes." Livejournal.com

18 "The Health and Environmental Problems with Clothes Dyes." Natural-environment.com

19 "What are Clothing Fabric Dyes Made Of?" Fibers.com

20 Ballad. "Is Flame-Resistant Clothing Safe For Children?" Livestrong.com

21 Reinhart. "What Makes Clothing Fire Retardant?" Ehow.com

22 "Formaldehyde: It's not just for embalming anymore." Home-ec101.com

23 "WakeUP and Smell the Formaldehyde." Organicclothing.com

24 Ibid.

25 Ibid.

26 "'Greener' stain-resistant coatings developed; avoid PFOA." Innovations-report.com

27 "Perfluorinated Compounds (PFCs)." Pollutioninpeople.org

28 "Is rayon bad for the environment?" Greenanswers.com

29 "Synthetic Clothing—Friend or Foe?" Strocel.com

30 Skinner. "How "Green" is your Gear? The Environmental Impact of Nylon." Trailcenter.org

31 "Synthetic Clothing—Friend or Foe?" Strocel.com

32 "Facts about the Fur Trade." Infurmation.com

33 Ibid.

34 "Leather: Animals Abused and Killed for Their Skins." Peta2.com

35 Ibid.

36 "Vegan Fashion=Compassionate Threads." Happycow.net

37 "Silk Series: Peace Silk." Trueup.net

38 Larkman. "Eco-friendly Bamboo: The hard facts behind the fiber." Curl.co.nz

39 "Bamboo: Facts behind the fiber." Organicclothing.blogs.com

40 Das, Dr. Subrata. "Bamboo—21st century eco fiber: Application in towel sector." Fibre2fashion.com

41 Larkman. "Eco-friendly Bamboo: The hard facts behind the fiber." Curl.co.nz

42 Ibid.

43 Ibid.

44 "FTC Blows The Whistle On Bamboo-Based Textiles' Green Claims." Sincerelysustainable.com

45 Henderson, Georgie. "Hypoallergenic Properties of Bamboo Flooring." Suite101.com

46 "Are Leading Brand Laundry Detergents Environmentally Friendly?" Laundry-alternative.com

47 "Buy Organic Cotton Jeans." Greenyour.com

48 Ibid.

49 Gutierrez. "Pests invade GM cotton crops in China." Naturalnews.com

50 "Comprehensive Rules For Ecological And Socially Responsible Textile Production." Global-standard.org

51 Clarren, Rebecca. "Not-so-green-jeans: Organic cotton is a leap ahead for the garment industry—not so the toxic dyes and finishing agents used in trendy eco-jeans." Salon.com

52 Agarwal, Sandeep. "Vintage Denim—At What Cost To Environment?" Denimsandjeans.com

53 "A Lot To Say Eco T-Shirt Line: The Revolution." Alototsay.com

54 "What makes polyurethane (PE) or polypropylene (PP) or PET more sustainable?" Cr4globalspec.com

55 Richter, Morgan. "Real Fur Vs. Faux." Ehow.com

56 "Are Leading Brand Laundry Detergents Environmentally Friendly?" Laundry-alternative.com

57 Kassem, Noreen. "Allergens and Toxins in Laundry Detergents. Synthetic Ingredients That Are Harmful to People and the Environment." Suite101.com

58 "Benzene." En.wikipedia.org

59 "Are Leading Brand Laundry Detergents Environmentally Friendly?" Laundry-alternative.com

60 "Laundry Supplies: The Problems With Conventional." Ecoeveryday.com

61 Juniper. "Greenhouse effects: dishwasher tablets. Consumers need to take action themselves as cleaning agents for dishwashers often have a high phosphate content." Timesonline.co.uk

62 "The Health Dangers of Phenols Found in Common Household Cleaners." Sixwise.com

63 "The Health Dangers of Phenols Found in Common Household Cleaners." Sixwise.com

64 "Optical Brightener." En.wikipedia.org

65 "Shedding Some Light on Optical Brighteners." Seventhgeneration.com

66 Maurer. "Green Laundry Detergent Packs Mean Less Waste." Associatedcontent.com

67 "How to Conserve Energy at Home." Northwest Arkansas Community College. Nwacc.edu

68 Herbst. "How to green your garb. From shopping to washing, from drying to dry cleaning, let MNN show you how to green your sleeves." Mnn.com

69 Perchloroethylene." Healthychild.org

70 "Dry cleaning." En.wikipedia.org

71 Loux. *Easy Green Living*, 254

72 Manning, Jennifer. "Looking Good, Feeling Bad; or, What's the Problem with Perc (Percholorethylene)?" Environmentalchemistry.com

73"Green Dry Cleaning." Treehugger.com

74 Barley. "If cows wore shoes...they'd wear these. The newest vegan shoes are fun comfy, stylish and affordable. Hard to believe, huh?" Vegetarian Times, posted on findarticles.com

75 "Leather." Idausa.org

76 Ibid.

77 "Chlorophenols Other Than Pentachlorophenol." International Programme on Chemical Safety. Inchem.org

78 Barley. "If cows wore shoes...they'd wear these. The newest vegan shoes are fun comfy, stylish and affordable. Hard to believe, huh?" Vegetarian Times, posted on findarticles.com

79 "Absolutely Scandalous." Animalaid.org.uk

80 Fletcher. "Lead Found in Women's Handbags. ABC News Exclusive: Retailers Agree to Test Purses for Lead Levels." Abcnews.go.com

81 Lacroix. "Eco-Friendly Handbags and Footwear— Surprising Facts About Leather and PVC." Ezinearticles.com

INDEX